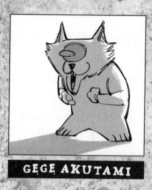

GEGE AKUTAMI

Smart gorillas hide their nipples!

GEGE AKUTAMI published a few short works before starting *Jujutsu Kaisen*, which began serialization in *Weekly Shonen Jump* in 2018.

JUJUTSU KAISEN

VOLUME 12
SHONEN JUMP MANGA EDITION

BY GEGE AKUTAMI

TRANSLATION Stefan Koza
TOUCH-UP ART & LETTERING Snir Aharon
DESIGN Joy Zhang
EDITOR John Bae
CONSULTING EDITOR Erika Onabe

First published in Japan in 2018 by SHUEISHA Inc., Tokyo.
English translation rights arranged by SHUEISHA Inc.

Printed in Italy

Published by VIZ Media, LLC
P.O. Box 77010
San Francisco, CA 94107

10 9 8 7 6 5 4 3
First printing, October 2021
Third printing, October 2021

VIZ MEDIA
viz.com

SHONEN JUMP

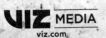

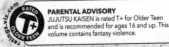

JUJUTSU KAISEN 12

THE SHIBU
INCIDENT
—SUMMON

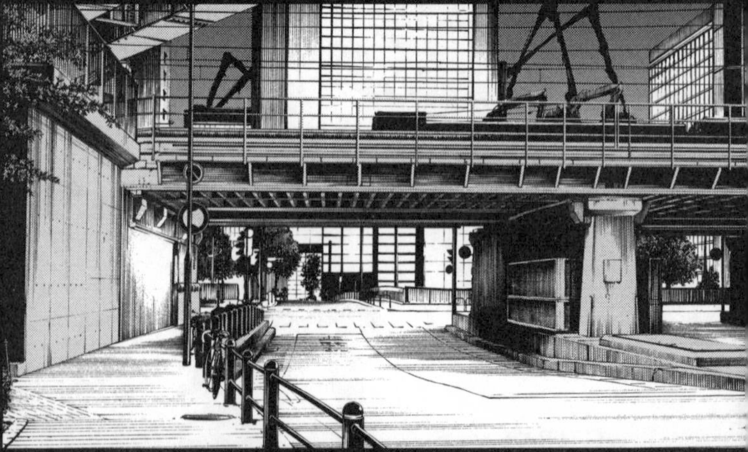

STORY AND ART BY GEGE AKUTAMI

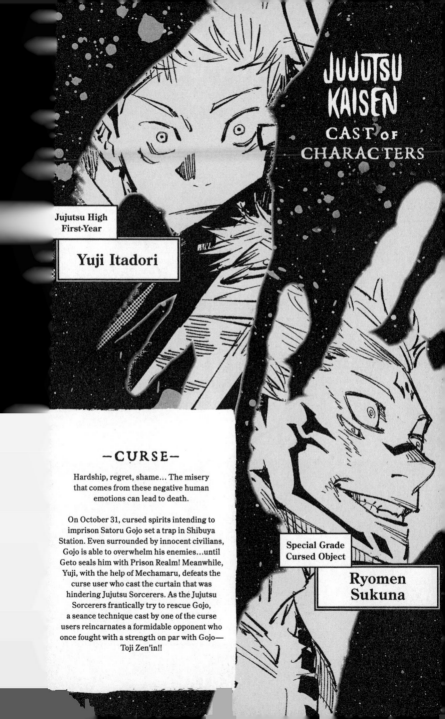

JUJUTSU KAISEN
CAST OF CHARACTERS

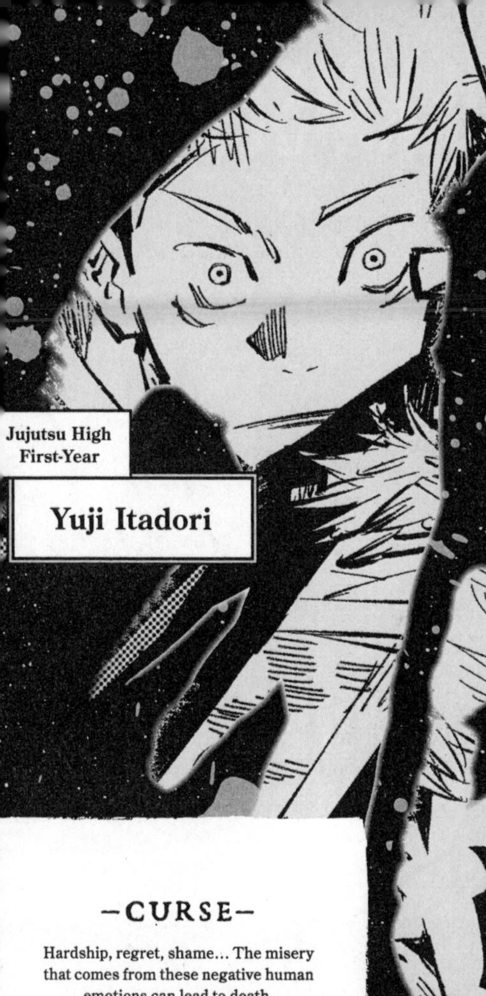

Jujutsu High
First-Year

Yuji Itadori

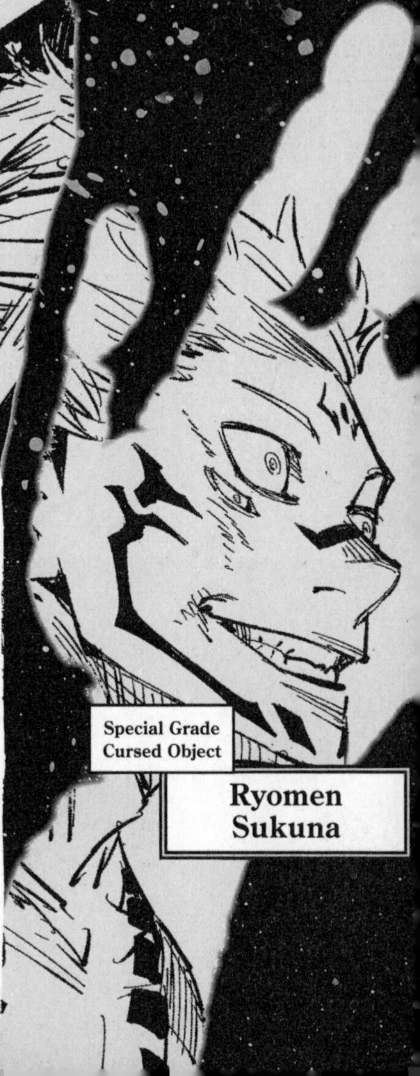

Special Grade
Cursed Object

Ryomen Sukuna

—CURSE—

Hardship, regret, shame... The misery that comes from these negative human emotions can lead to death.

On October 31, cursed spirits intending to imprison Satoru Gojo set a trap in Shibuya Station. Even surrounded by innocent civilians, Gojo is able to overwhelm his enemies...until Geto seals him with Prison Realm! Meanwhile, Yuji, with the help of Mechamaru, defeats the curse user who cast the curtain that was hindering Jujutsu Sorcerers. As the Jujutsu Sorcerers frantically try to rescue Gojo, a seance technique cast by one of the curse users reincarnates a formidable opponent who once fought with a strength on par with Gojo—Toji Zen'in!!

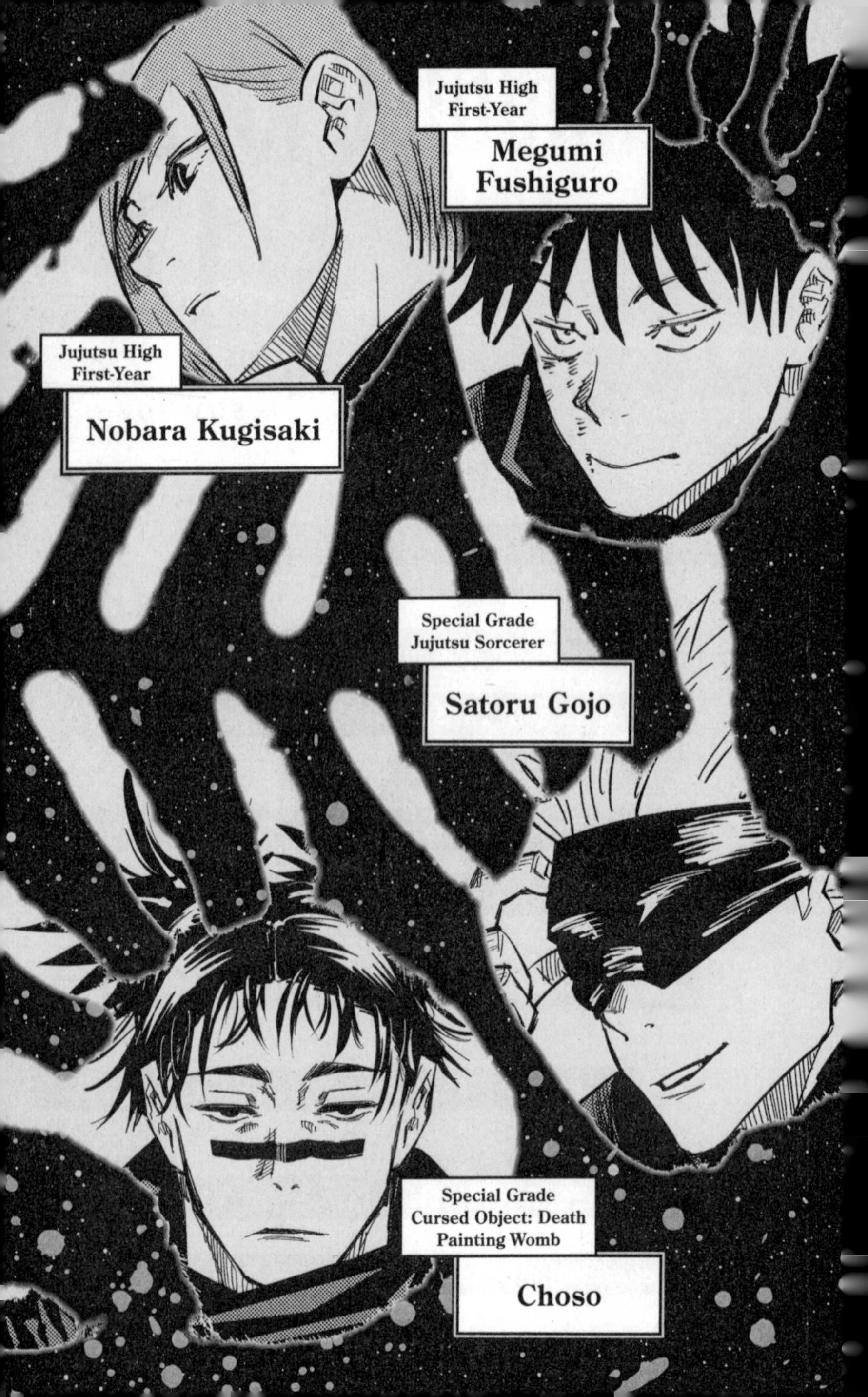
Jujutsu High
First-Year
Megumi
Fushiguro
Jujutsu High
First-Year
Nobara Kugisaki
Special Grade
Jujutsu Sorcerer
Satoru Gojo
Special Grade
Cursed Object: Death
Painting Womb
Choso

JUJUTSU KAISEN

12

THE SHIBUYA INCIDENT —SUMMON—

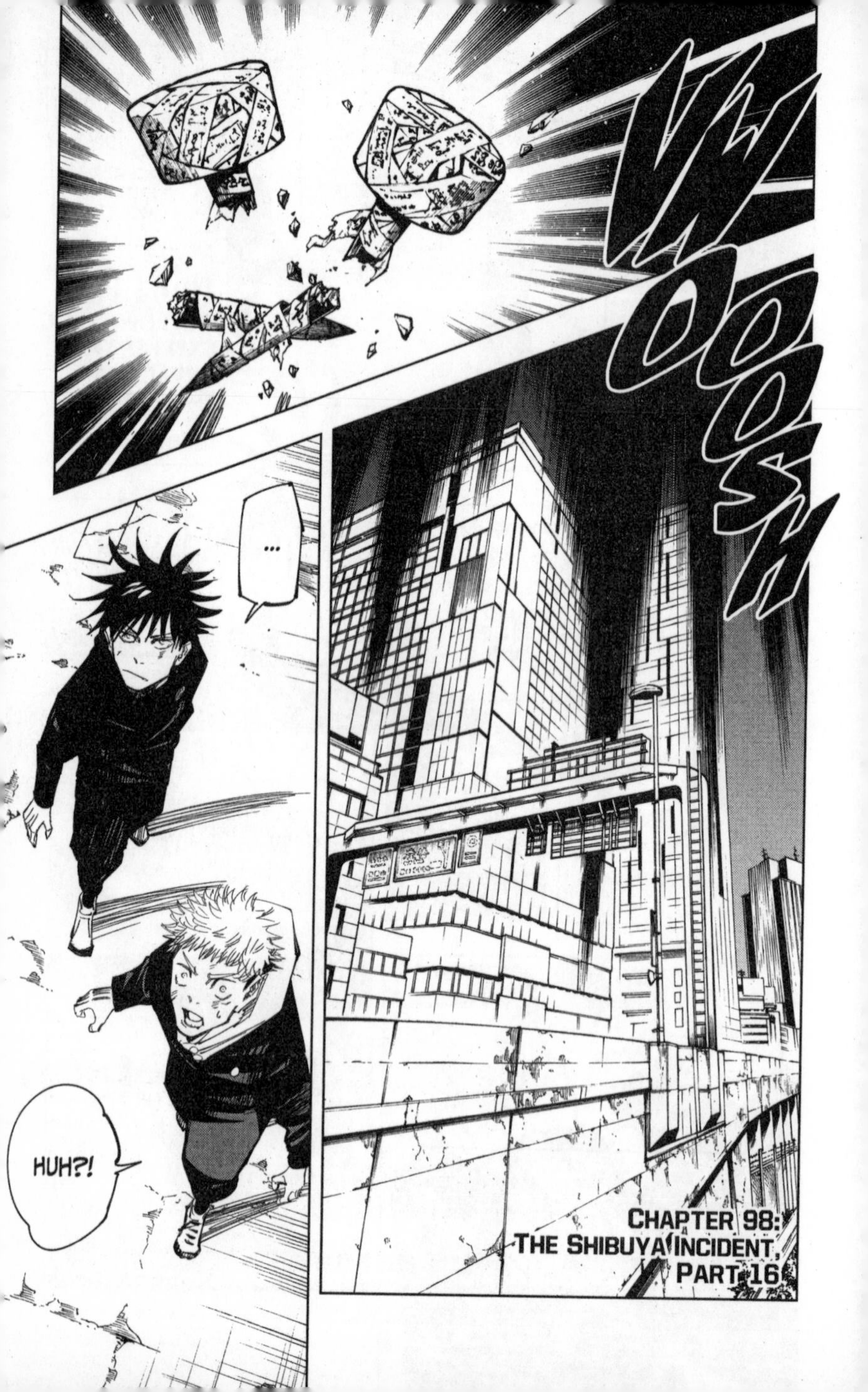
WHOOOSH
CHAPTER 98: THE SHIBUYA INCIDENT, PART 16
...
HUH?!

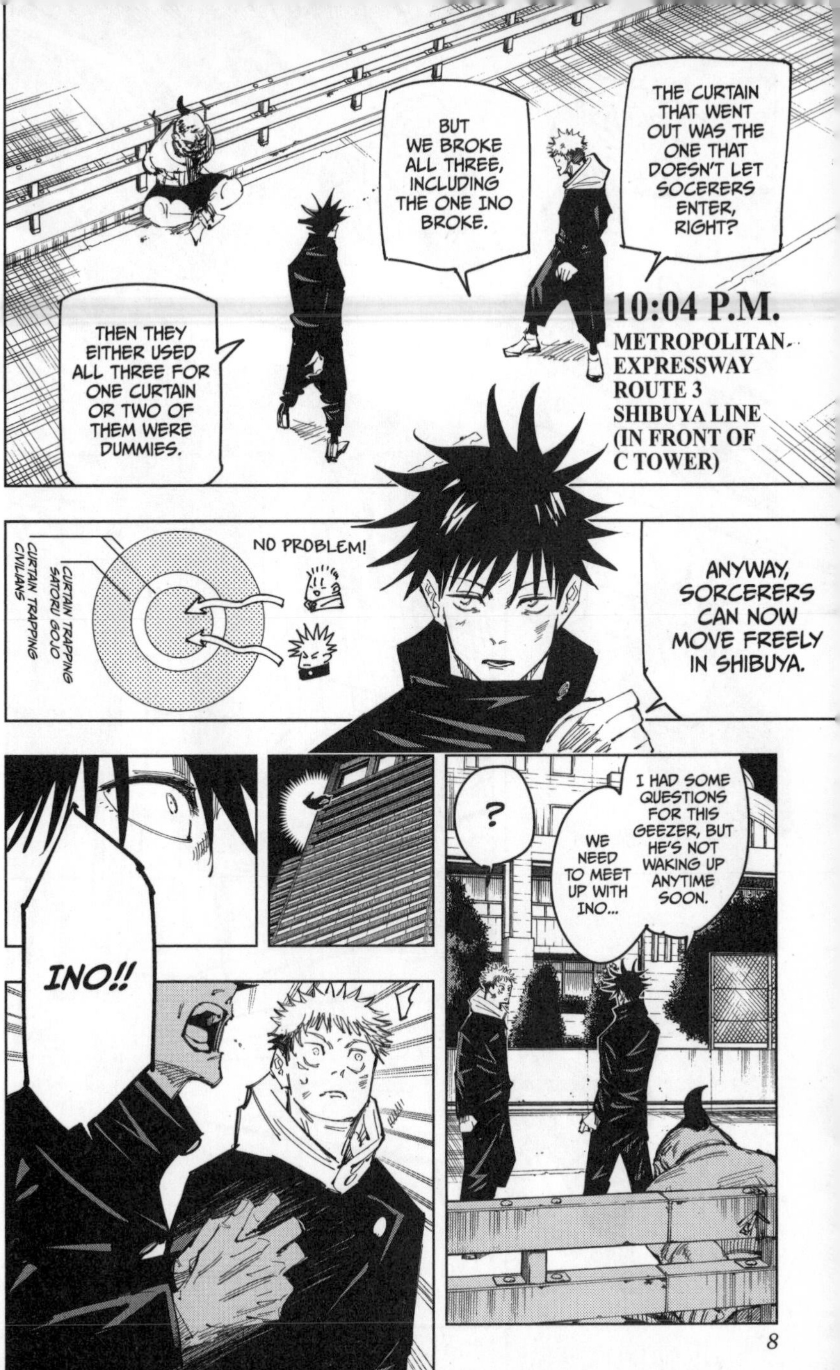
THE CURTAIN THAT WENT OUT WAS THE ONE THAT DOESN'T LET SOCERERS ENTER, RIGHT?
BUT WE BROKE ALL THREE, INCLUDING THE ONE INO BROKE.
10:04 P.M. METROPOLITAN EXPRESSWAY ROUTE 3 SHIBUYA LINE (IN FRONT OF C TOWER)
THEN THEY EITHER USED ALL THREE FOR ONE CURTAIN OR TWO OF THEM WERE DUMMIES.
ANYWAY, SORCERERS CAN NOW MOVE FREELY IN SHIBUYA.
NO PROBLEM!
CURTAIN TRAPPING SATORU GOJO
CURTAIN TRAPPING CIVILIANS
I HAD SOME QUESTIONS FOR THIS GEEZER, BUT HE'S NOT WAKING UP ANYTIME SOON.
WE NEED TO MEET UP WITH INO...
?
INO!!

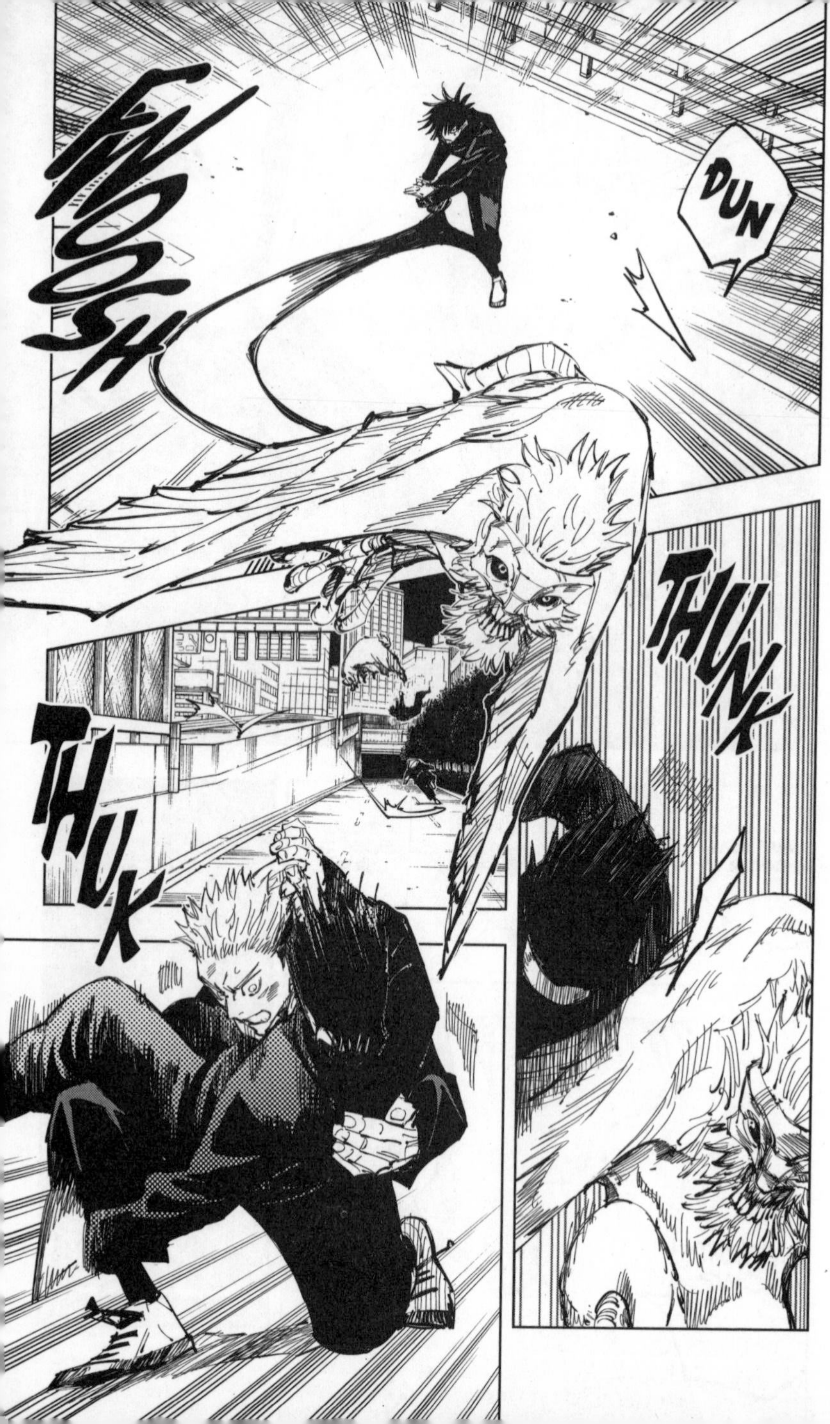
DUN
SWOOSH
THUNK
THUNK

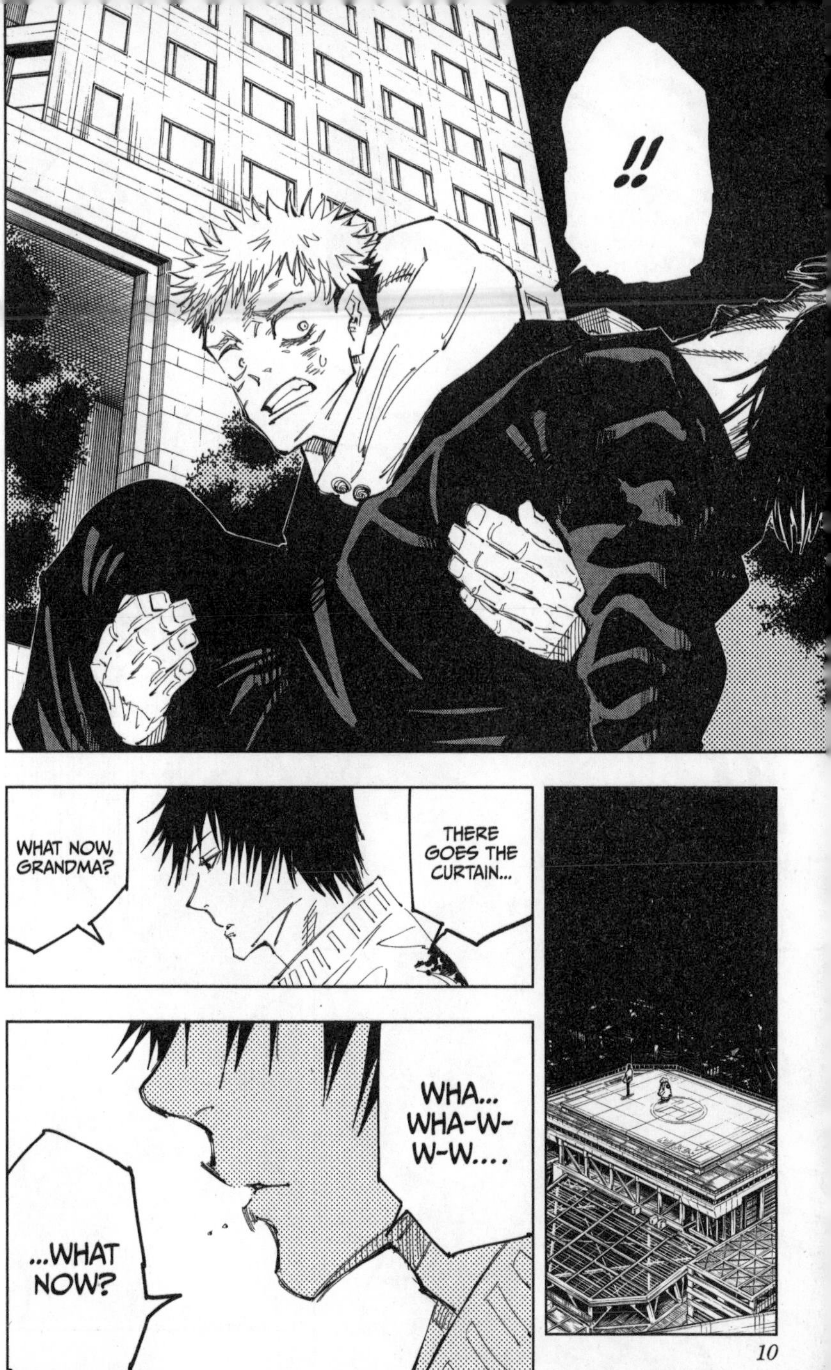
!!
THERE GOES THE CURTAIN...
WHAT NOW, GRANDMA?
WHA... WHA-W-W-W....
...WHAT NOW?

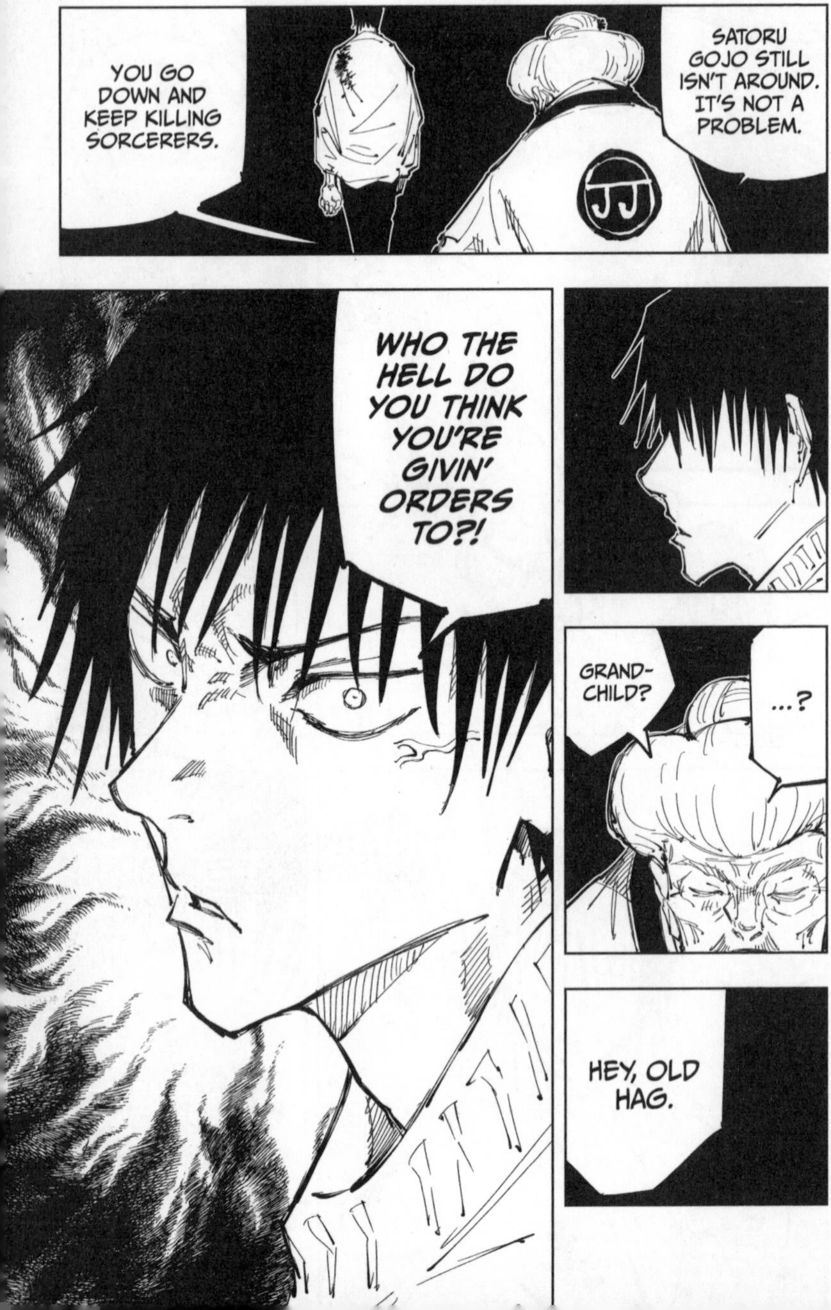
SATORU GOJO STILL ISN'T AROUND. IT'S NOT A PROBLEM.
YOU GO DOWN AND KEEP KILLING SORCERERS.
...?
GRAND-CHILD?
HEY, OLD HAG.
WHO THE HELL DO YOU THINK YOU'RE GIVIN' ORDERS TO?!

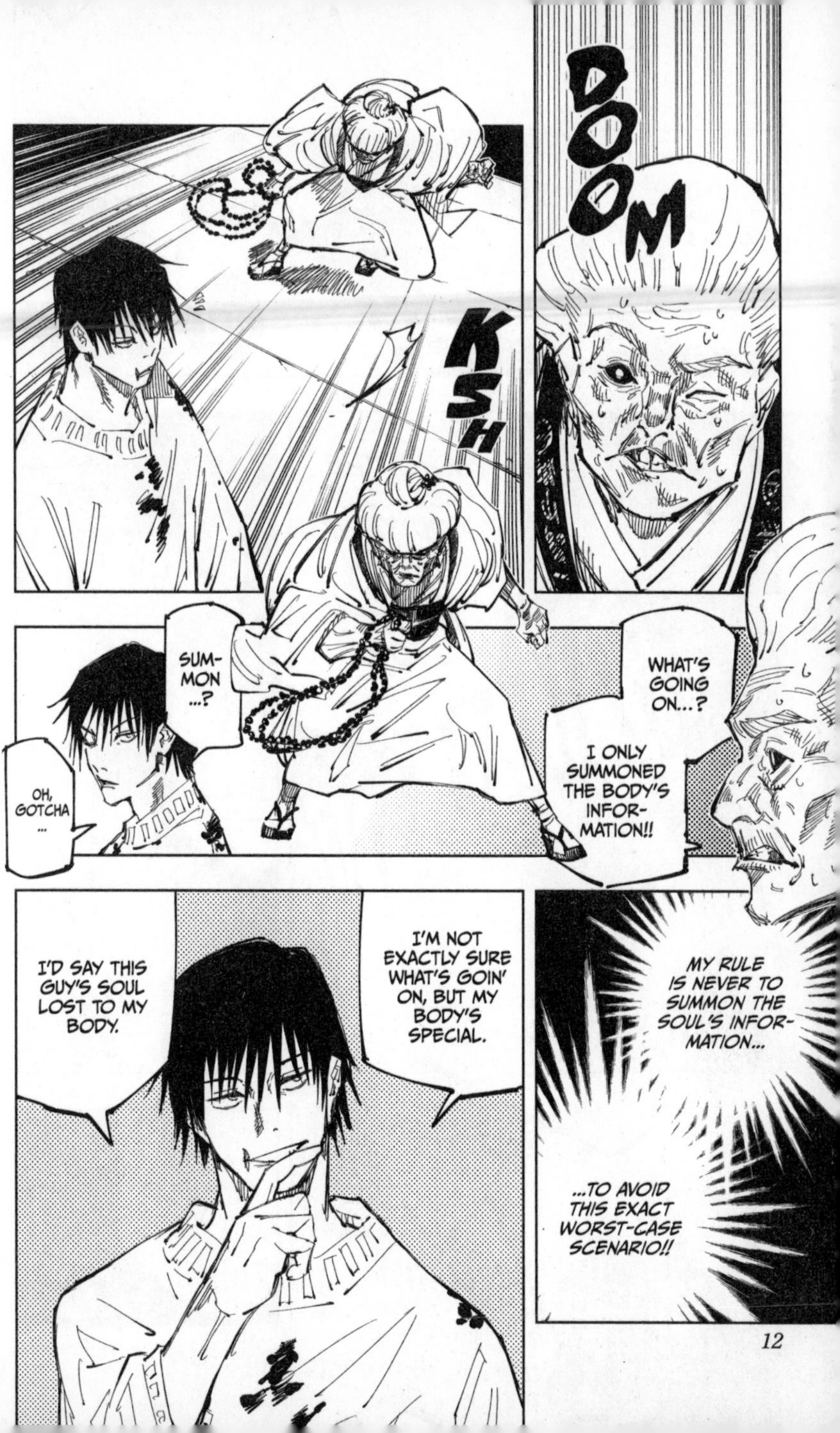
DOOM
KSH
WHAT'S GOING ON...?
I ONLY SUMMONED THE BODY'S INFORMATION!!
SUMMON...?
OH, GOTCHA...
MY RULE IS NEVER TO SUMMON THE SOUL'S INFORMATION...
...TO AVOID THIS EXACT WORST-CASE SCENARIO!!
I'M NOT EXACTLY SURE WHAT'S GOIN' ON, BUT MY BODY'S SPECIAL.
I'D SAY THIS GUY'S SOUL LOST TO MY BODY.

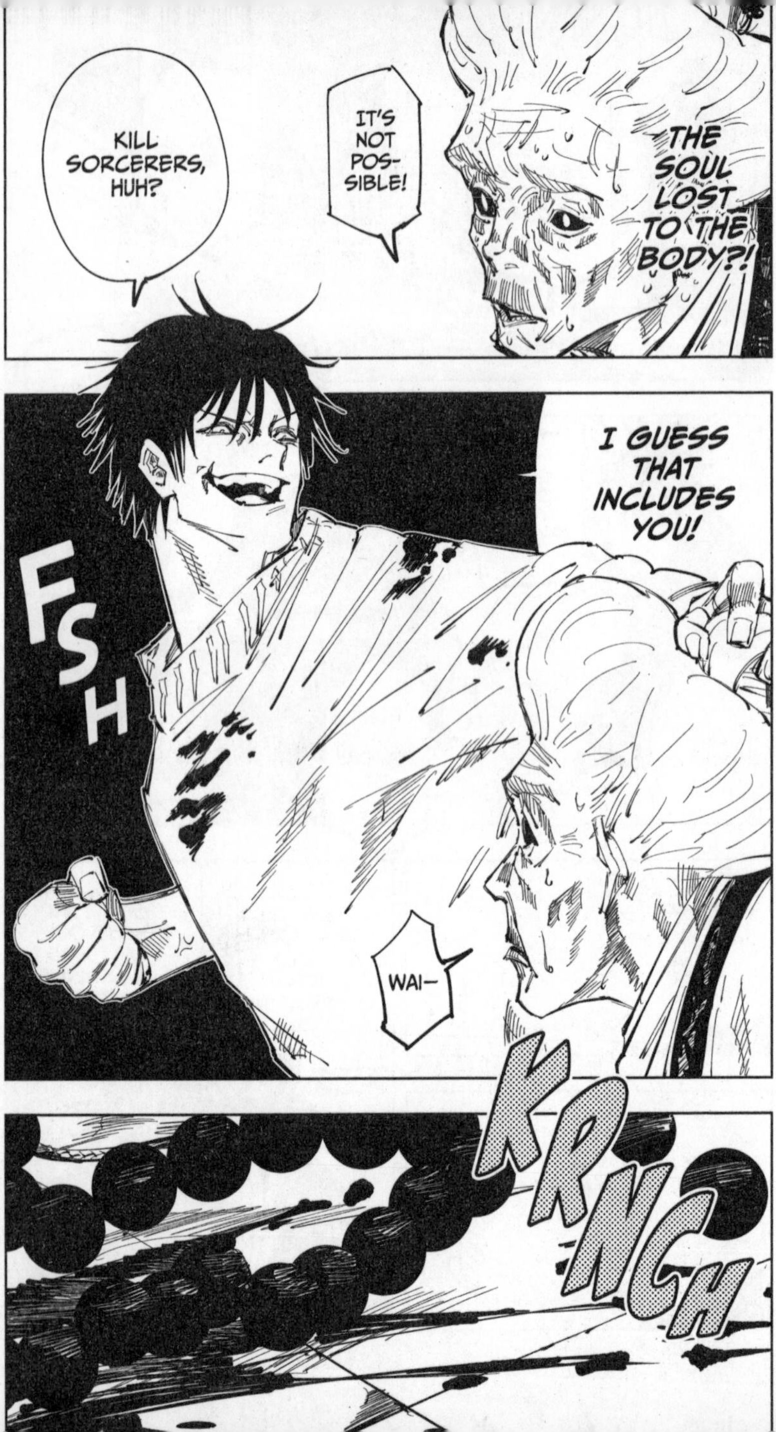
THE SOUL LOST TO THE BODY?!
IT'S NOT POS-SIBLE!
KILL SORCERERS, HUH?
I GUESS THAT INCLUDES YOU!
FSH
WAI—
KRNCH

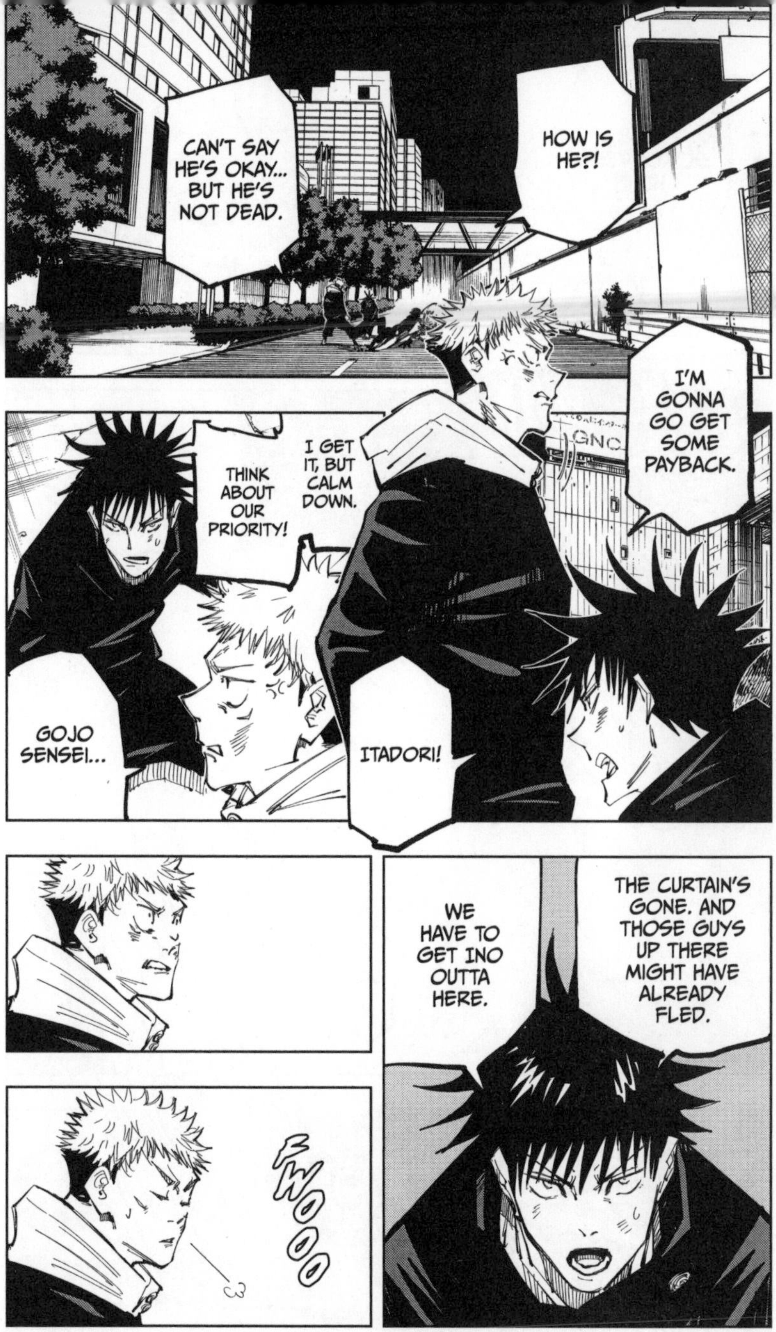
HOW IS HE?!
CAN'T SAY HE'S OKAY... BUT HE'S NOT DEAD.
I'M GONNA GO GET SOME PAYBACK.
ITADORI!
I GET IT, BUT CALM DOWN.
THINK ABOUT OUR PRIORITY!
GOJO SENSEI...
THE CURTAIN'S GONE. AND THOSE GUYS UP THERE MIGHT HAVE ALREADY FLED.
WE HAVE TO GET INO OUTTA HERE.
FWOOO

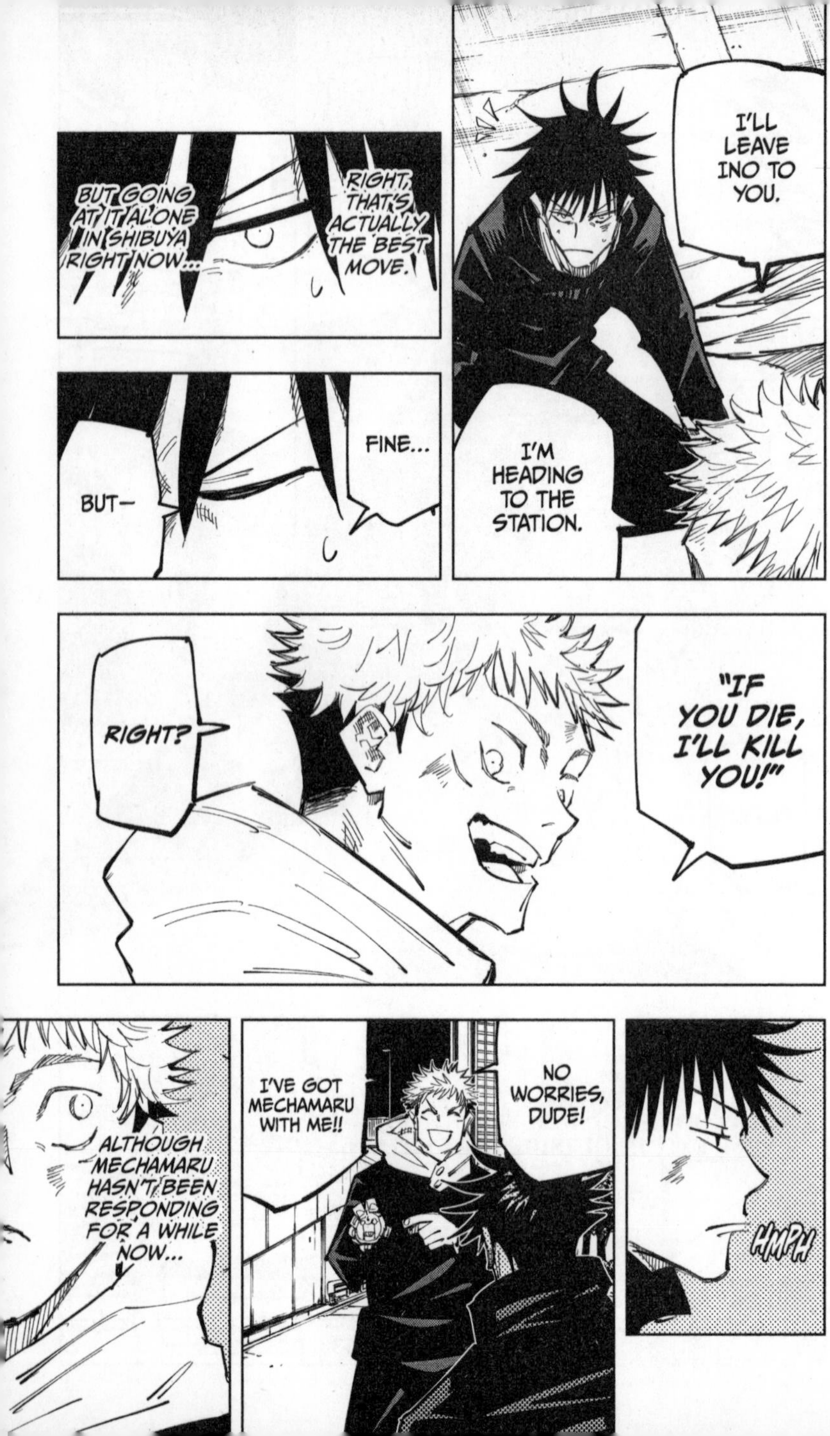
I'LL LEAVE INO TO YOU.
I'M HEADING TO THE STATION.
RIGHT, THAT'S ACTUALLY THE BEST MOVE.
BUT GOING AT IT ALONE IN SHIBUYA RIGHT NOW...
FINE...
BUT—
"IF YOU DIE, I'LL KILL YOU!"
RIGHT?
HMPH
NO WORRIES, DUDE!
I'VE GOT MECHAMARU WITH ME!!
ALTHOUGH MECHAMARU HASN'T BEEN RESPONDING FOR A WHILE NOW...

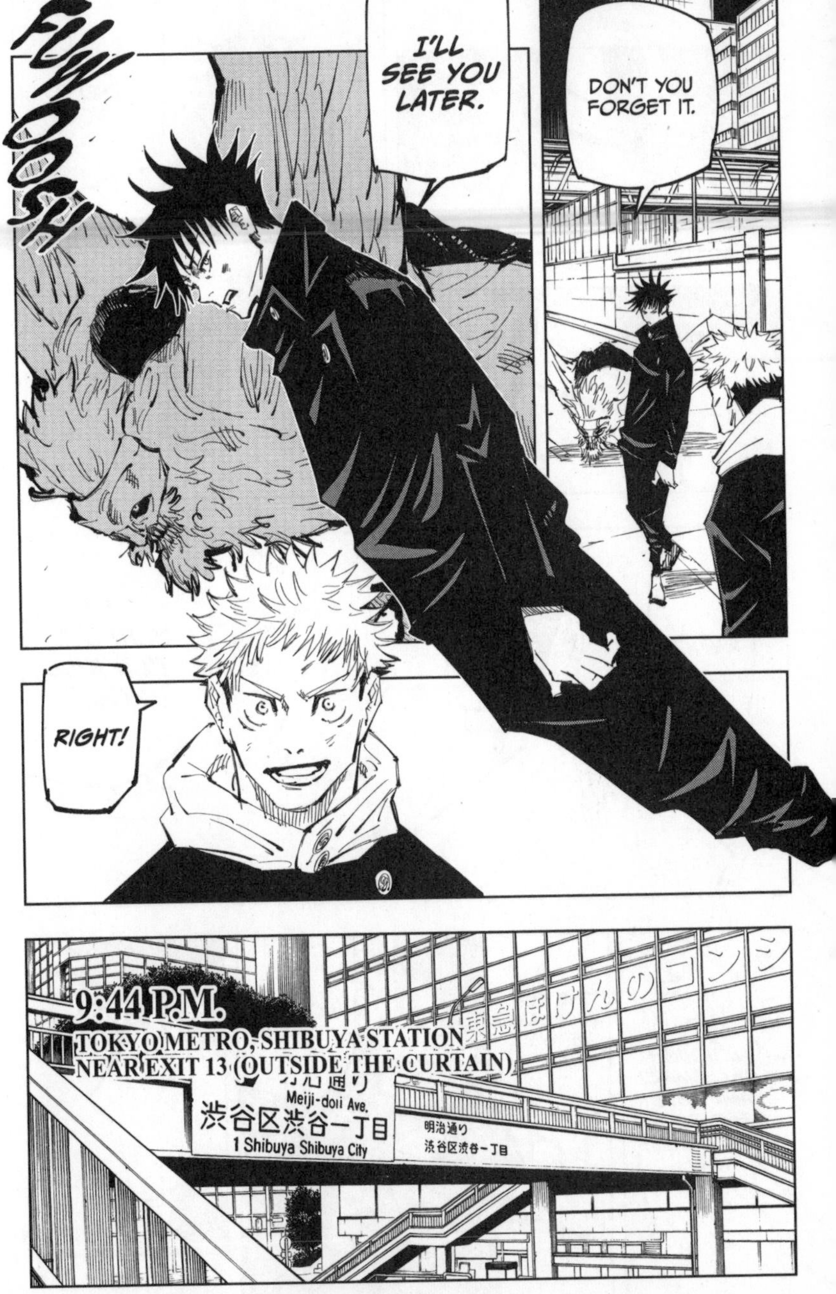
DON'T YOU FORGET IT.
I'LL SEE YOU LATER.
FWOOSH
RIGHT!
9:44 P.M.
TOKYO METRO, SHIBUYA STATION
NEAR EXIT 13 (OUTSIDE THE CURTAIN)
東急ほけんのコンシ
Meiji-dori Ave.
渋谷区渋谷一丁目
1 Shibuya Shibuya City
明治通り
渋谷区渋谷一丁目

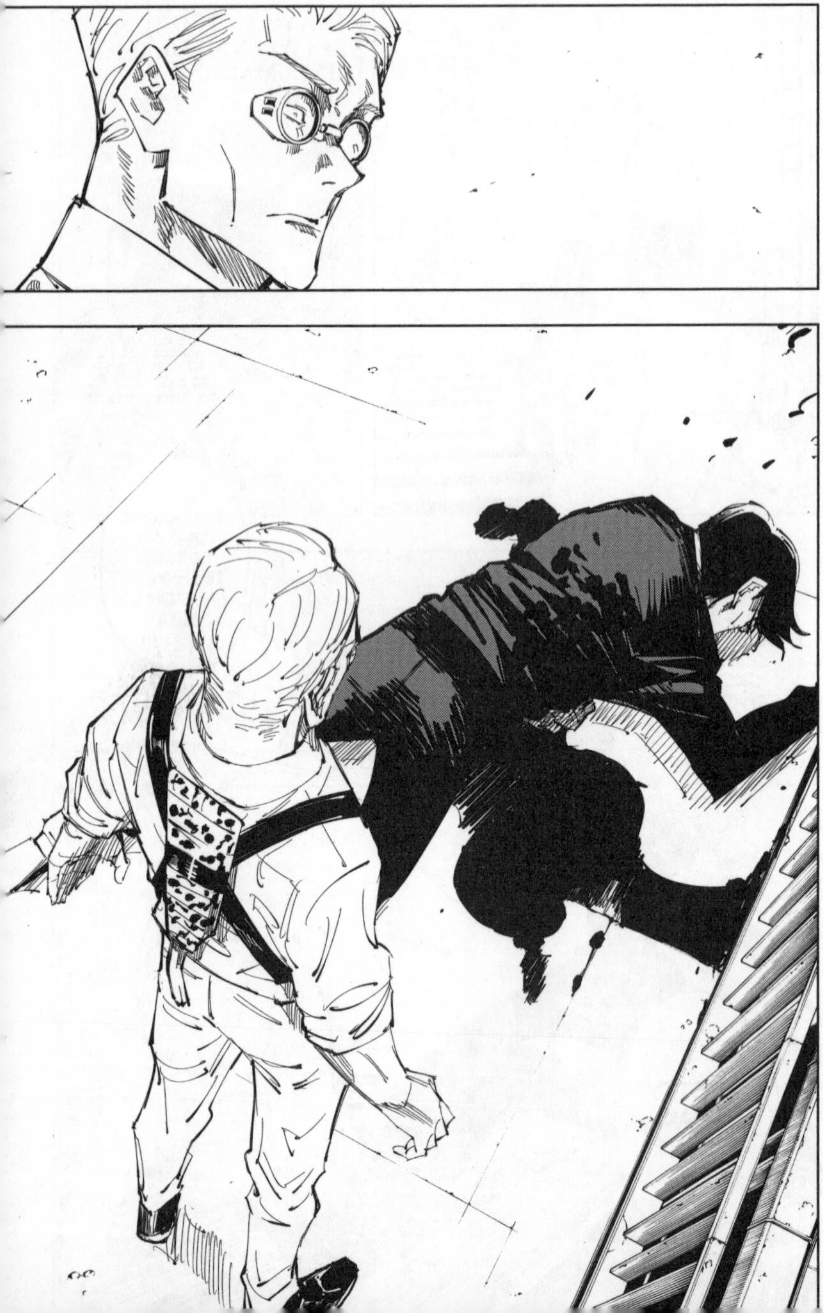

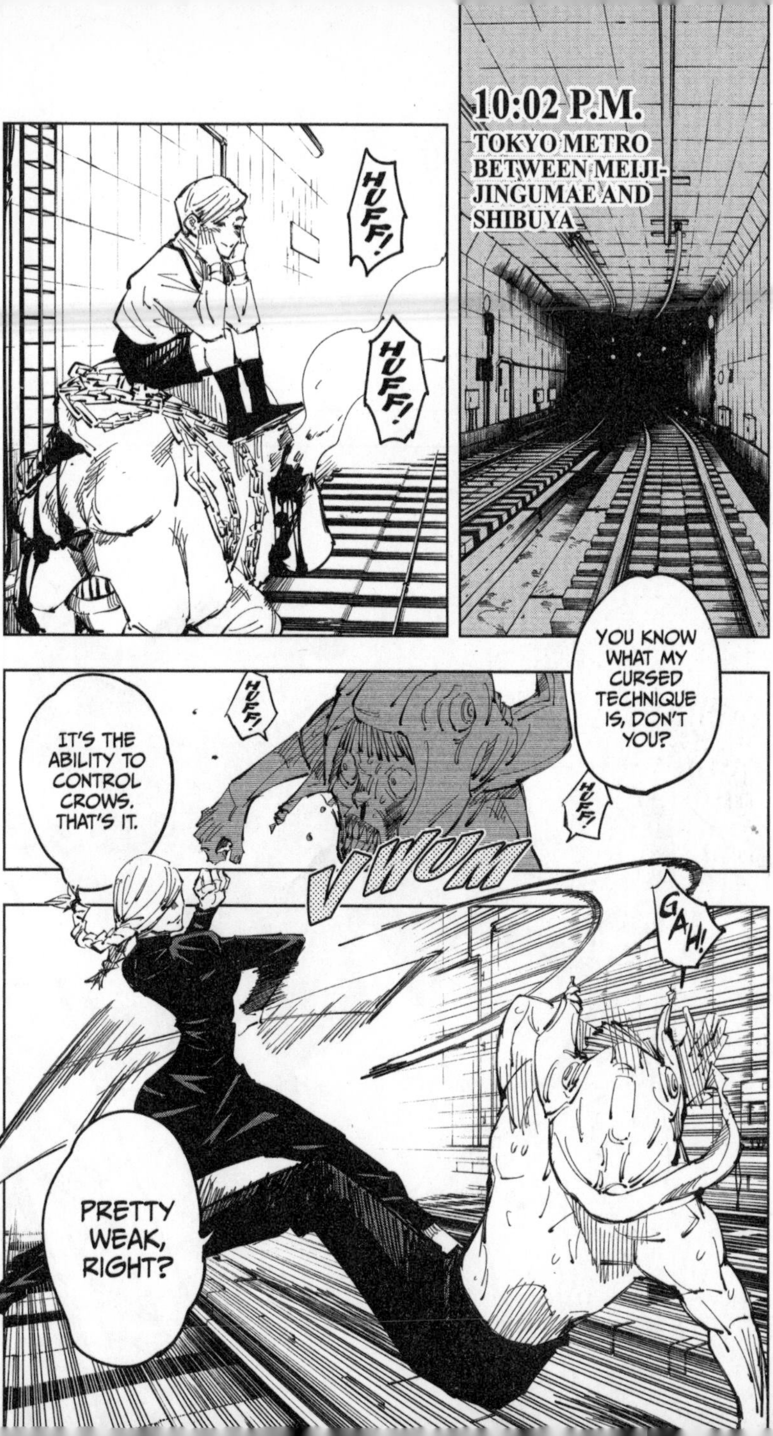
10:02 P.M.
TOKYO METRO BETWEEN MEIJI-JINGUMAE AND SHIBUYA
HUFF!
HUFF!
YOU KNOW WHAT MY CURSED TECHNIQUE IS, DON'T YOU?
HUFF!
HUFF!
IT'S THE ABILITY TO CONTROL CROWS. THAT'S IT.
VWUM
GAH!
PRETTY WEAK, RIGHT?

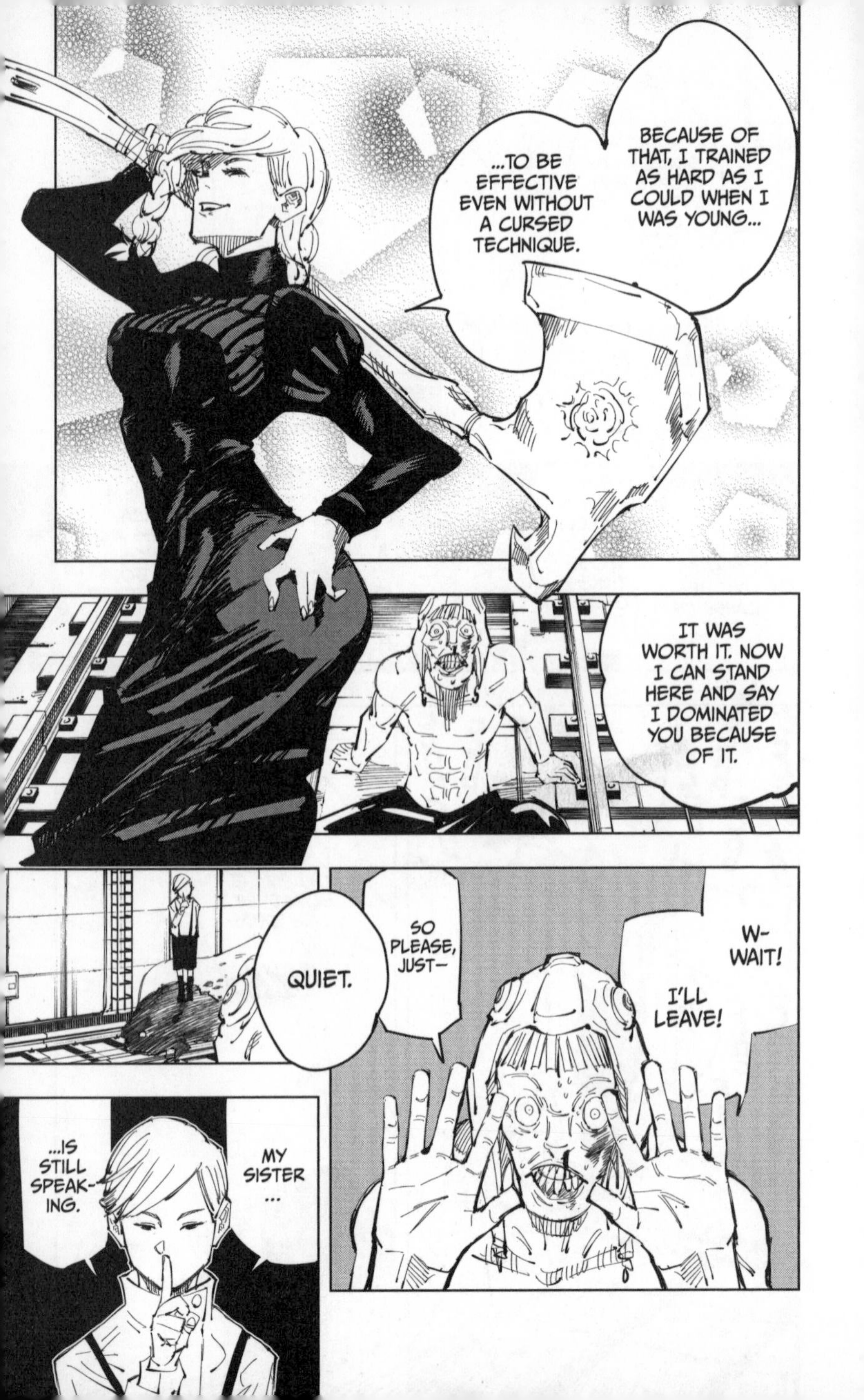
BECAUSE OF THAT, I TRAINED AS HARD AS I COULD WHEN I WAS YOUNG...
...TO BE EFFECTIVE EVEN WITHOUT A CURSED TECHNIQUE.
IT WAS WORTH IT. NOW I CAN STAND HERE AND SAY I DOMINATED YOU BECAUSE OF IT.
W-WAIT!
I'LL LEAVE!
SO PLEASE, JUST—
QUIET.
MY SISTER...
...IS STILL SPEAKING.

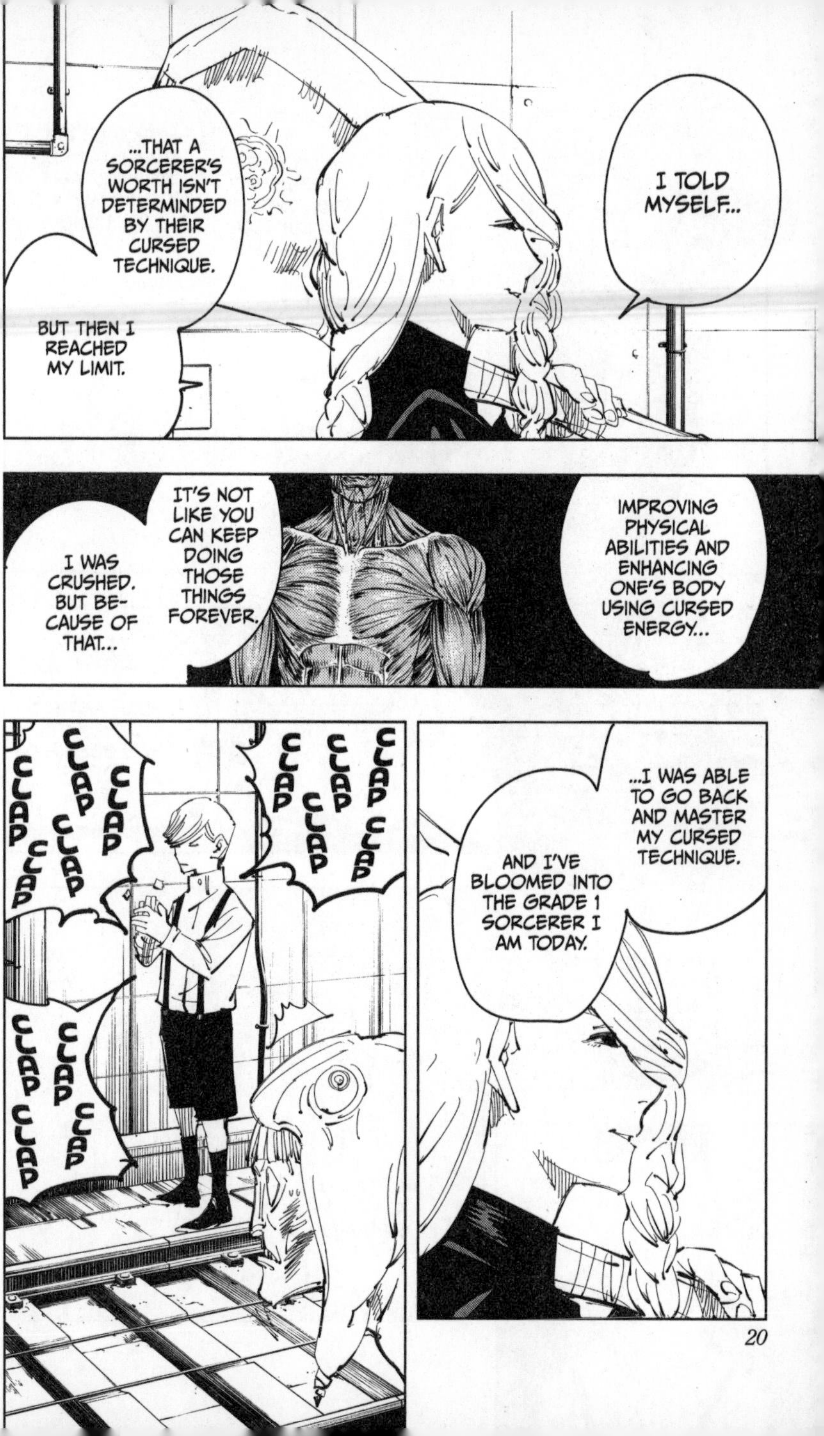
I TOLD MYSELF...
...THAT A SORCERER'S WORTH ISN'T DETERMINDED BY THEIR CURSED TECHNIQUE.
BUT THEN I REACHED MY LIMIT.
IMPROVING PHYSICAL ABILITIES AND ENHANCING ONE'S BODY USING CURSED ENERGY...
IT'S NOT LIKE YOU CAN KEEP DOING THOSE THINGS FOREVER.
I WAS CRUSHED. BUT BE-CAUSE OF THAT...
...I WAS ABLE TO GO BACK AND MASTER MY CURSED TECHNIQUE.
AND I'VE BLOOMED INTO THE GRADE 1 SORCERER I AM TODAY.
CLAP CLAP
CLAP
CLAP CLAP
CLAP
CLAP
CLAP
CLAP CLAP
CLAP
CLAP
CLAP CLAP
CLAP CLAP
CLAP

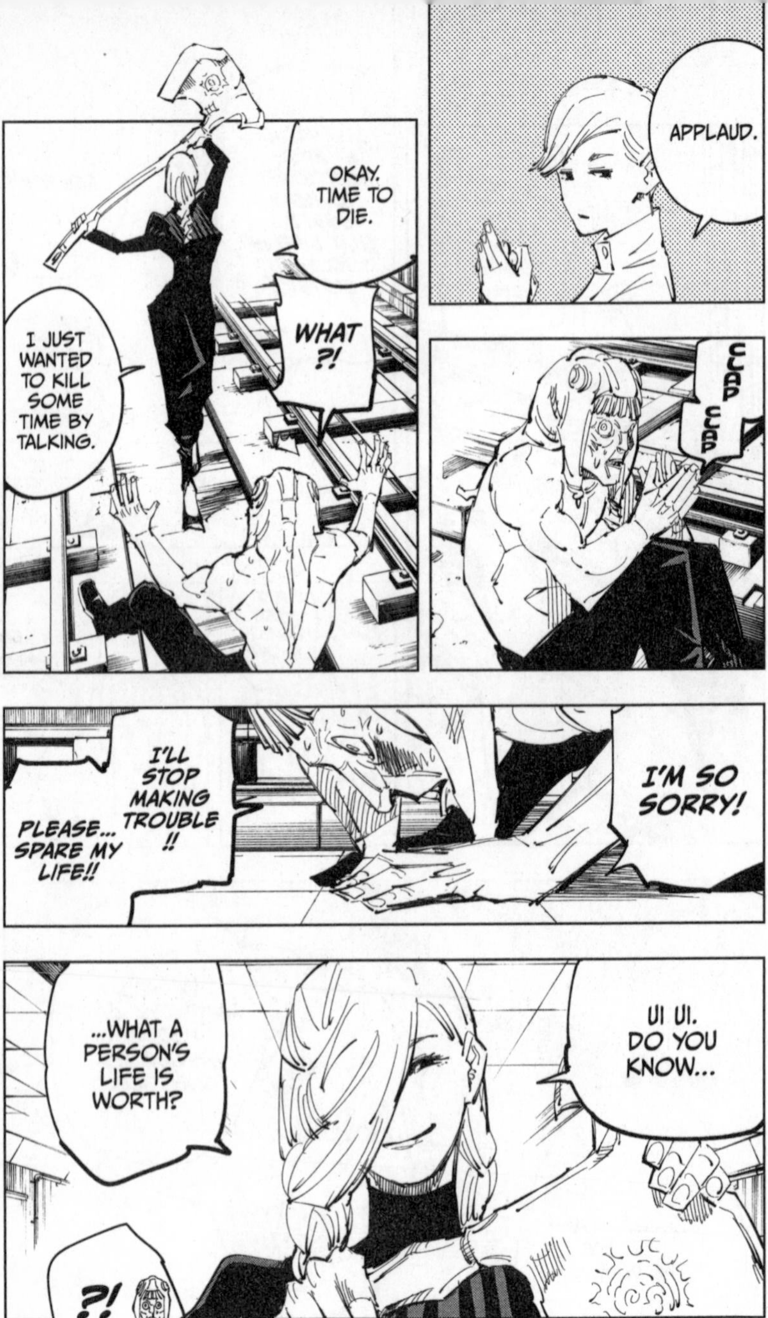
APPLAUD.
CLAP CLAP
OKAY. TIME TO DIE.
WHAT ?!
I JUST WANTED TO KILL SOME TIME BY TALKING.
I'M SO SORRY!
I'LL STOP MAKING TROUBLE !!
PLEASE... SPARE MY LIFE!!
UI UI. DO YOU KNOW...
...WHAT A PERSON'S LIFE IS WORTH?
?!

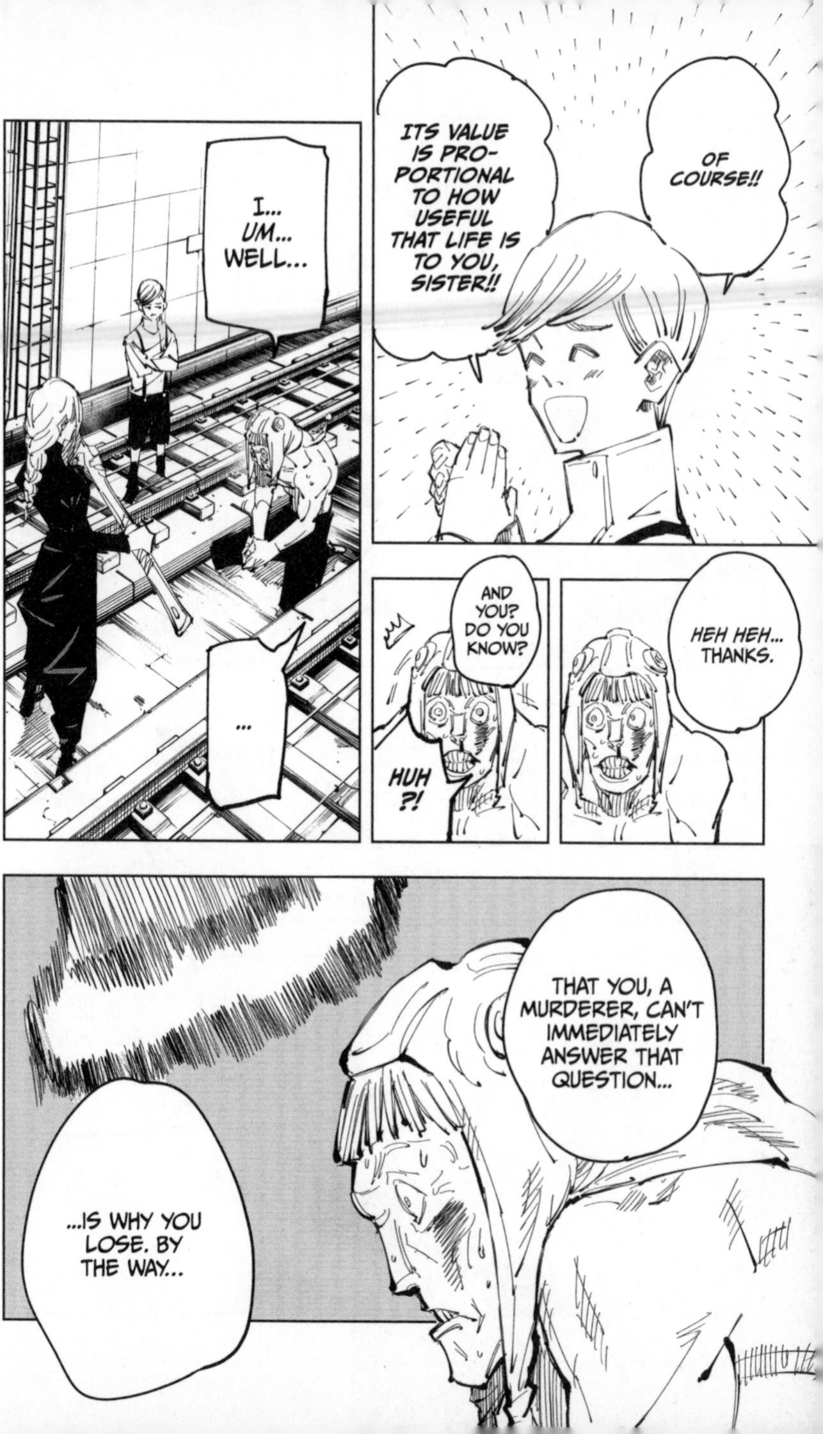
OF COURSE!!
ITS VALUE IS PRO- PORTIONAL TO HOW USEFUL THAT LIFE IS TO YOU, SISTER!!
HEH HEH... THANKS.
AND YOU? DO YOU KNOW?
HUH ?!
I... UM... WELL...
...
THAT YOU, A MURDERER, CAN'T IMMEDIATELY ANSWER THAT QUESTION...
...IS WHY YOU LOSE. BY THE WAY...

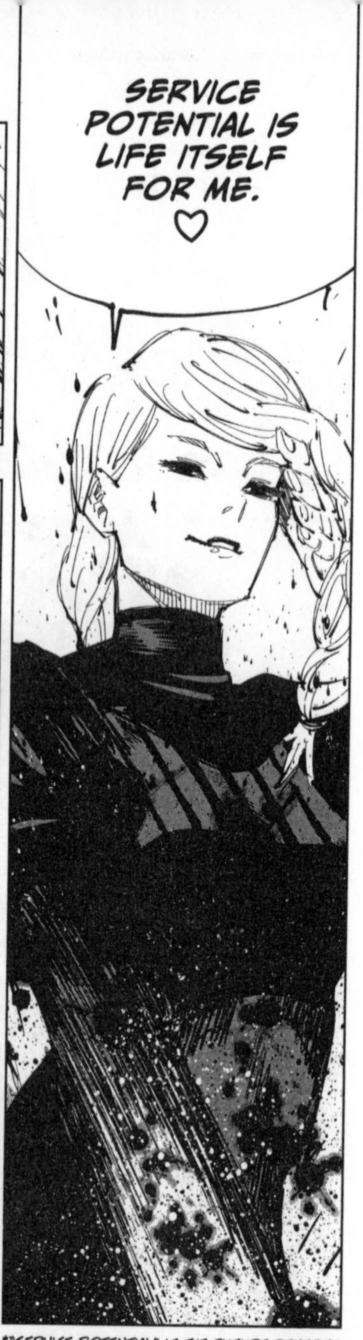
SERVICE POTENTIAL IS LIFE ITSELF FOR ME. ♡

*"SERVICE POTENTIAL" IS THE FUTURE BENEFITS THAT AN ASSET CAN BE EXPECTED TO BRING. THIS CONCEPT IS NOT APPLICABLE TO HUMANS. PROBABLY.

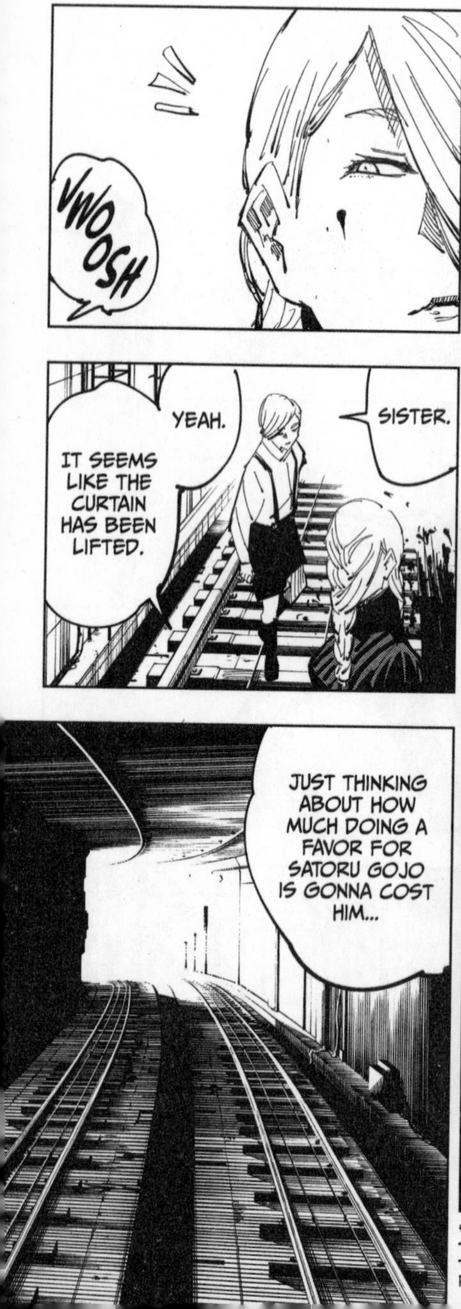
VWOOSH
SISTER.
YEAH.
IT SEEMS LIKE THE CURTAIN HAS BEEN LIFTED.
JUST THINKING ABOUT HOW MUCH DOING A FAVOR FOR SATORU GOJO IS GONNA COST HIM...

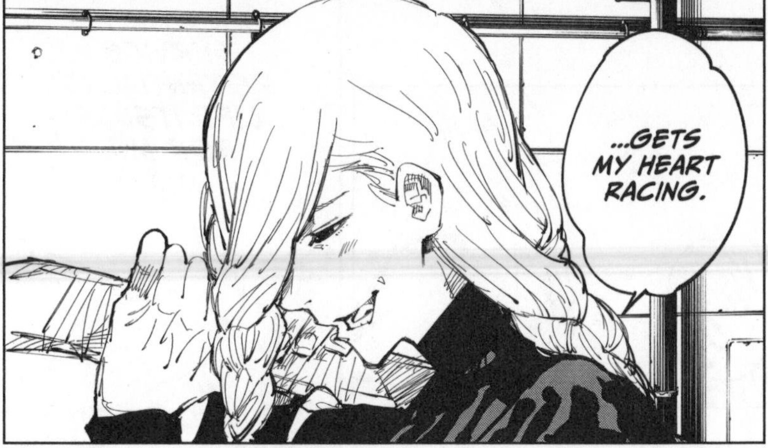
...GETS MY HEART RACING.
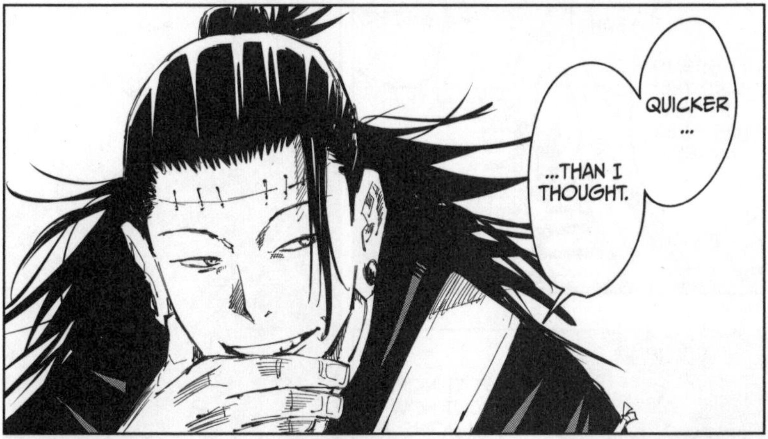
QUICKER ...
...THAN I THOUGHT.
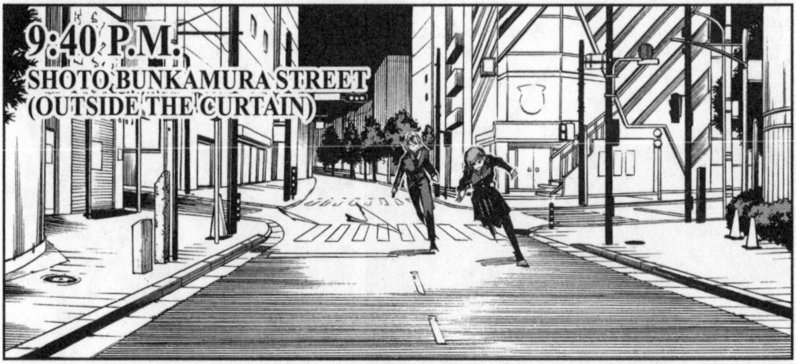
9:40 P.M.
SHOTO BUNKAMURA STREET (OUTSIDE THE CURTAIN)

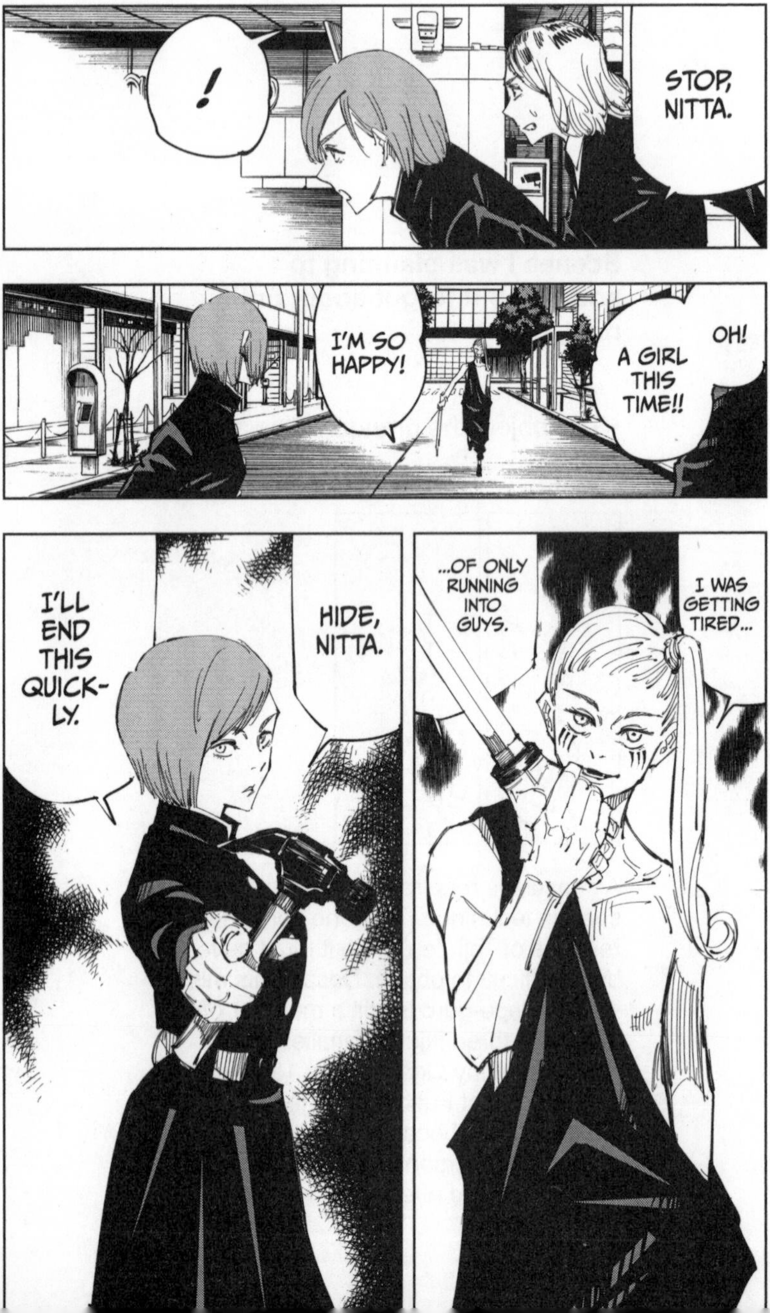
STOP, NITTA.
!
OH! A GIRL THIS TIME!!
I'M SO HAPPY!
I WAS GETTING TIRED...
...OF ONLY RUNNING INTO GUYS.
HIDE, NITTA.
I'LL END THIS QUICK-LY.

Scenes I was planning to address but forgot about until now, part 1

• The object the grandchild swallowed

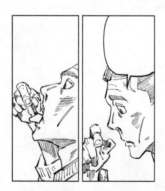

A capsule is required for Granny Ogami's seance technique. This one contained the remains of Toji Zen'in, so it must have been difficult to obtain. Despite his misfit status, Papa-guro is still a member of one of the big three jujutsu families. The reason Granny Ogami refers to him as Zen'in and not Fushiguro when summoning is because invoking the name used by the person at the height of their powers is more effective in necromancy.

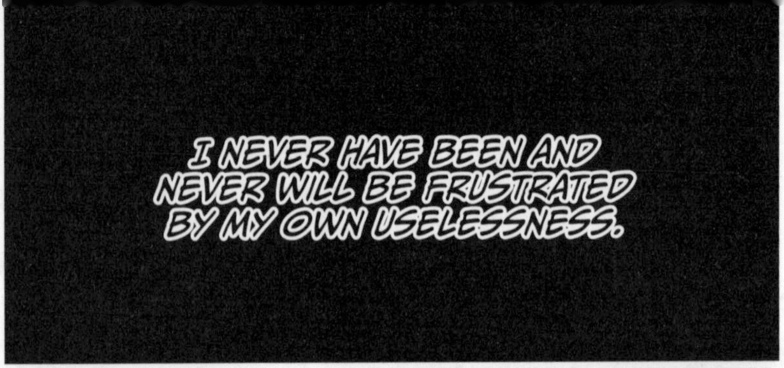
I NEVER HAVE BEEN AND NEVER WILL BE FRUSTRATED BY MY OWN USELESSNESS.

Chapter 99: The Shibuya Incident, Part 17

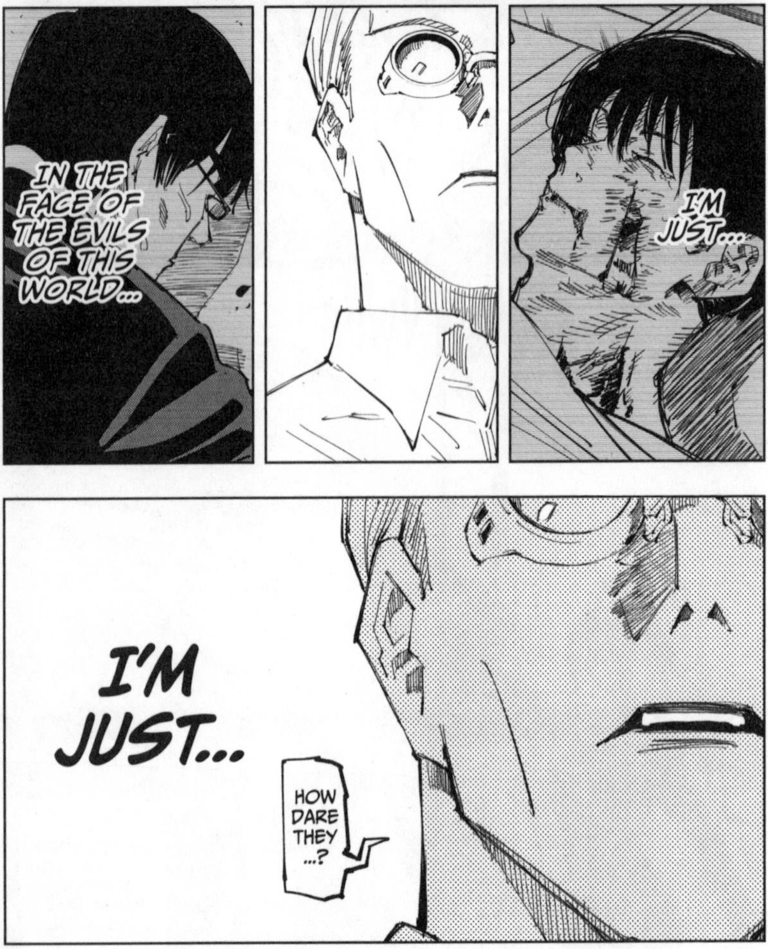
I'M JUST...
IN THE FACE OF THE EVILS OF THIS WORLD...
HOW DARE THEY ...?
I'M JUST...

Chapter 99: The Shibuya Incident, Part 17

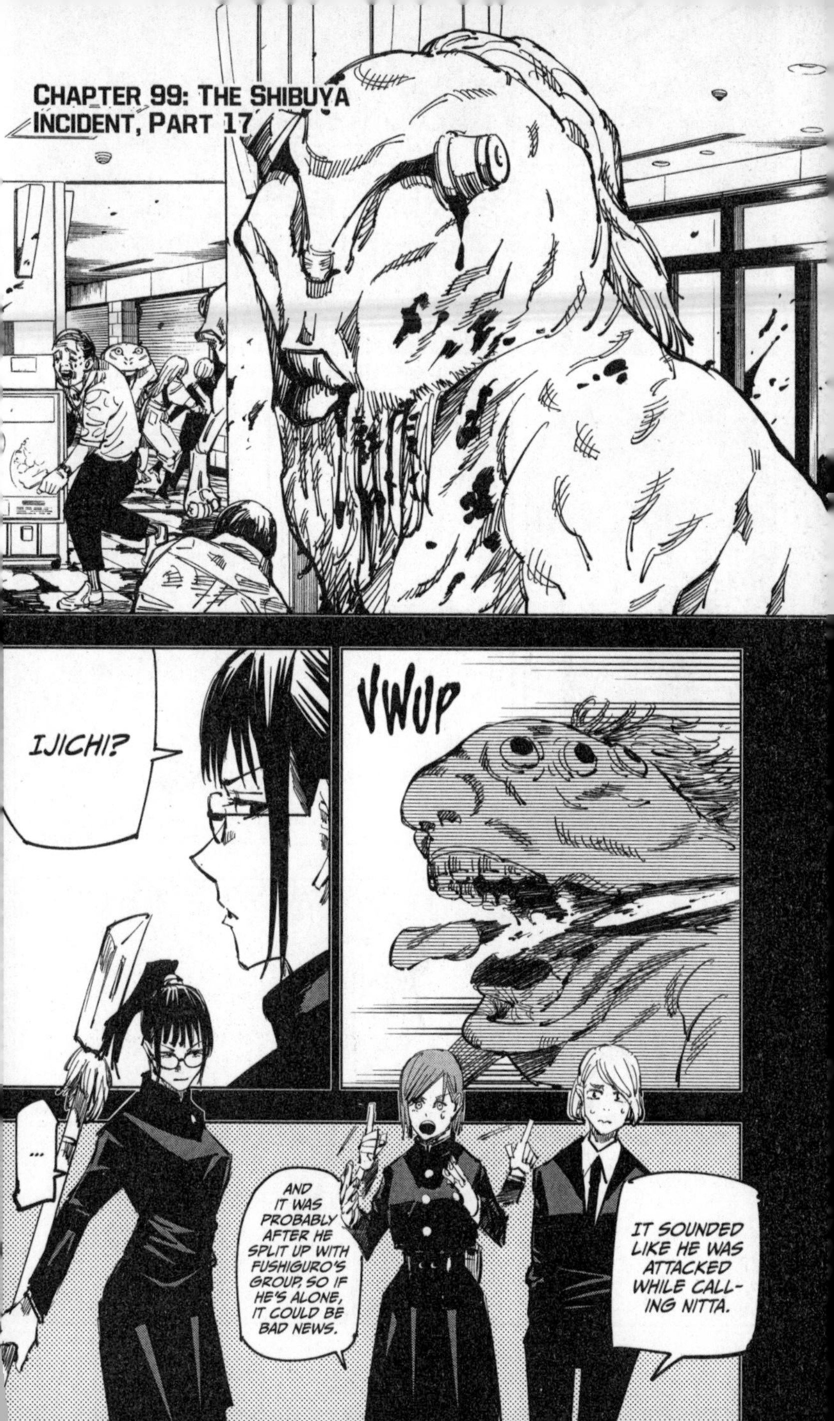
VWUP
IJICHI?
IT SOUNDED LIKE HE WAS ATTACKED WHILE CALLING NITTA.
AND IT WAS PROBABLY AFTER HE SPLIT UP WITH FUSHIGURO'S GROUP, SO IF HE'S ALONE, IT COULD BE BAD NEWS.
...

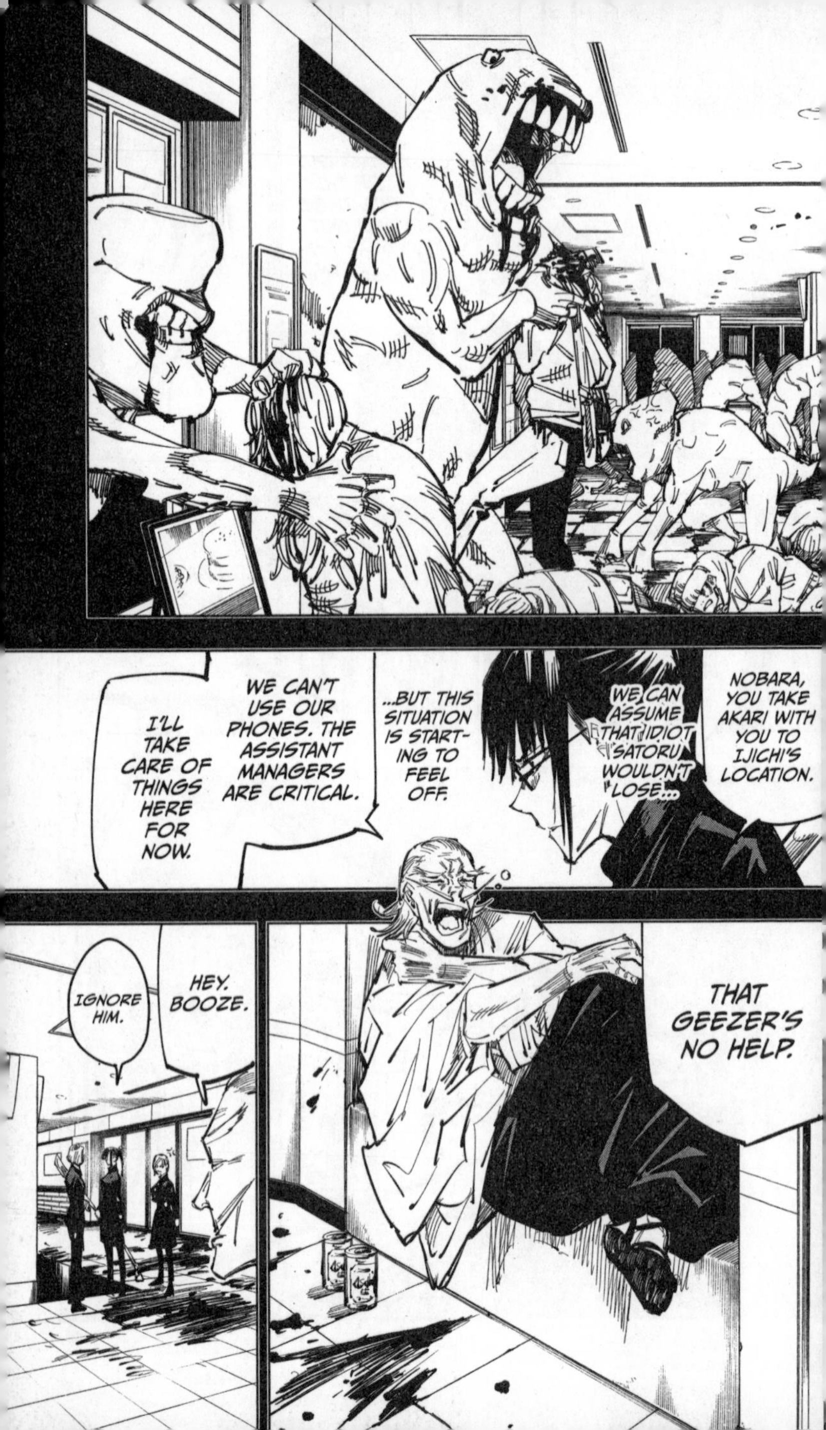
NOBARA, YOU TAKE AKARI WITH YOU TO IJICHI'S LOCATION.
WE CAN ASSUME THAT IDIOT SATORU WOULDN'T LOSE...
...BUT THIS SITUATION IS STARTING TO FEEL OFF.
WE CAN'T USE OUR PHONES. THE ASSISTANT MANAGERS ARE CRITICAL.
I'LL TAKE CARE OF THINGS HERE FOR NOW.
THAT GEEZER'S NO HELP.
HEY. BOOZE.
IGNORE HIM.

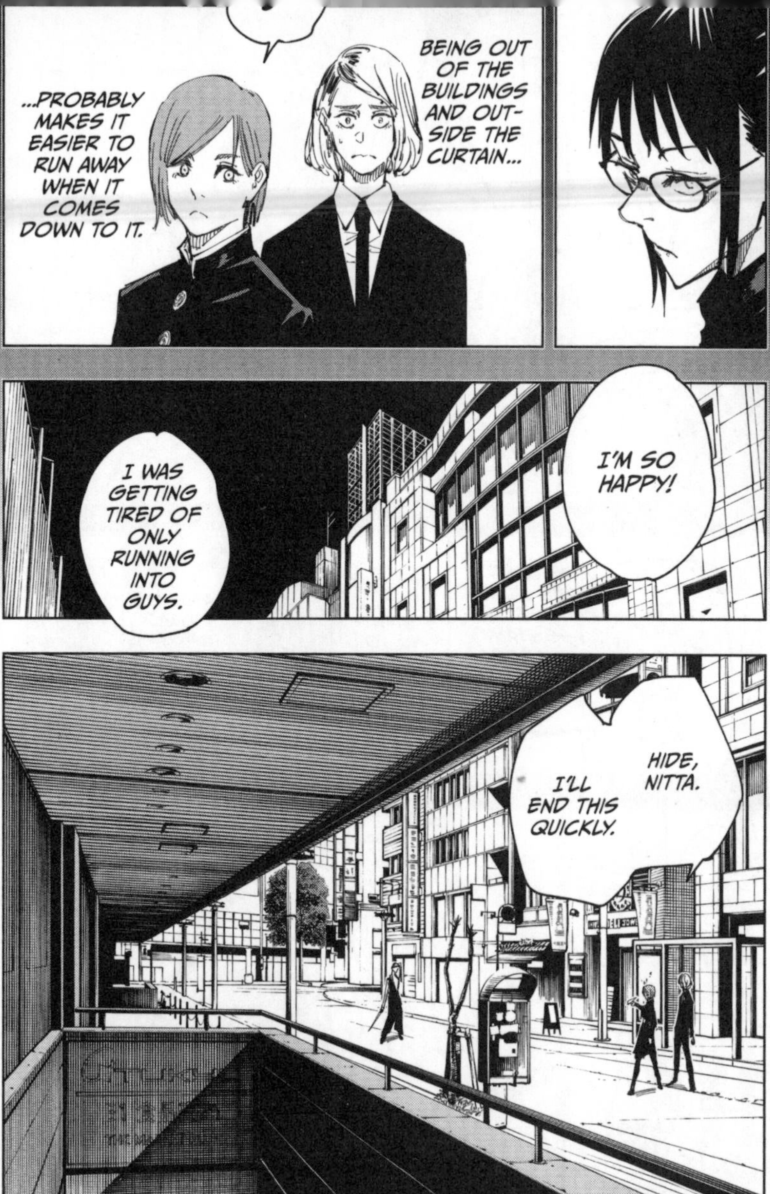
BEING OUT OF THE BUILDINGS AND OUT-SIDE THE CURTAIN...
...PROBABLY MAKES IT EASIER TO RUN AWAY WHEN IT COMES DOWN TO IT.
I'M SO HAPPY!
I WAS GETTING TIRED OF ONLY RUNNING INTO GUYS.
HIDE, NITTA.
I'LL END THIS QUICKLY.

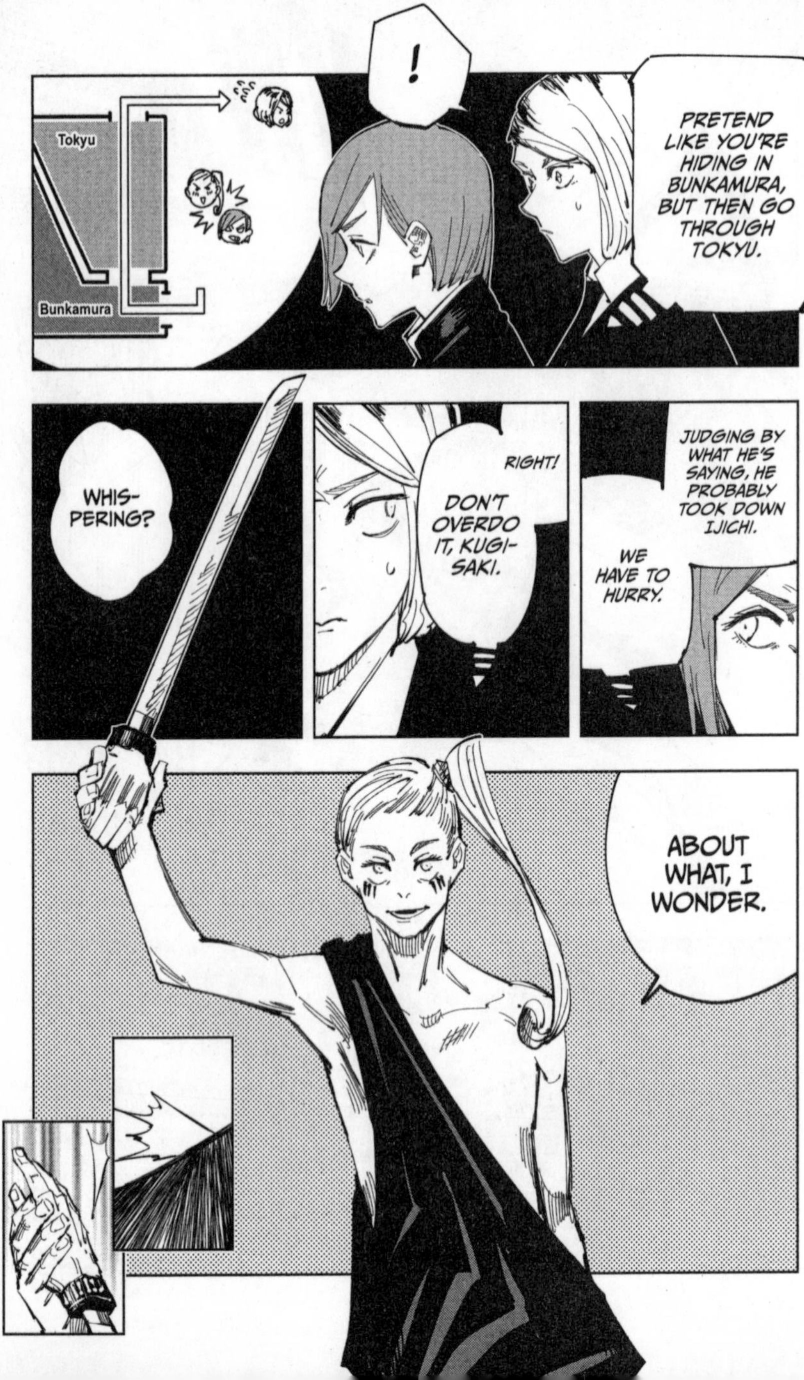
PRETEND LIKE YOU'RE HIDING IN BUNKAMURA, BUT THEN GO THROUGH TOKYU.
!
Tokyu
Bunkamura
JUDGING BY WHAT HE'S SAYING, HE PROBABLY TOOK DOWN IJICHI.
WE HAVE TO HURRY.
RIGHT!
DON'T OVERDO IT, KUGI-SAKI.
WHIS-PERING?
ABOUT WHAT, I WONDER.

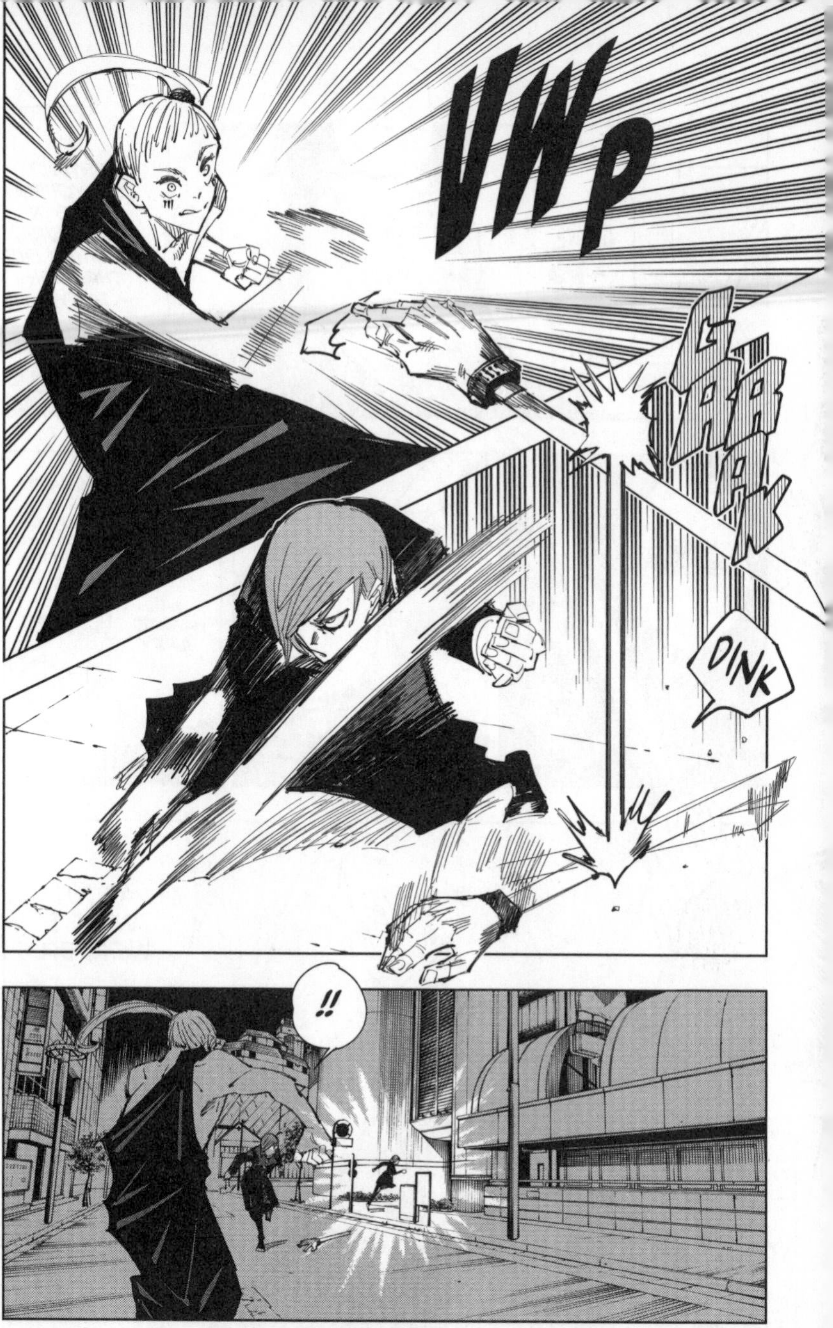
VWP
CAAAK
DINK
!!

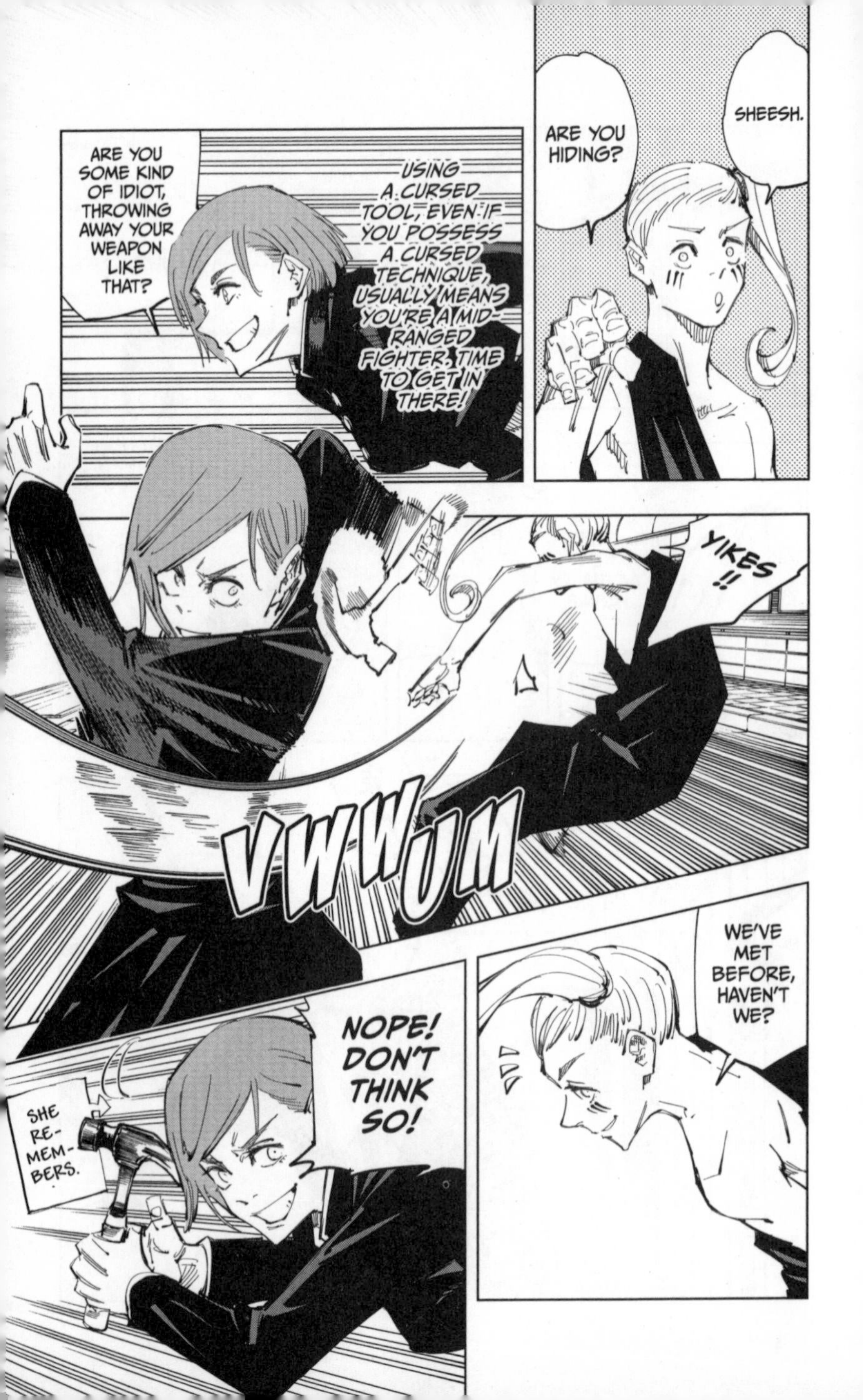
SHEESH.
ARE YOU HIDING?
USING A CURSED TOOL, EVEN IF YOU POSSESS A CURSED TECHNIQUE, USUALLY MEANS YOU'RE A MID-RANGED FIGHTER. TIME TO GET IN THERE!
ARE YOU SOME KIND OF IDIOT, THROWING AWAY YOUR WEAPON LIKE THAT?
YIKES!!
VWWUUM
WE'VE MET BEFORE, HAVEN'T WE?
NOPE! DON'T THINK SO!
SHE RE-MEM-BERS.

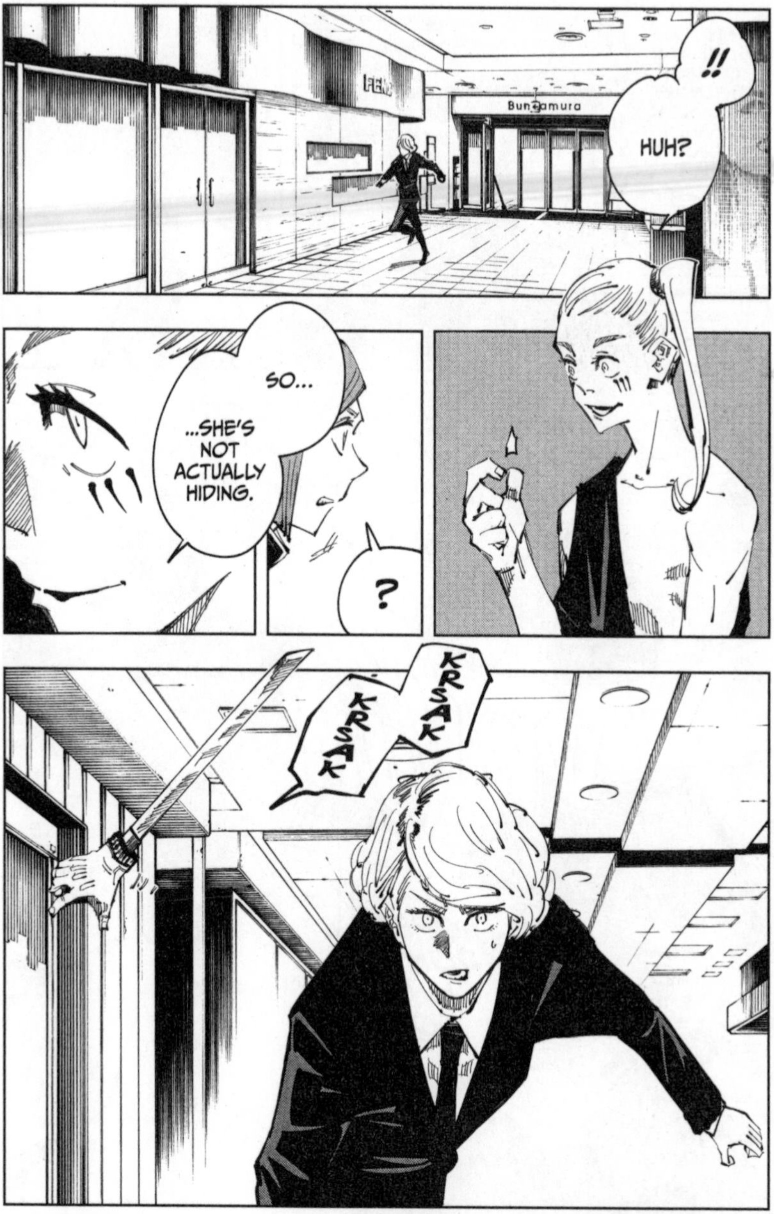
!!
HUH?
?
SO...
...SHE'S NOT ACTUALLY HIDING.
KRSAK
KRSAK

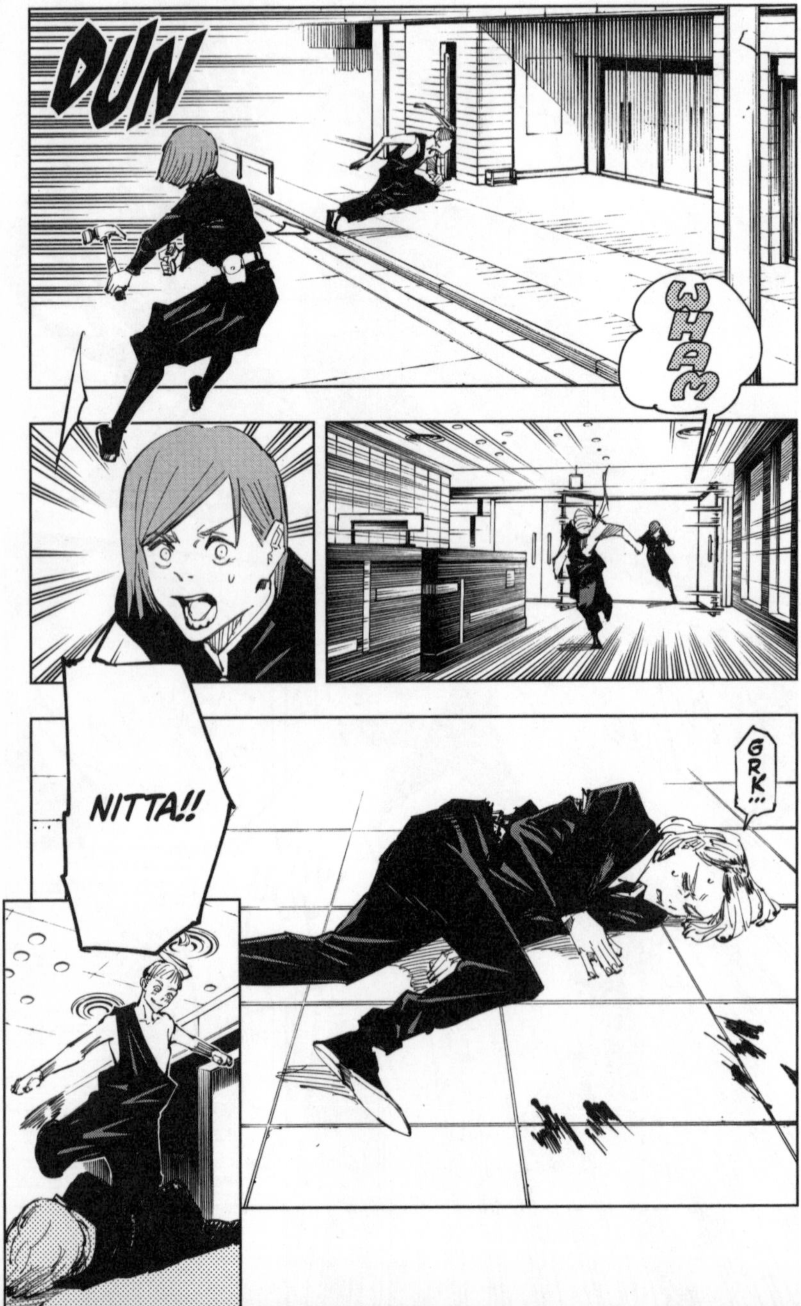
DUN
WHAM
NITTA!!
GRK...

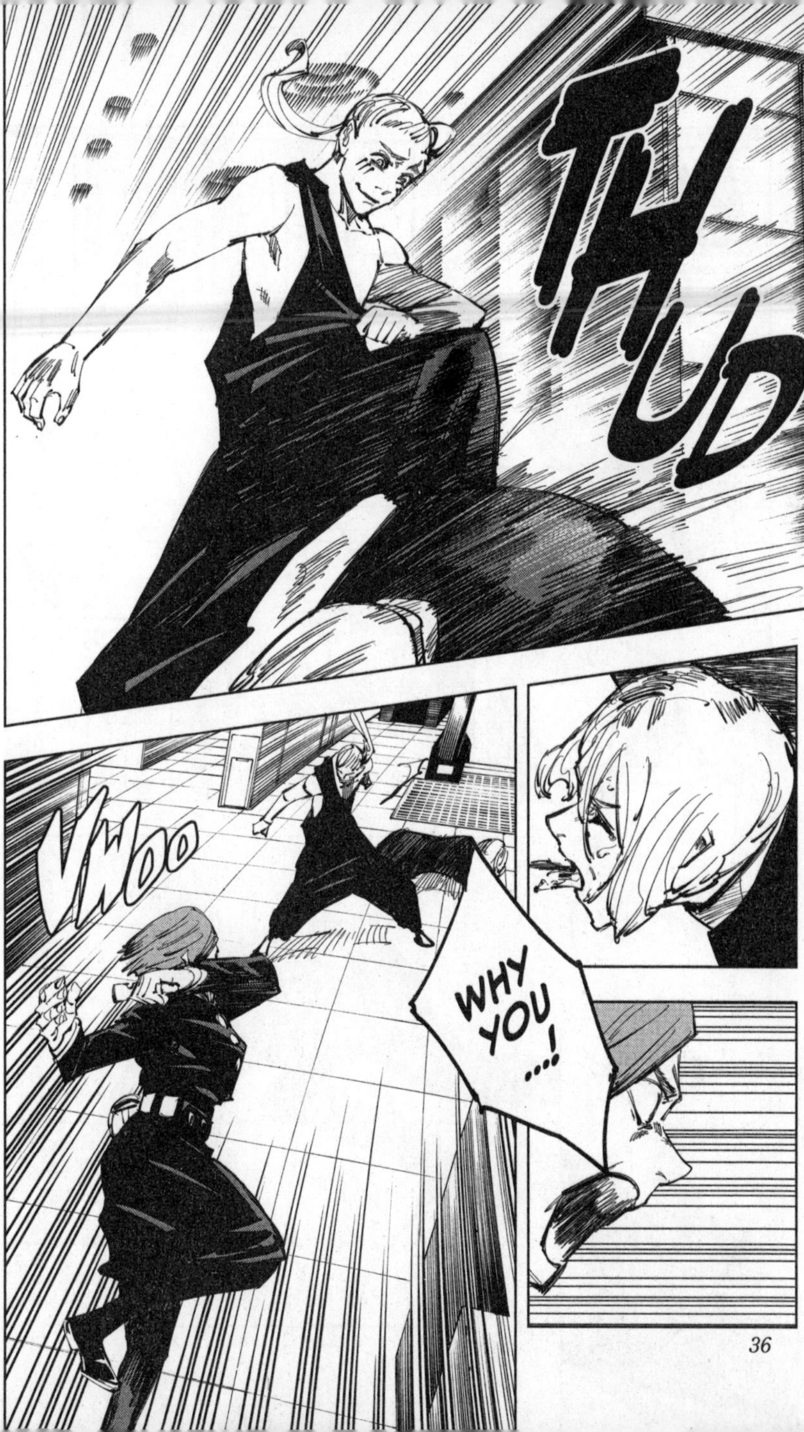
THUD
WHY YOU ...!
VWOO

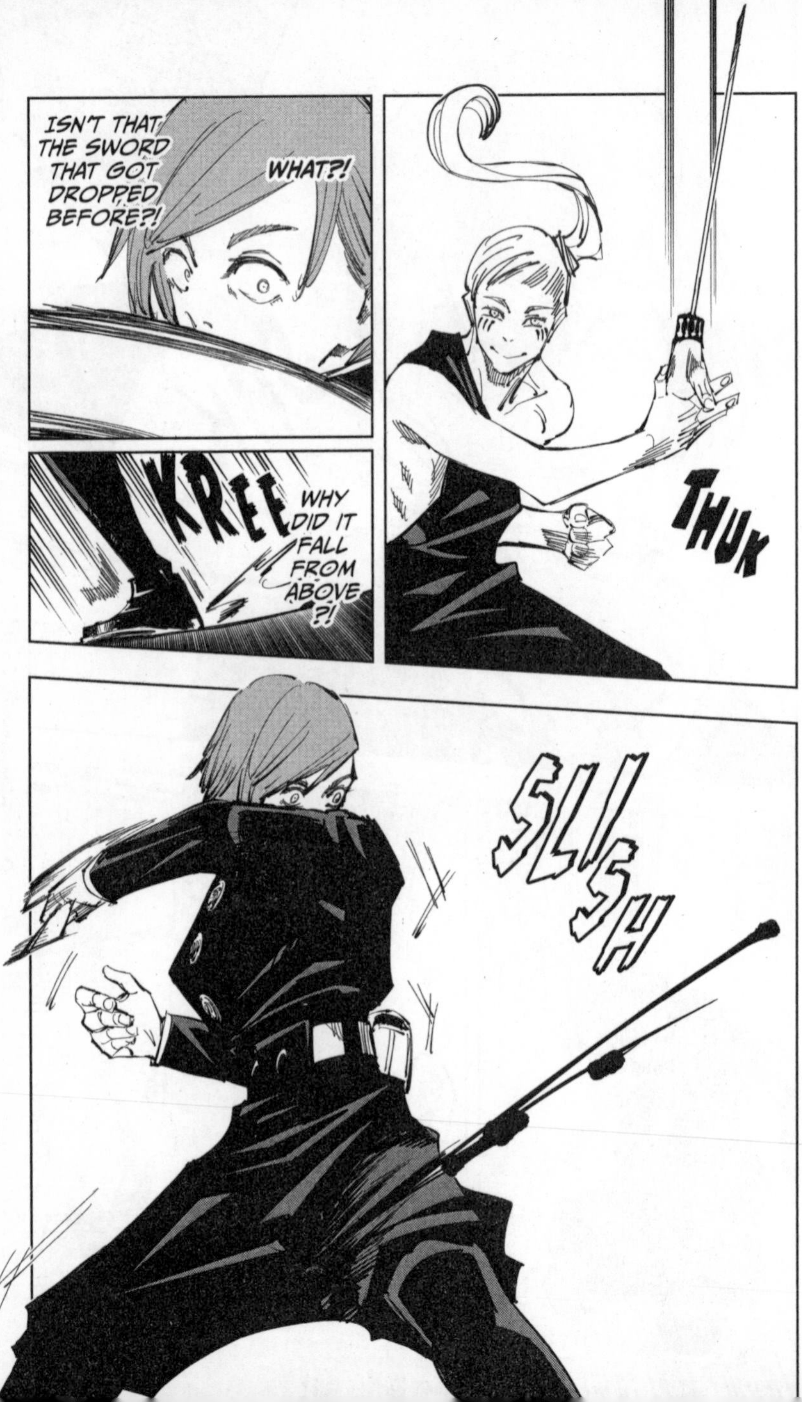
THUK
WHAT?!
ISN'T THAT THE SWORD THAT GOT DROPPED BEFORE?!
WHY DID IT FALL FROM ABOVE ?!
KREE
SLISH

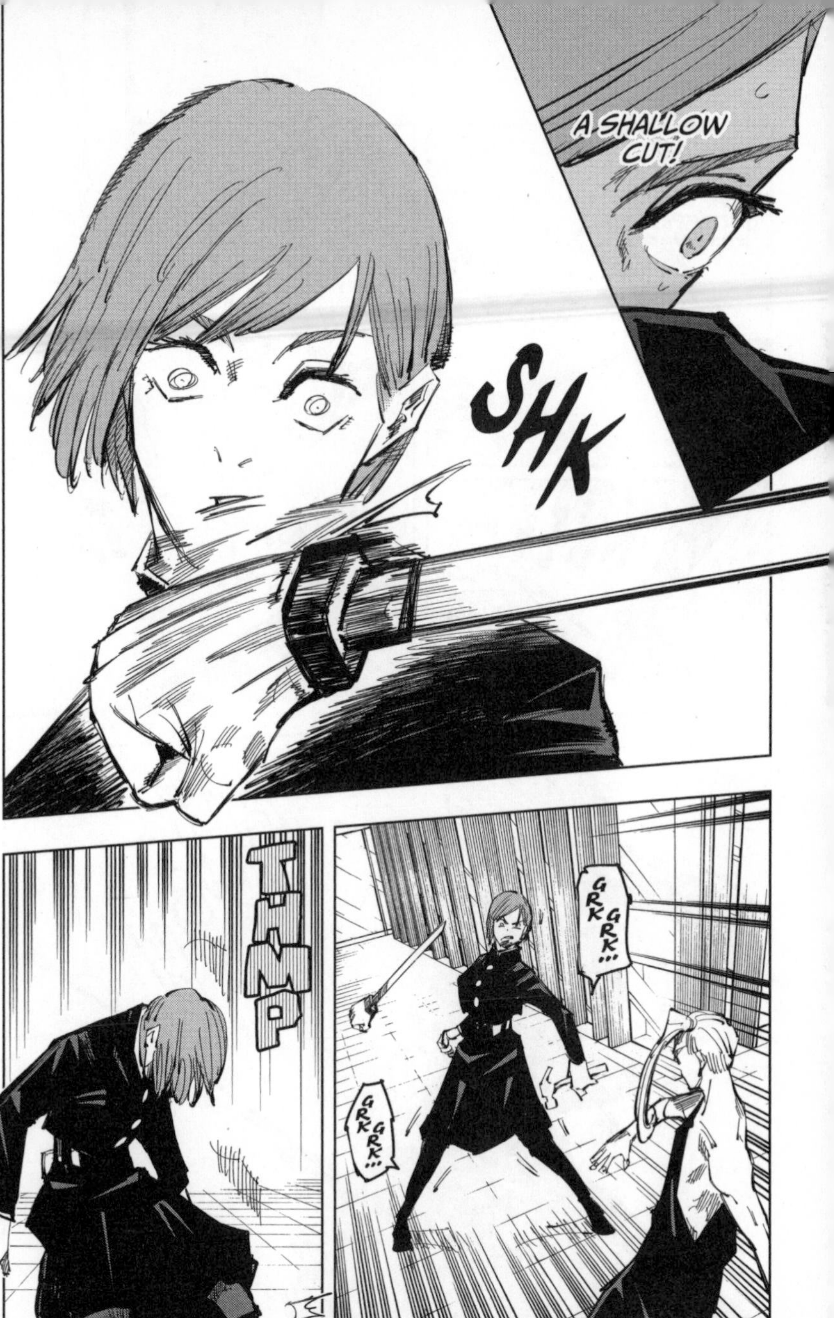
A SHALLOW CUT!
SHK
GRK GRK...
GRK GRK...
THMP

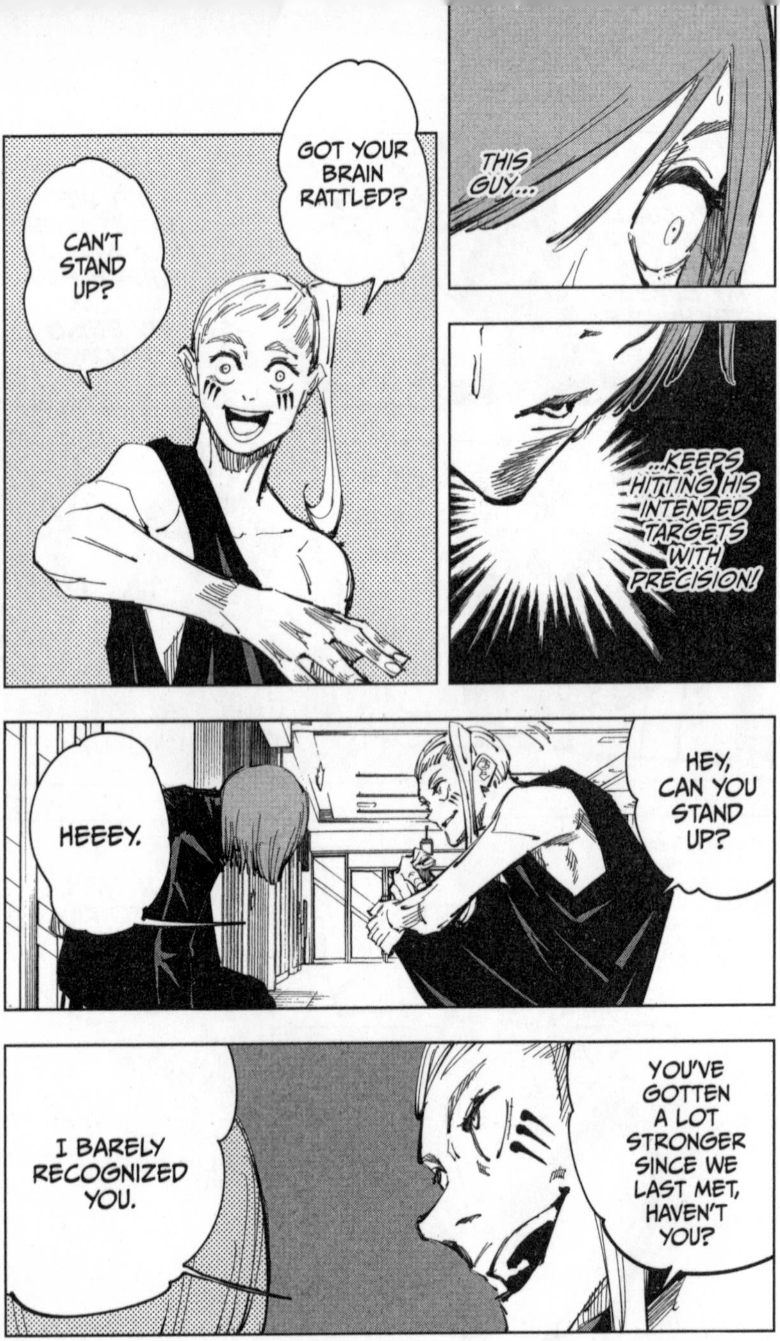
THIS GUY...
...KEEPS HITTING HIS INTENDED TARGETS WITH PRECISION!
GOT YOUR BRAIN RATTLED?
CAN'T STAND UP?
HEY, CAN YOU STAND UP?
HEEEY.
YOU'VE GOTTEN A LOT STRONGER SINCE WE LAST MET, HAVEN'T YOU?
I BARELY RECOGNIZED YOU.

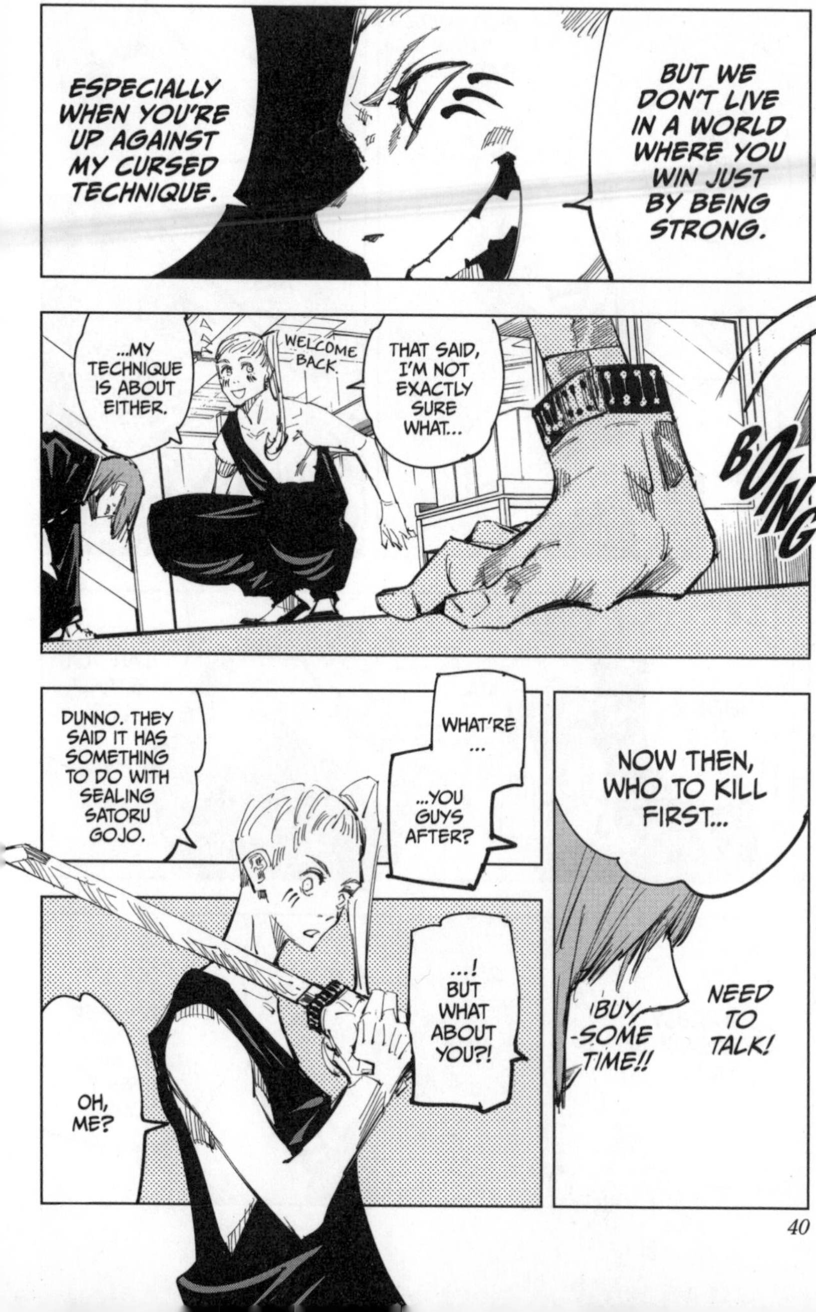
BUT WE DON'T LIVE IN A WORLD WHERE YOU WIN JUST BY BEING STRONG.
ESPECIALLY WHEN YOU'RE UP AGAINST MY CURSED TECHNIQUE.
BOING
THAT SAID, I'M NOT EXACTLY SURE WHAT...
WELCOME BACK.
...MY TECHNIQUE IS ABOUT EITHER.
NOW THEN, WHO TO KILL FIRST...
NEED TO TALK!
BUY SOME TIME!!
WHAT'RE ...
...YOU GUYS AFTER?
DUNNO. THEY SAID IT HAS SOMETHING TO DO WITH SEALING SATORU GOJO.
...! BUT WHAT ABOUT YOU?!
OH, ME?

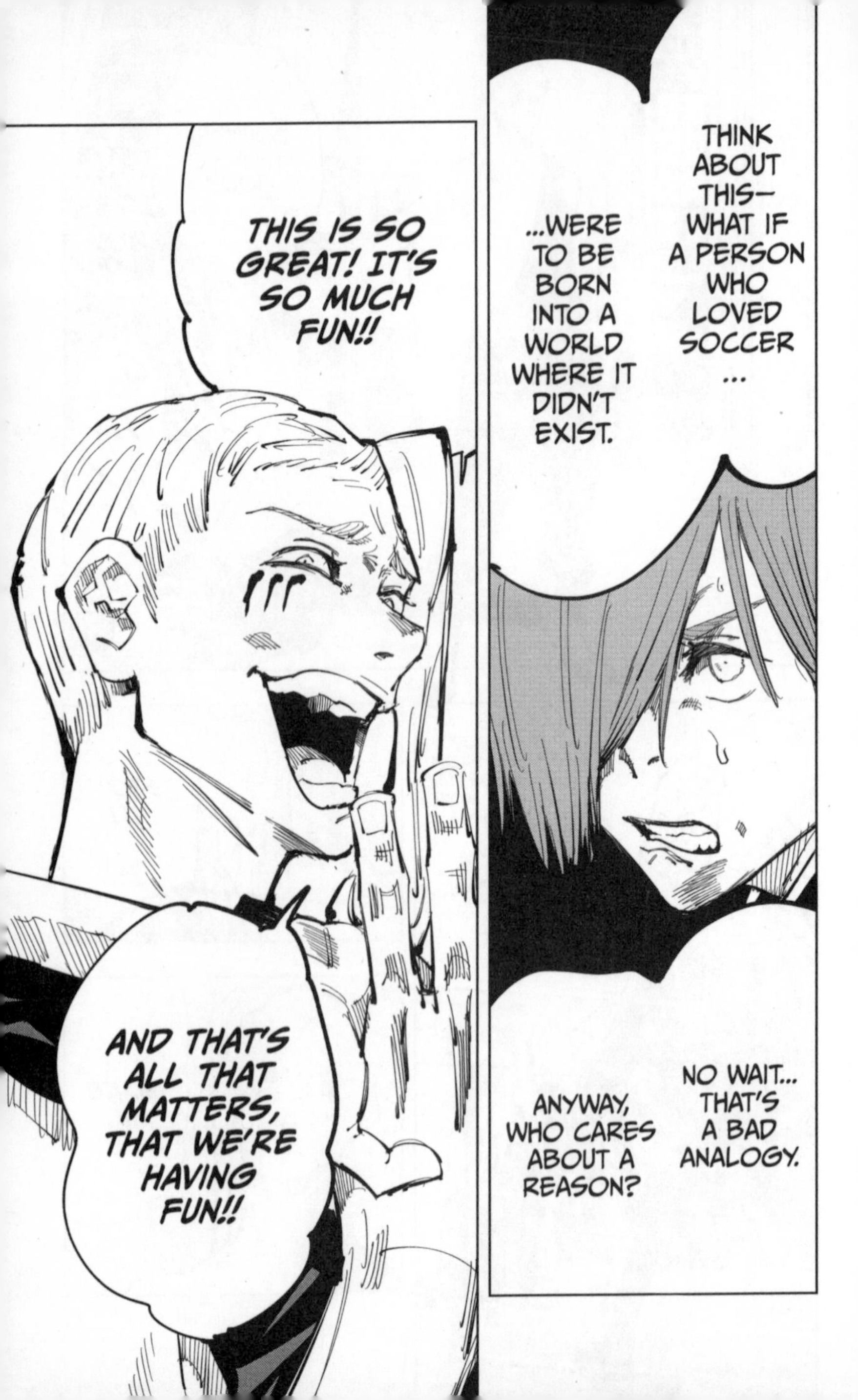
THINK ABOUT THIS— WHAT IF A PERSON WHO LOVED SOCCER ...
...WERE TO BE BORN INTO A WORLD WHERE IT DIDN'T EXIST.
NO WAIT... THAT'S A BAD ANALOGY.
ANYWAY, WHO CARES ABOUT A REASON?
THIS IS SO GREAT! IT'S SO MUCH FUN!!
AND THAT'S ALL THAT MATTERS, THAT WE'RE HAVING FUN!!

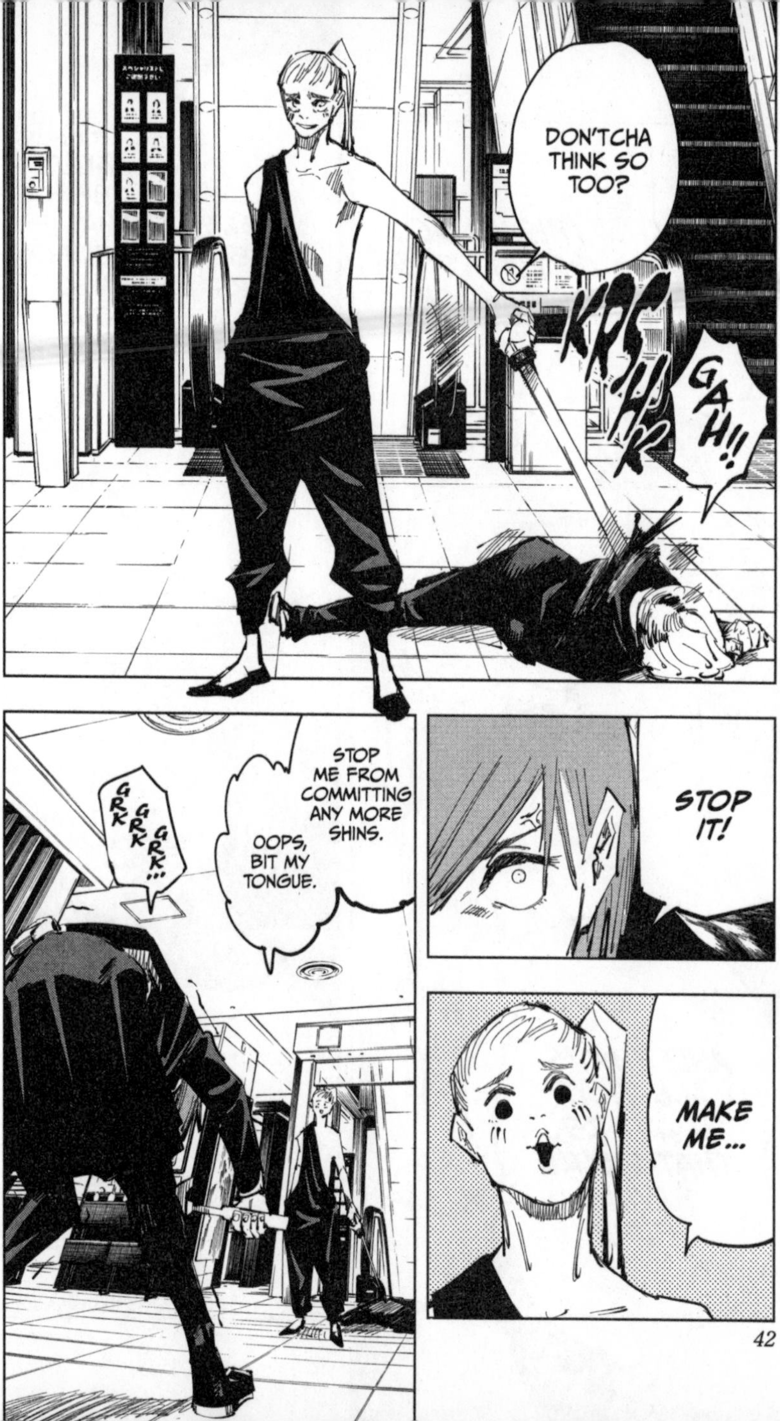
DON'TCHA THINK SO TOO?
KRSHHK
GAH!!
STOP IT!
MAKE ME...
STOP ME FROM COMMITTING ANY MORE SHINS.
OOPS, BIT MY TONGUE.
GRK GRK GRK...

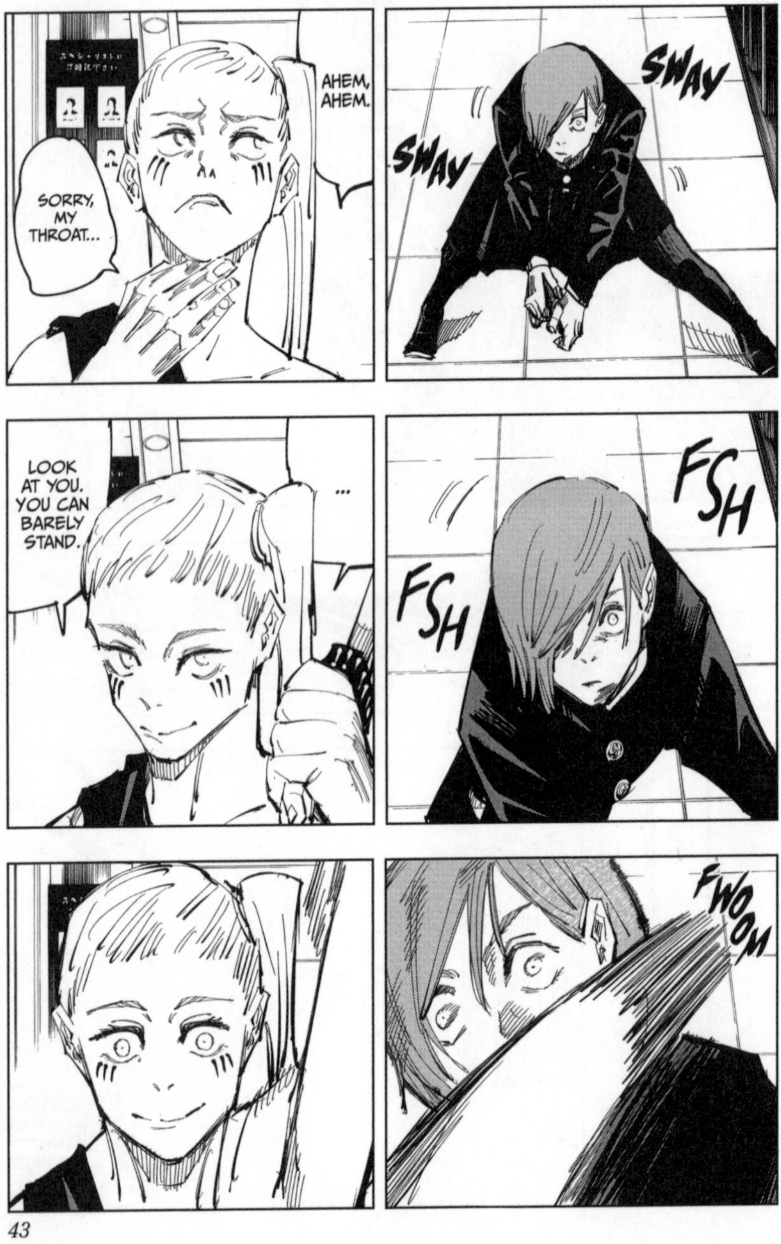
SWAY
SWAY
AHEM, AHEM.
SORRY, MY THROAT...
FSH
FSH
...
LOOK AT YOU. YOU CAN BARELY STAND.
FWOOM

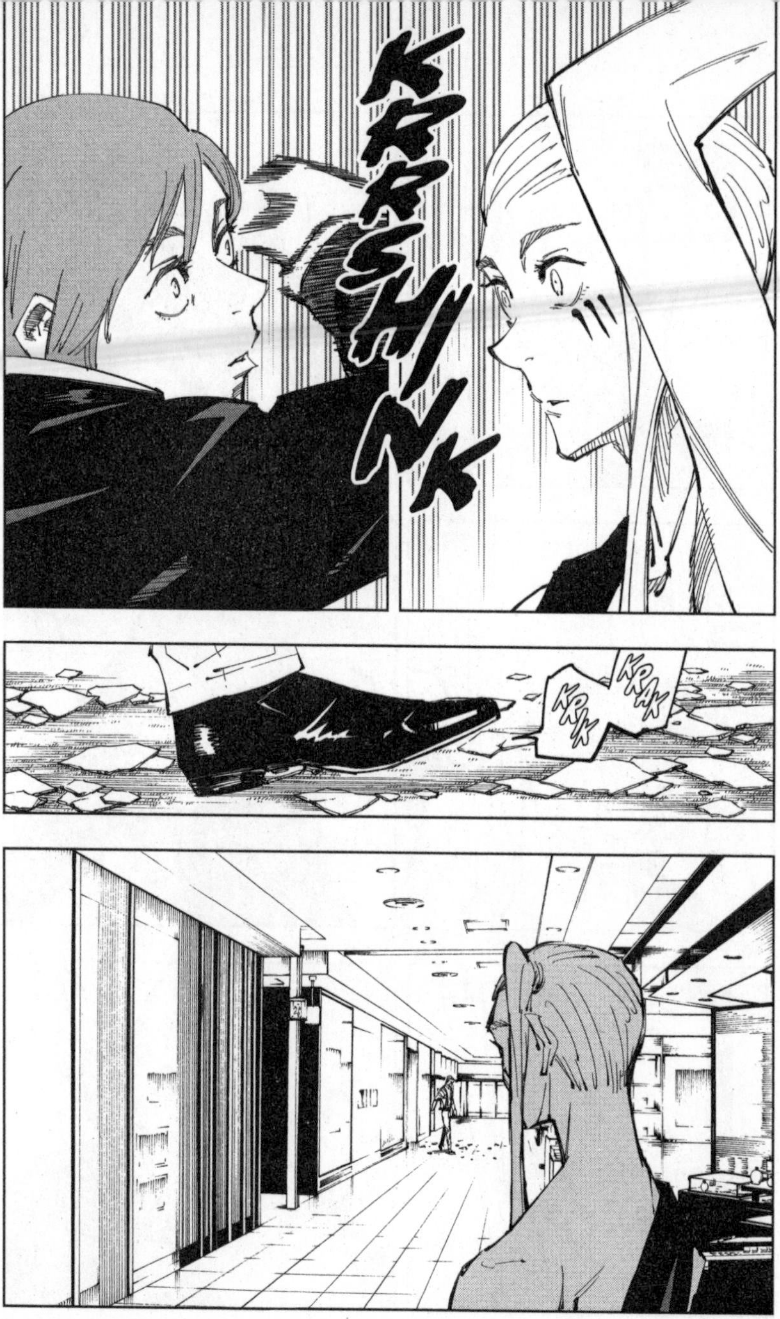

KRRSHINK
KRAK
KRIK

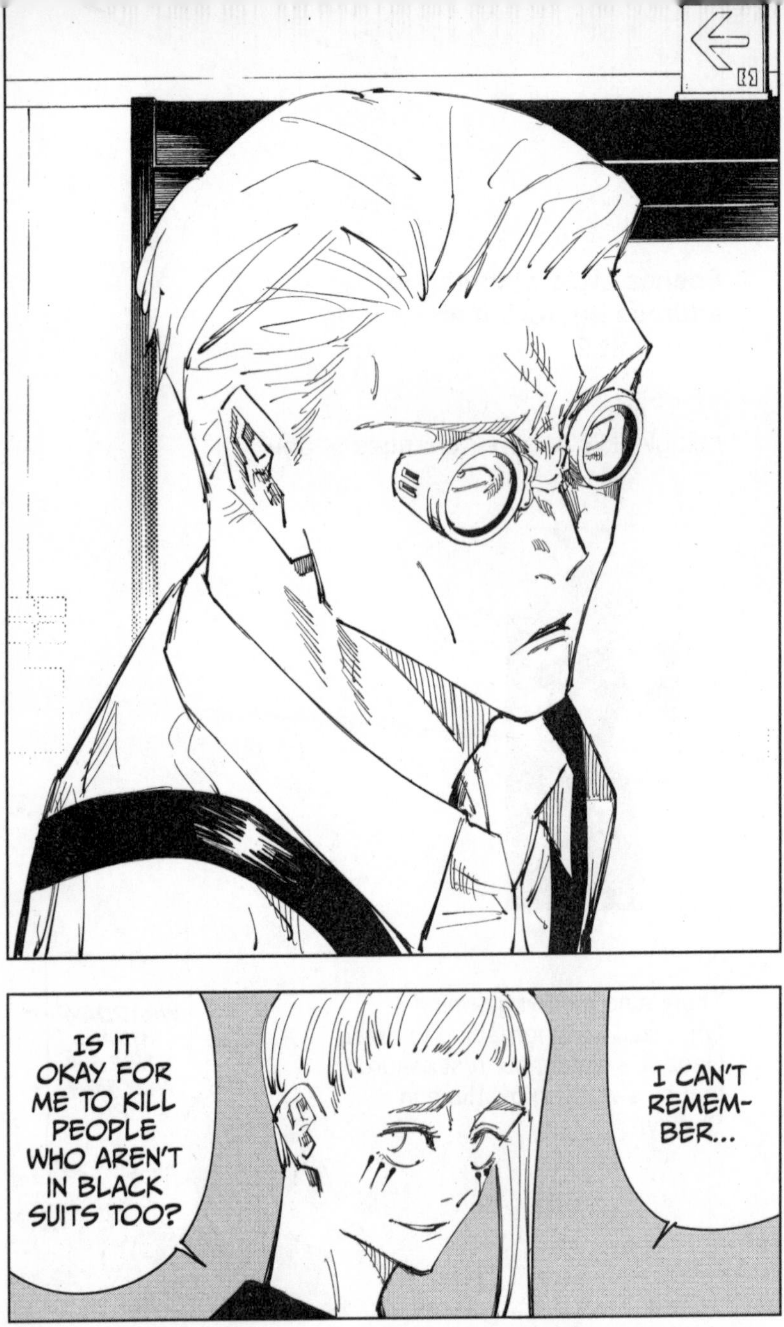
I CAN'T REMEM-BER...
IS IT OKAY FOR ME TO KILL PEOPLE WHO AREN'T IN BLACK SUITS TOO?

Scenes I was planning to address but forgot about until now, part 2

• Kugisaki's hammer changes shape

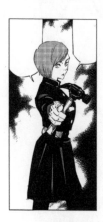

There's no meaning behind it. Oh, I also keep forgetting to draw Nanami's watch, but rest assured that he's working overtime in Shibuya.

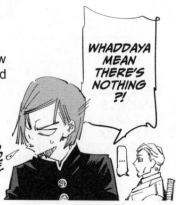

WHADDAYA MEAN THERE'S NOTHING ?!

PTOOEY

....

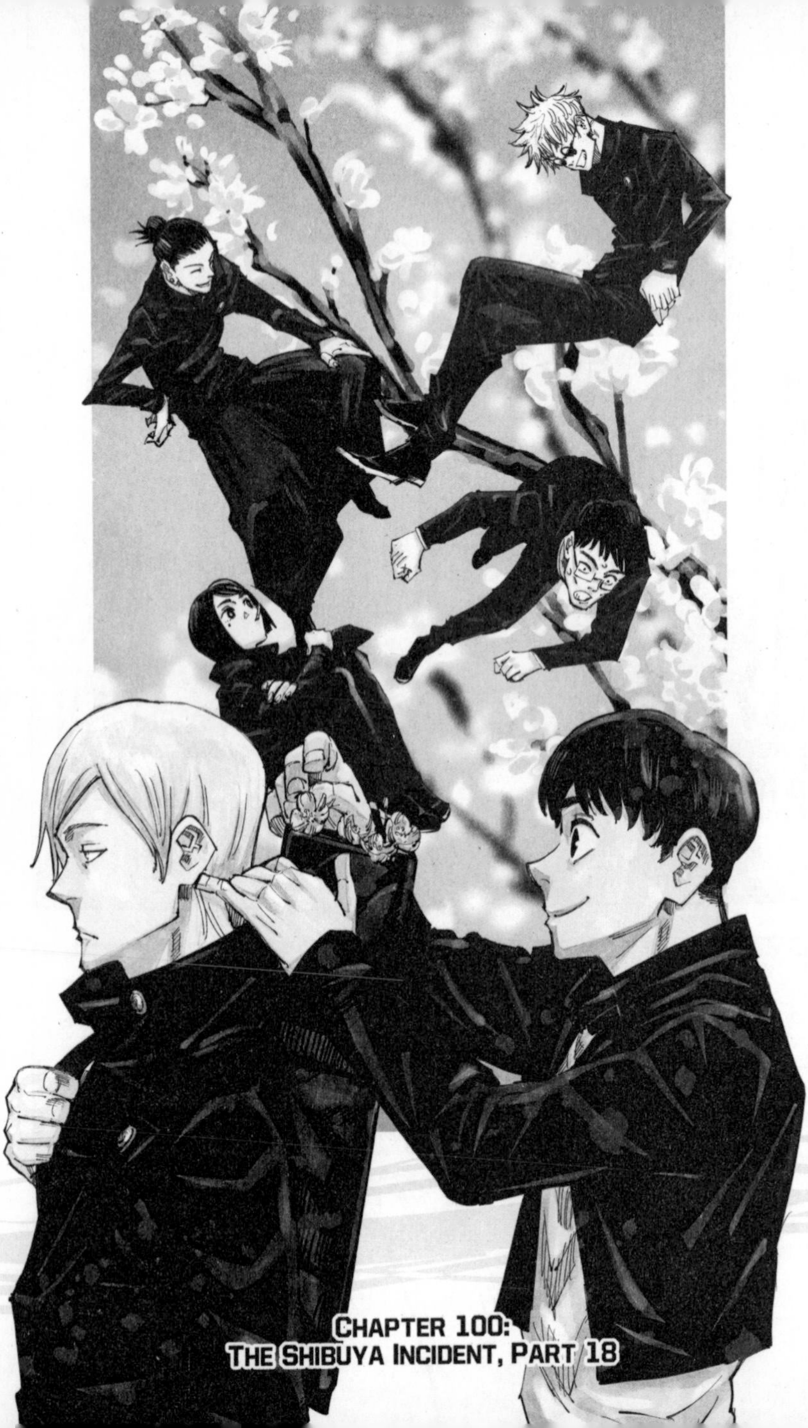
Chapter 100:
The Shibuya Incident, Part 18

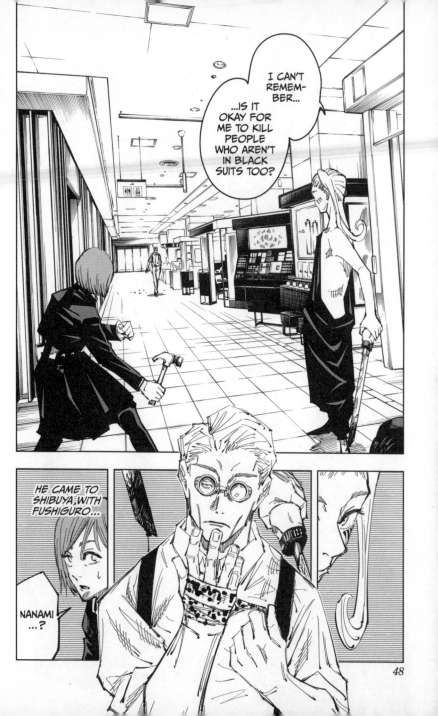

48

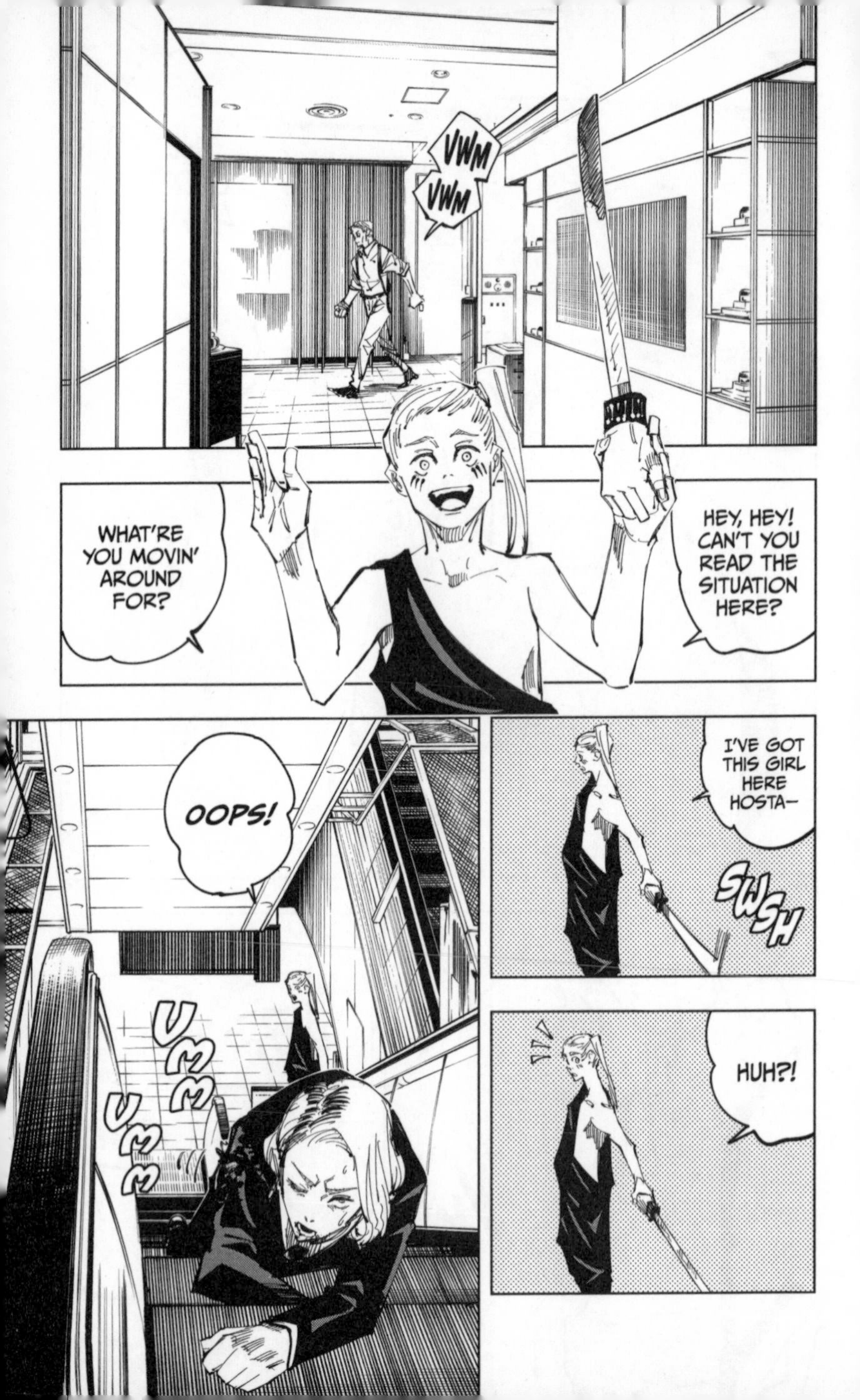
VWM
VWM
HEY, HEY! CAN'T YOU READ THE SITUATION HERE?
WHAT'RE YOU MOVIN' AROUND FOR?
I'VE GOT THIS GIRL HERE HOSTA-
SWSH
HUH?!
OOPS!
VMM
VMM

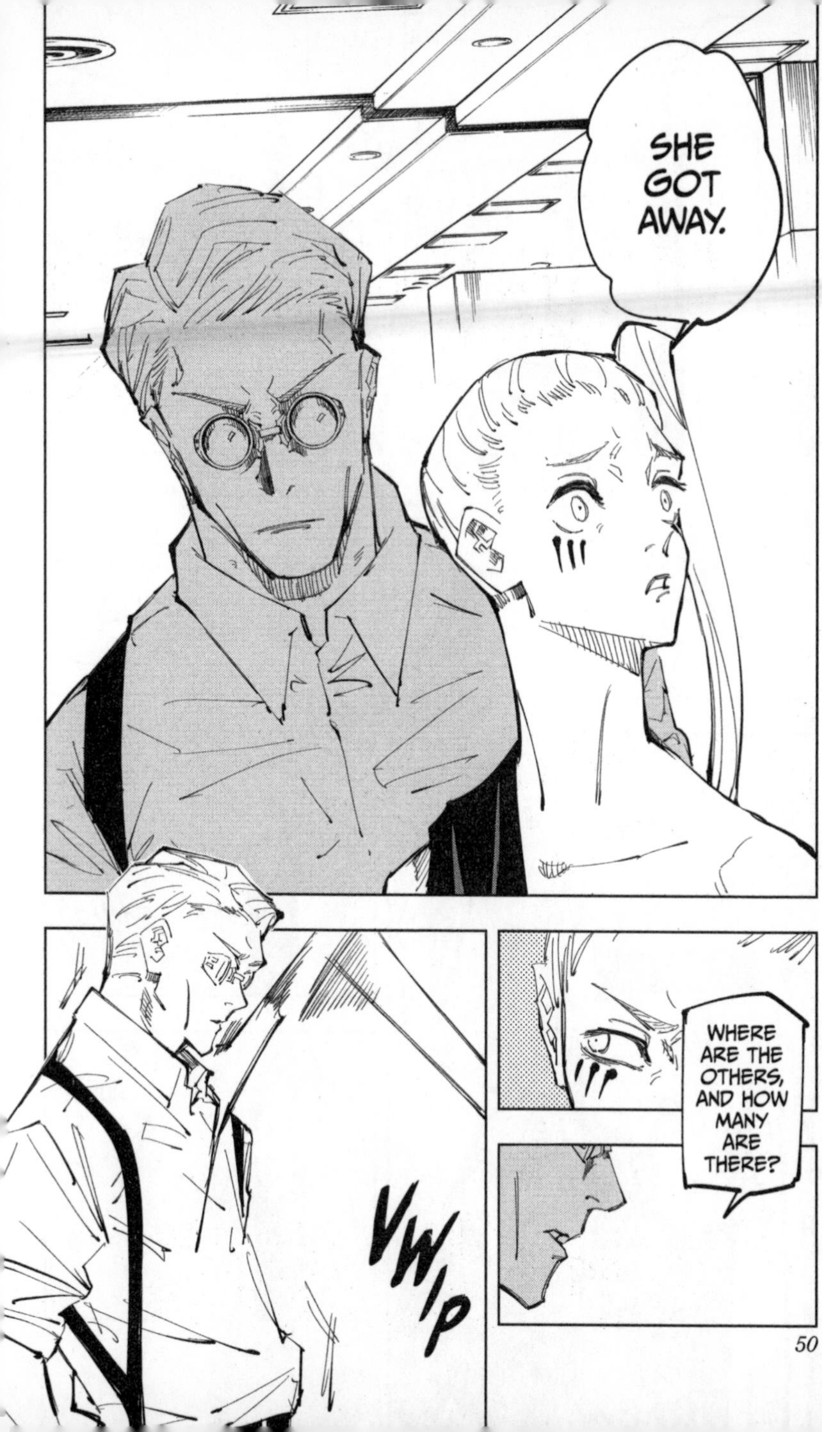
SHE GOT AWAY.
WHERE ARE THE OTHERS, AND HOW MANY ARE THERE?
VWIP

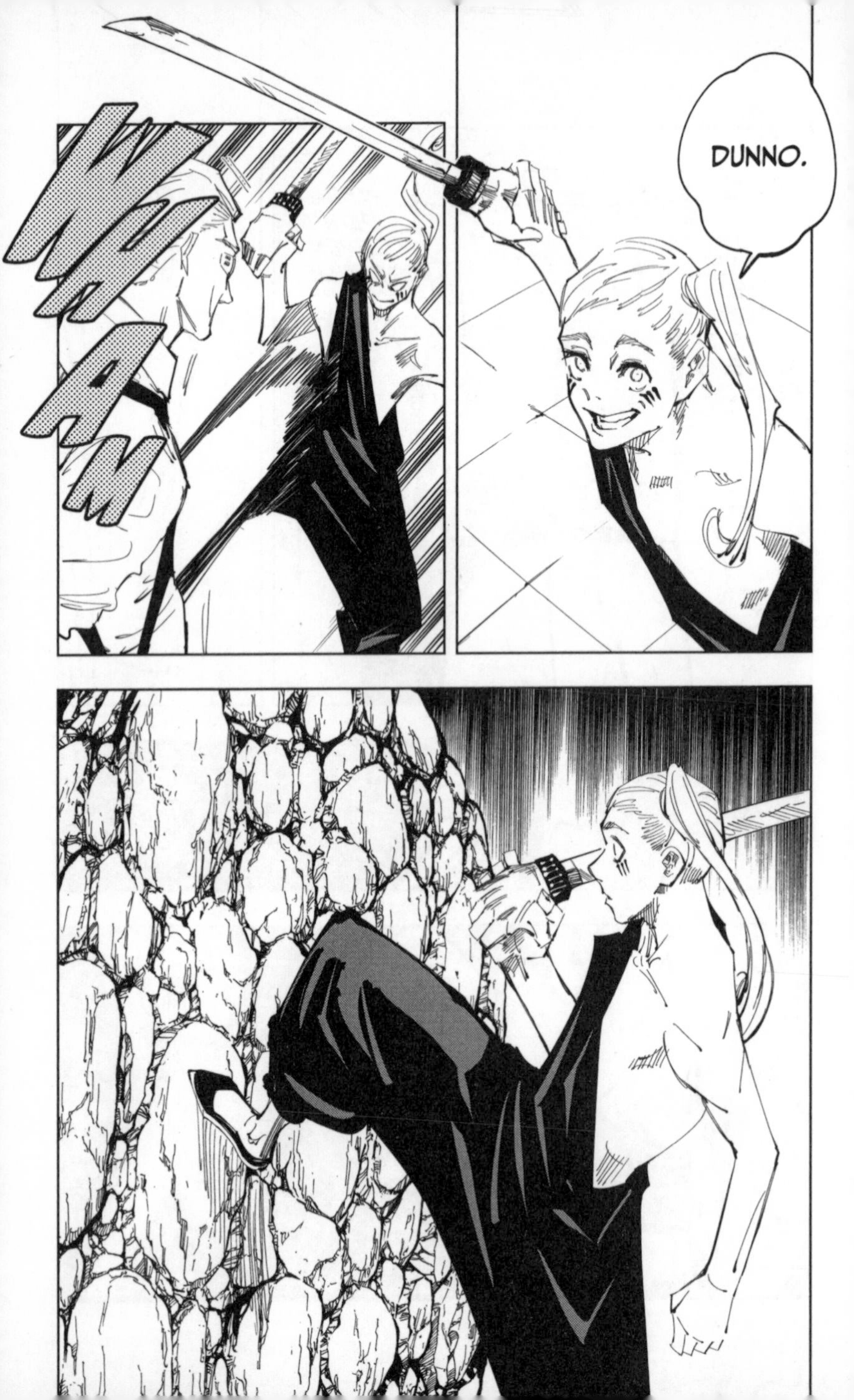
DUNNO.
WHAM

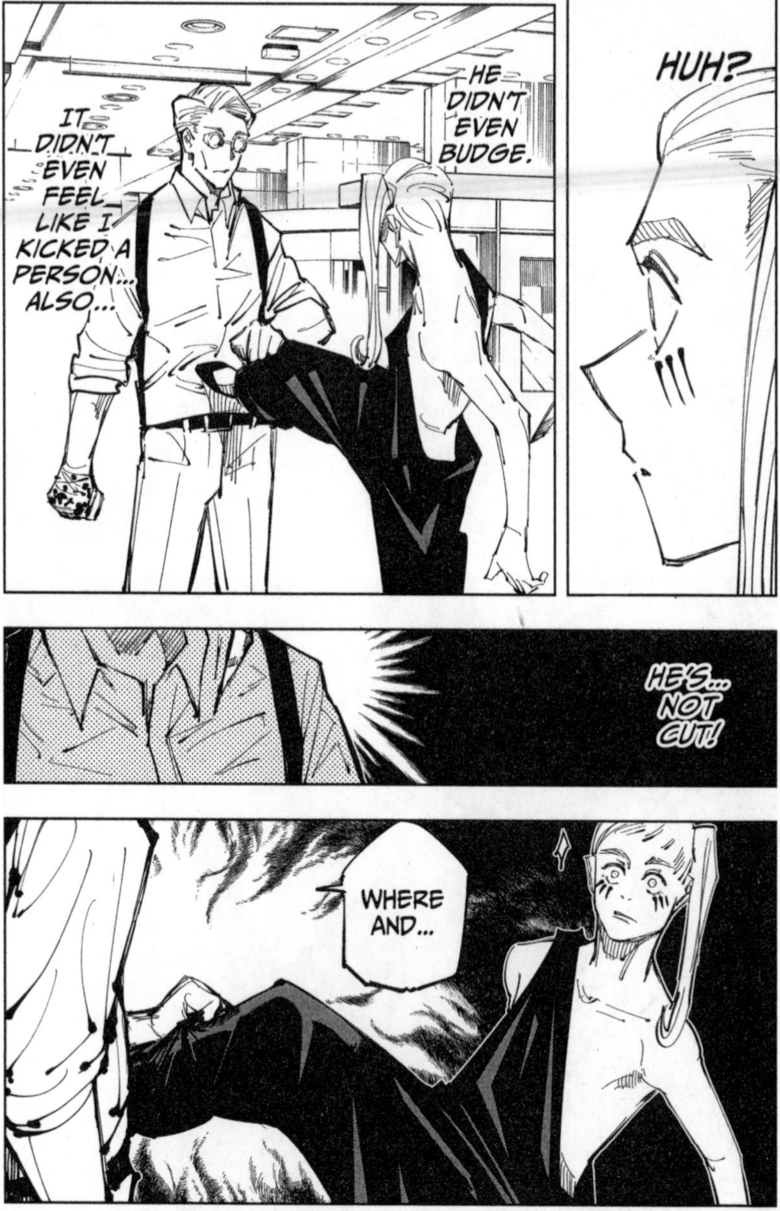
HUH?
HE DIDN'T EVEN BUDGE.
IT DIDN'T EVEN FEEL LIKE I KICKED A PERSON... ALSO...
HE'S... NOT CUT!
WHERE AND...

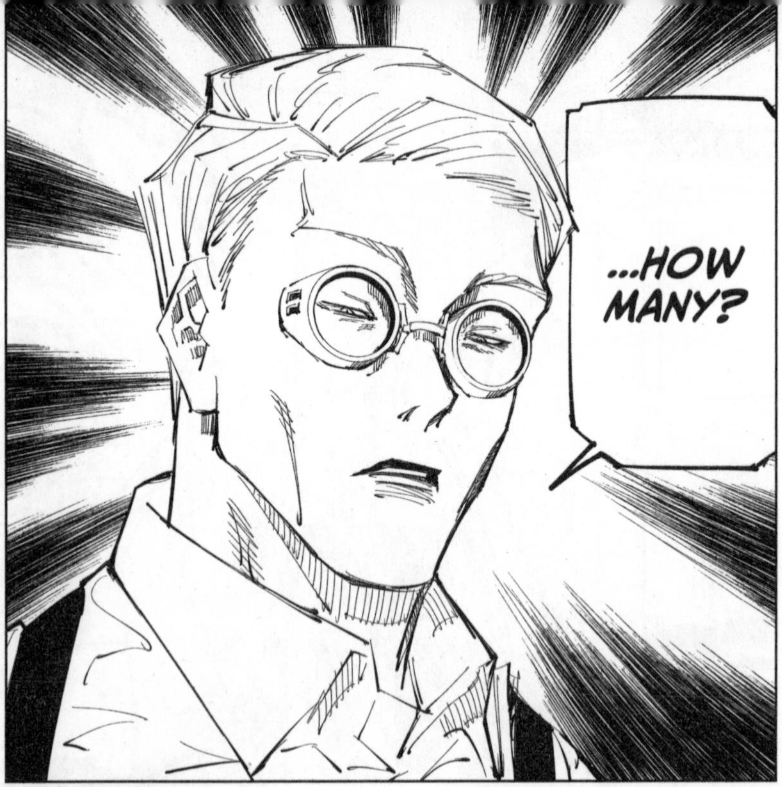
...HOW MANY?
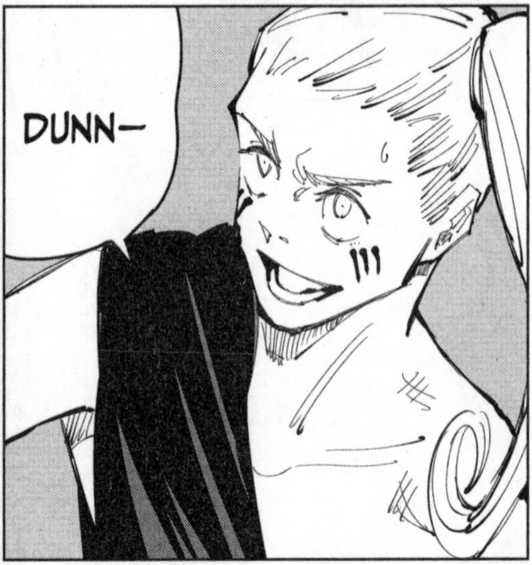
DUNN-
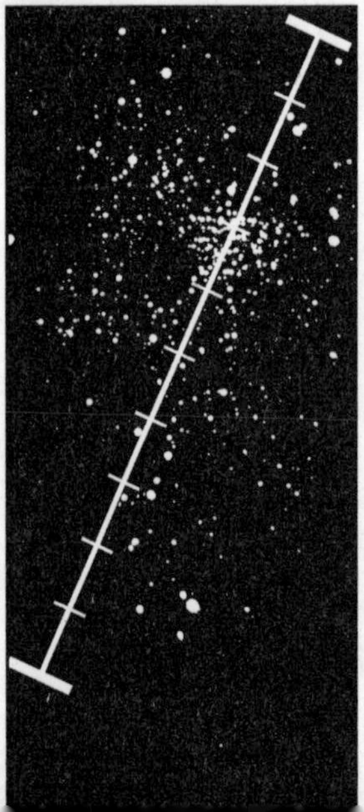

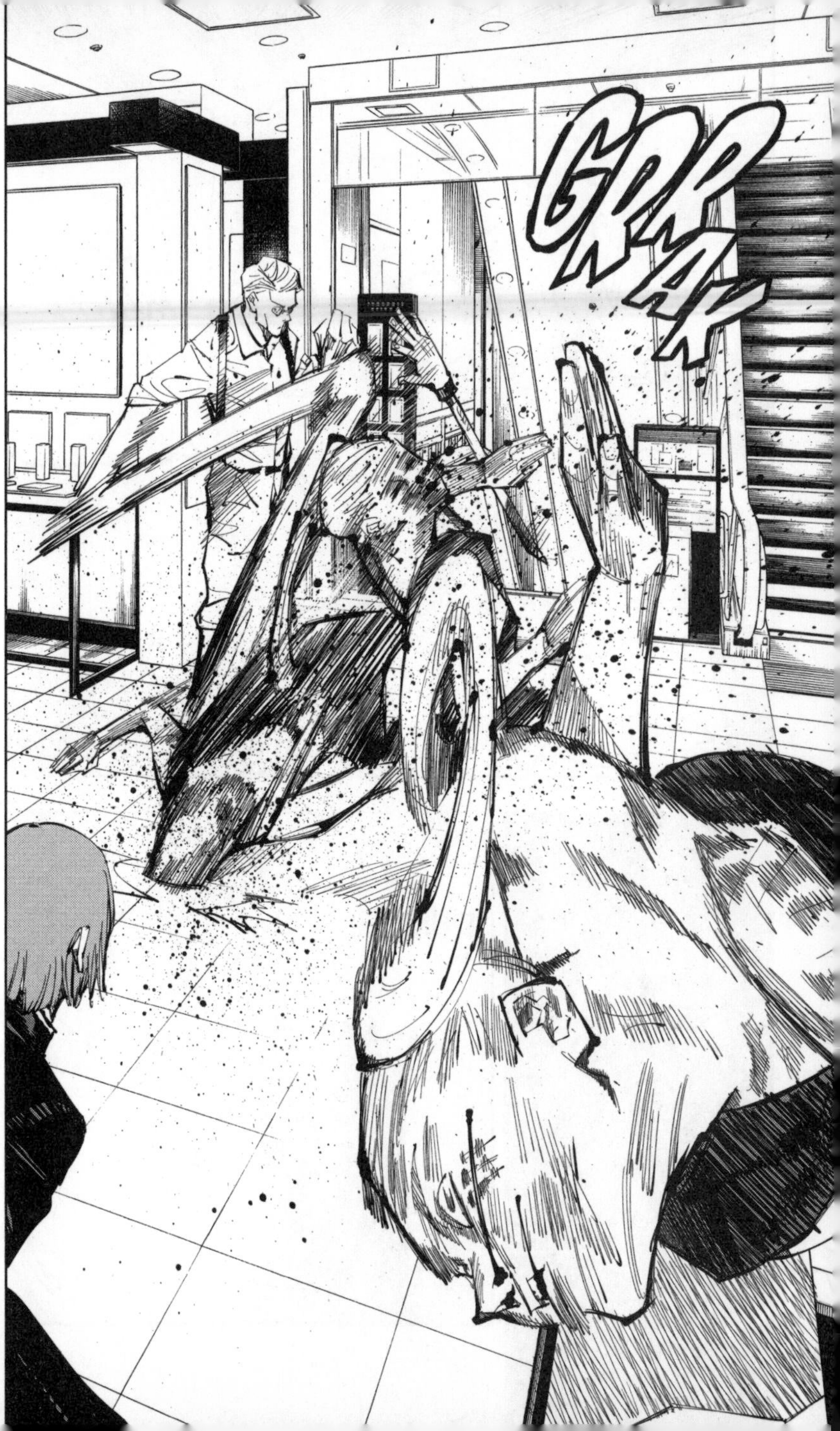
GRRAK

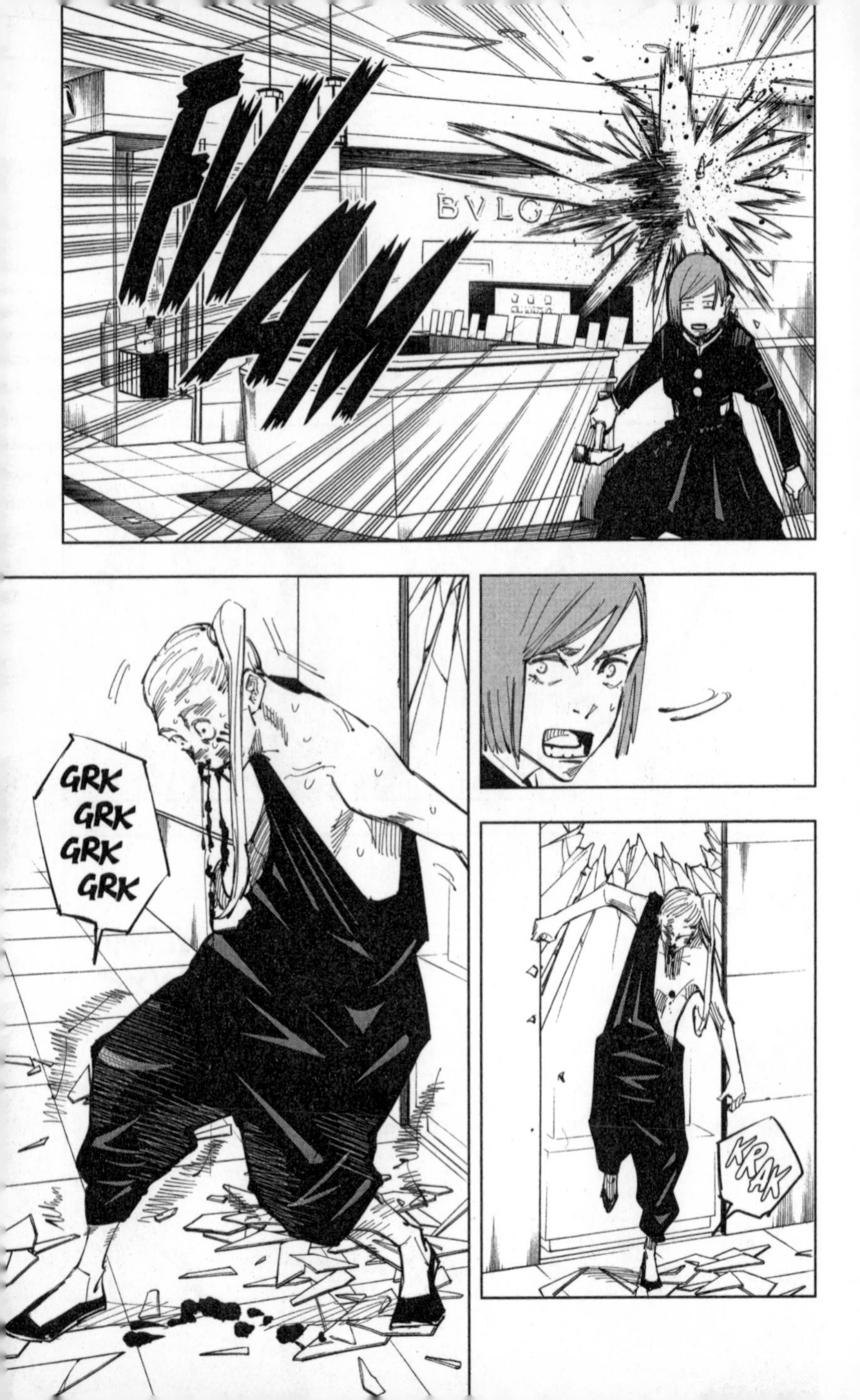
FWAM
BVLGA
KRAK
GRK GRK GRK GRK

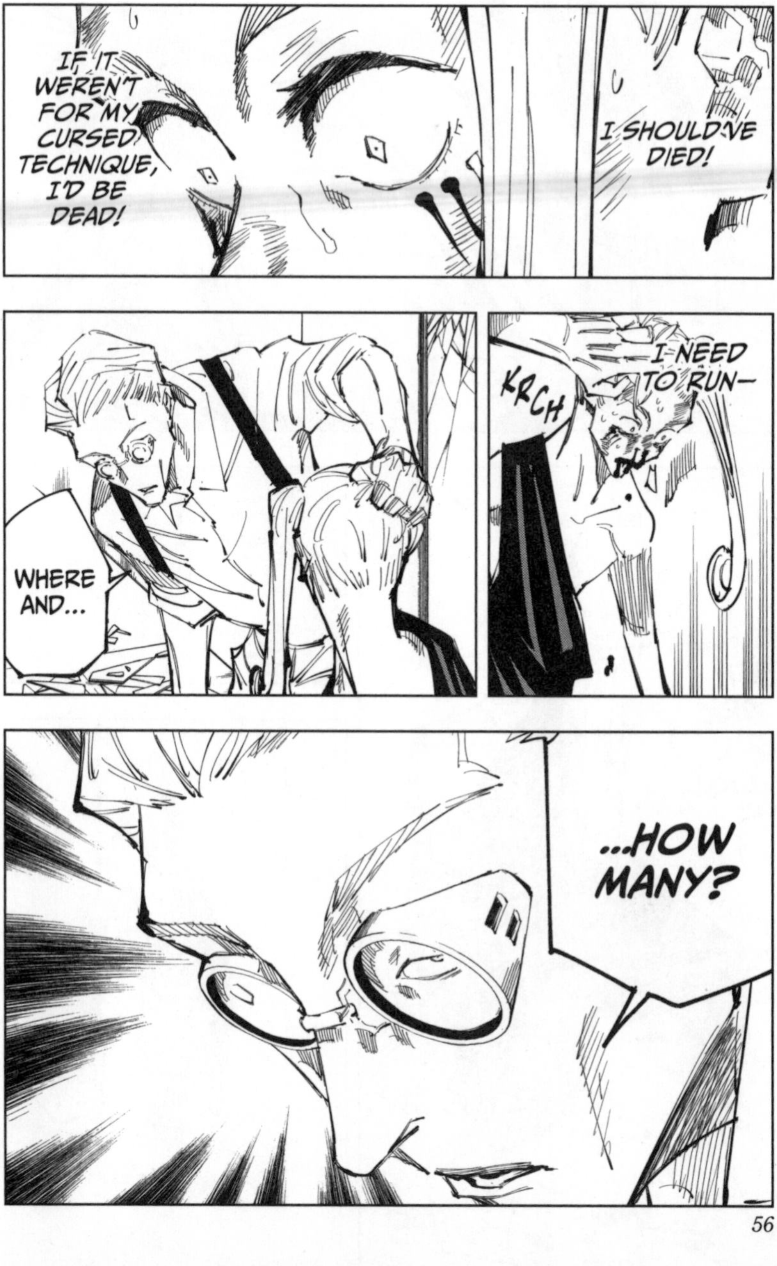
I SHOULD'VE DIED!
IF IT WEREN'T FOR MY CURSED TECHNIQUE, I'D BE DEAD!
KRCH
I NEED TO RUN—
WHERE AND...
...HOW MANY?

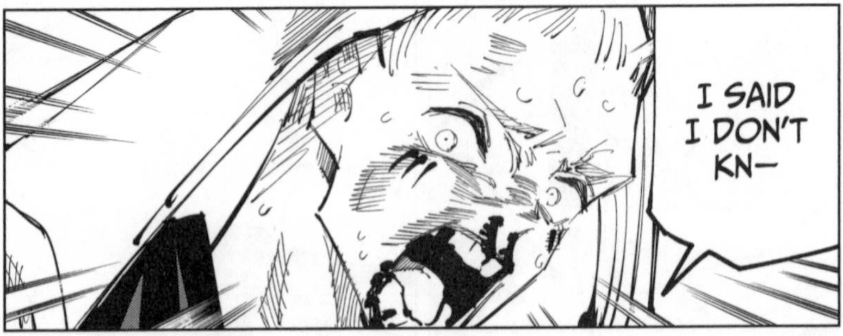
I SAID I DON'T KN—

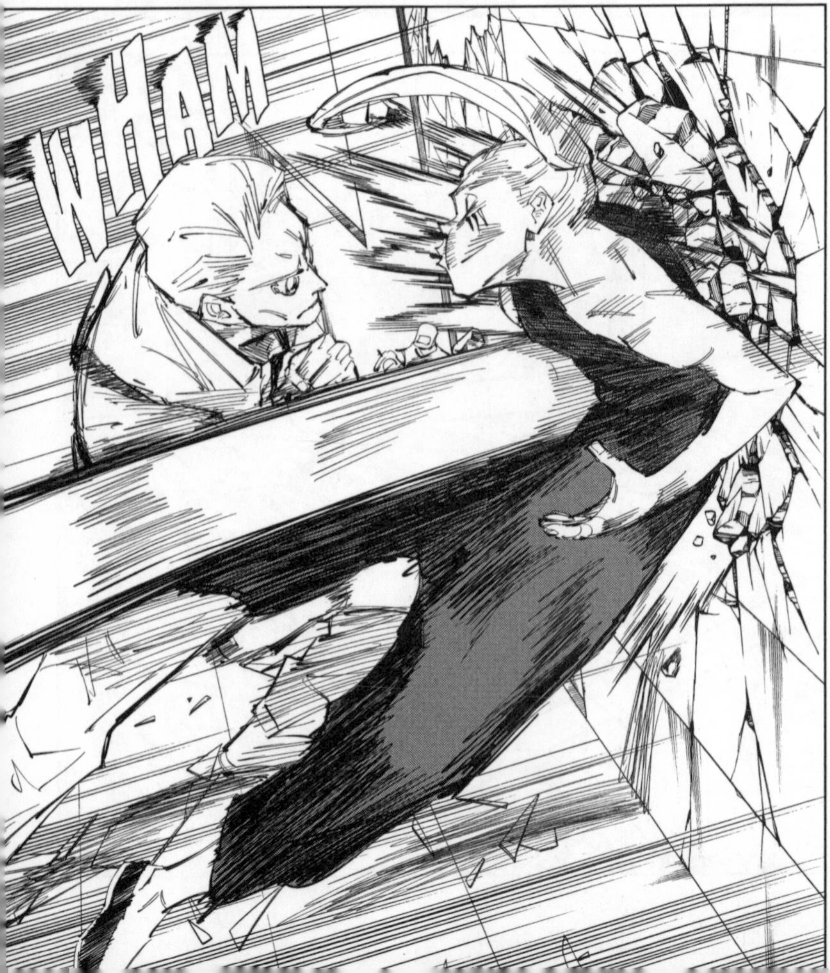
WHAM

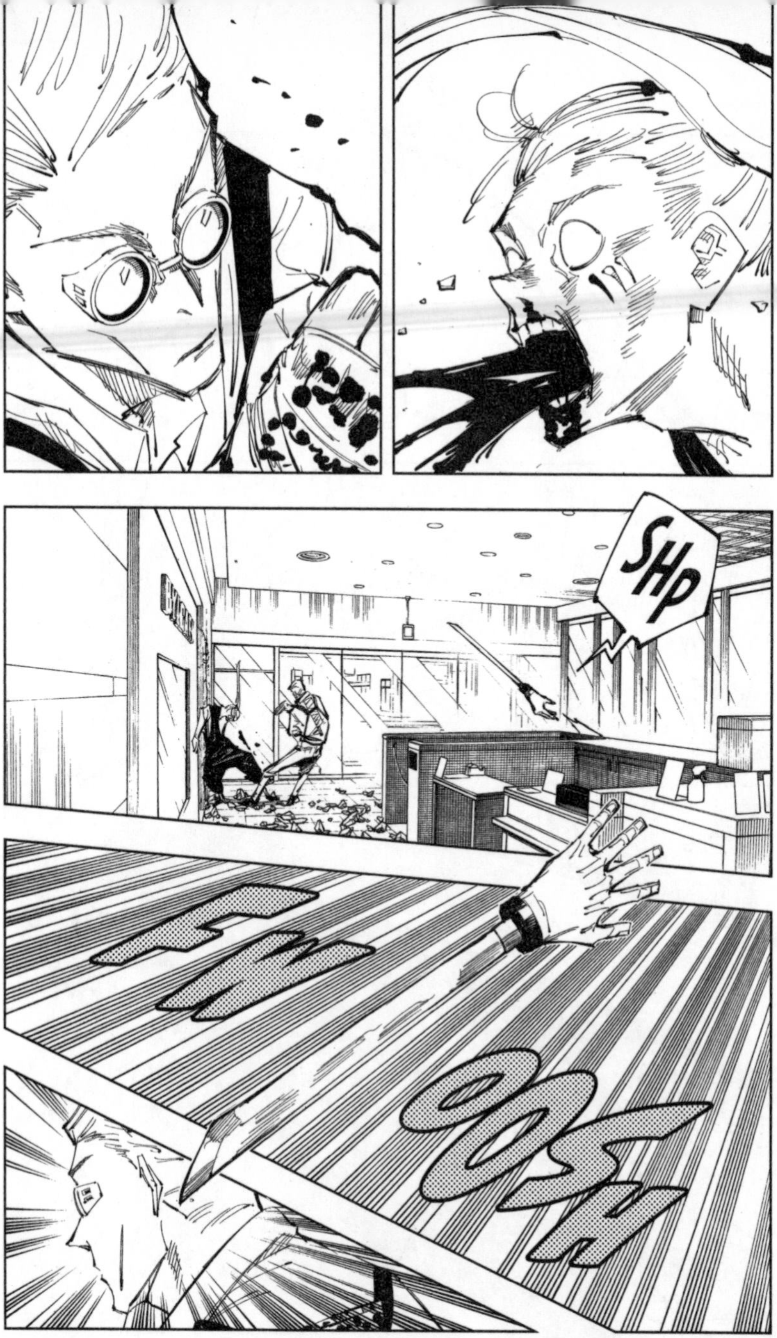
SHP
WHOOSH

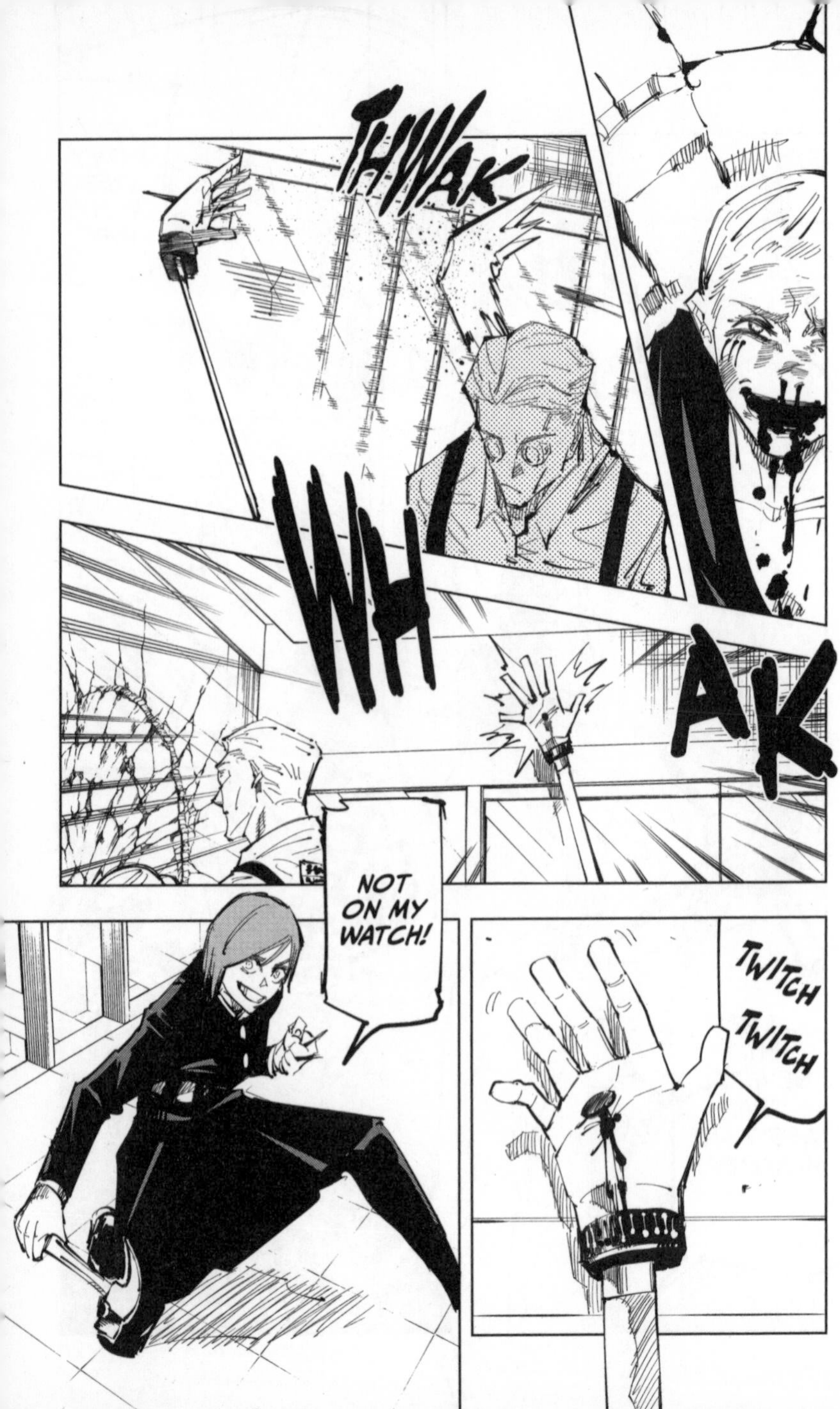
THWAK
WHAK
TWITCH
TWITCH
NOT ON MY WATCH!

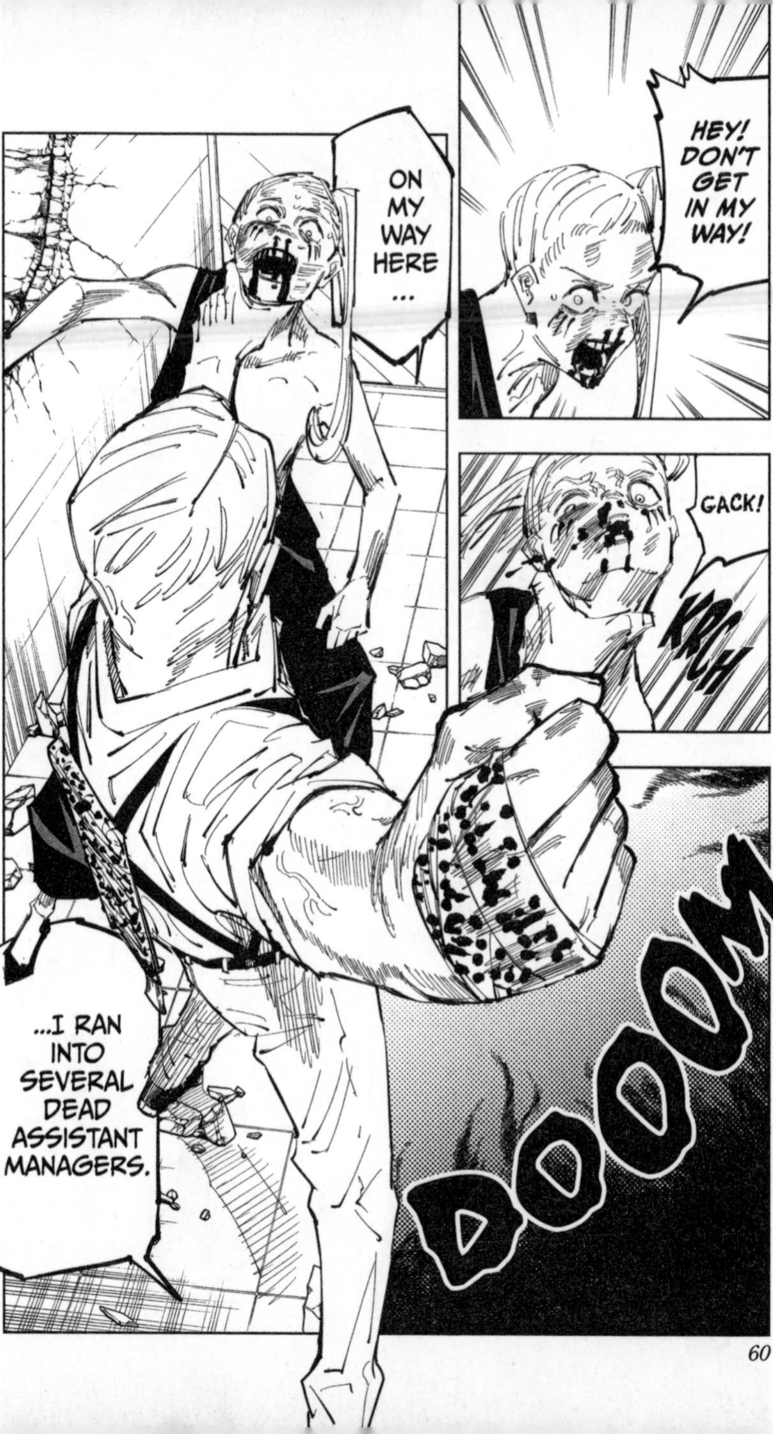
HEY! DON'T GET IN MY WAY!
GACK!
KRCH
DOOOM
ON MY WAY HERE...
...I RAN INTO SEVERAL DEAD ASSISTANT MANAGERS.

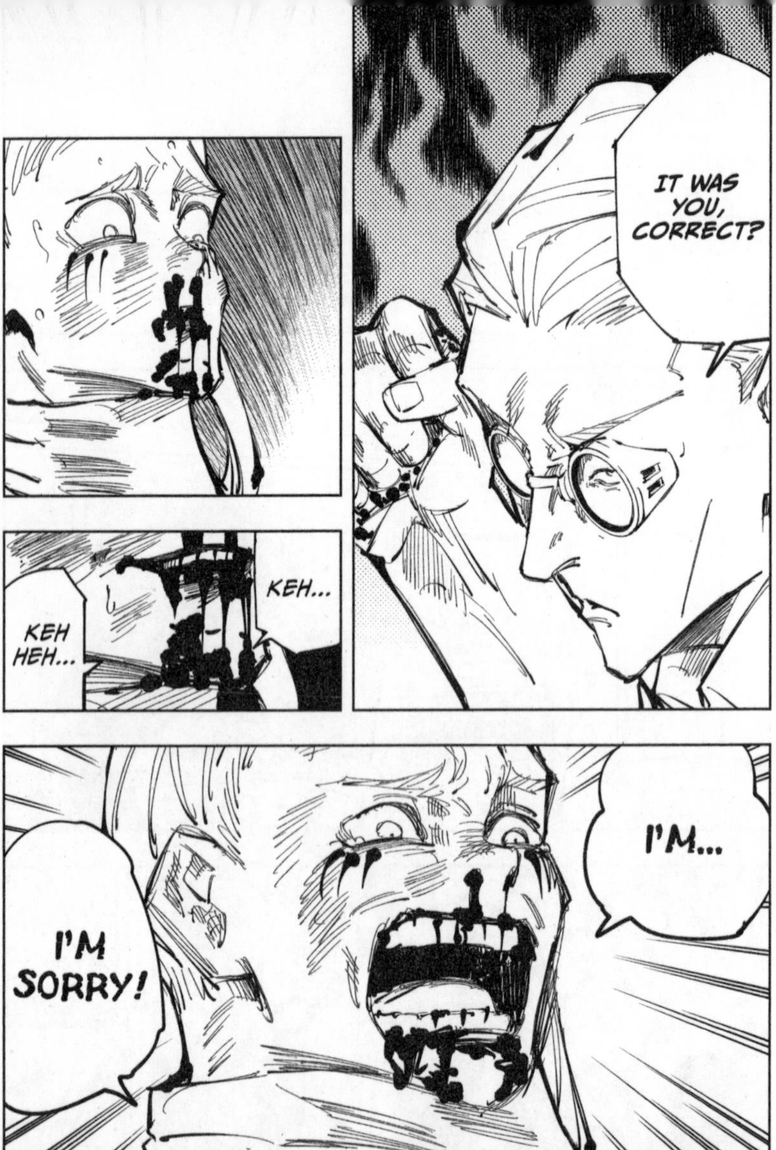
IT WAS YOU, CORRECT?
KEH...
KEH HEH...
I'M...
I'M SORRY!

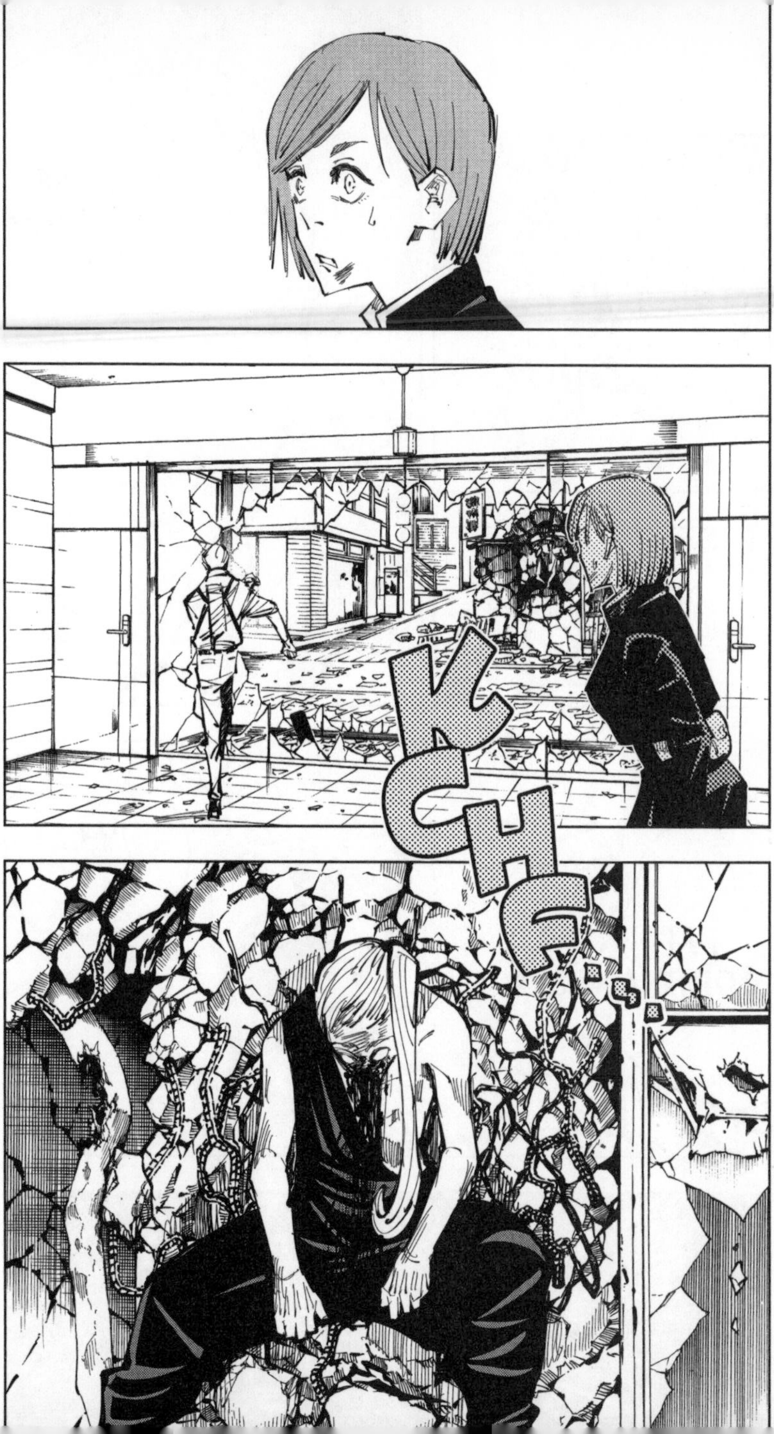
KCHC...

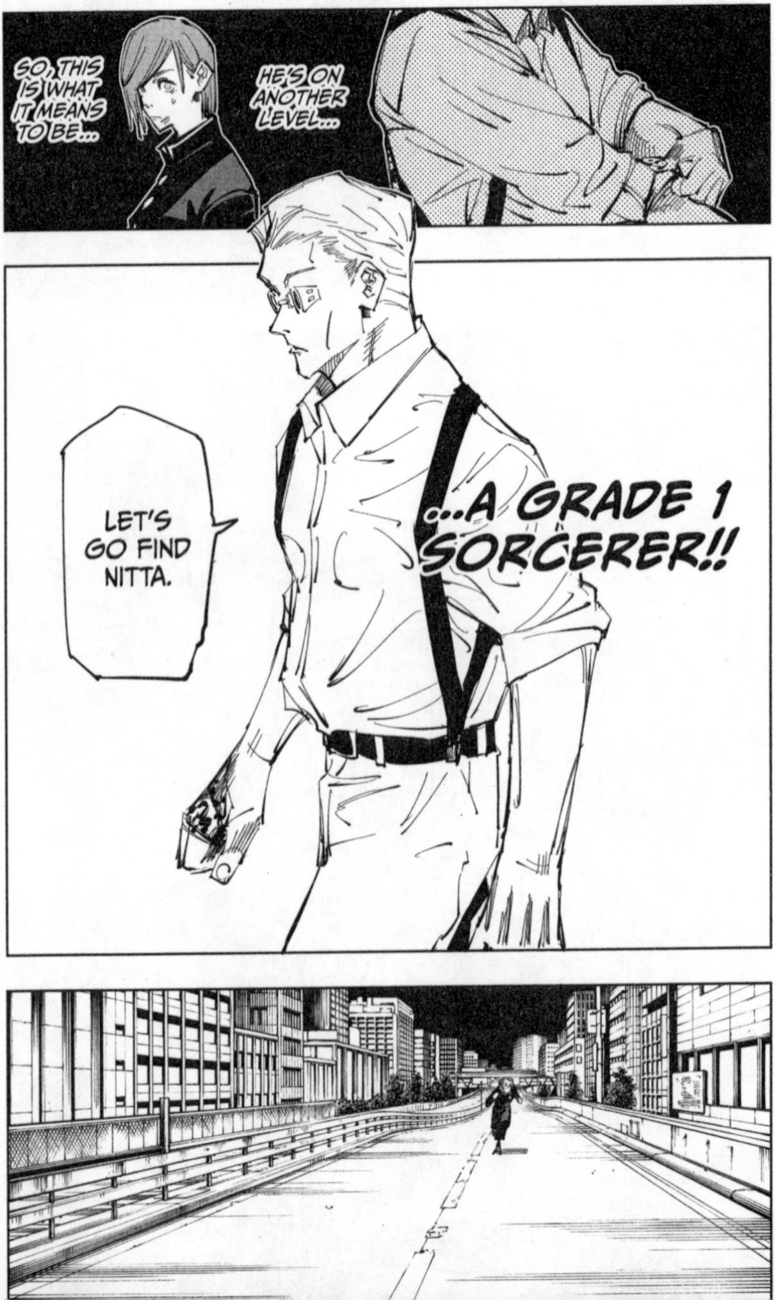
HE'S ON ANOTHER LEVEL...
SO, THIS IS WHAT IT MEANS TO BE...
...A GRADE 1 SORCERER!!
LET'S GO FIND NITTA.

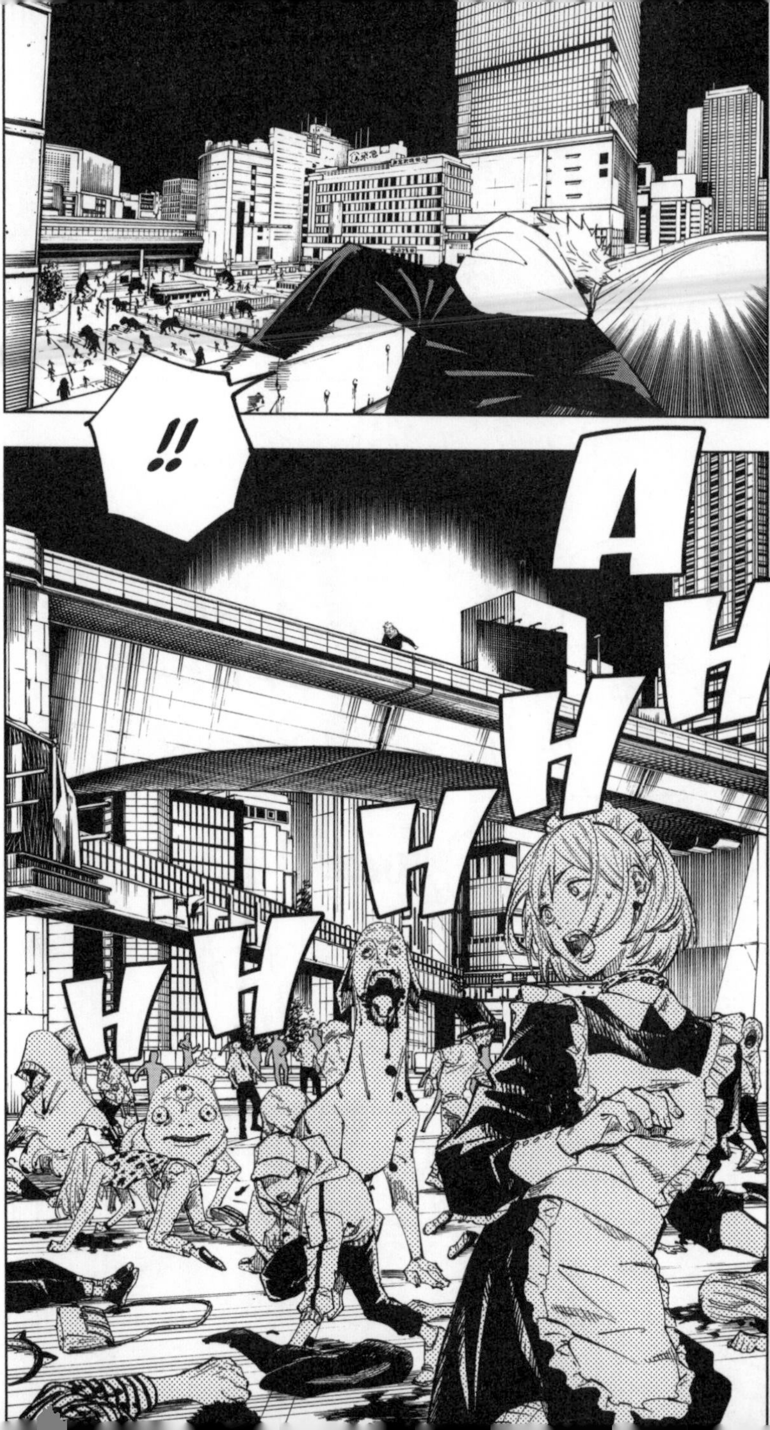
!!
AHHHHH

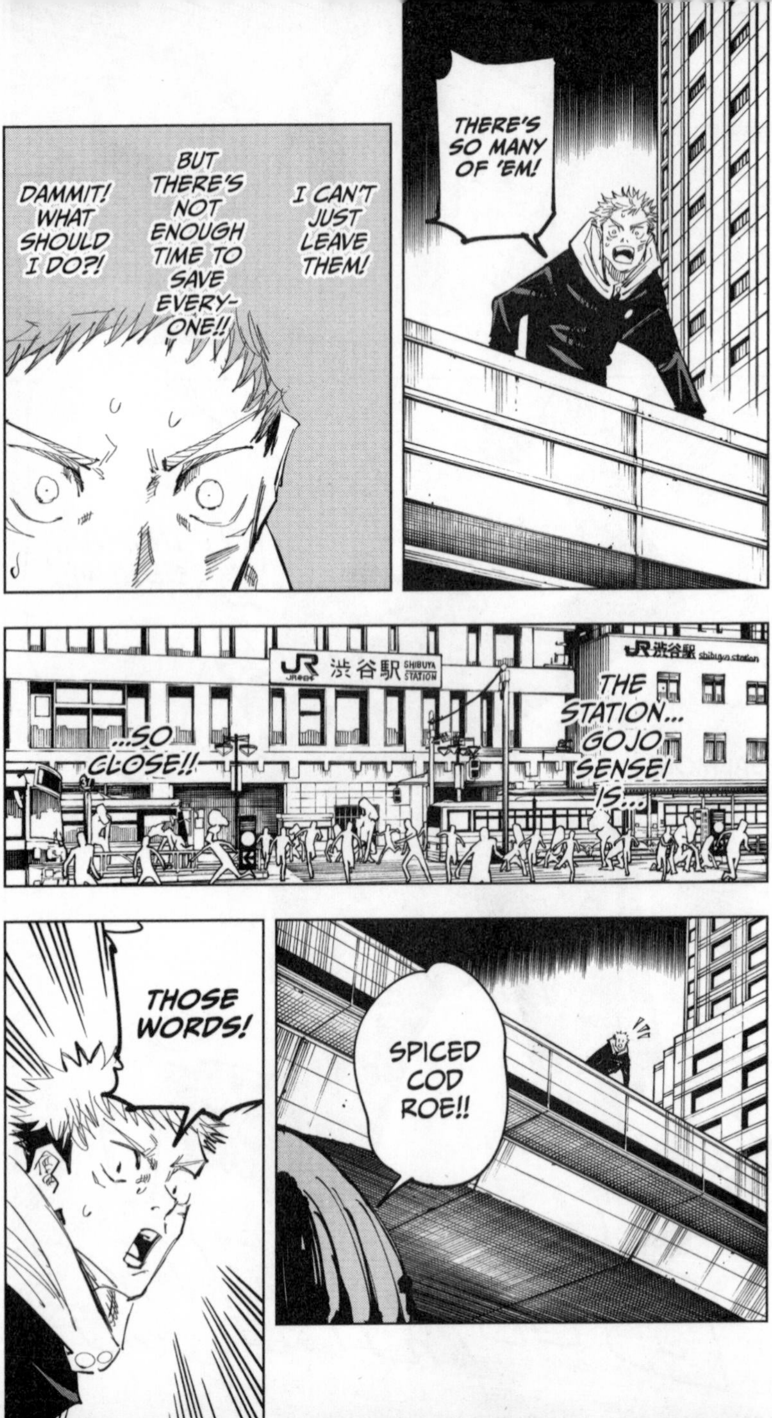
THERE'S SO MANY OF 'EM!
I CAN'T JUST LEAVE THEM!
BUT THERE'S NOT ENOUGH TIME TO SAVE EVERY-ONE!!
DAMMIT! WHAT SHOULD I DO?!
JR 渋谷駅 shibuya station
THE STATION... GOJO SENSEI IS...
JR 渋谷駅 SHIBUYA STATION
...SO CLOSE!!
SPICED COD ROE!!
THOSE WORDS!

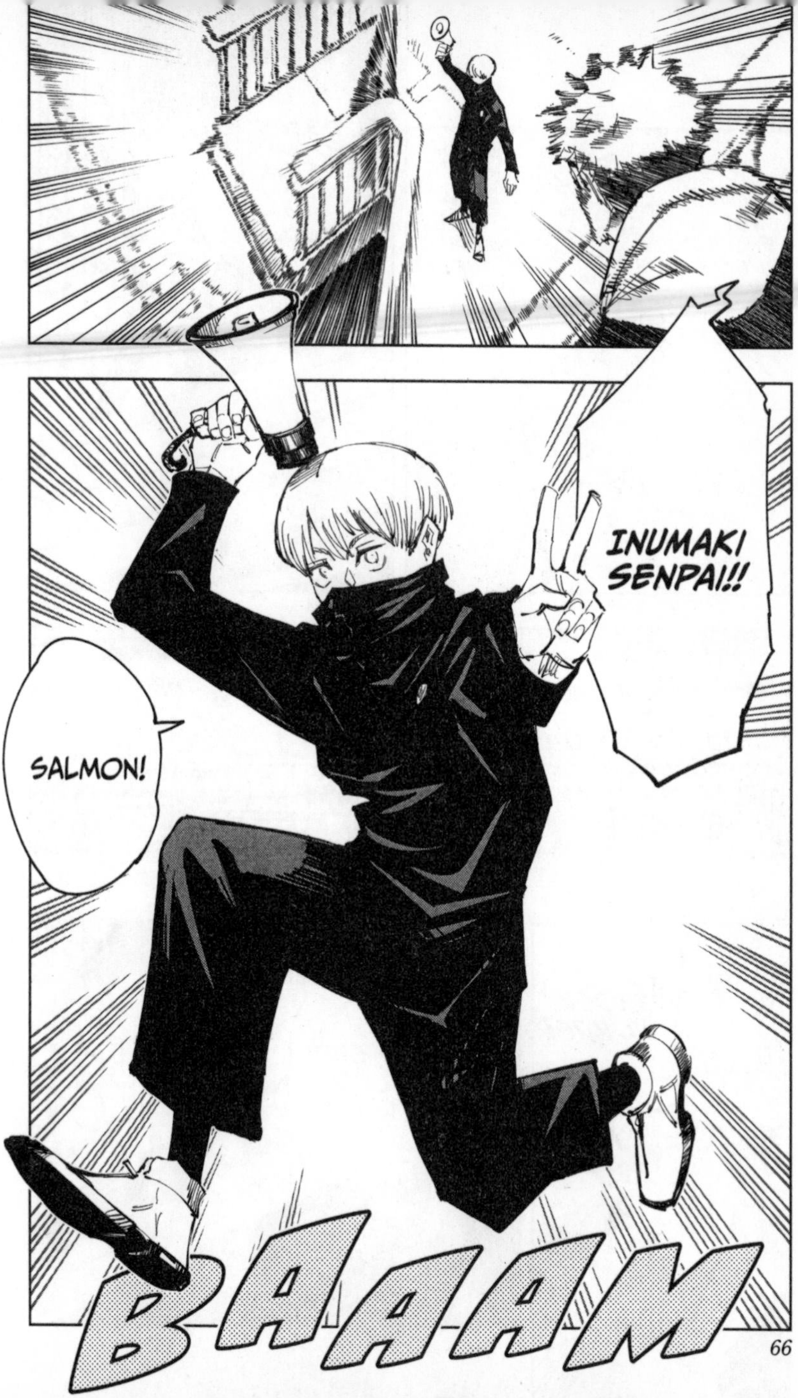
INUMAKI SENPAI!!
SALMON!
BAAAM

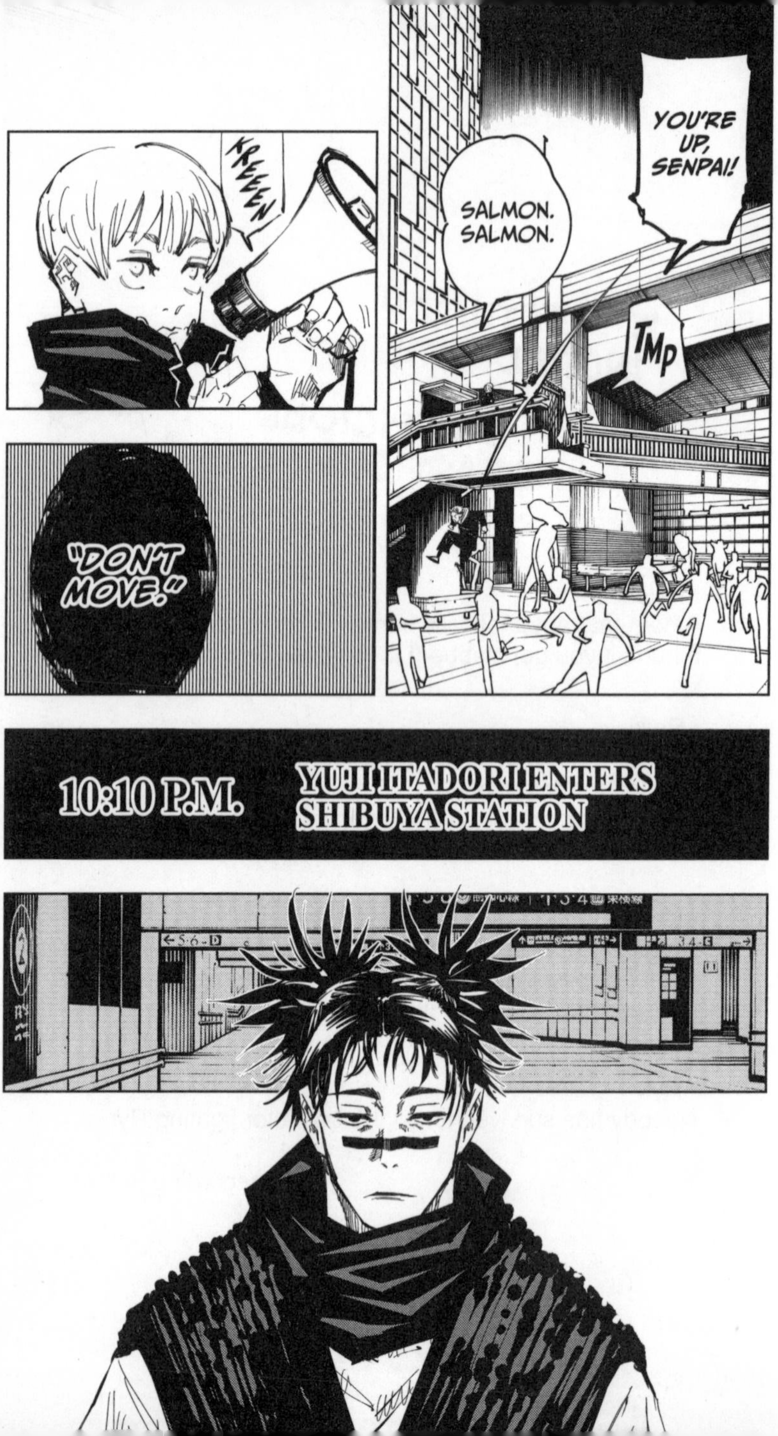
YOU'RE UP, SENPAI!
SALMON. SALMON.
TMP
KREEEN
"DON'T MOVE."
10:10 P.M.
YUJI ITADORI ENTERS SHIBUYA STATION

IT'S ACTUALLY INCREDIBLE!

AUSPICIOUS BEAST SUMMON

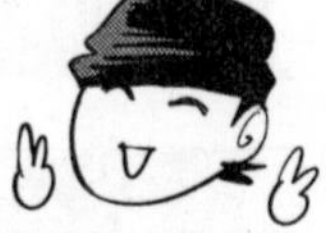

• Kaichi
A horn that automatically homes in on its target!
It hurts if you get stabbed! It can even draw blood!

• Reiki
Cursed water that covers your body! Use it as a cushion for defense!
If you cover your feet with it, you can move by sliding around!

• Kirin
Drugs the brain! Feeling body pains? Magically gone like poof! For those of you who can't afford to take the day off!
Beware the crash after the effects wear off!

• Ryu
Nobody has survived to tell the tale after fighting Ryu…

(According to Ino)

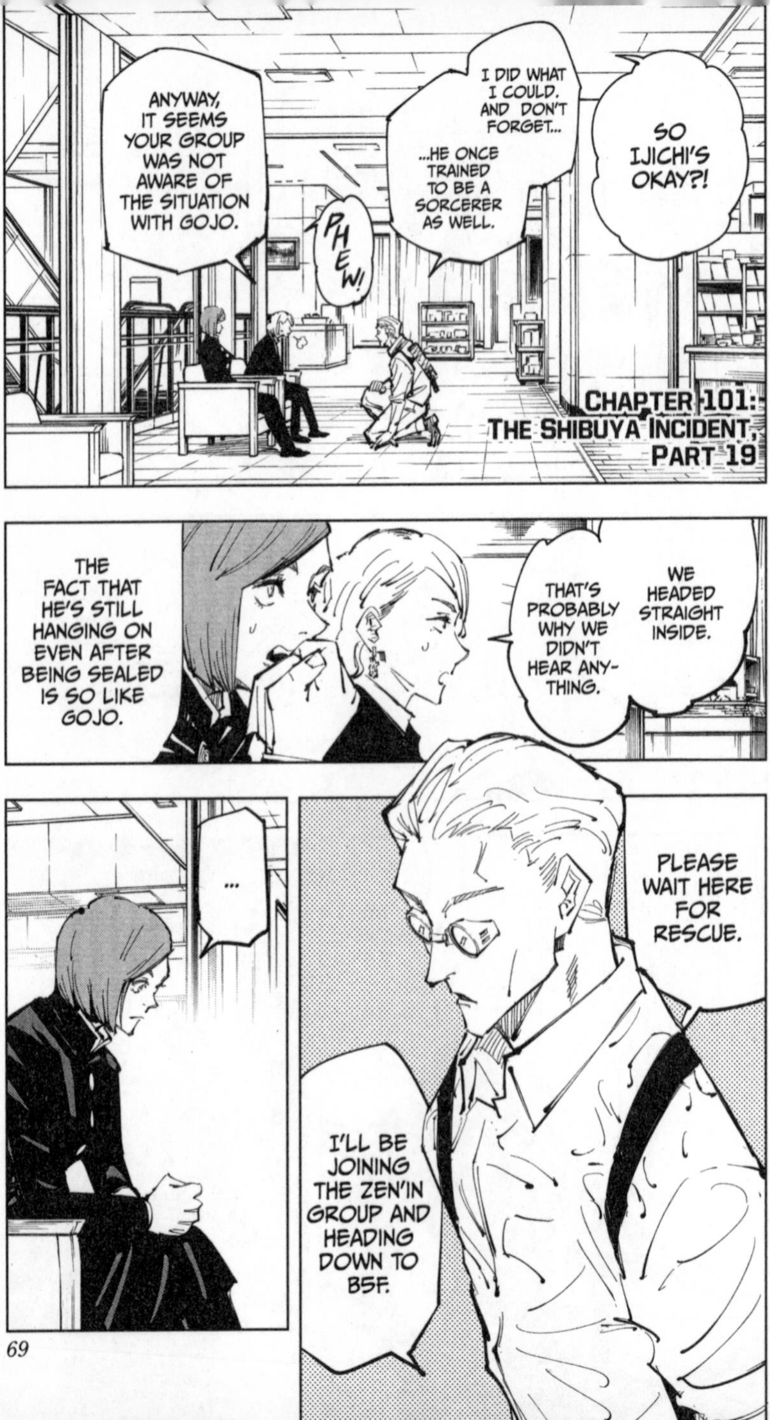
SO IJICHI'S OKAY?!
I DID WHAT I COULD. AND DON'T FORGET...
...HE ONCE TRAINED TO BE A SORCERER AS WELL.
PHEW!
ANYWAY, IT SEEMS YOUR GROUP WAS NOT AWARE OF THE SITUATION WITH GOJO.
CHAPTER 101: THE SHIBUYA INCIDENT, PART 19
WE HEADED STRAIGHT INSIDE.
THAT'S PROBABLY WHY WE DIDN'T HEAR ANY-THING.
THE FACT THAT HE'S STILL HANGING ON EVEN AFTER BEING SEALED IS SO LIKE GOJO.
PLEASE WAIT HERE FOR RESCUE.
I'LL BE JOINING THE ZEN'IN GROUP AND HEADING DOWN TO B5F.
...

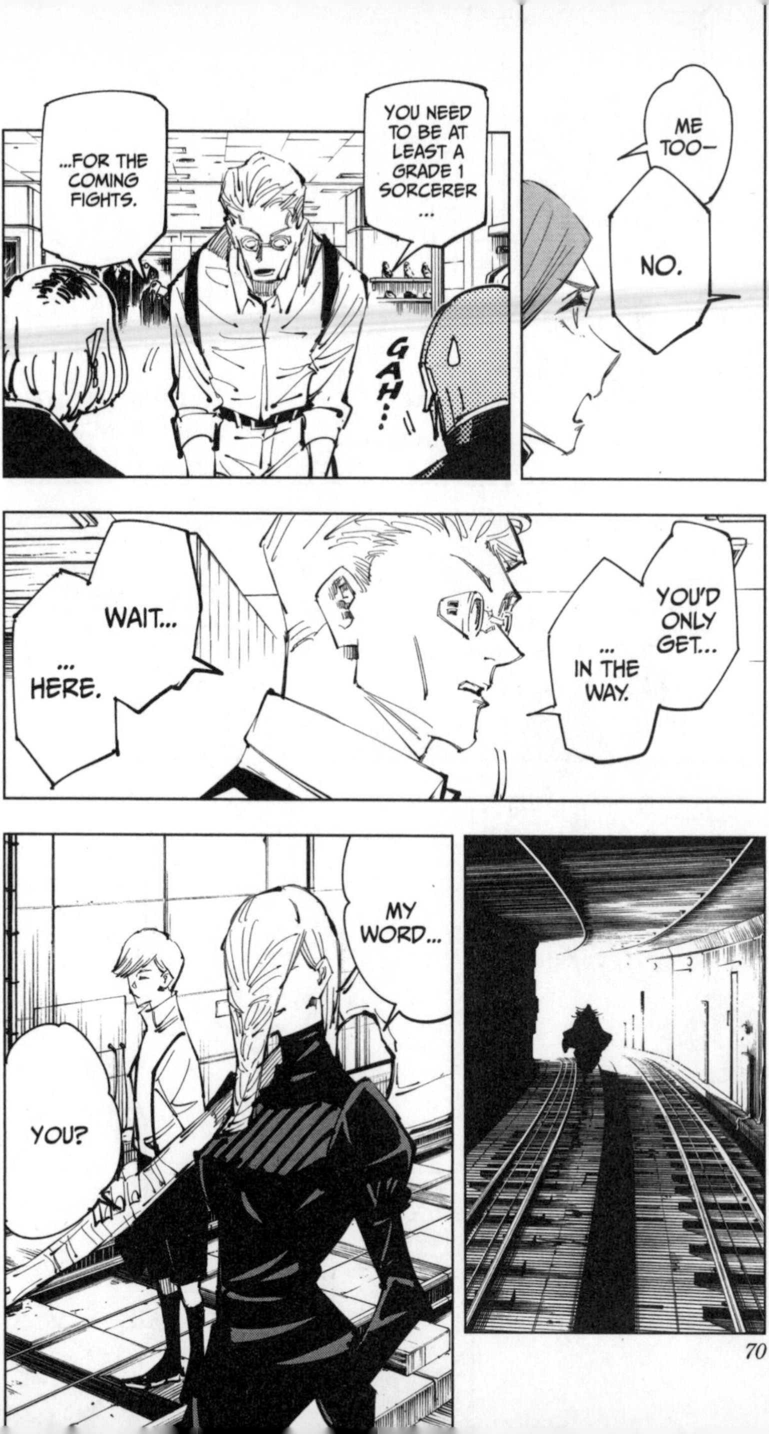
ME TOO—
NO.
YOU NEED TO BE AT LEAST A GRADE 1 SORCERER ...
...FOR THE COMING FIGHTS.
GAH...
YOU'D ONLY GET...
... IN THE WAY.
WAIT...
... HERE.
MY WORD...
YOU?

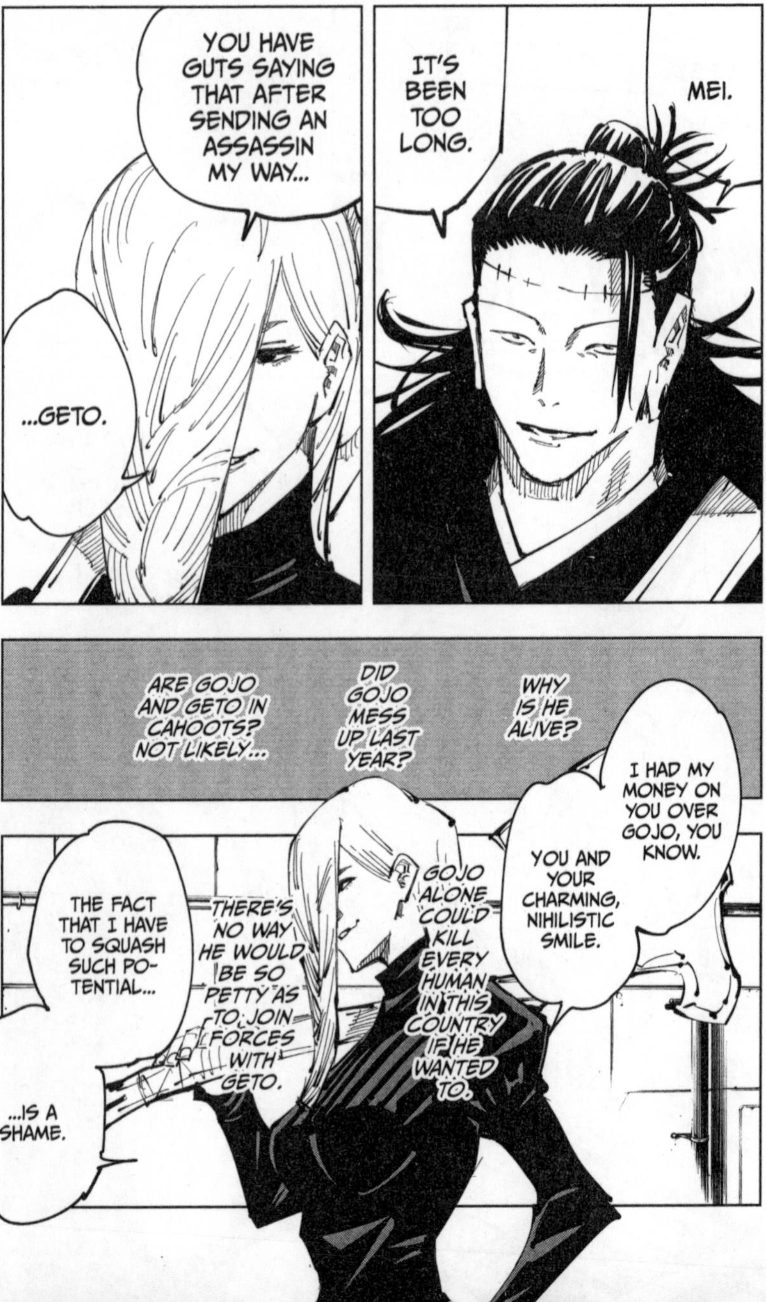
MEI.
IT'S BEEN TOO LONG.
YOU HAVE GUTS SAYING THAT AFTER SENDING AN ASSASSIN MY WAY...
...GETO.
WHY IS HE ALIVE?
DID GOJO MESS UP LAST YEAR?
ARE GOJO AND GETO IN CAHOOTS? NOT LIKELY...
I HAD MY MONEY ON YOU OVER GOJO, YOU KNOW.
YOU AND YOUR CHARMING, NIHILISTIC SMILE.
GOJO ALONE COULD KILL EVERY HUMAN IN THIS COUNTRY IF HE WANTED TO.
THERE'S NO WAY HE WOULD BE SO PETTY AS TO JOIN FORCES WITH GETO.
THE FACT THAT I HAVE TO SQUASH SUCH PO- TENTIAL...
...IS A SHAME.

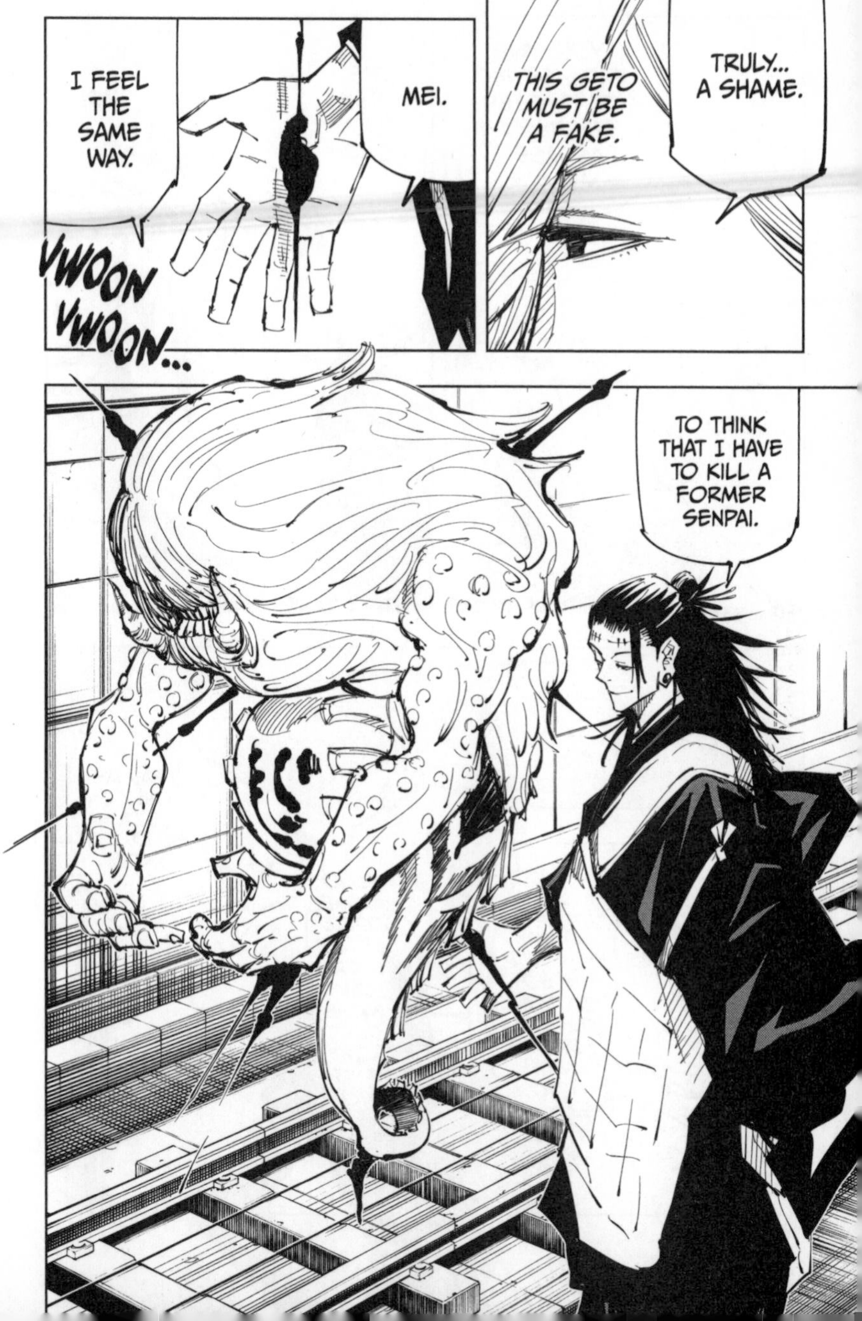
TRULY... A SHAME.
THIS GETO MUST BE A FAKE.
MEI.
I FEEL THE SAME WAY.
VWOON VWOON...
TO THINK THAT I HAVE TO KILL A FORMER SENPAI.

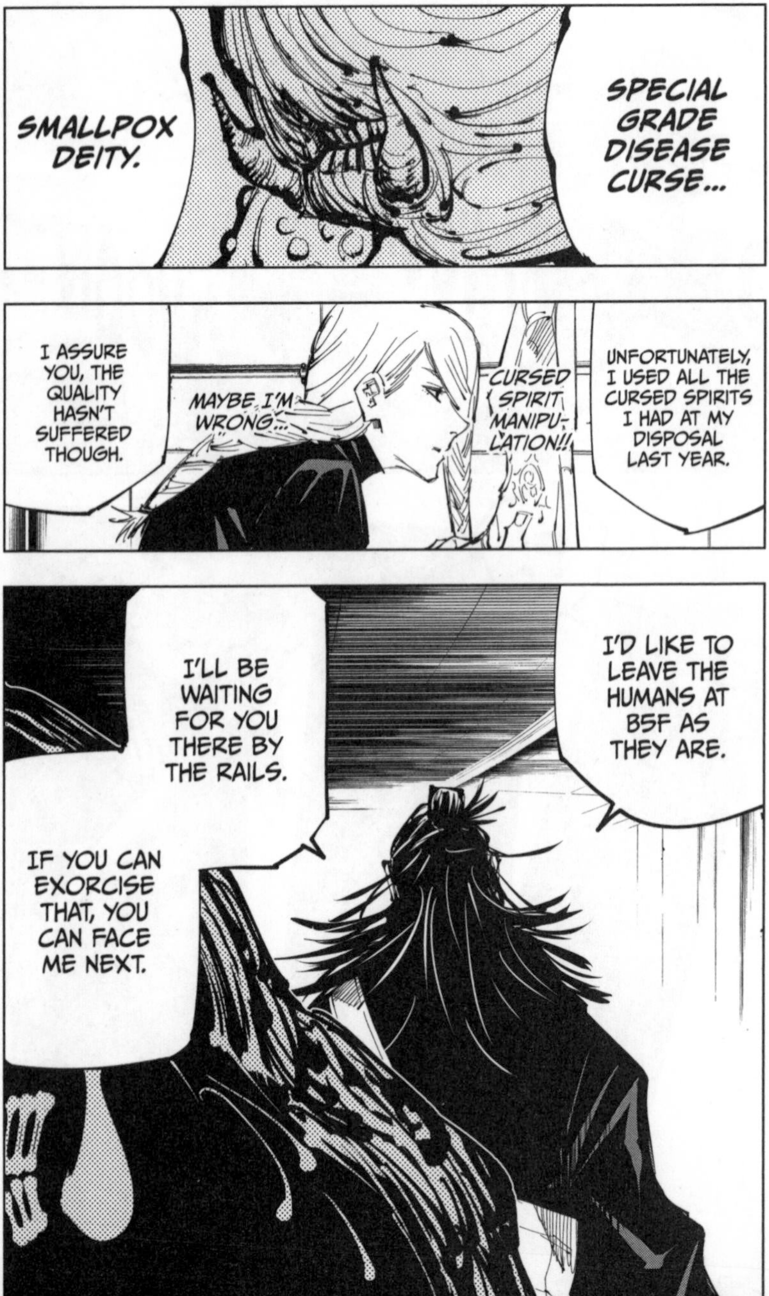
SPECIAL GRADE DISEASE CURSE...
SMALLPOX DEITY.
UNFORTUNATELY, I USED ALL THE CURSED SPIRITS I HAD AT MY DISPOSAL LAST YEAR.
CURSED SPIRIT MANIPULATION!!
MAYBE I'M WRONG...
I ASSURE YOU, THE QUALITY HASN'T SUFFERED THOUGH.
I'D LIKE TO LEAVE THE HUMANS AT B5F AS THEY ARE.
I'LL BE WAITING FOR YOU THERE BY THE RAILS.
IF YOU CAN EXORCISE THAT, YOU CAN FACE ME NEXT.

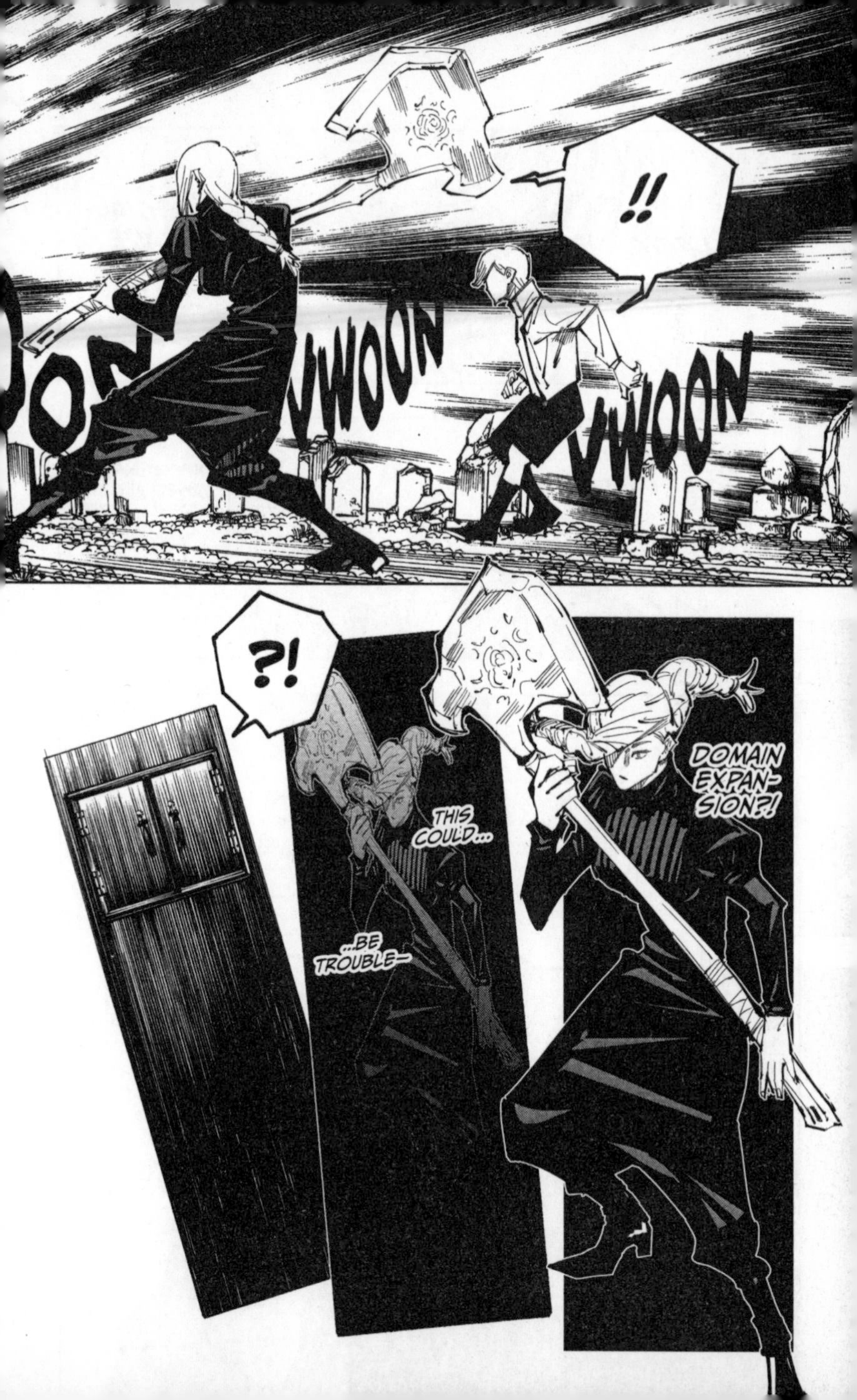
!!
VWOON
VWOON
DOMAIN EXPAN-SION?!
THIS COULD...
...BE TROUBLE—
?!

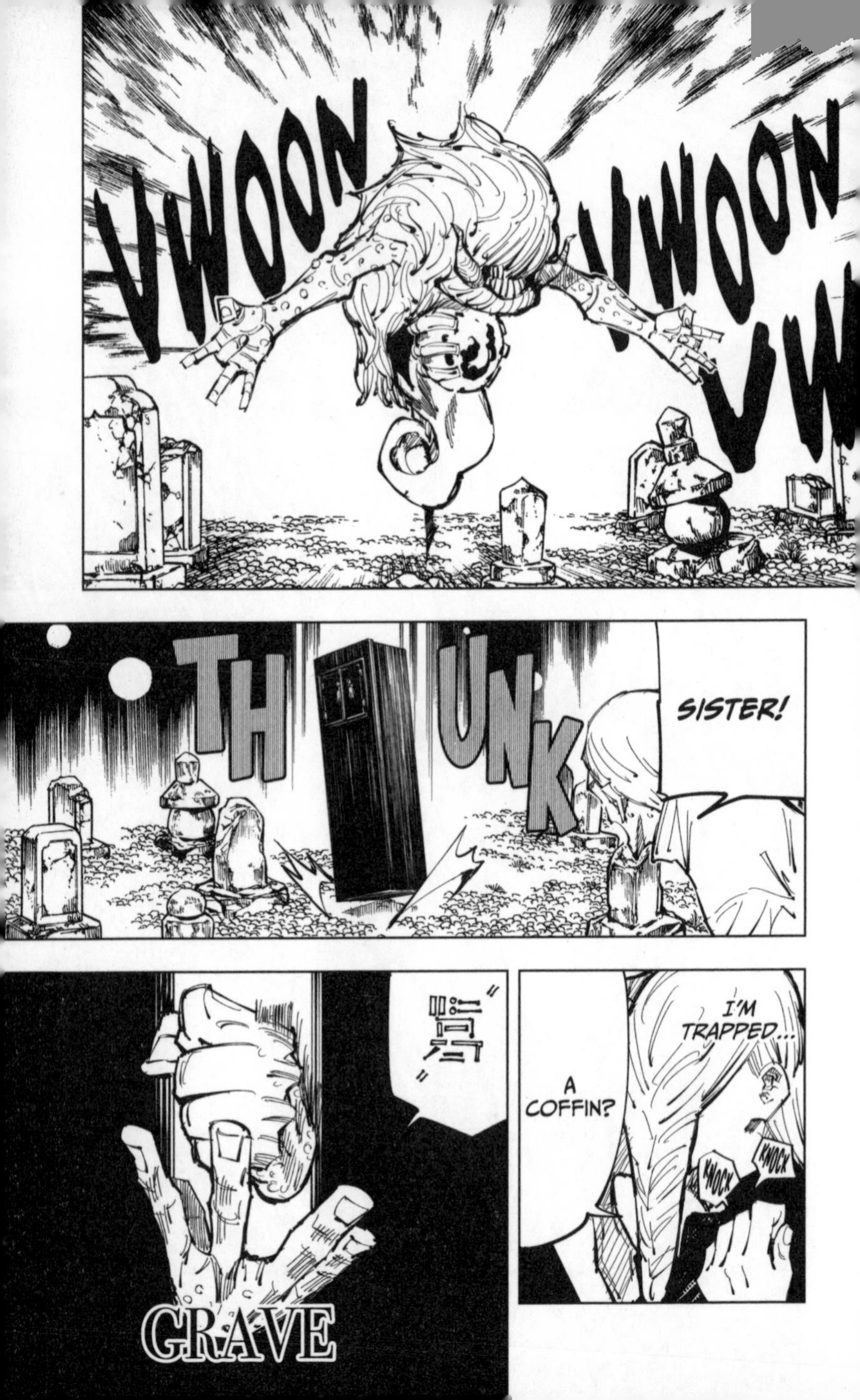
VWOON
VW
VWOON
SISTER!
THUNK
I'M TRAPPED...
KNOCK
KNOCK
A COFFIN?
GRAVE

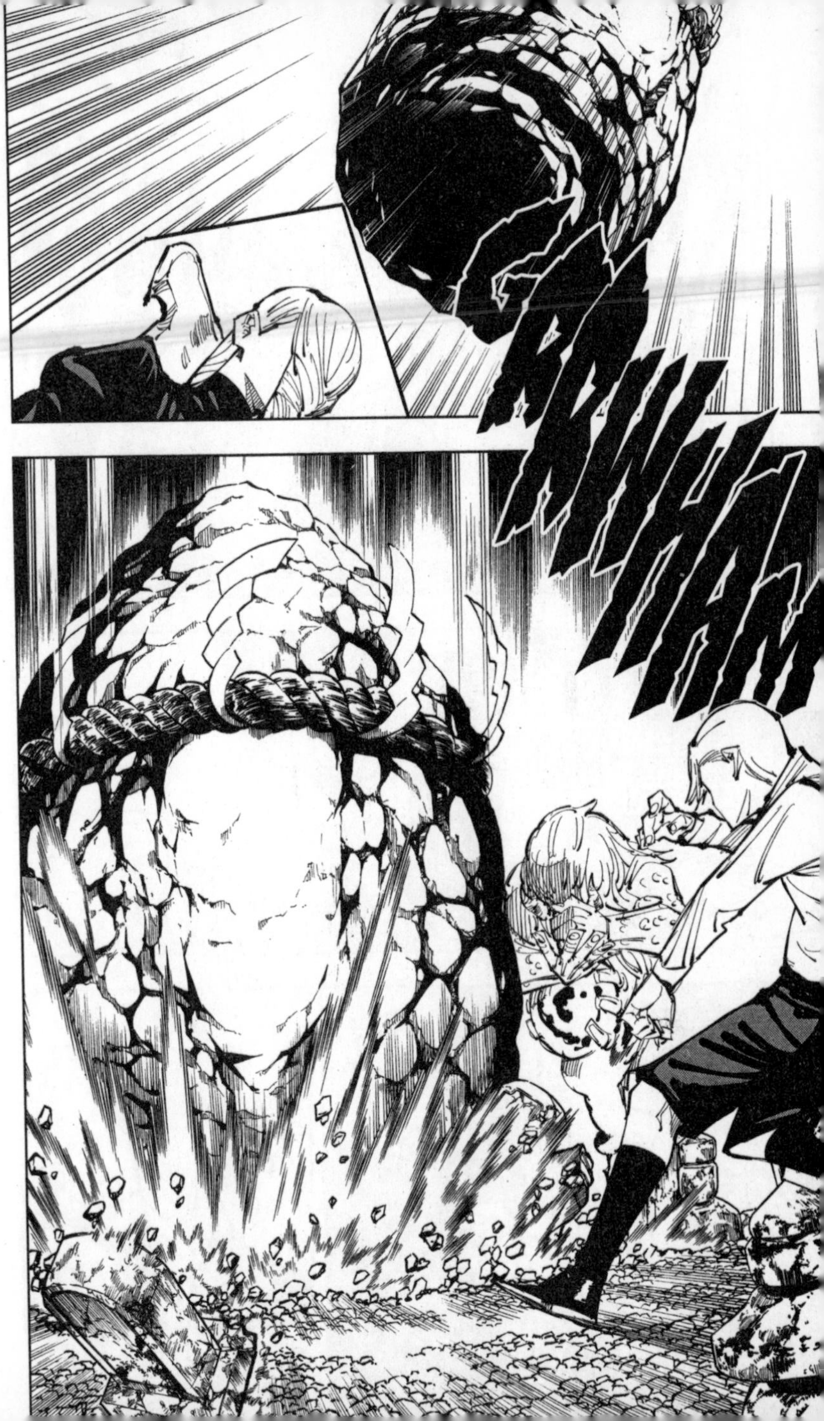

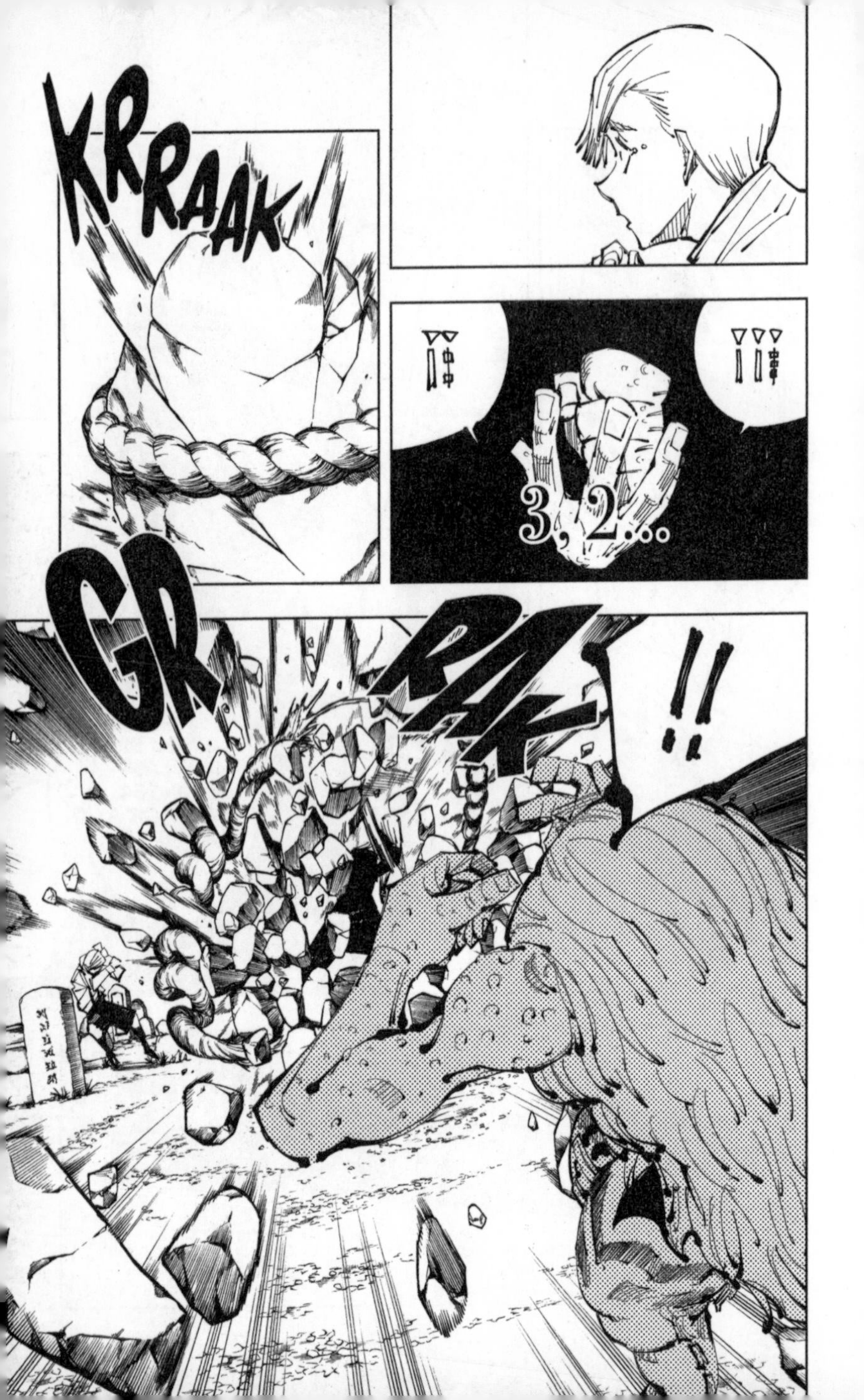
3, 2...
KRRAAK
GRRAK!!

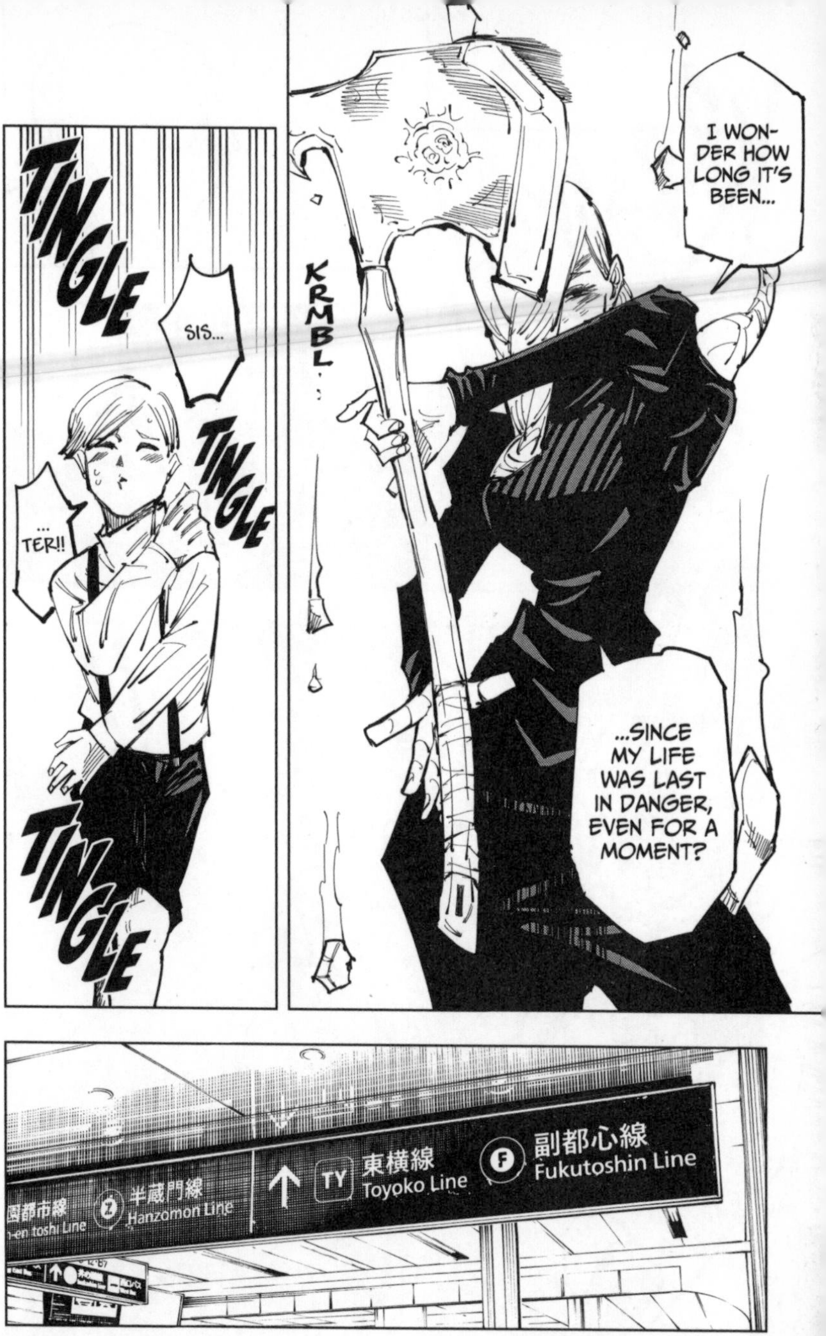
I WONDER HOW LONG IT'S BEEN...
KRMBL
...SINCE MY LIFE WAS LAST IN DANGER, EVEN FOR A MOMENT?
TINGLE
SIS...
TINGLE
...TER!!
TINGLE
副都心線 Fukutoshin Line
TY 東横線 Toyoko Line
半蔵門線 Hanzomon Line

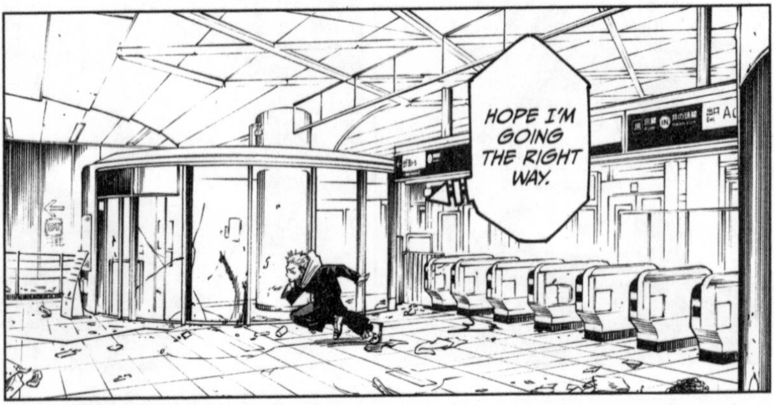
HOPE I'M GOING THE RIGHT WAY.

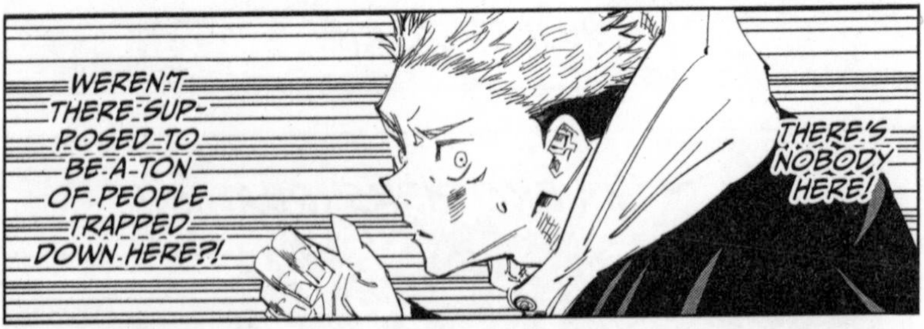
THERE'S NOBODY HERE!
WEREN'T THERE SUPPOSED TO BE A TON OF PEOPLE TRAPPED DOWN HERE?!

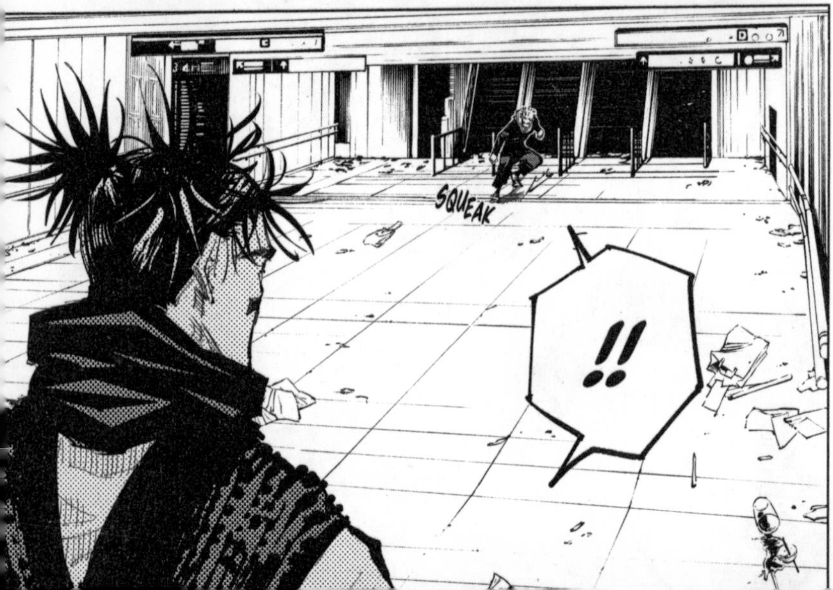
SQUEAK
!!

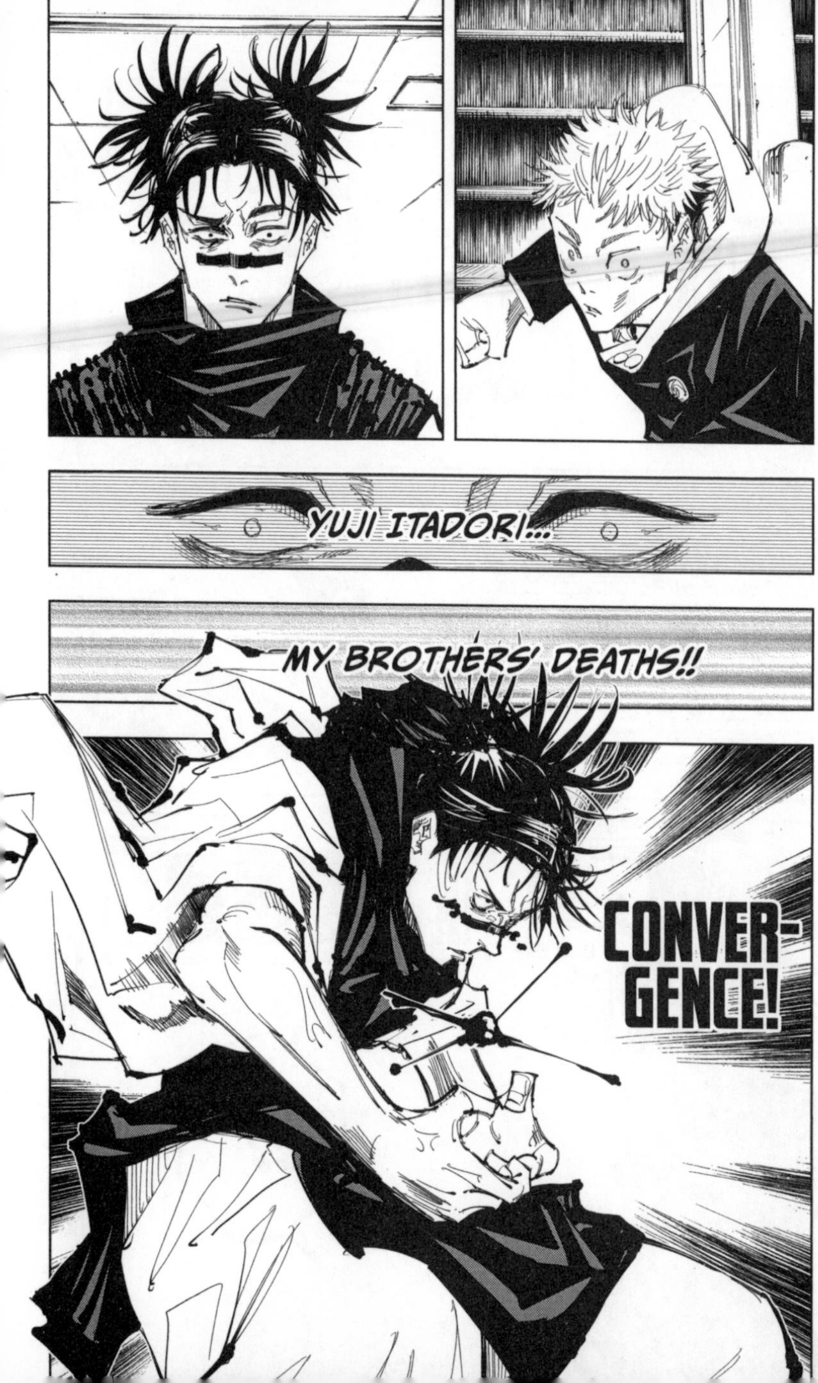
YUJI ITADORI...
MY BROTHERS' DEATHS!!
CONVER-GENCE!

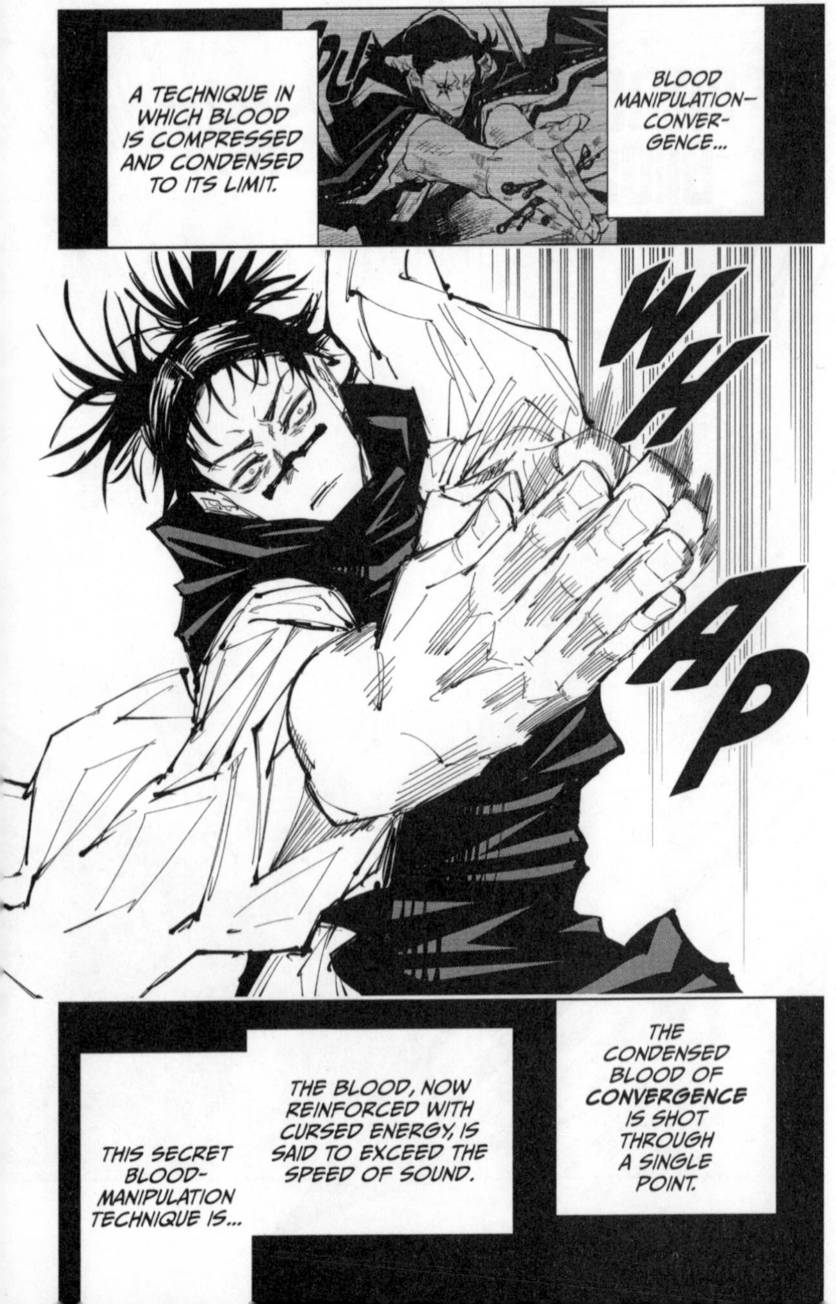
BLOOD MANIPULATION—CONVERGENCE...
A TECHNIQUE IN WHICH BLOOD IS COMPRESSED AND CONDENSED TO ITS LIMIT.
WHAAP
THE CONDENSED BLOOD OF **CONVERGENCE** IS SHOT THROUGH A SINGLE POINT.
THE BLOOD, NOW REINFORCED WITH CURSED ENERGY, IS SAID TO EXCEED THE SPEED OF SOUND.
THIS SECRET BLOOD-MANIPULATION TECHNIQUE IS...

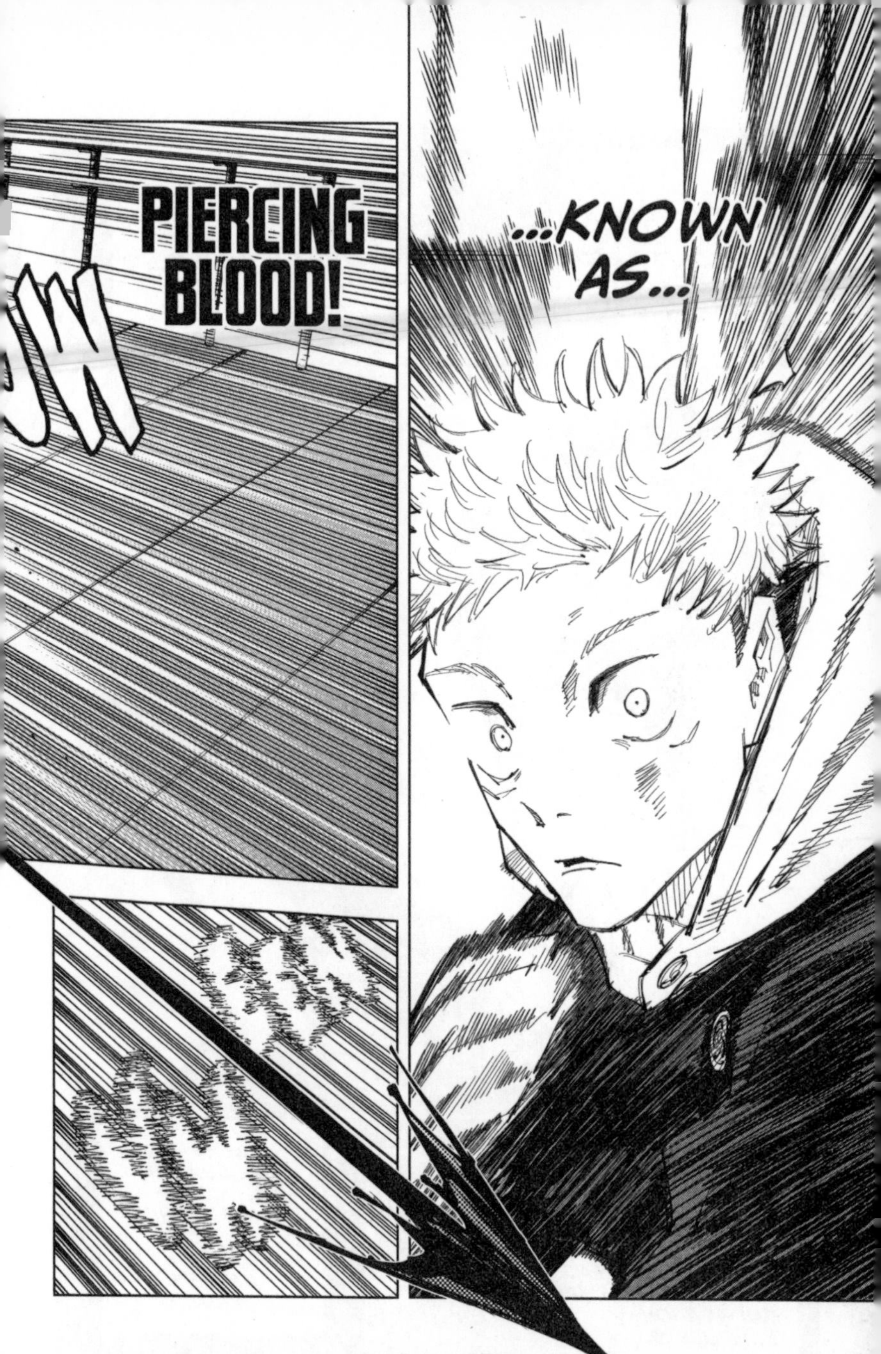
...KNOWN AS...
PIERCING BLOOD!

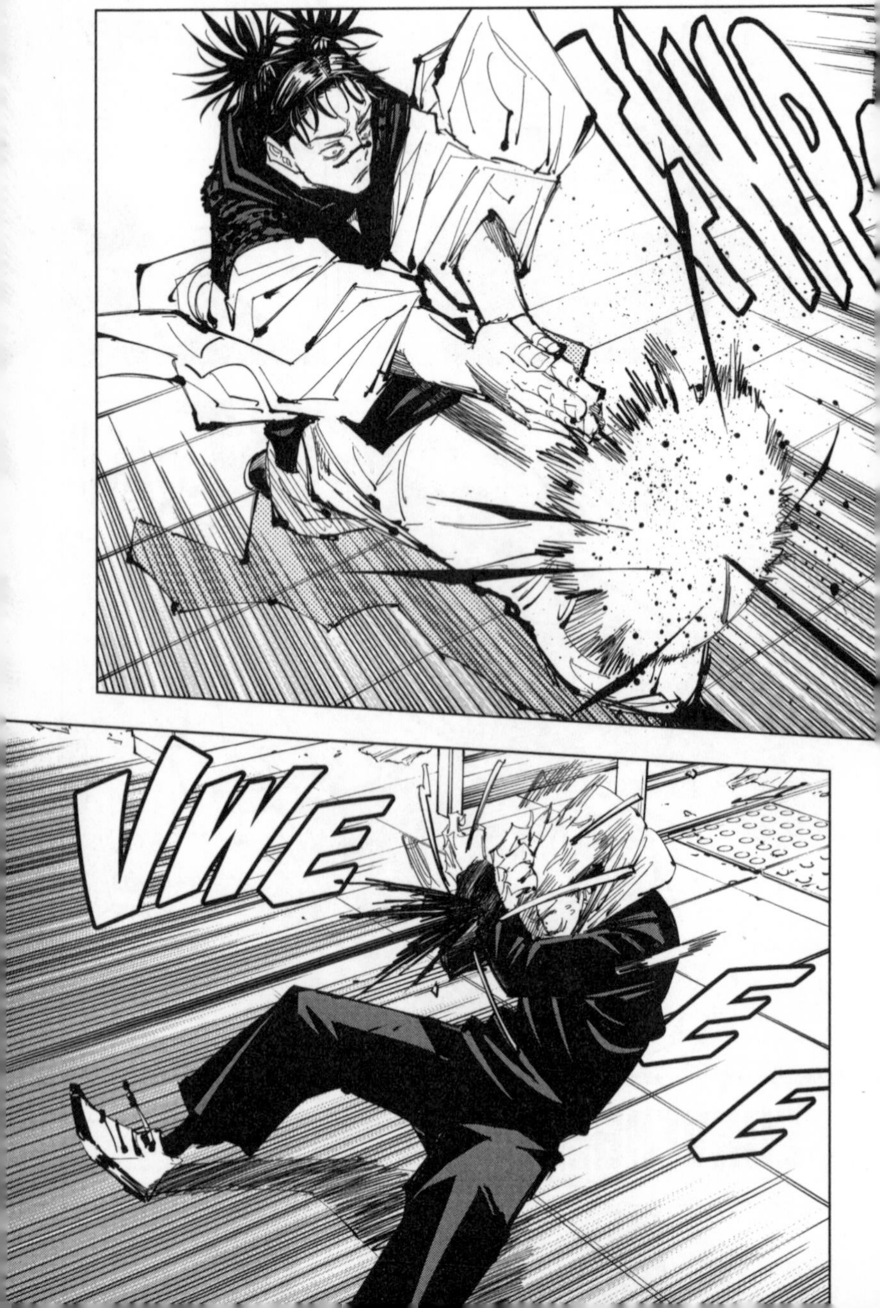
VWEEE

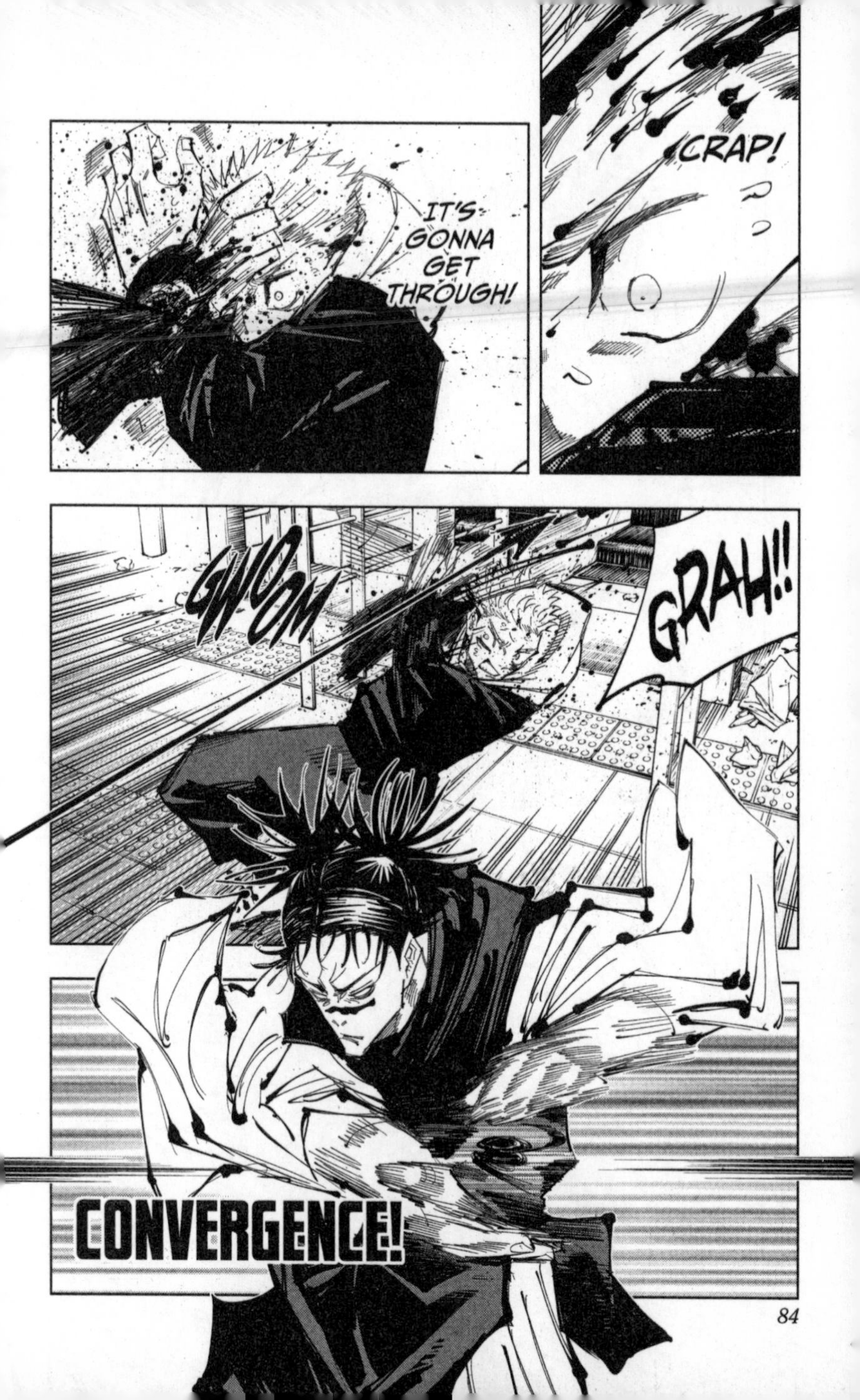
CRAP!
IT'S GONNA GET THROUGH!
GRAH!!
GWOOM
CONVERGENCE!

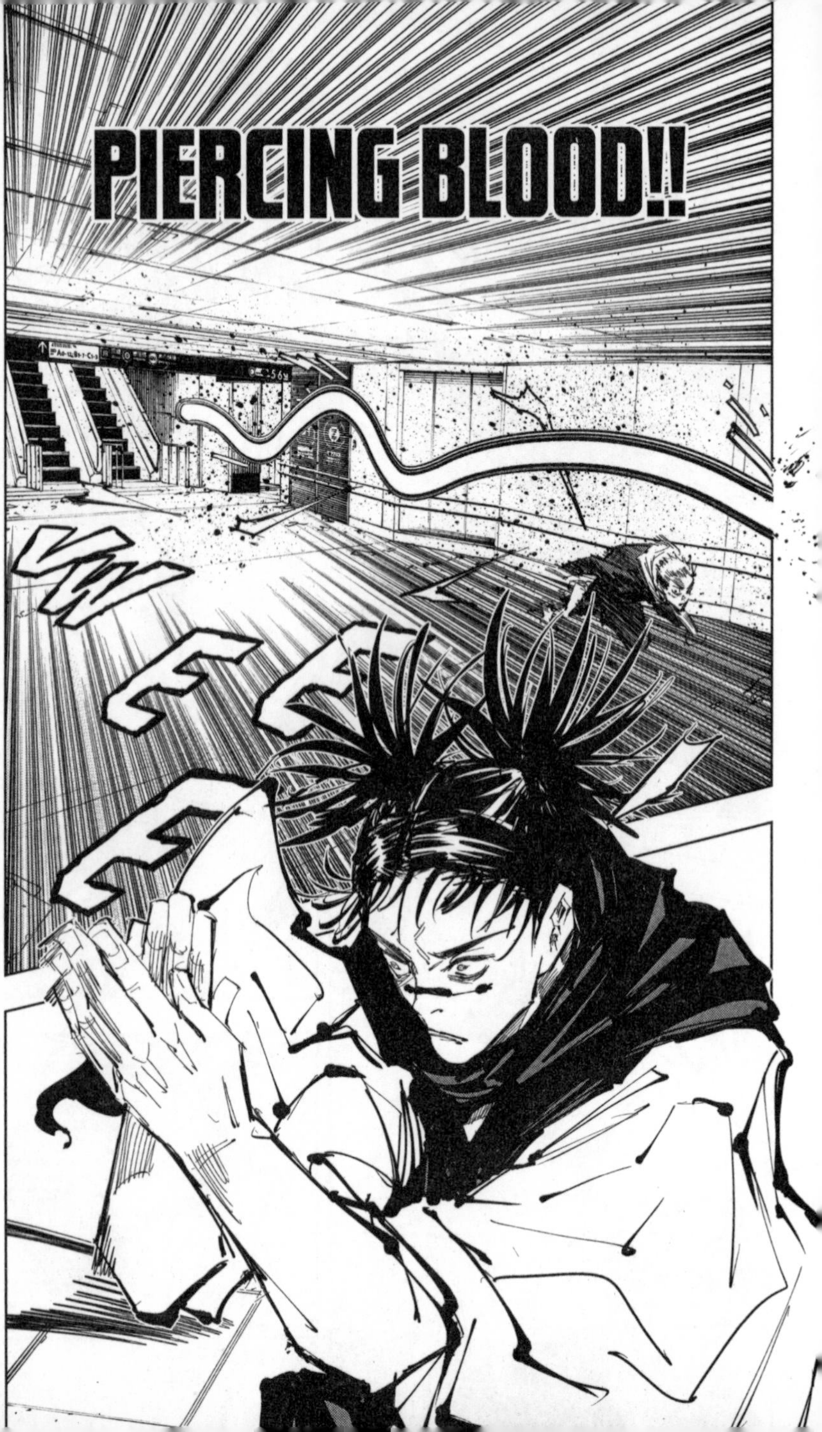
PIERCING BLOOD!!
VWFFF

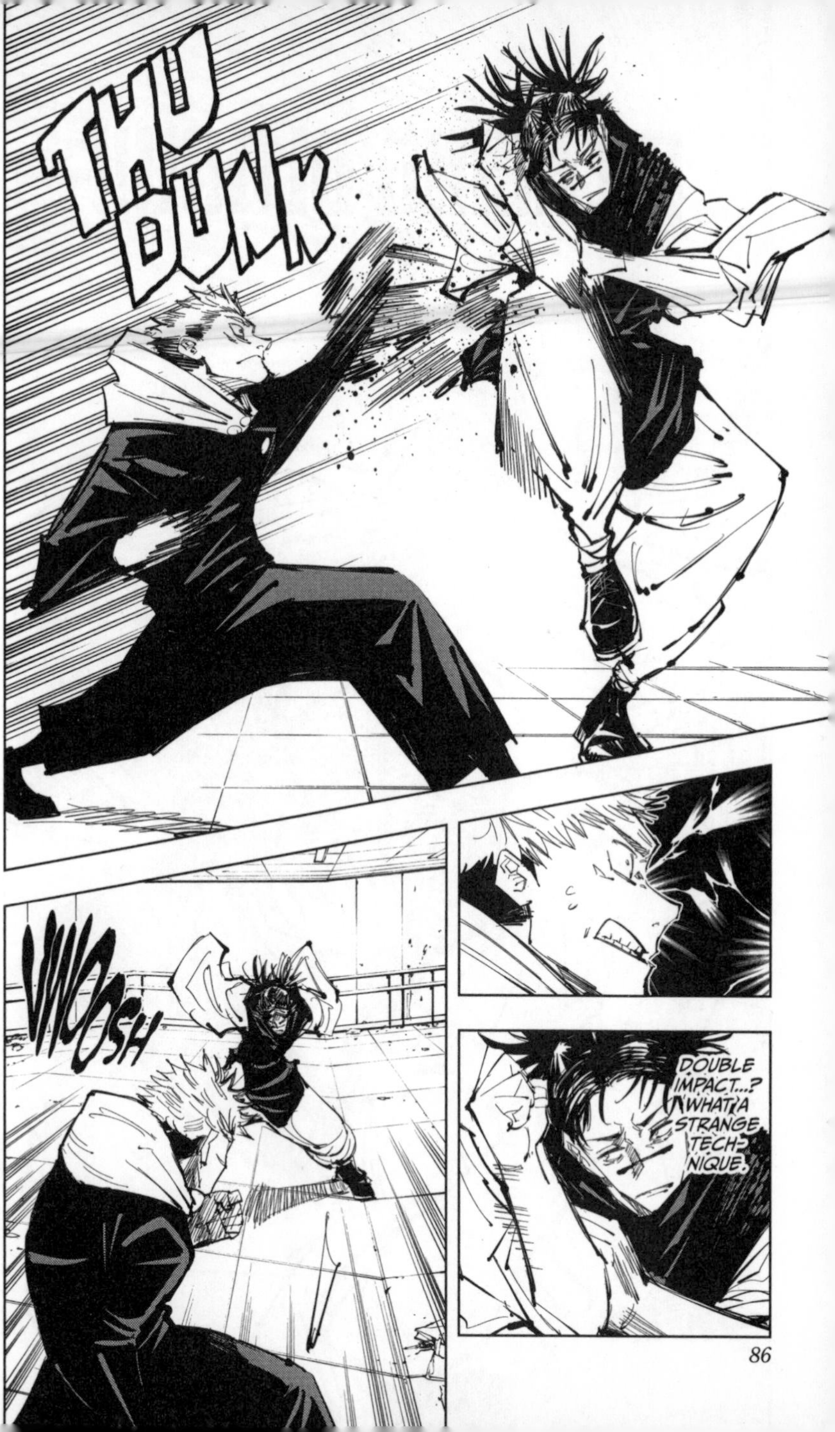
THU DUNK
DOUBLE IMPACT...? WHAT A STRANGE TECH-NIQUE.
VWOOSH

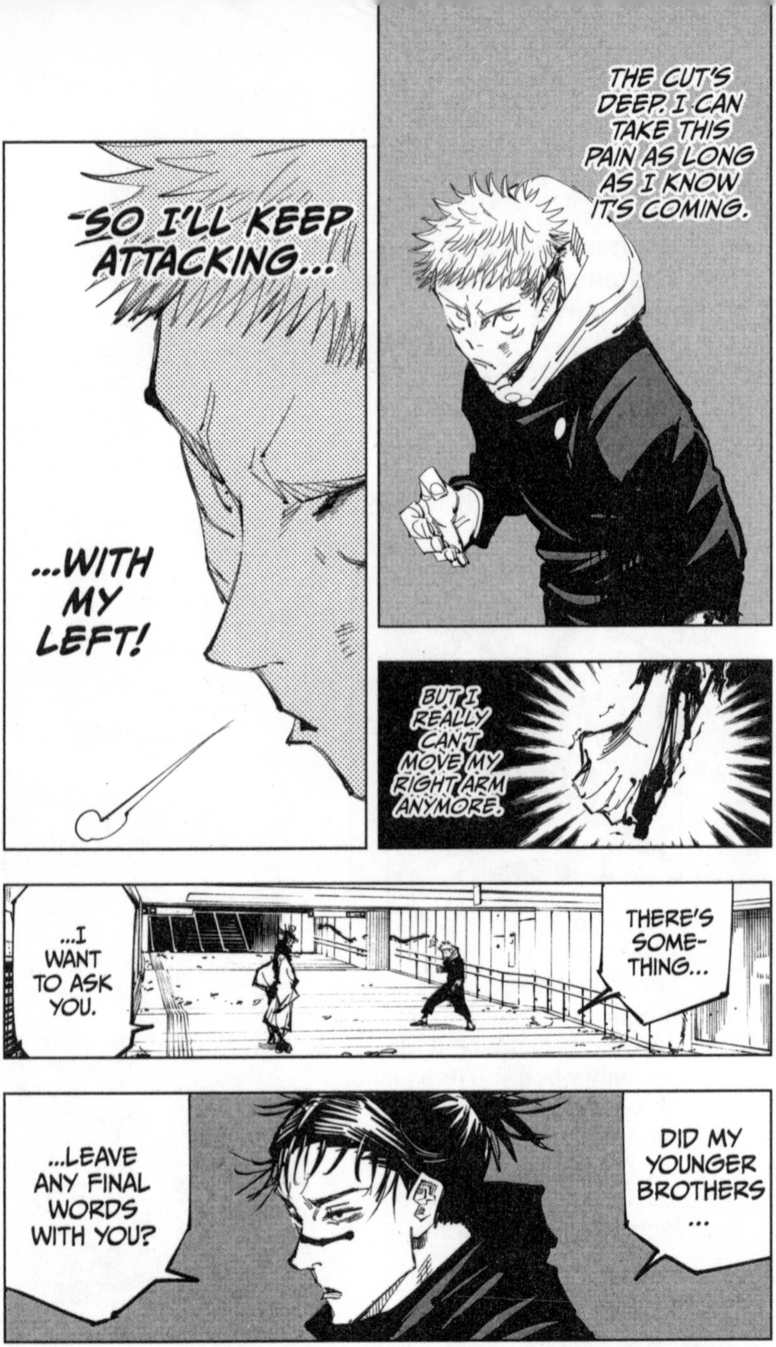
THE CUT'S DEEP. I CAN TAKE THIS PAIN AS LONG AS I KNOW IT'S COMING.
BUT I REALLY CAN'T MOVE MY RIGHT ARM ANYMORE.
-SO I'LL KEEP ATTACKING...
...WITH MY LEFT!
THERE'S SOME-THING...
...I WANT TO ASK YOU.
DID MY YOUNGER BROTHERS ...
...LEAVE ANY FINAL WORDS WITH YOU?

Scenes I was planning to address but forgot about until now, part 3

• Summer uniforms

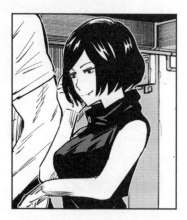

There isn't much of a difference between the summer and winter uniforms (although one is more breathable). After all, it's dangerous to not be dressed properly when you're a jujutsu sorcerer. But, if you put in a request for a customized uniform, they'll make it for you.

Nobara didn't know this.

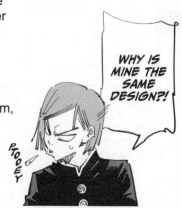

WHY IS MINE THE SAME DESIGN?!

PTOOEY

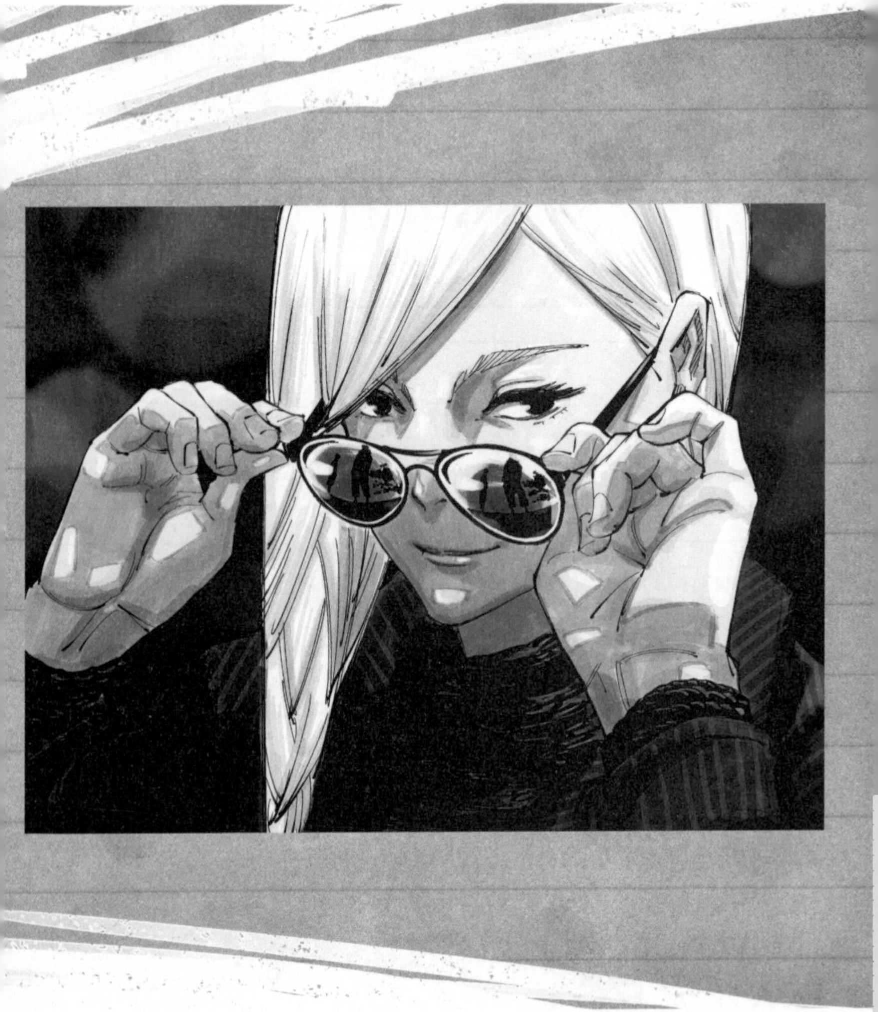

CHAPTER 102:
THE SHIBUYA INCIDENT, PART 20

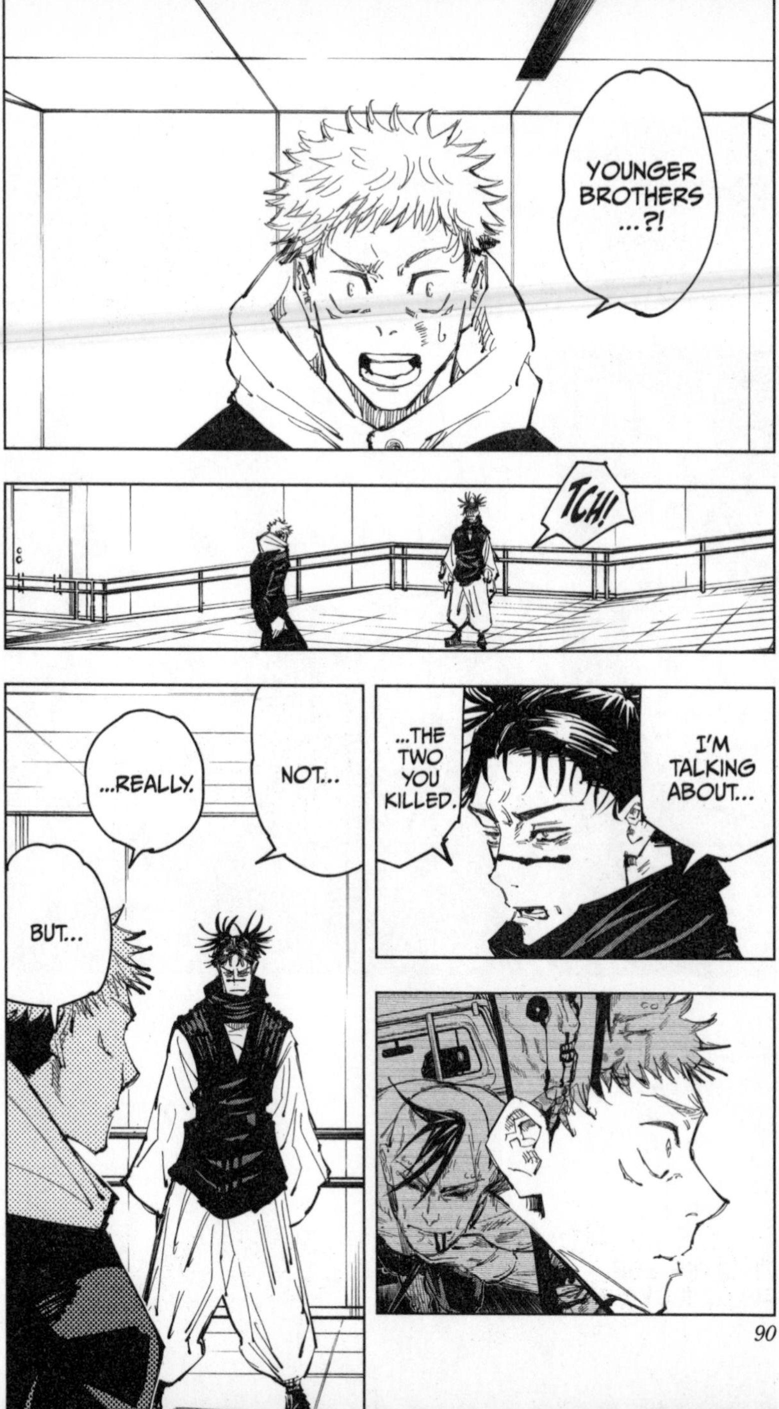
YOUNGER BROTHERS ...?!
TCH!
I'M TALKING ABOUT...
...THE TWO YOU KILLED.
NOT...
...REALLY.
BUT...

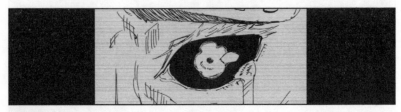

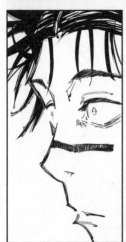

...THEY DID CRY.

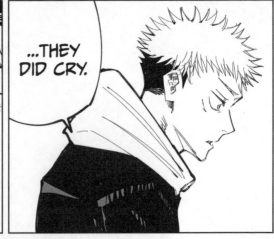

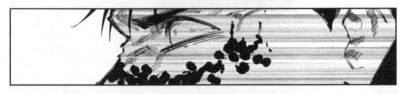

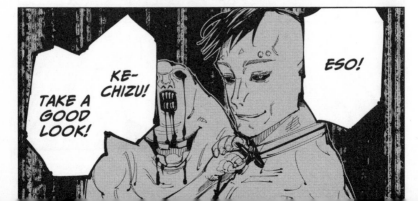

TAKE A GOOD LOOK!

KE-CHIZU!

ESO!

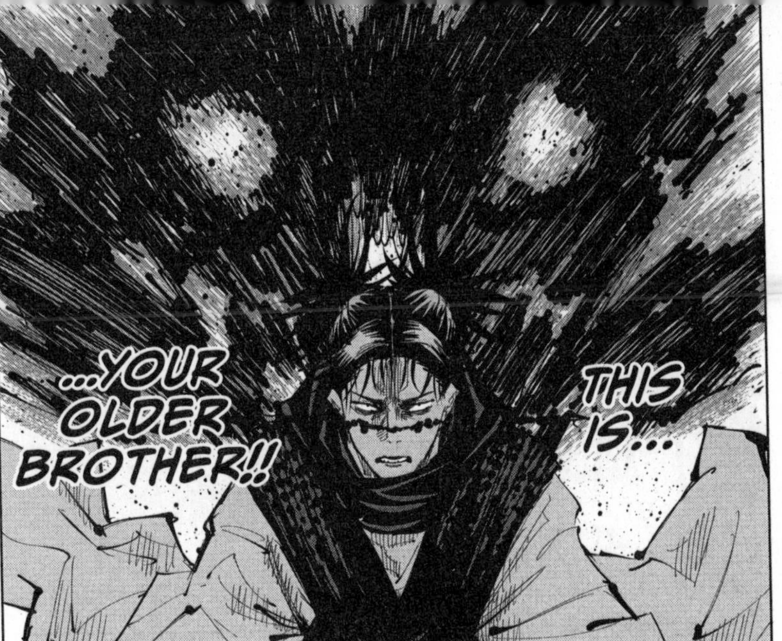
THIS IS...
...YOUR OLDER BROTHER!!
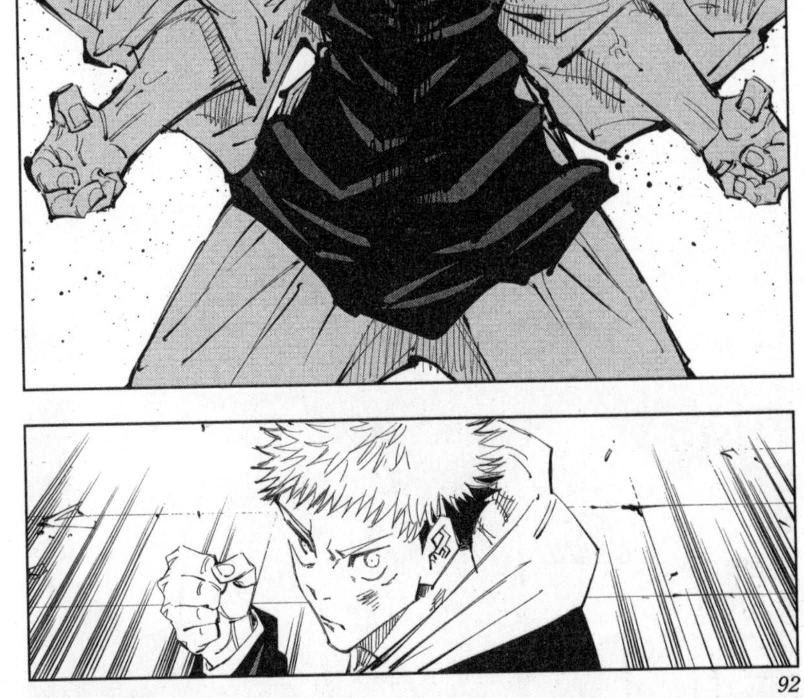

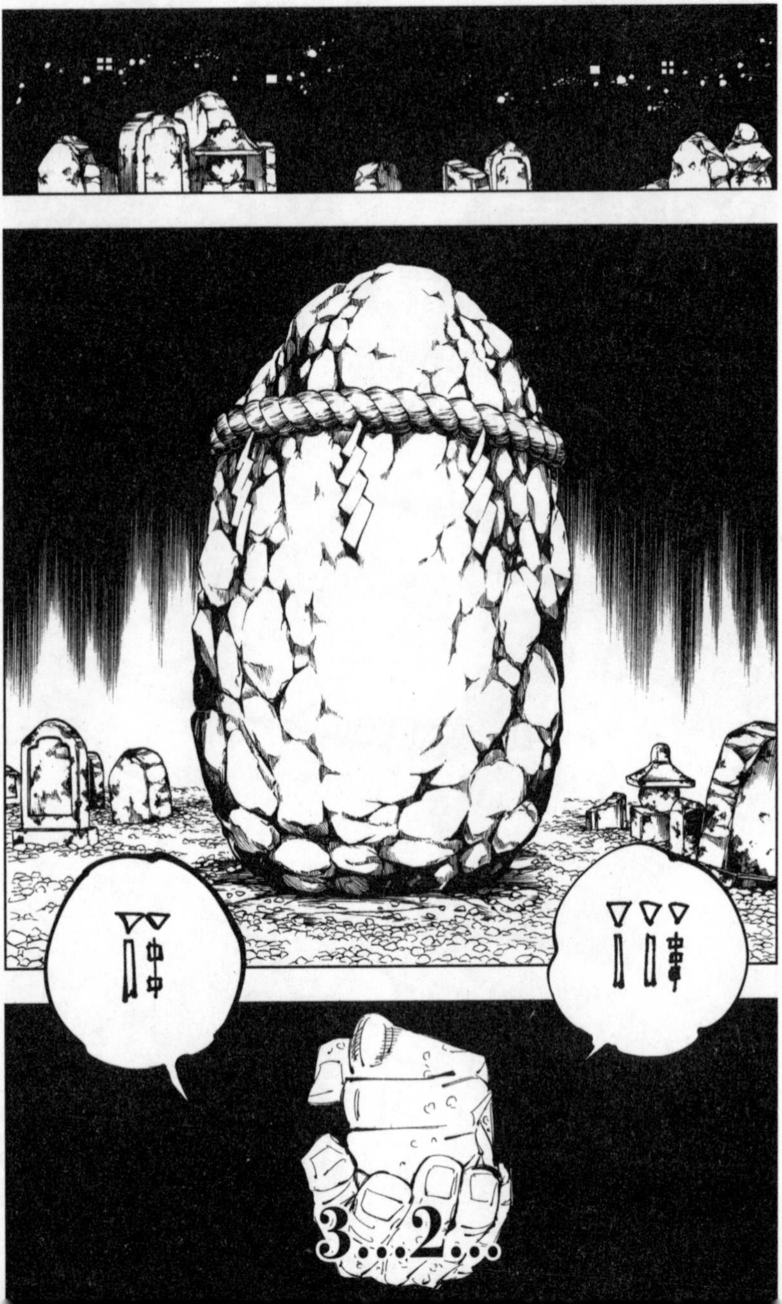
3...2...

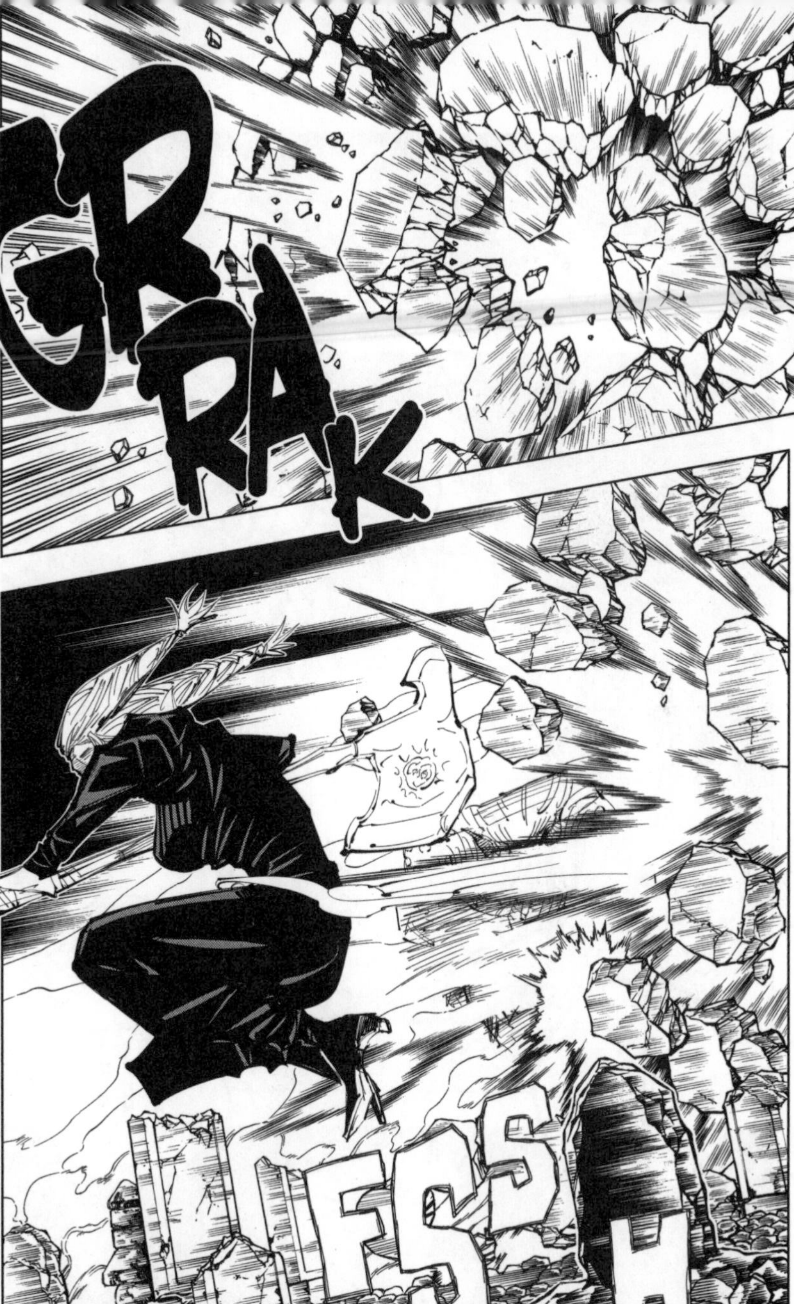
GRRAK
FSSH

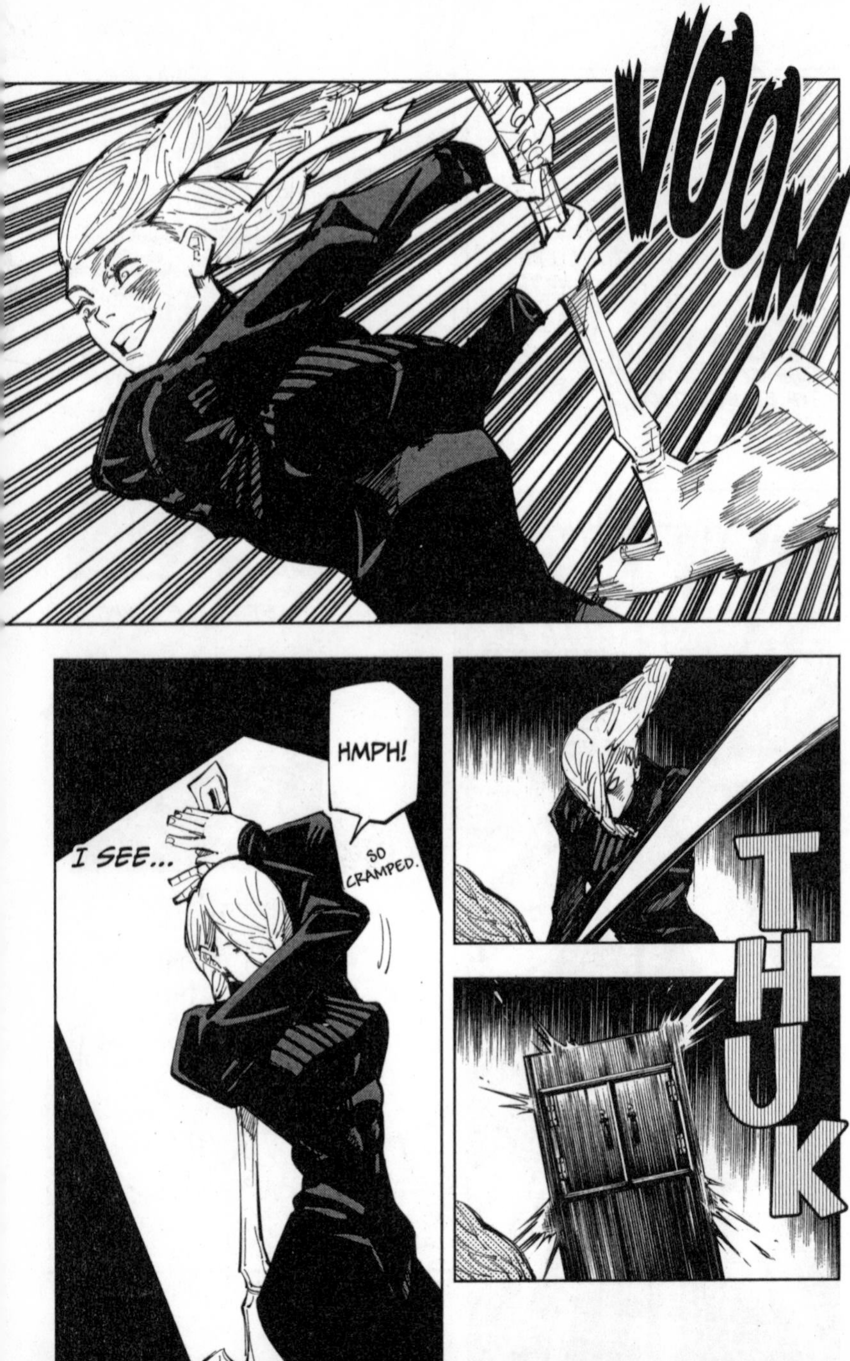
VOOM
THUNK
HMPH!
SO CRAMPED.
I SEE...

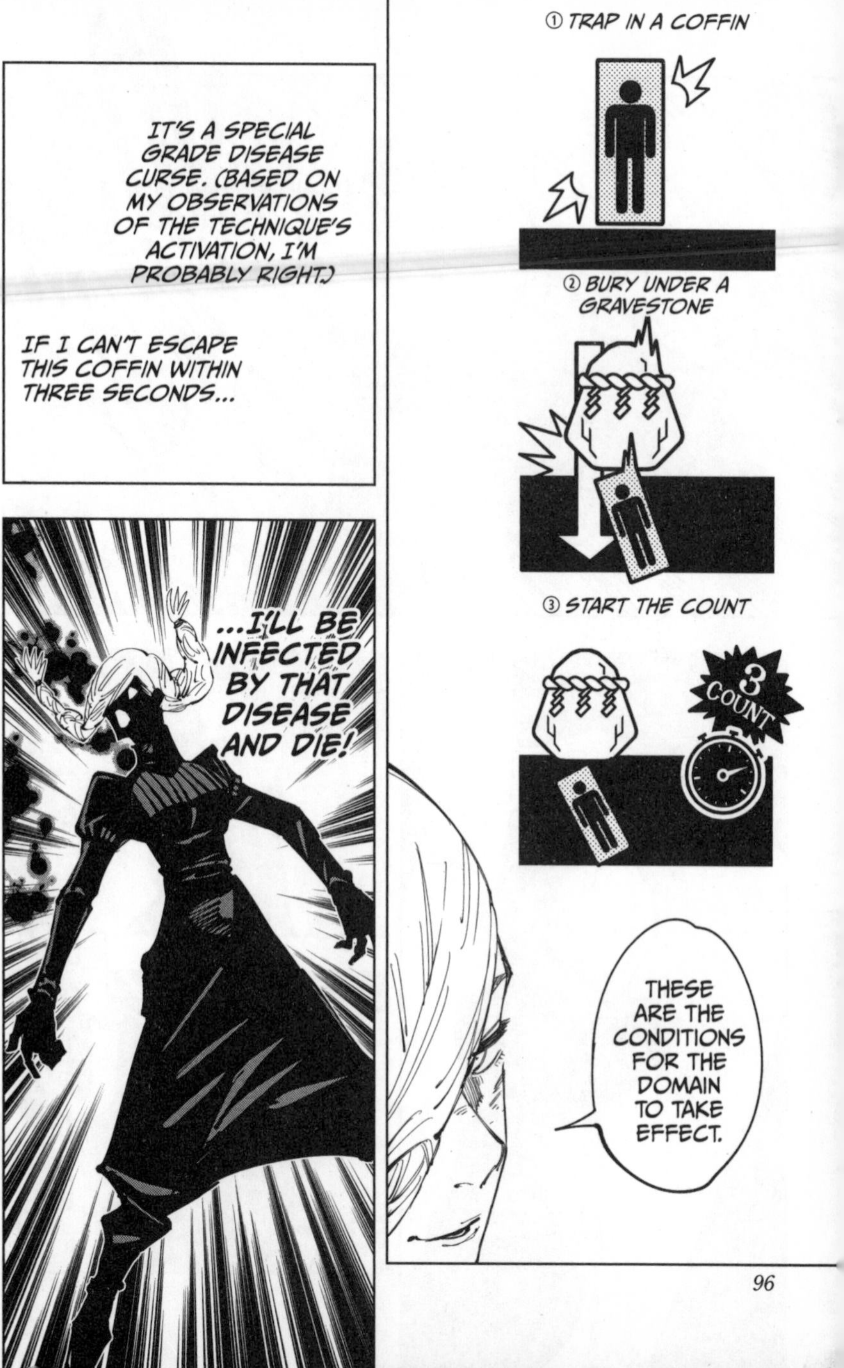
① TRAP IN A COFFIN
② BURY UNDER A GRAVESTONE
③ START THE COUNT
3 COUNT
THESE ARE THE CONDITIONS FOR THE DOMAIN TO TAKE EFFECT.
IT'S A SPECIAL GRADE DISEASE CURSE. (BASED ON MY OBSERVATIONS OF THE TECHNIQUE'S ACTIVATION, I'M PROBABLY RIGHT.)
IF I CAN'T ESCAPE THIS COFFIN WITHIN THREE SECONDS...
...I'LL BE INFECTED BY THAT DISEASE AND DIE!

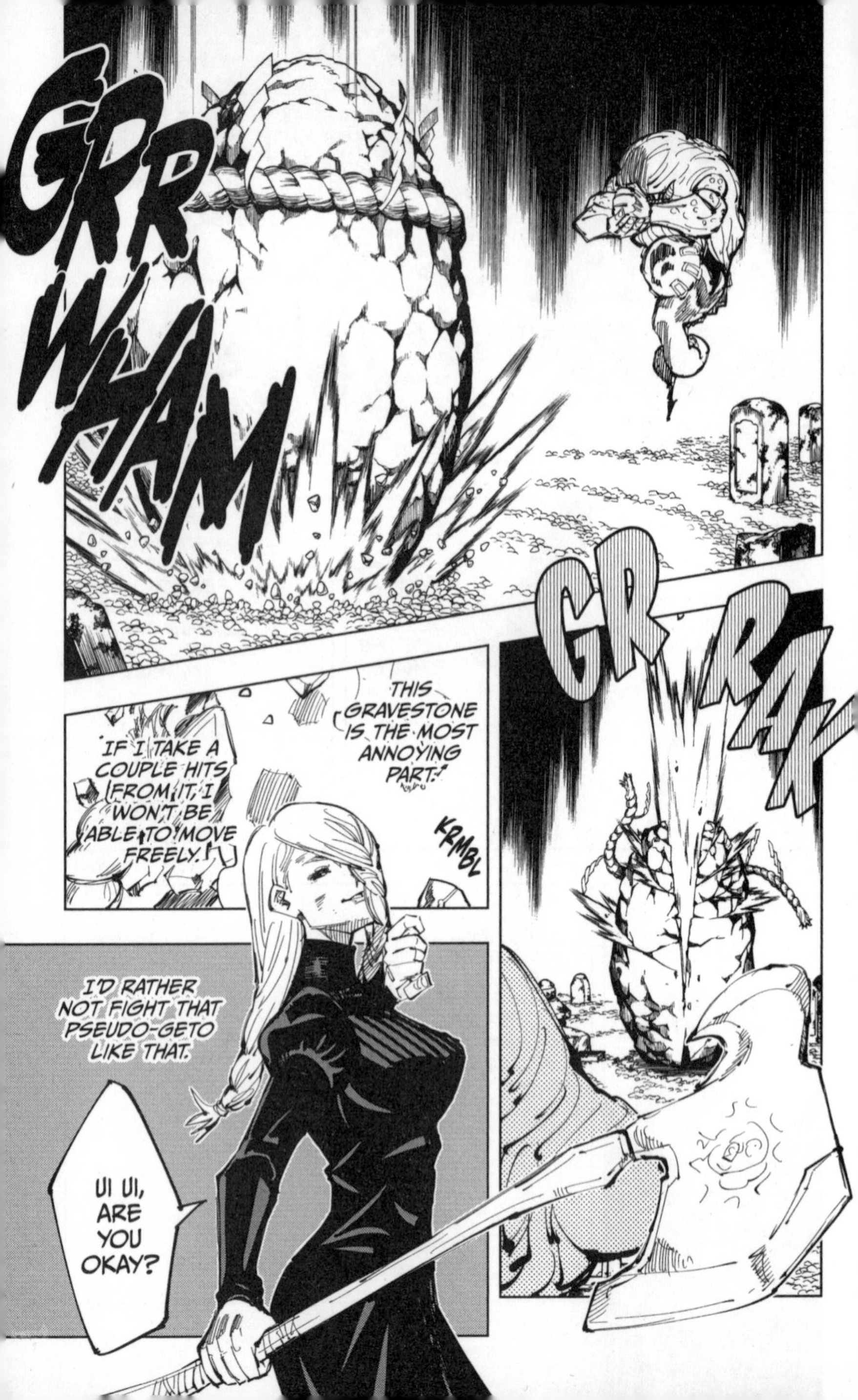
GRR WHAM
GRRAK
THIS GRAVESTONE IS THE MOST ANNOYING PART.
IF I TAKE A COUPLE HITS FROM IT, I WON'T BE ABLE TO MOVE FREELY.
KRMBL
I'D RATHER NOT FIGHT THAT PSEUDO-GETO LIKE THAT.
UI UI, ARE YOU OKAY?

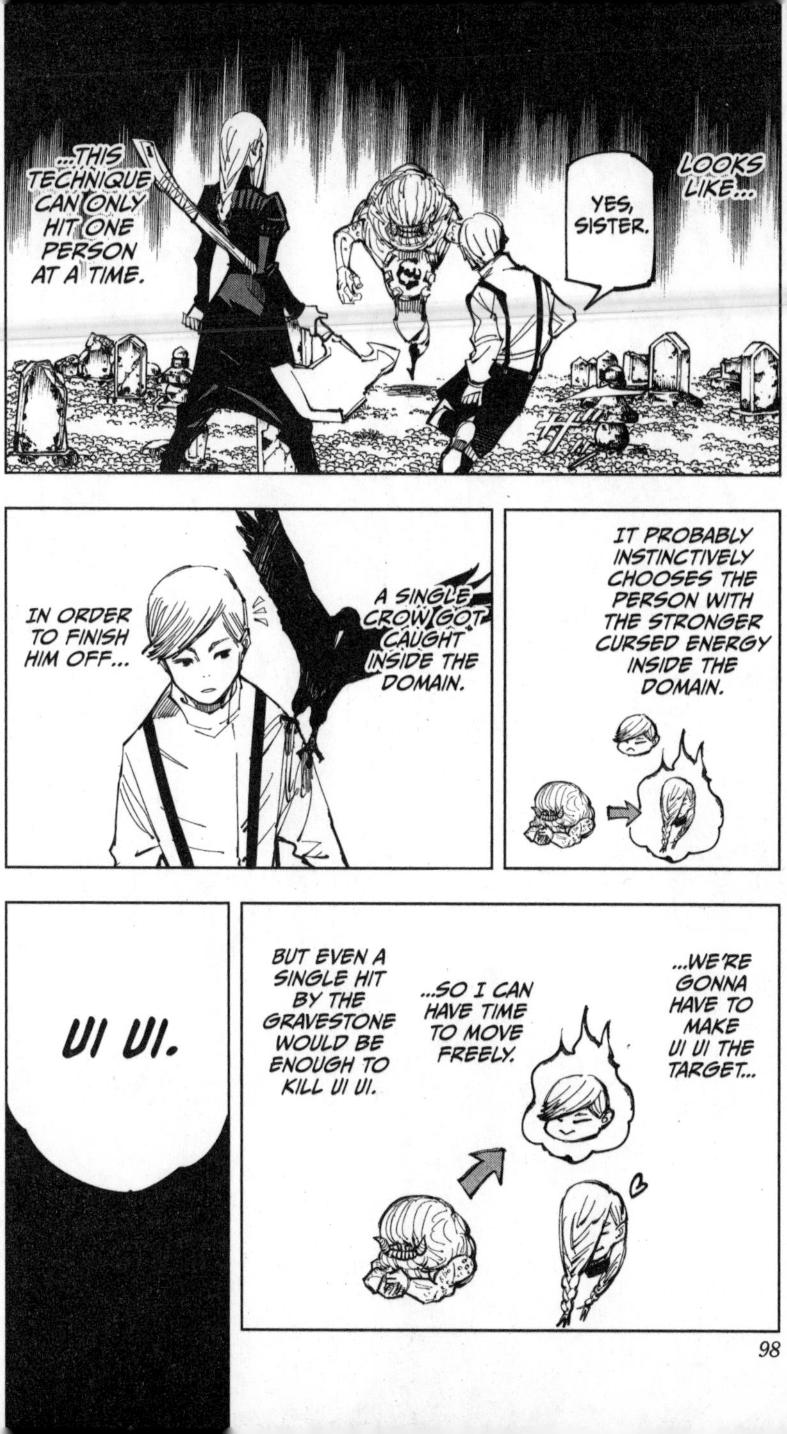
LOOKS LIKE...
YES, SISTER.
...THIS TECHNIQUE CAN ONLY HIT ONE PERSON AT A TIME.
IT PROBABLY INSTINCTIVELY CHOOSES THE PERSON WITH THE STRONGER CURSED ENERGY INSIDE THE DOMAIN.
A SINGLE CROW GOT CAUGHT INSIDE THE DOMAIN.
IN ORDER TO FINISH HIM OFF...
...WE'RE GONNA HAVE TO MAKE UI UI THE TARGET...
...SO I CAN HAVE TIME TO MOVE FREELY.
BUT EVEN A SINGLE HIT BY THE GRAVESTONE WOULD BE ENOUGH TO KILL UI UI.
UI UI.

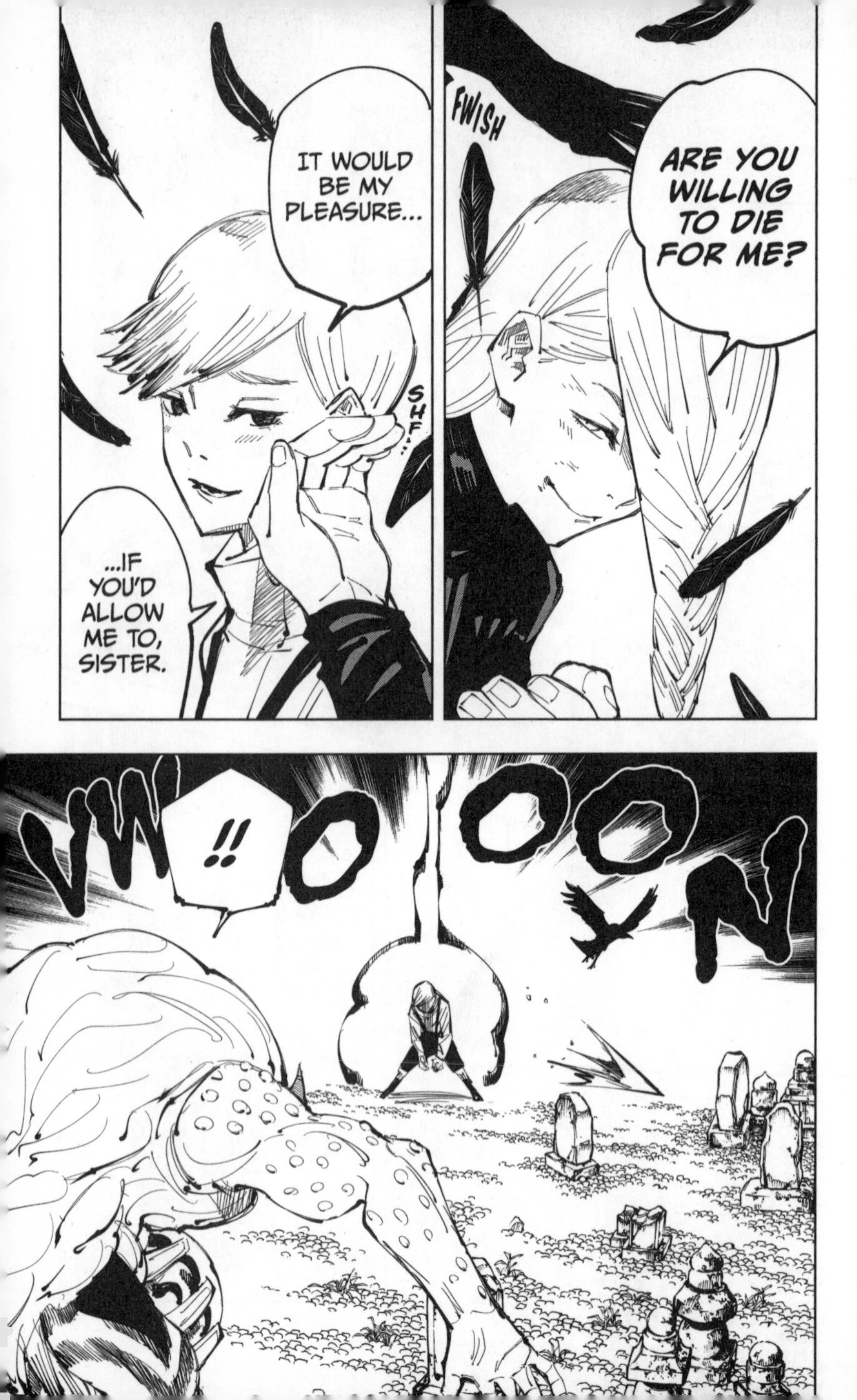
FWISH
ARE YOU WILLING TO DIE FOR ME?
IT WOULD BE MY PLEASURE...
SHF...
...IF YOU'D ALLOW ME TO, SISTER.
VWOOOON
!!

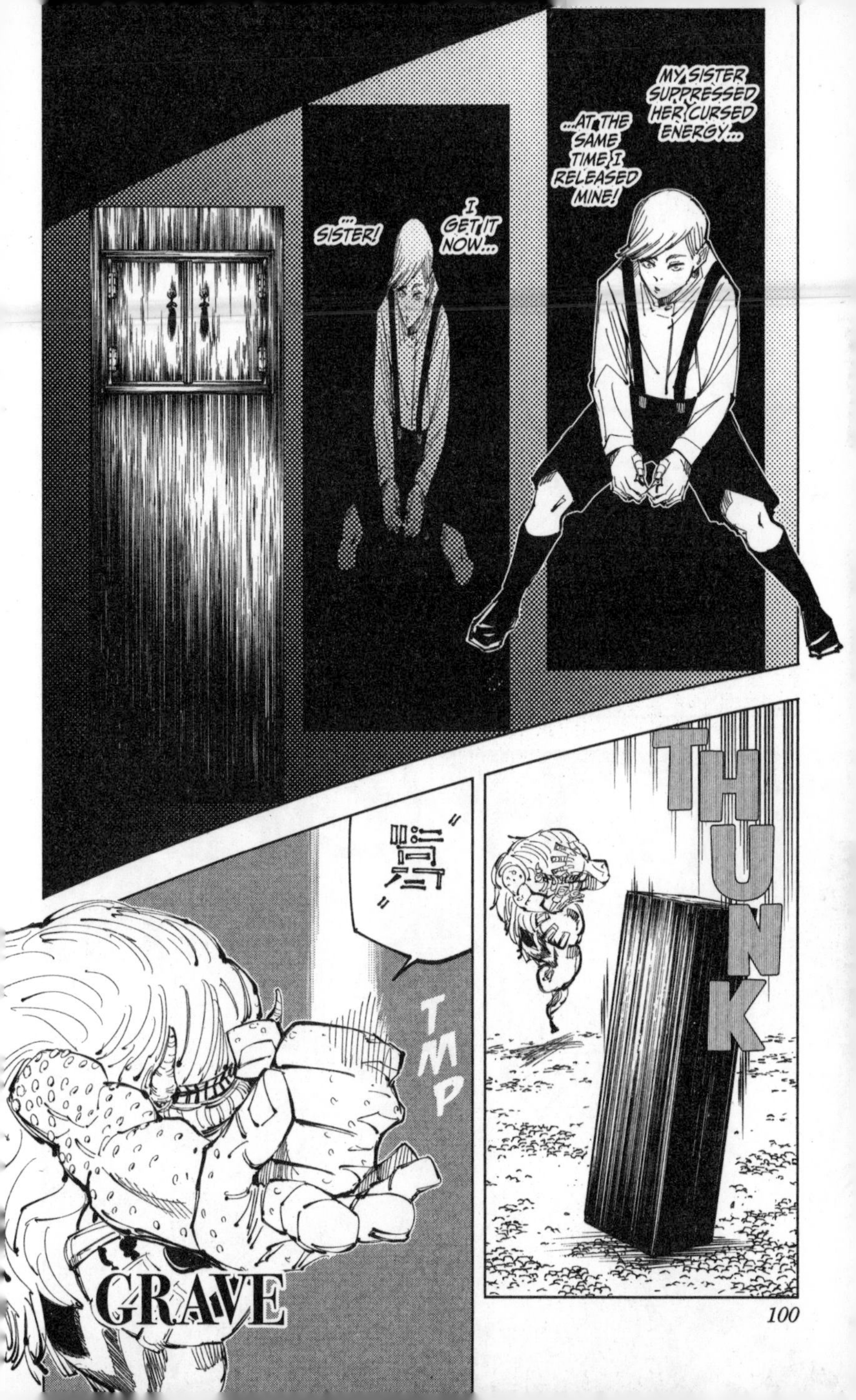
MY SISTER SUPPRESSED HER CURSED ENERGY...
...AT THE SAME TIME I RELEASED MINE!
I GET IT NOW...
...SISTER!
THUNK
TMP
GRAVE

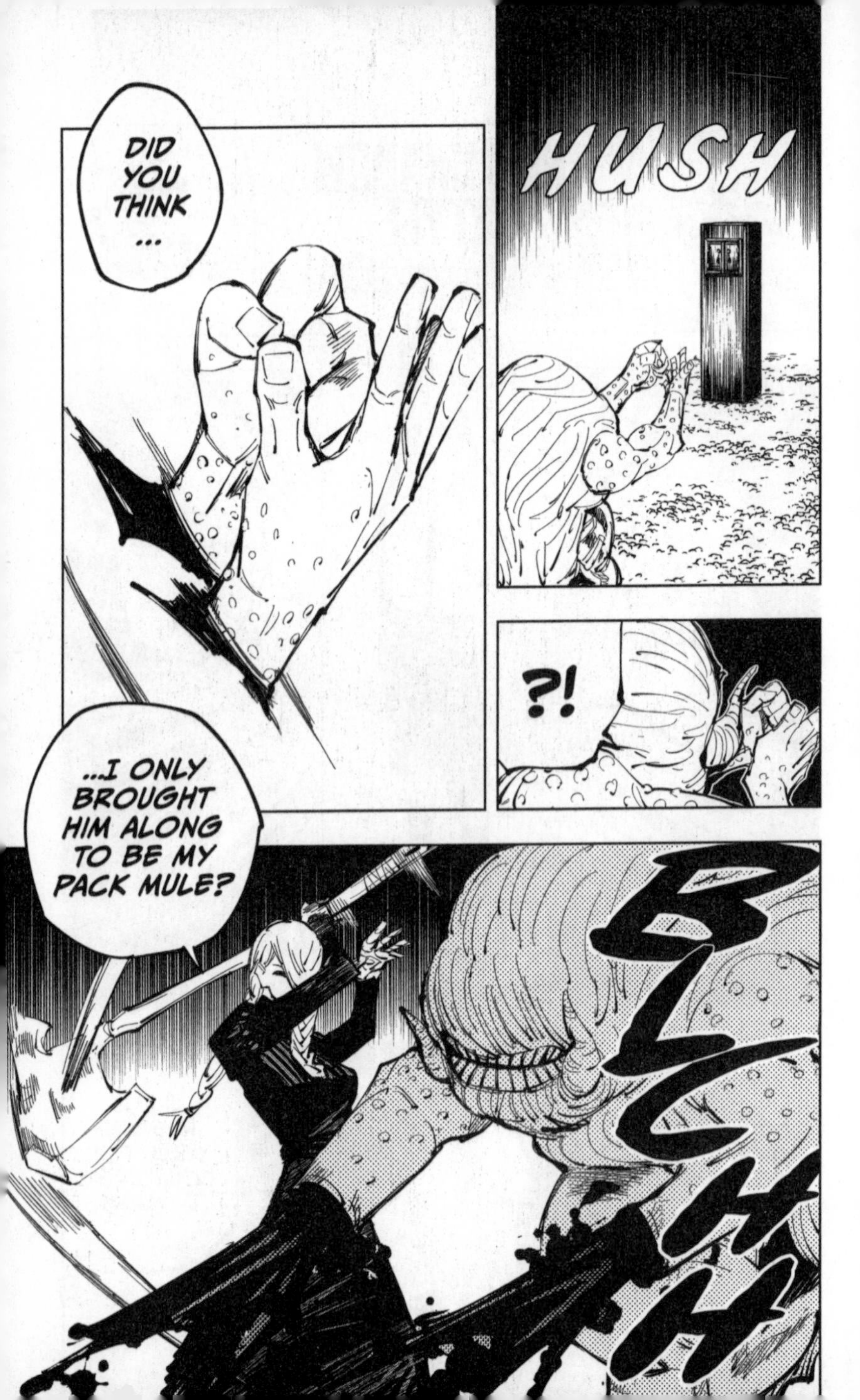
HUSH
?!
DID YOU THINK ...
...I ONLY BROUGHT HIM ALONG TO BE MY PACK MULE?
BLCHH

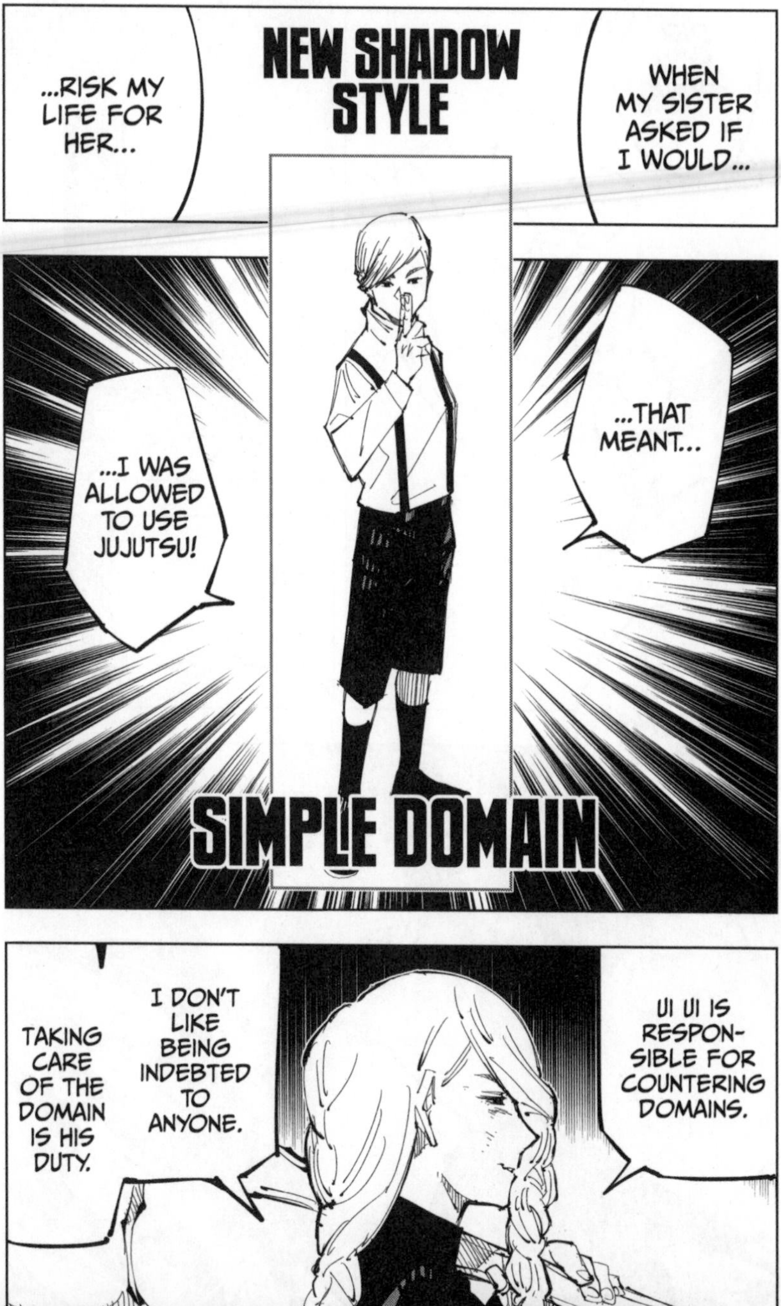
WHEN MY SISTER ASKED IF I WOULD...
NEW SHADOW STYLE
...RISK MY LIFE FOR HER...
...THAT MEANT...
...I WAS ALLOWED TO USE JUJUTSU!
SIMPLE DOMAIN
UI UI IS RESPON-SIBLE FOR COUNTERING DOMAINS.
I DON'T LIKE BEING INDEBTED TO ANYONE.
TAKING CARE OF THE DOMAIN IS HIS DUTY.

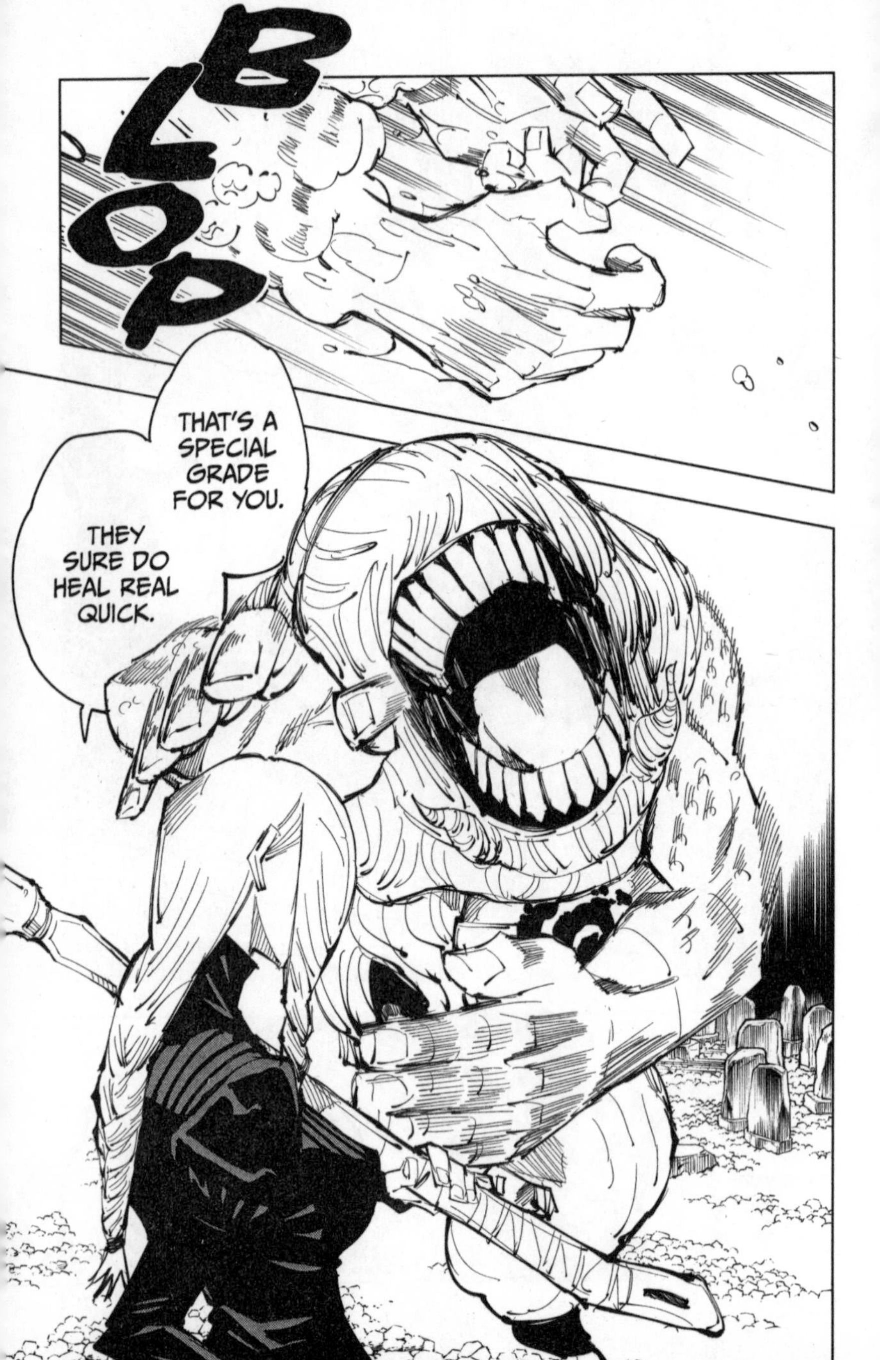
BLOP
THAT'S A SPECIAL GRADE FOR YOU.
THEY SURE DO HEAL REAL QUICK.

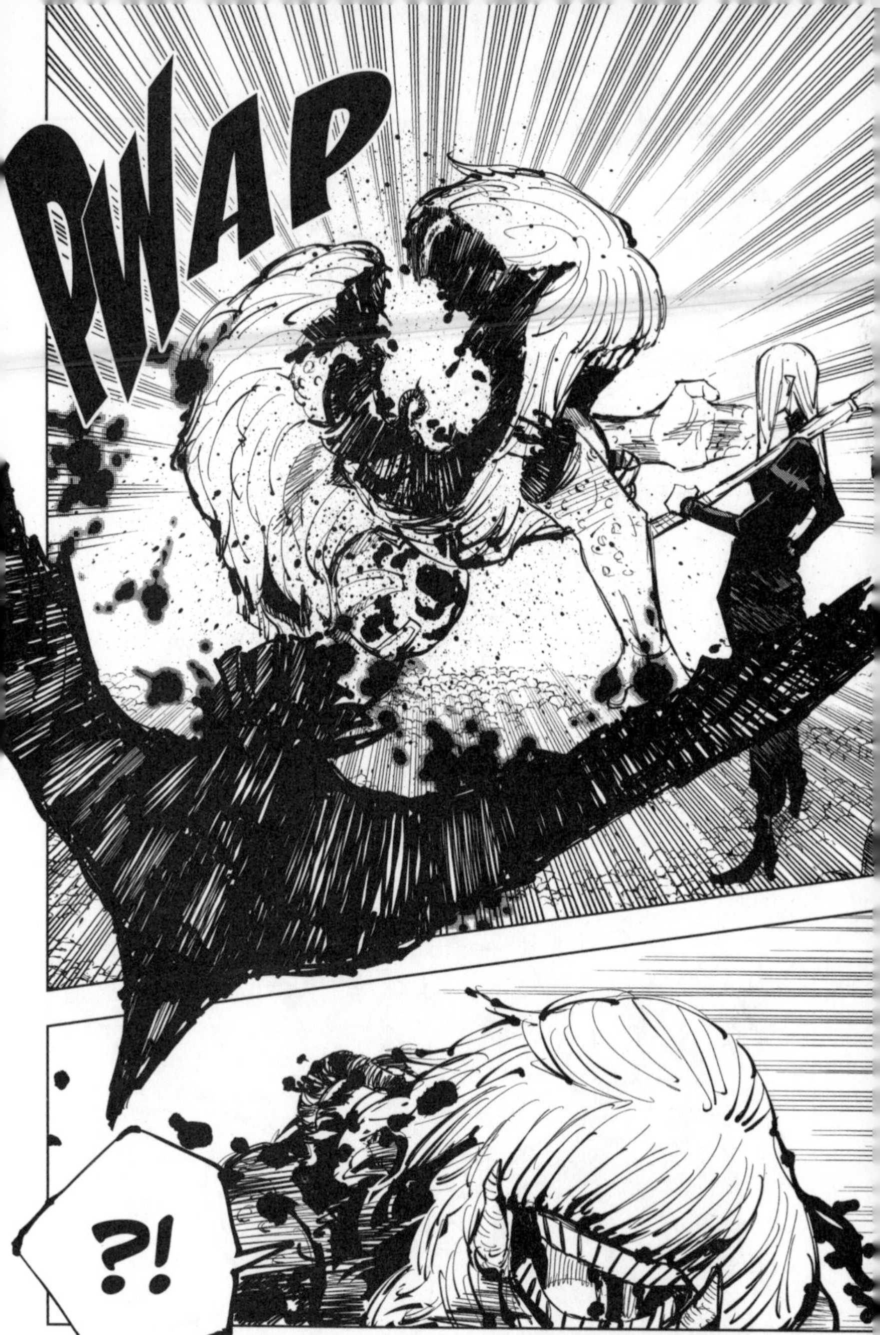
PWAP
?!

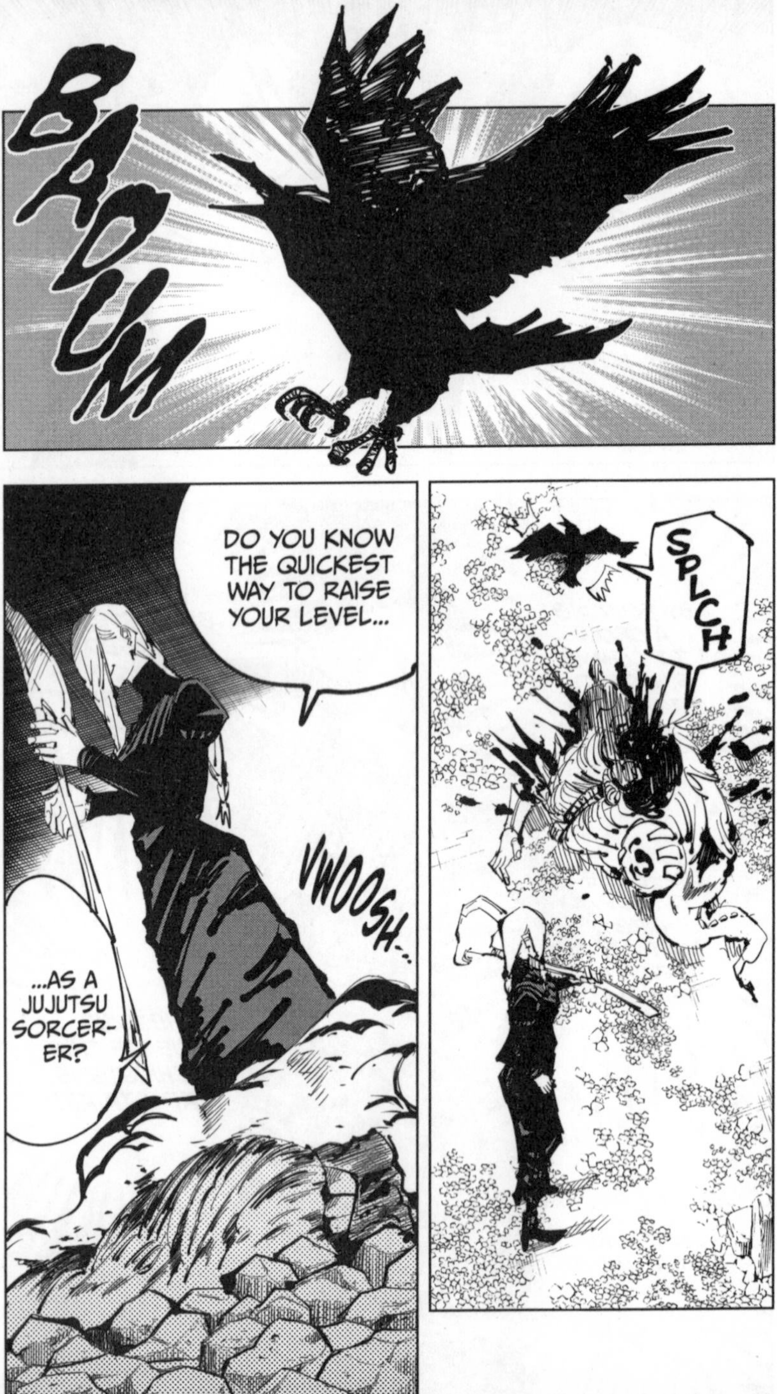
BADUM
SPLCH
DO YOU KNOW THE QUICKEST WAY TO RAISE YOUR LEVEL...
VWOOSH...
...AS A JUJUTSU SORCER-ER?

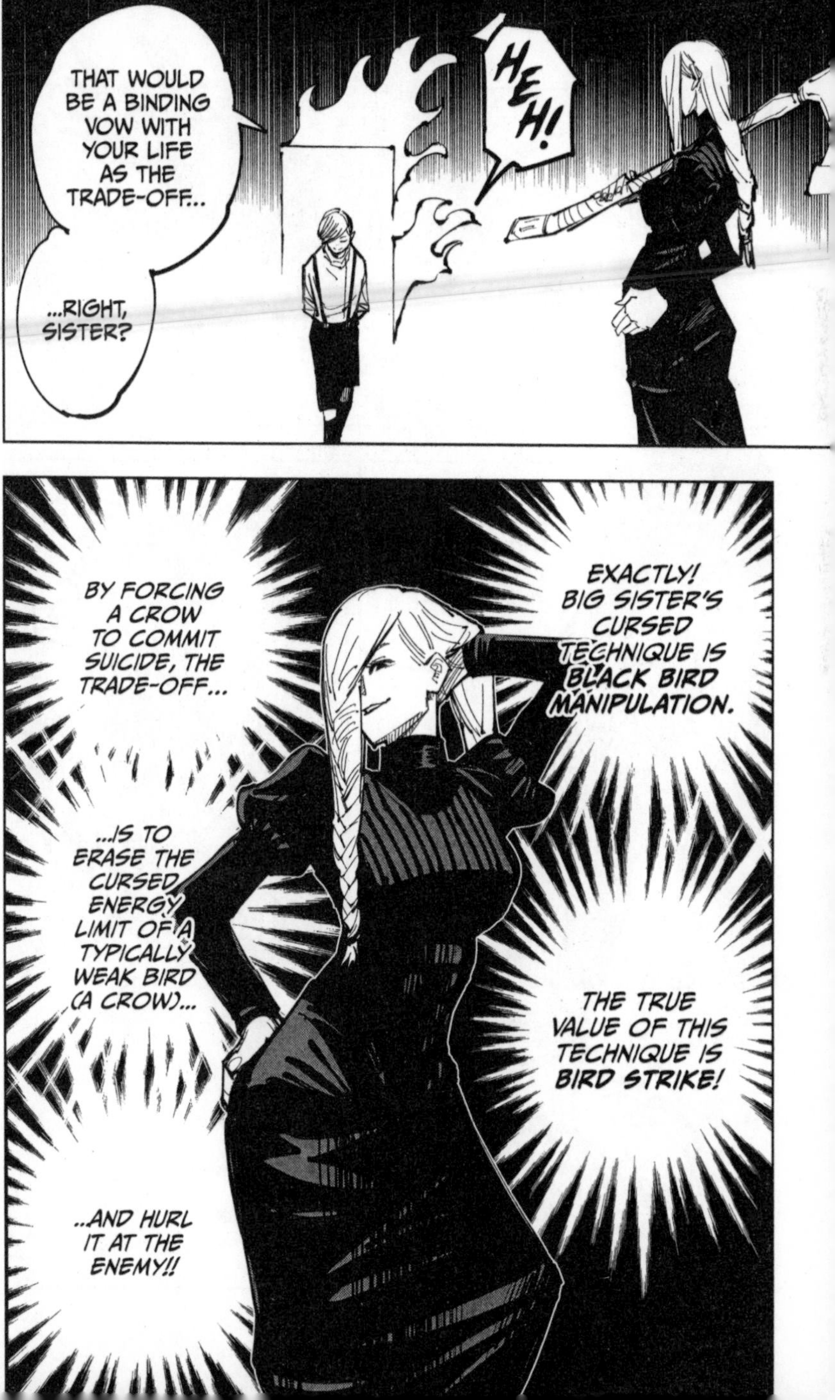
HEH!
THAT WOULD BE A BINDING VOW WITH YOUR LIFE AS THE TRADE-OFF...
...RIGHT, SISTER?
EXACTLY! BIG SISTER'S CURSED TECHNIQUE IS BLACK BIRD MANIPULATION.
BY FORCING A CROW TO COMMIT SUICIDE, THE TRADE-OFF...
...IS TO ERASE THE CURSED ENERGY LIMIT OF A TYPICALLY WEAK BIRD (A CROW)...
...AND HURL IT AT THE ENEMY!!
THE TRUE VALUE OF THIS TECHNIQUE IS BIRD STRIKE!

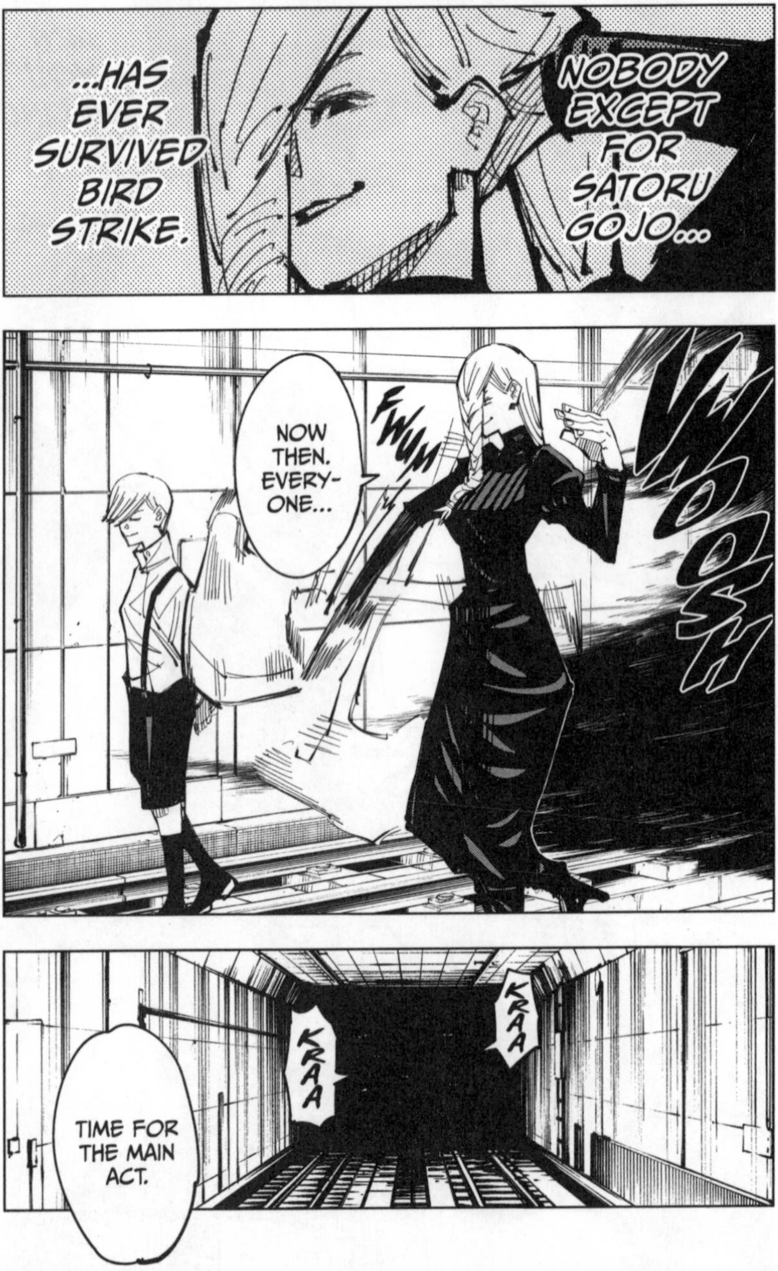
NOBODY EXCEPT FOR SATORU GOJO...
...HAS EVER SURVIVED BIRD STRIKE.
WHOOSH
FWUM
NOW THEN. EVERY-ONE...
KRAA
KRAA
TIME FOR THE MAIN ACT.

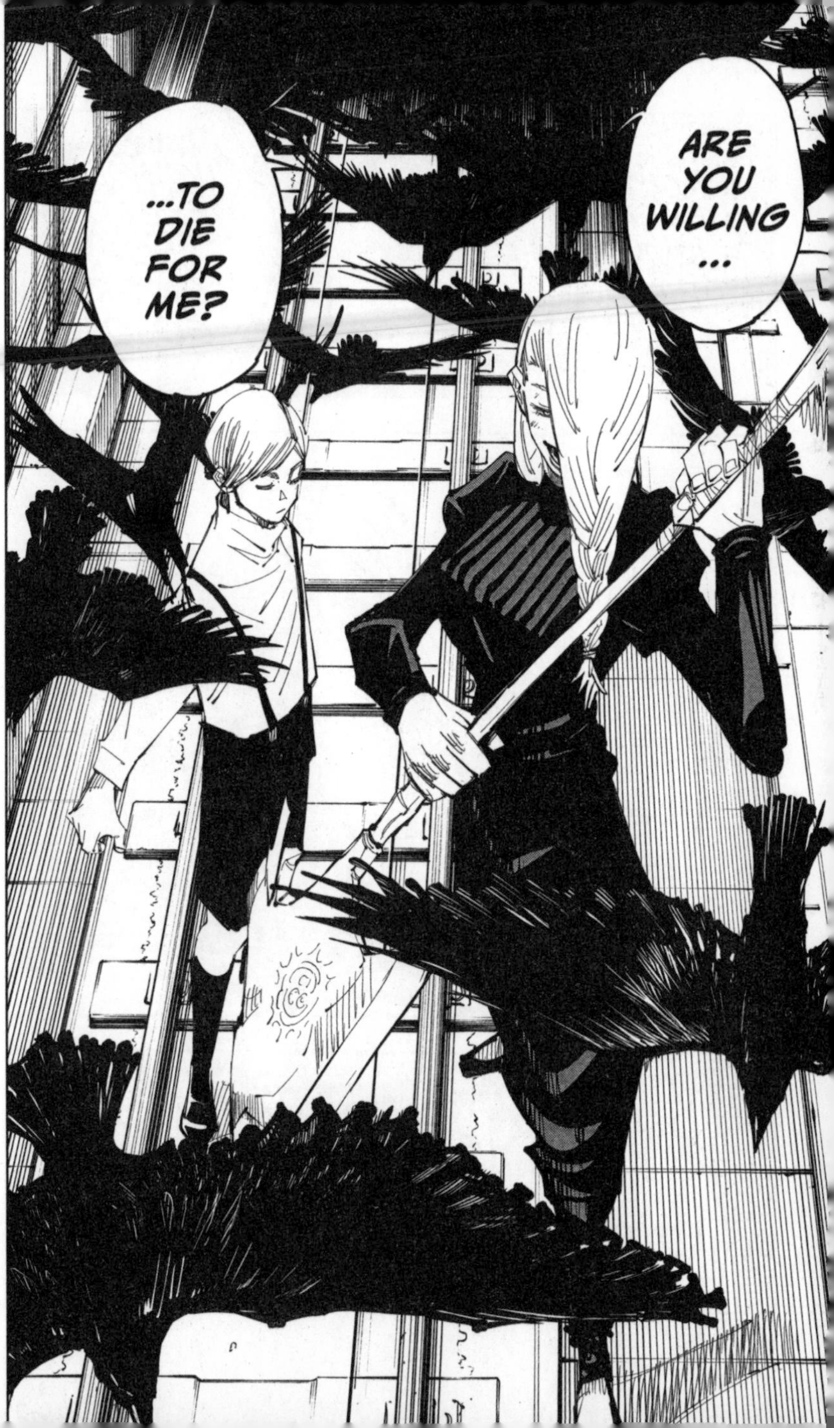
ARE YOU WILLING ...
...TO DIE FOR ME?

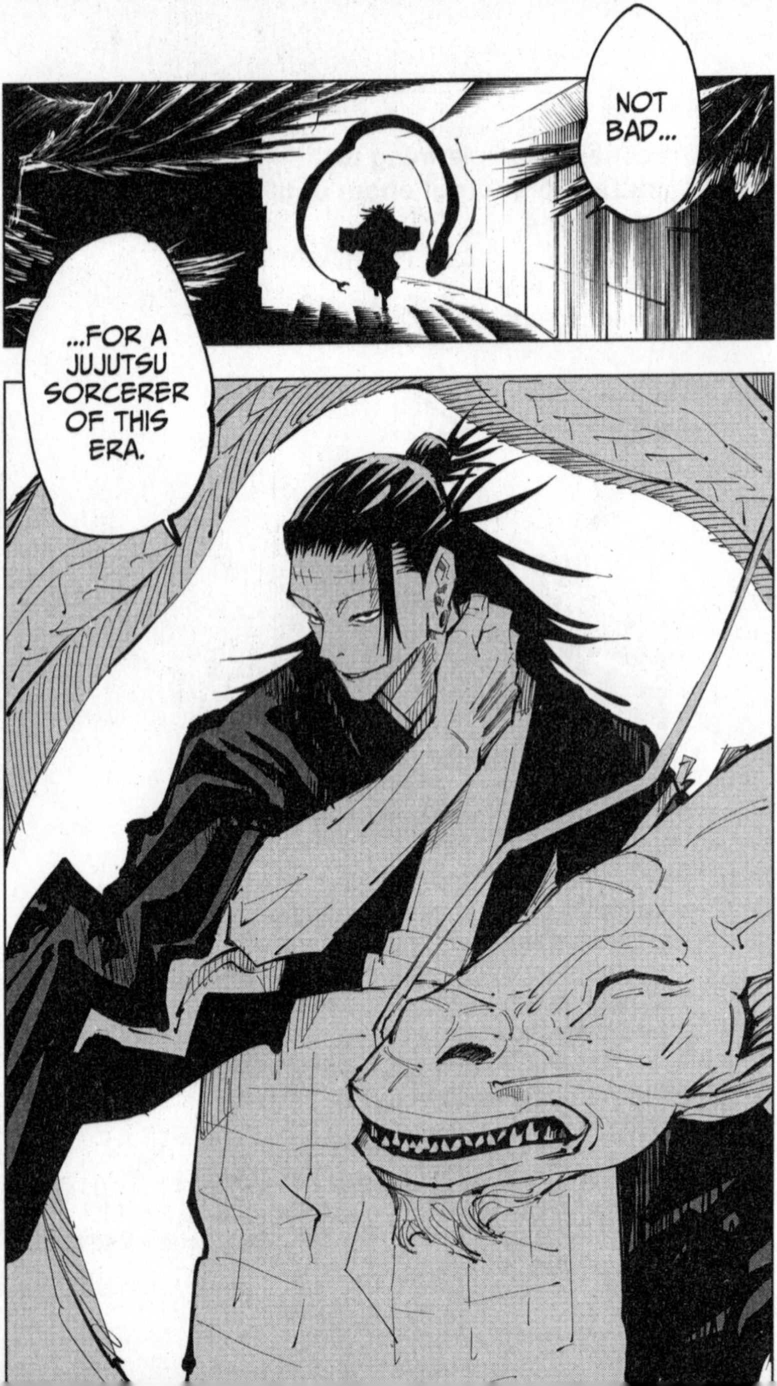
NOT BAD...
...FOR A JUJUTSU SORCERER OF THIS ERA.

Scenes I was planning to address but forgot about until now, part 4

• Disease curse

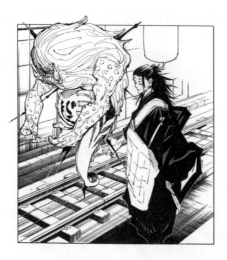

A curse born from a fear of a disease such as the plague. I didn't want to bring diseases that actually exist into the story out of respect to those who may be or have been affected by them. Smallpox has been eradicated, so I thought it might be okay to use. (This isn't about being allowed to use illnesses just because they no longer exist.)

Geto (?) is actually lying here. This cursed spirit isn't a smallpox deity, but rather a smallpox hag. If Mei Mei wasn't more familiar with disease curses, she could have been tricked.

Chapter 103:
The Shibuya Incident, Part 21

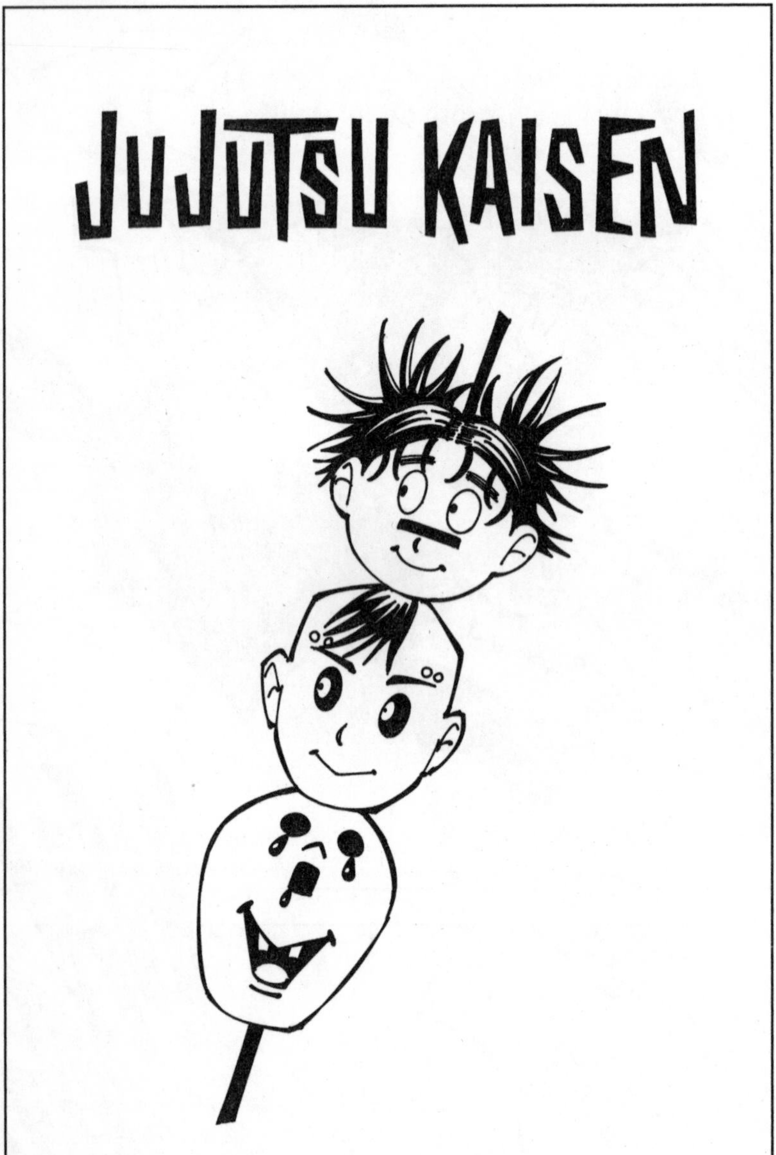
JUJUTSU KAISEN

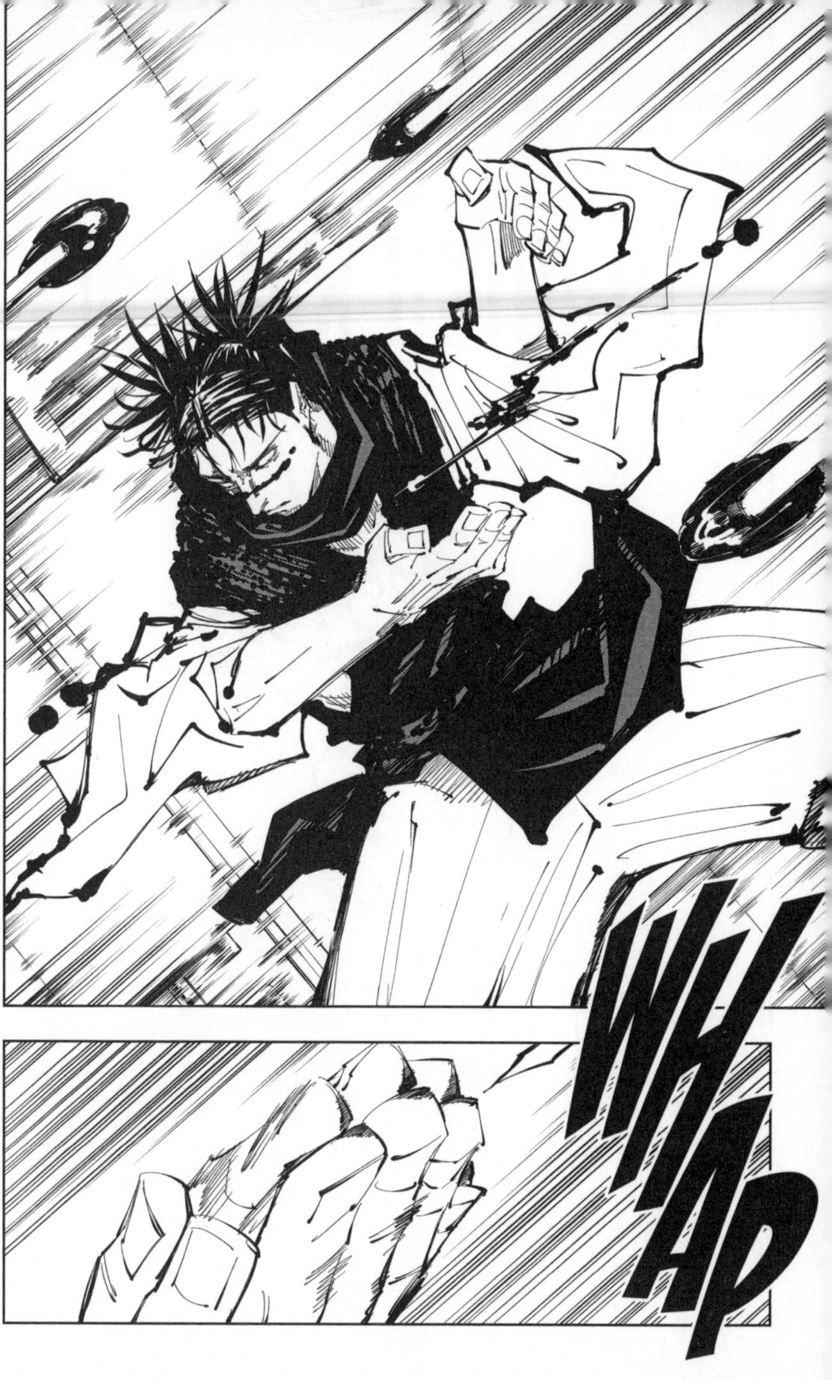
WHAP

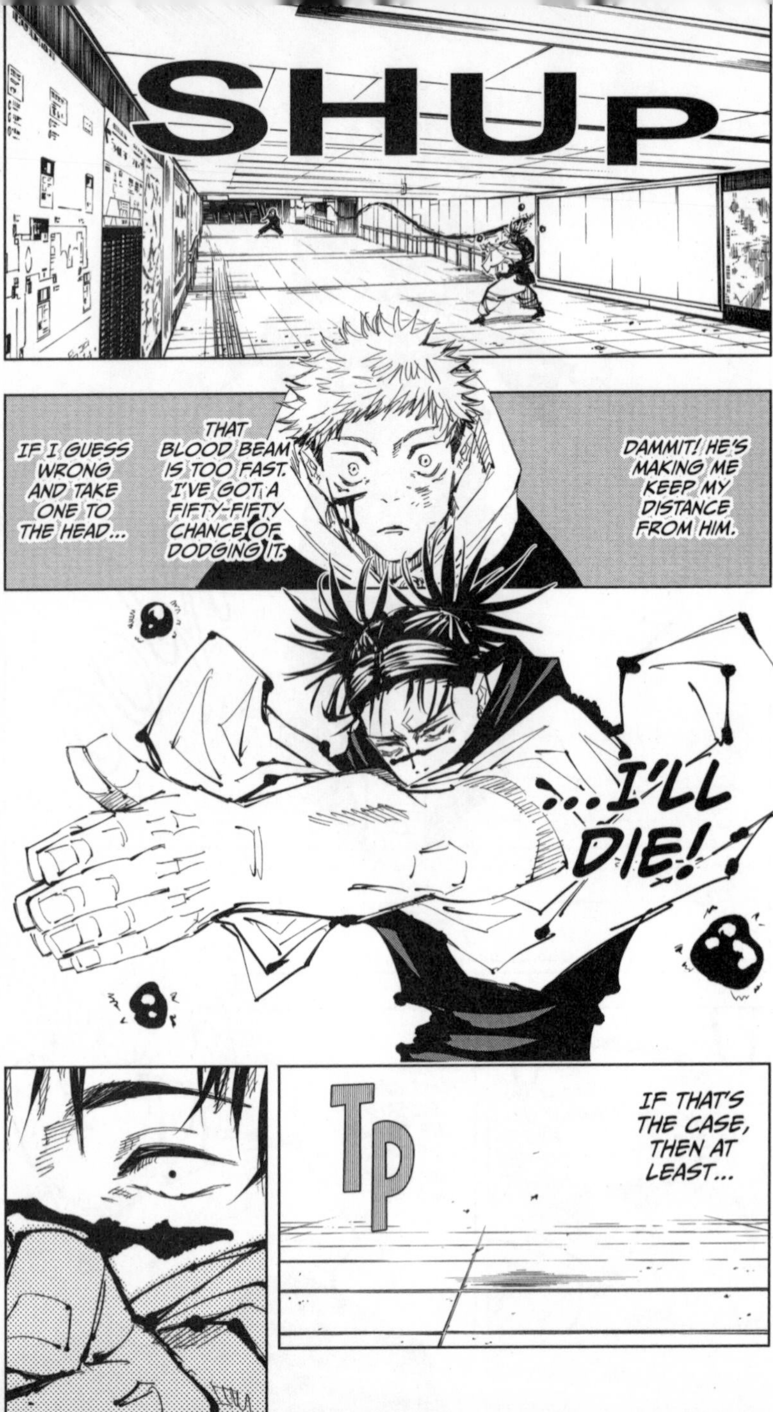
SHUP
DAMMIT! HE'S MAKING ME KEEP MY DISTANCE FROM HIM.
THAT BLOOD BEAM IS TOO FAST. I'VE GOT A FIFTY-FIFTY CHANCE OF DODGING IT.
IF I GUESS WRONG AND TAKE ONE TO THE HEAD...
...I'LL DIE!
IF THAT'S THE CASE, THEN AT LEAST...
TP

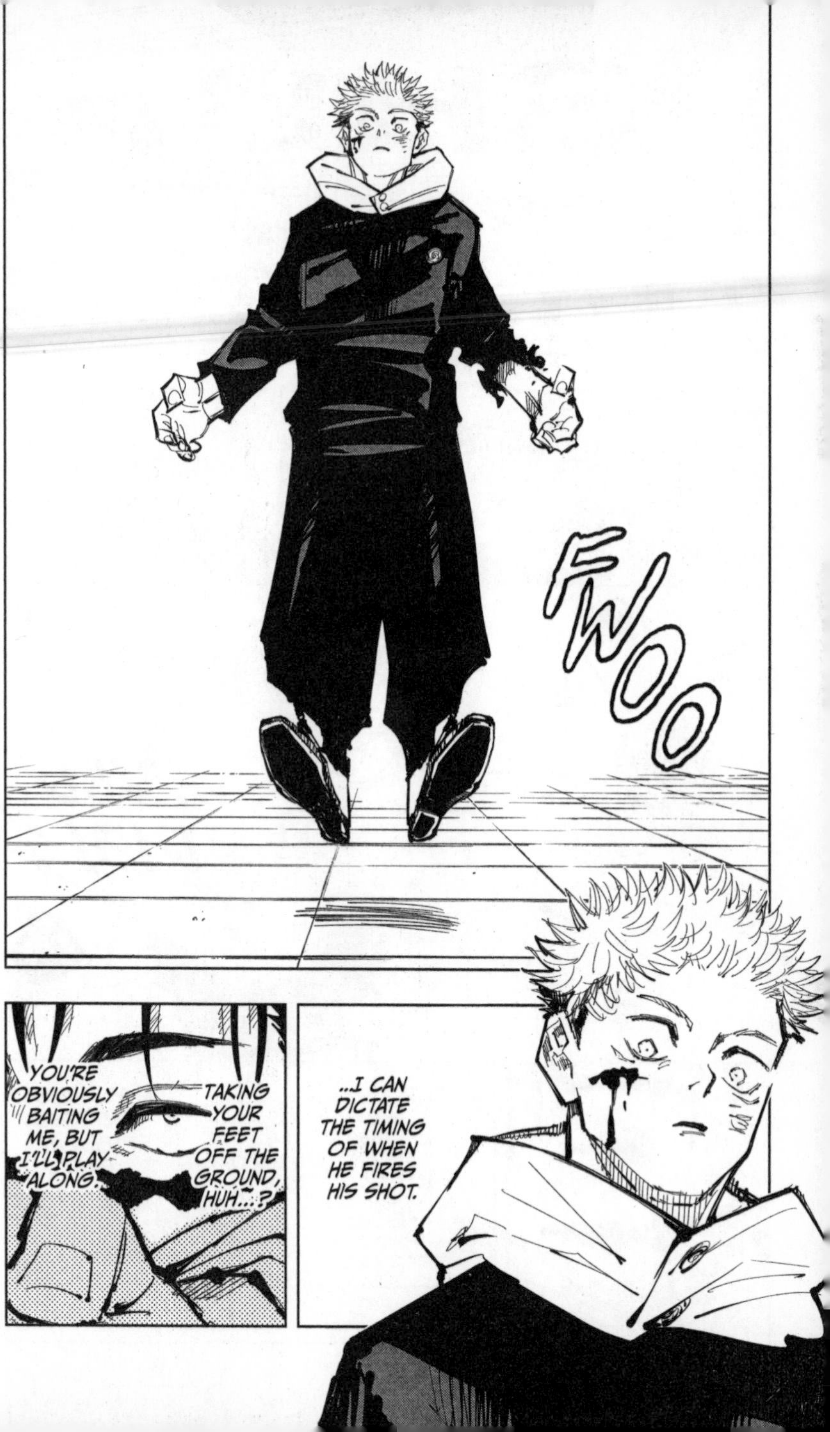
FWOO
...I CAN DICTATE THE TIMING OF WHEN HE FIRES HIS SHOT.
TAKING YOUR FEET OFF THE GROUND, HUH...?
YOU'RE OBVIOUSLY BAITING ME, BUT I'LL PLAY ALONG.

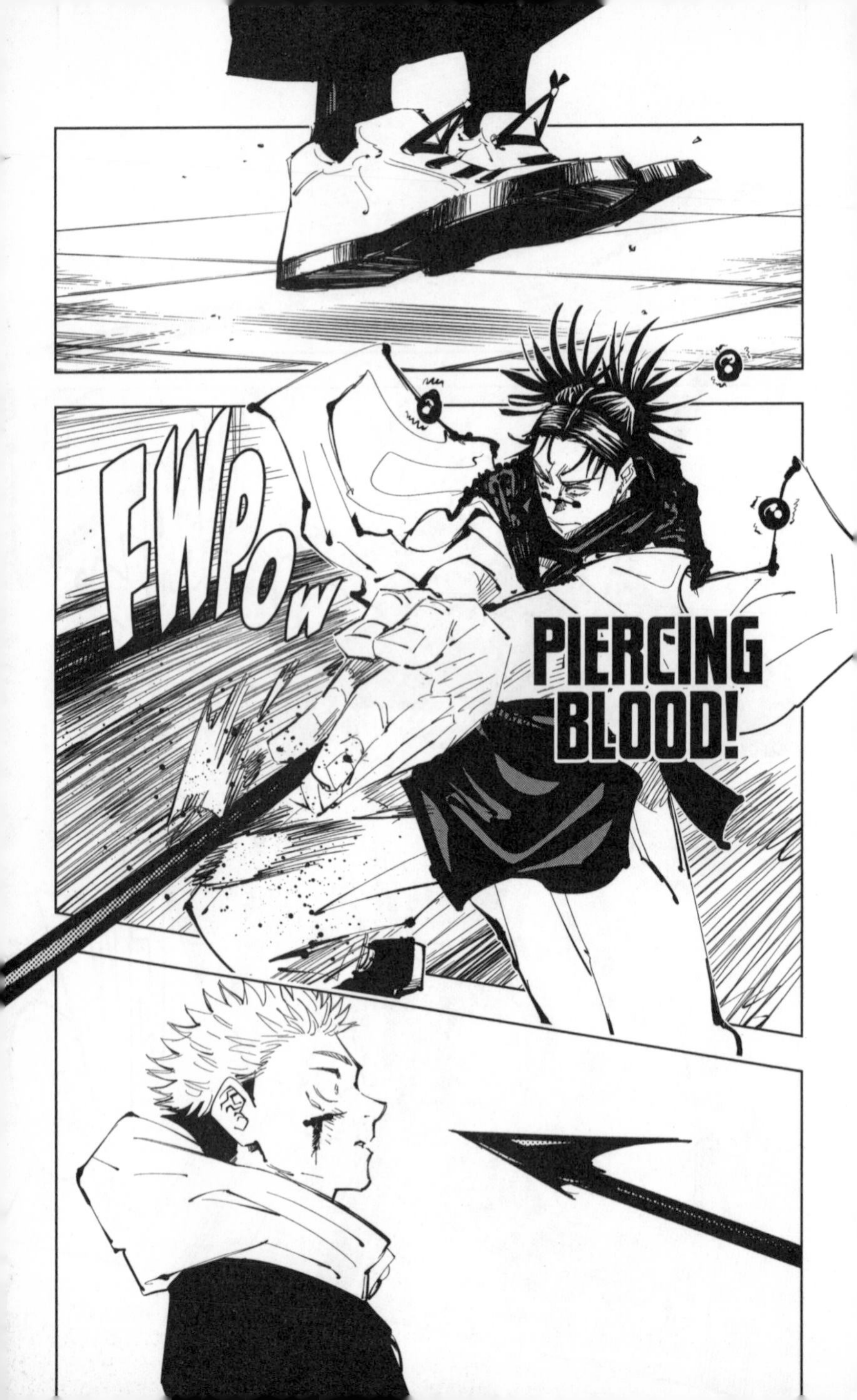
FWPOW
PIERCING BLOOD!

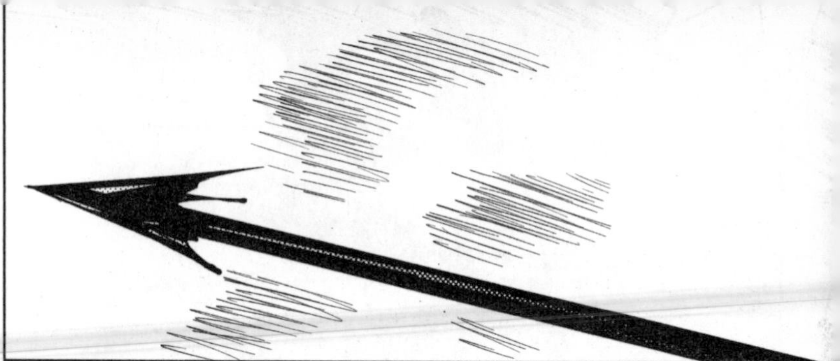

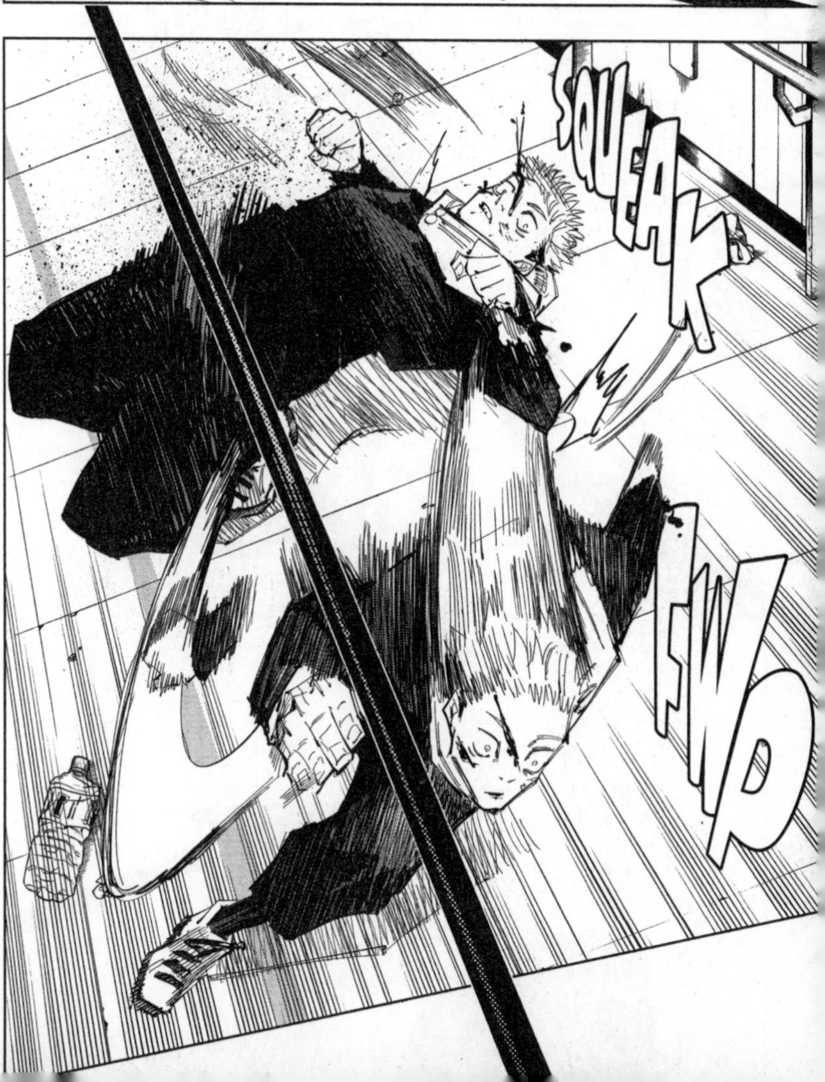
SQUEAK
FWIP

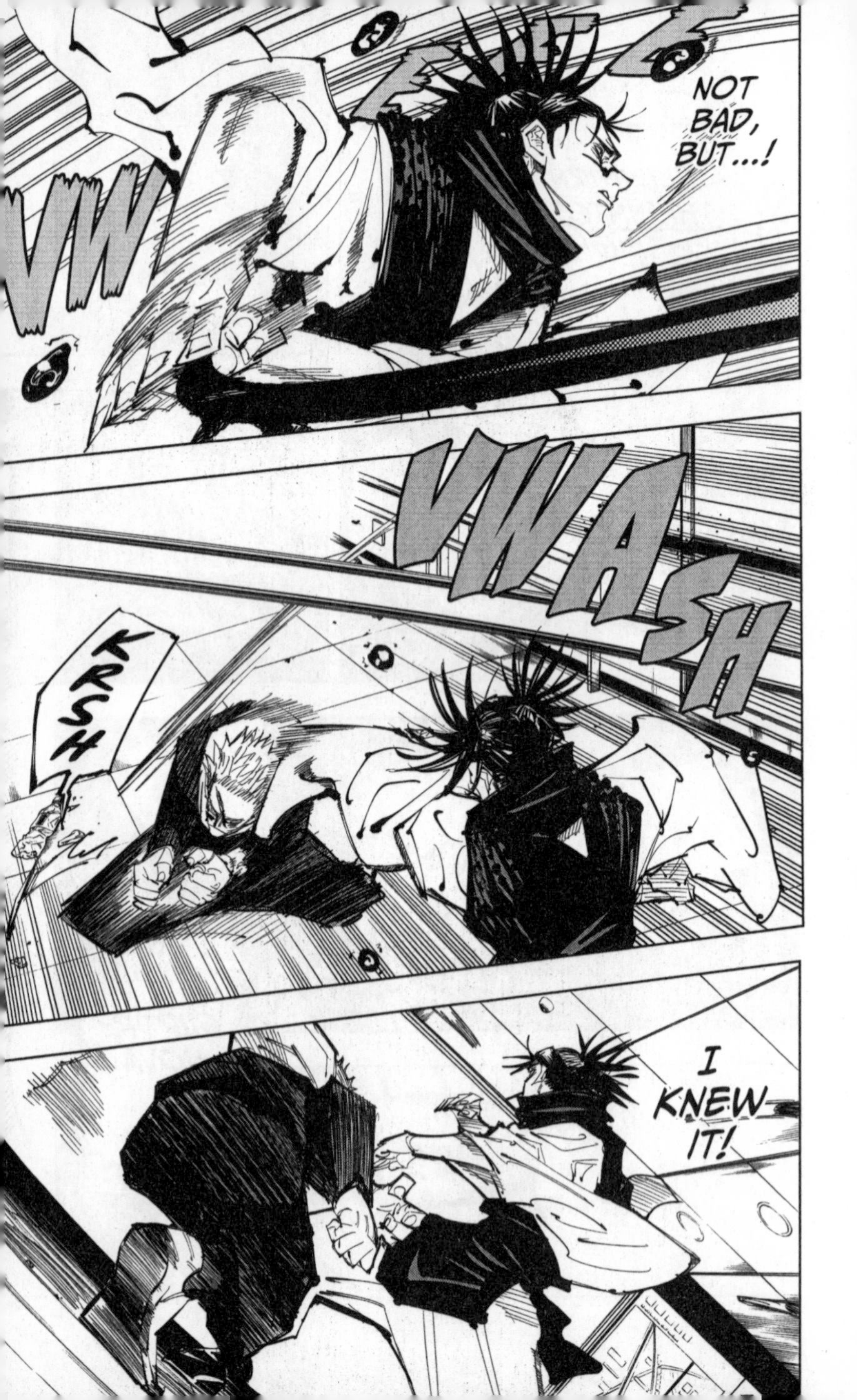
NOT BAD, BUT...!
VW
VWASH
KRSH
I KNEW IT!

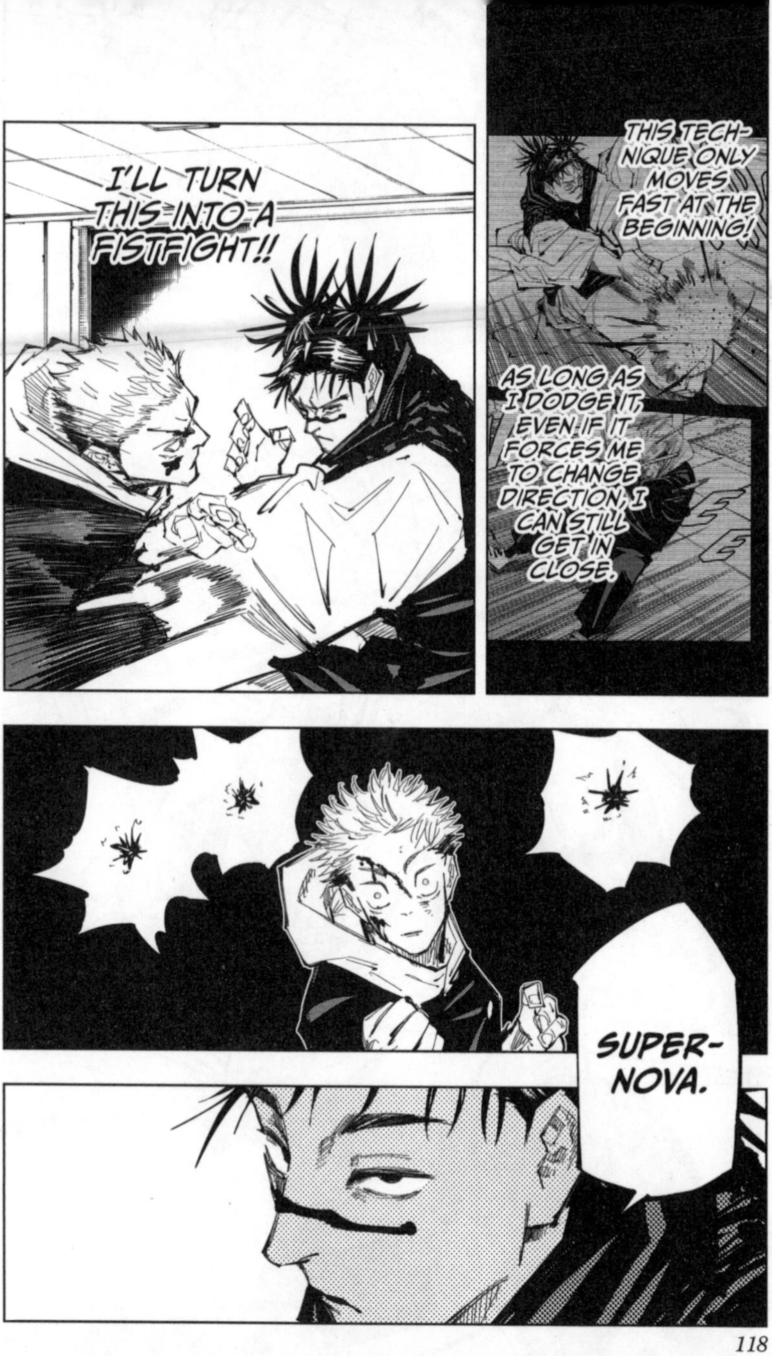
THIS TECH-NIQUE ONLY MOVES FAST AT THE BEGINNING!
AS LONG AS I DODGE IT, EVEN IF IT FORCES ME TO CHANGE DIRECTION, I CAN STILL GET IN CLOSE.
I'LL TURN THIS INTO A FISTFIGHT!!
SUPER-NOVA.

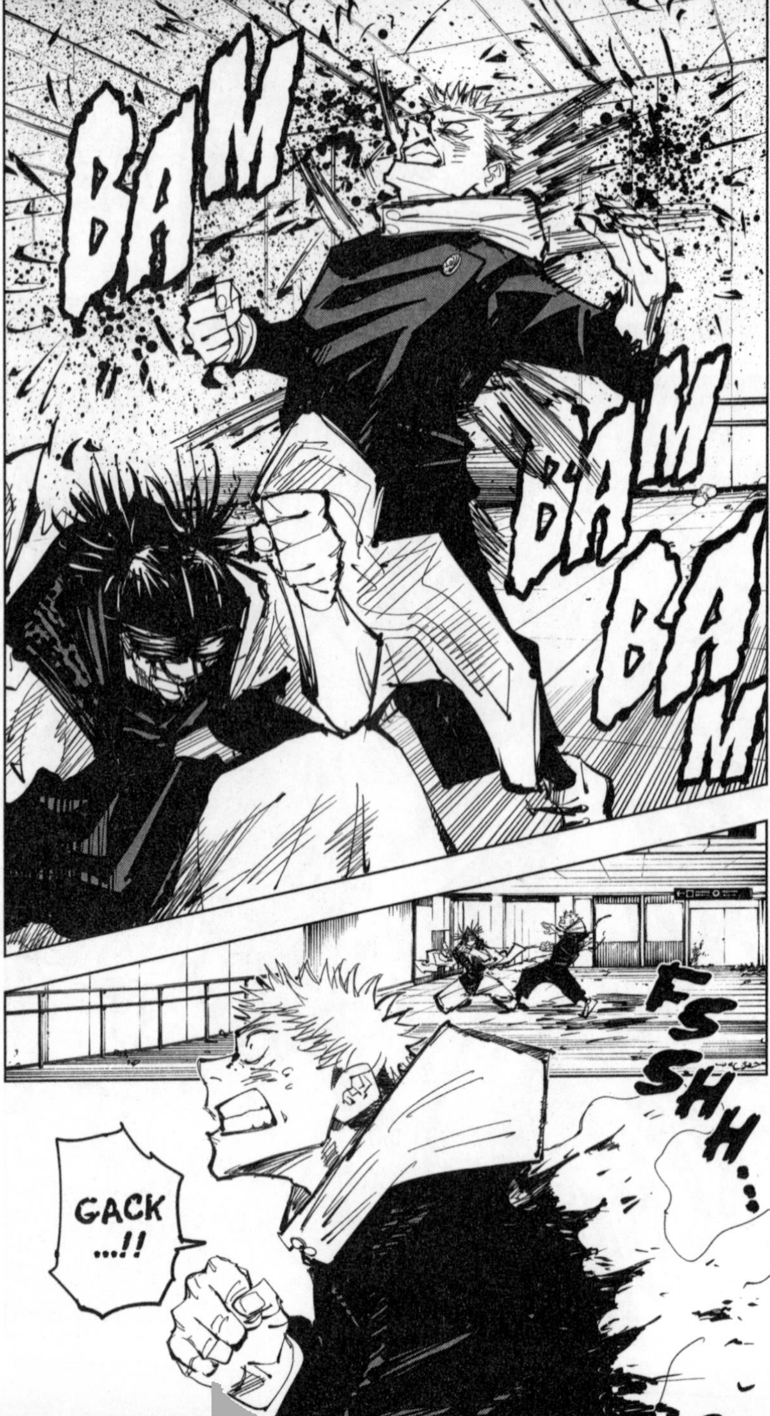
BAM
BAM
BAM
FSSHH...
GACK ...!!

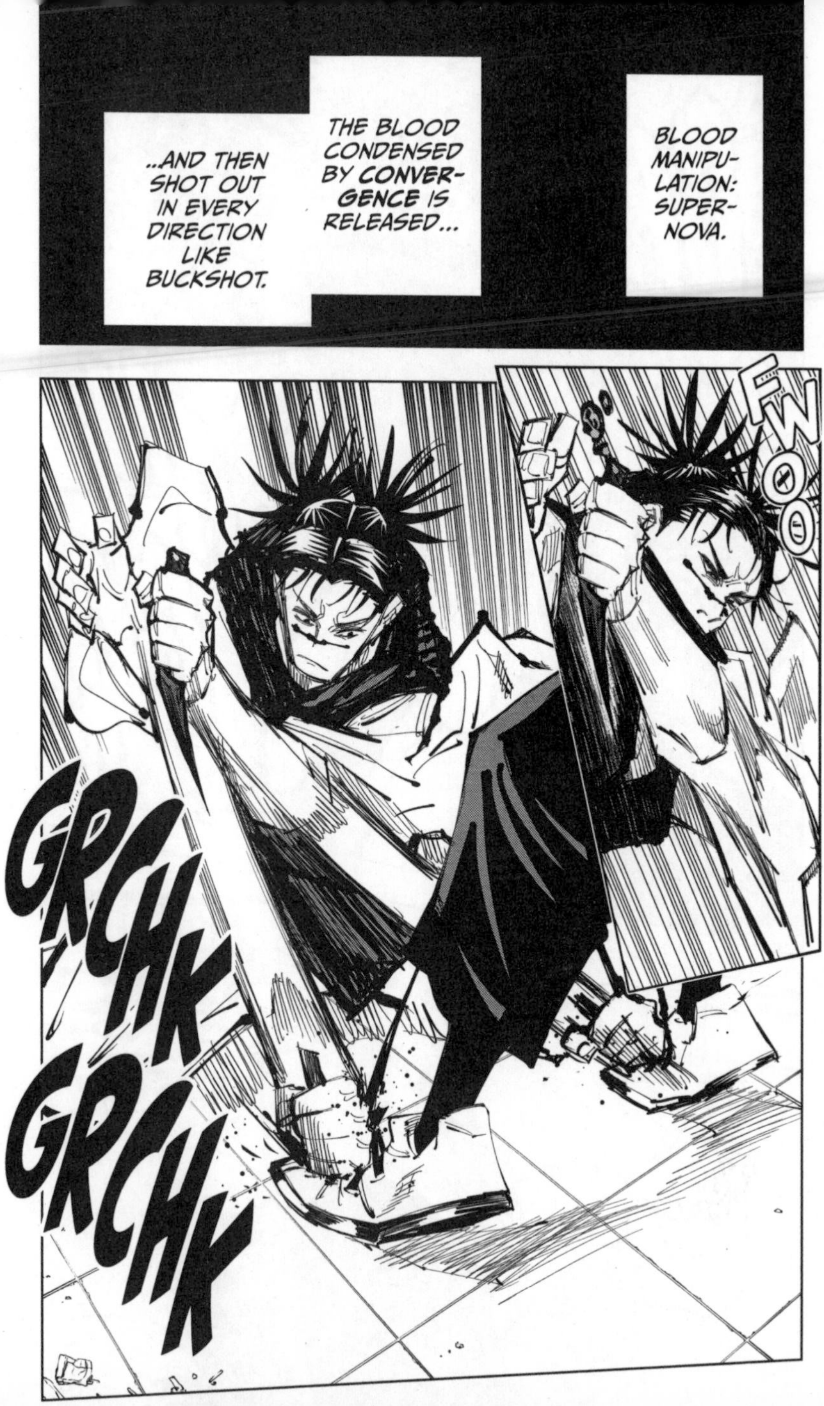
BLOOD MANIPULATION: SUPERNOVA.
THE BLOOD CONDENSED BY CONVERGENCE IS RELEASED...
...AND THEN SHOT OUT IN EVERY DIRECTION LIKE BUCKSHOT.
FWOOO
GRCHK GRCHK

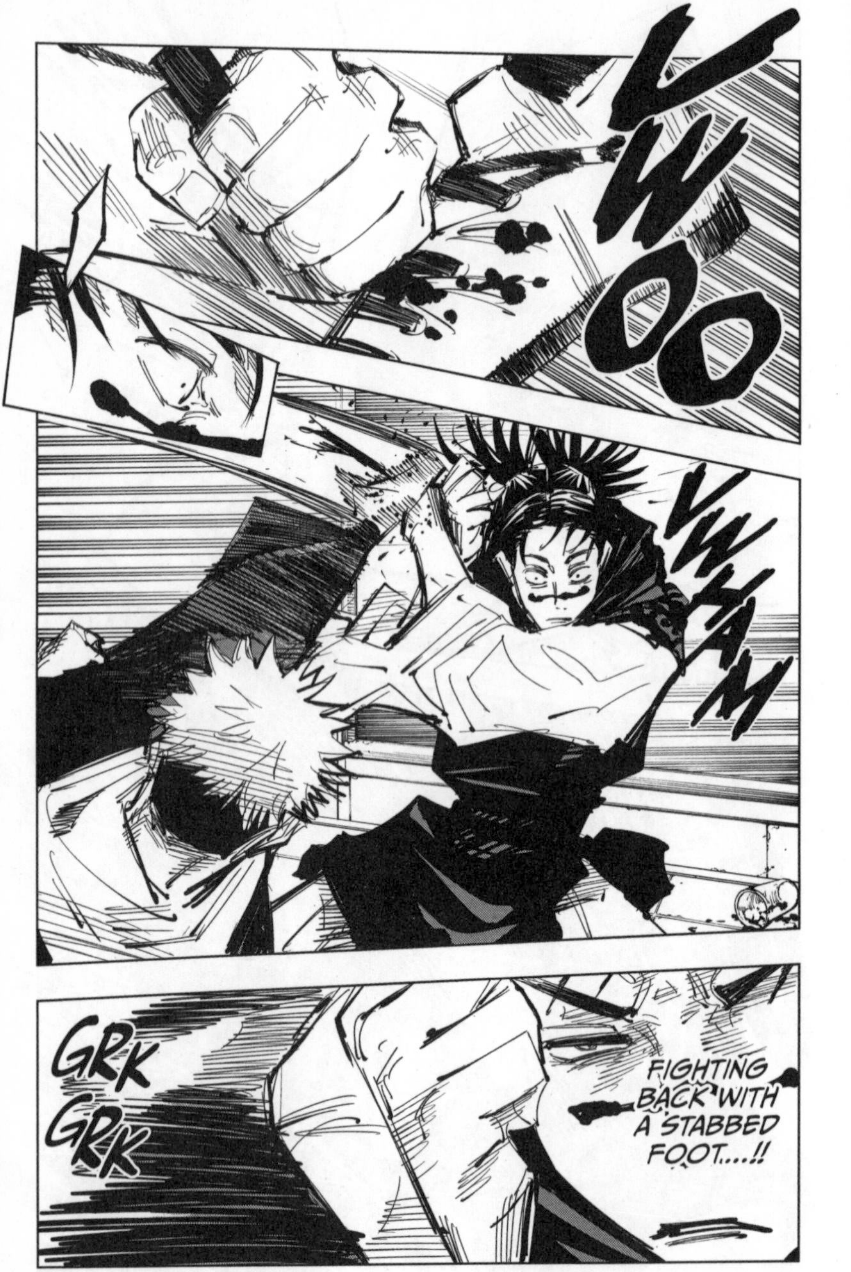
VWOO
VWHAM
FIGHTING BACK WITH A STABBED FOOT....!!
GRK GRK

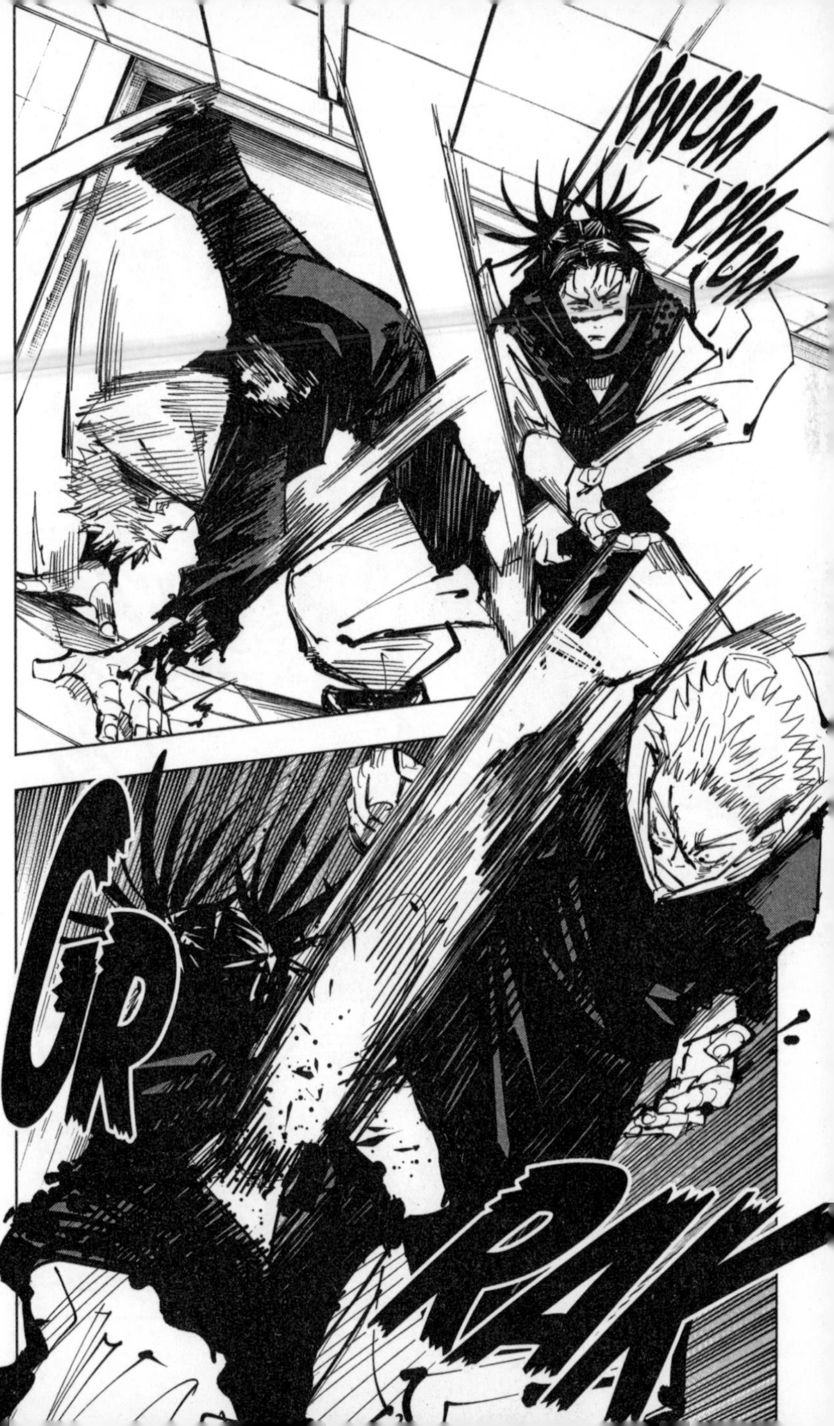
VWUM VWUM

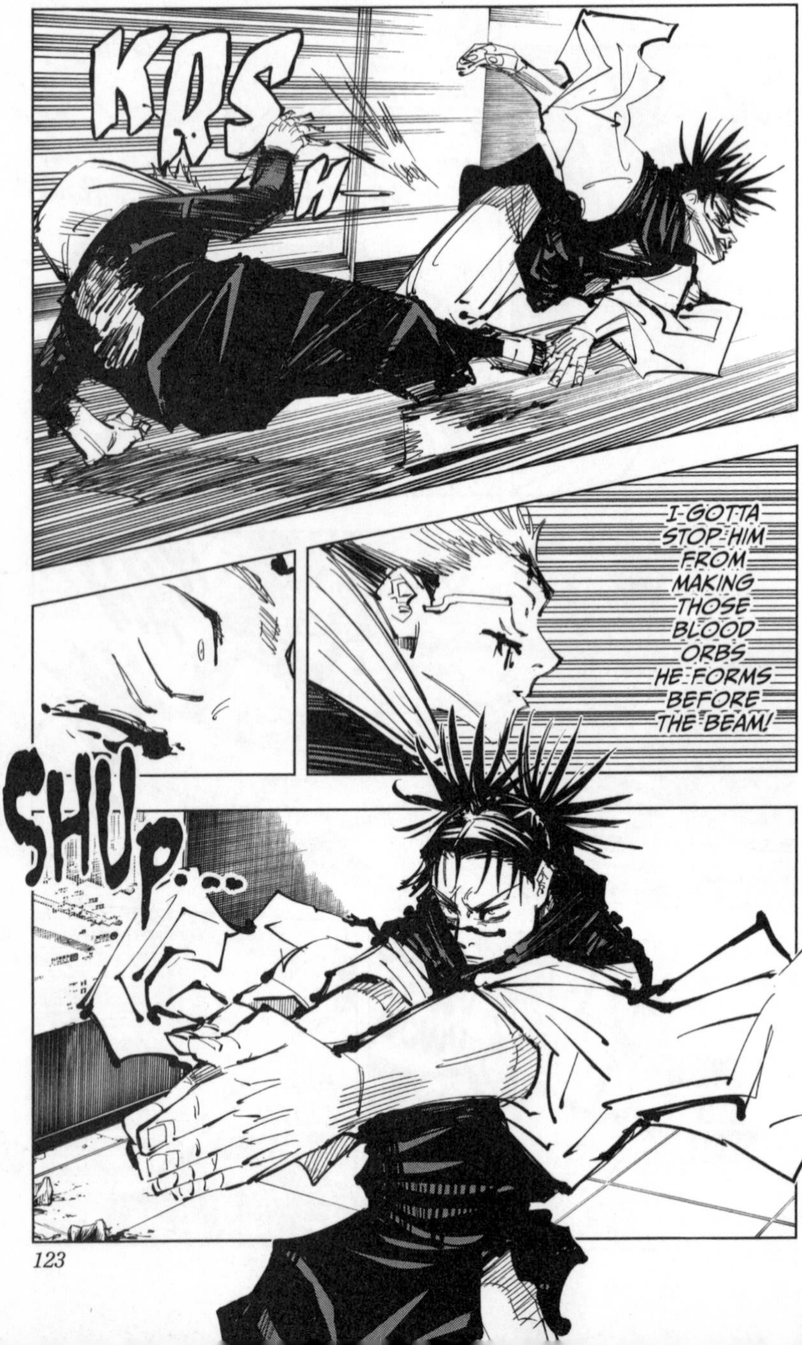
KRASH
I GOTTA STOP HIM FROM MAKING THOSE BLOOD ORBS HE FORMS BEFORE THE BEAM!
SHUP...

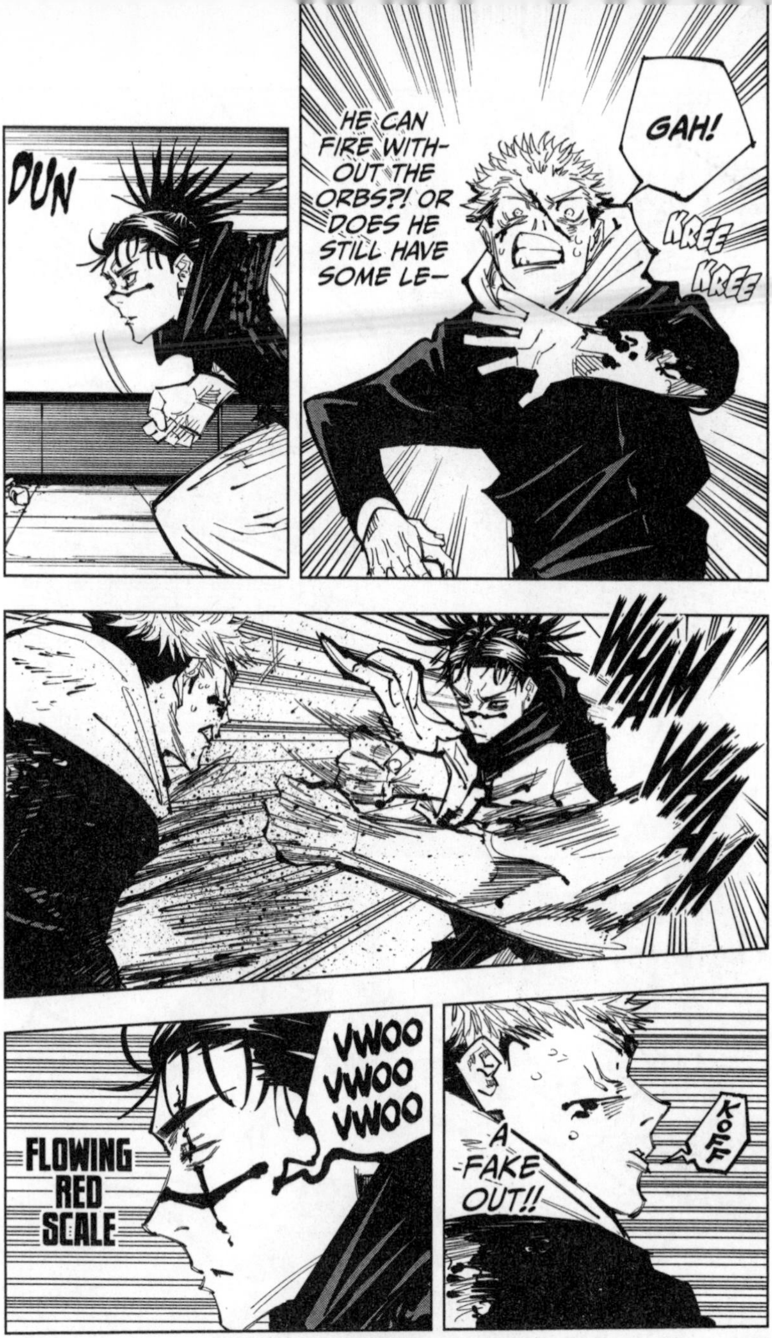
GAH!
KREE KREE
HE CAN FIRE WITH-OUT THE ORBS?! OR DOES HE STILL HAVE SOME LE—
DUN
WHAM WHAM
KOFF
A FAKE OUT!!
VWOO VWOO VWOO
FLOWING RED SCALE

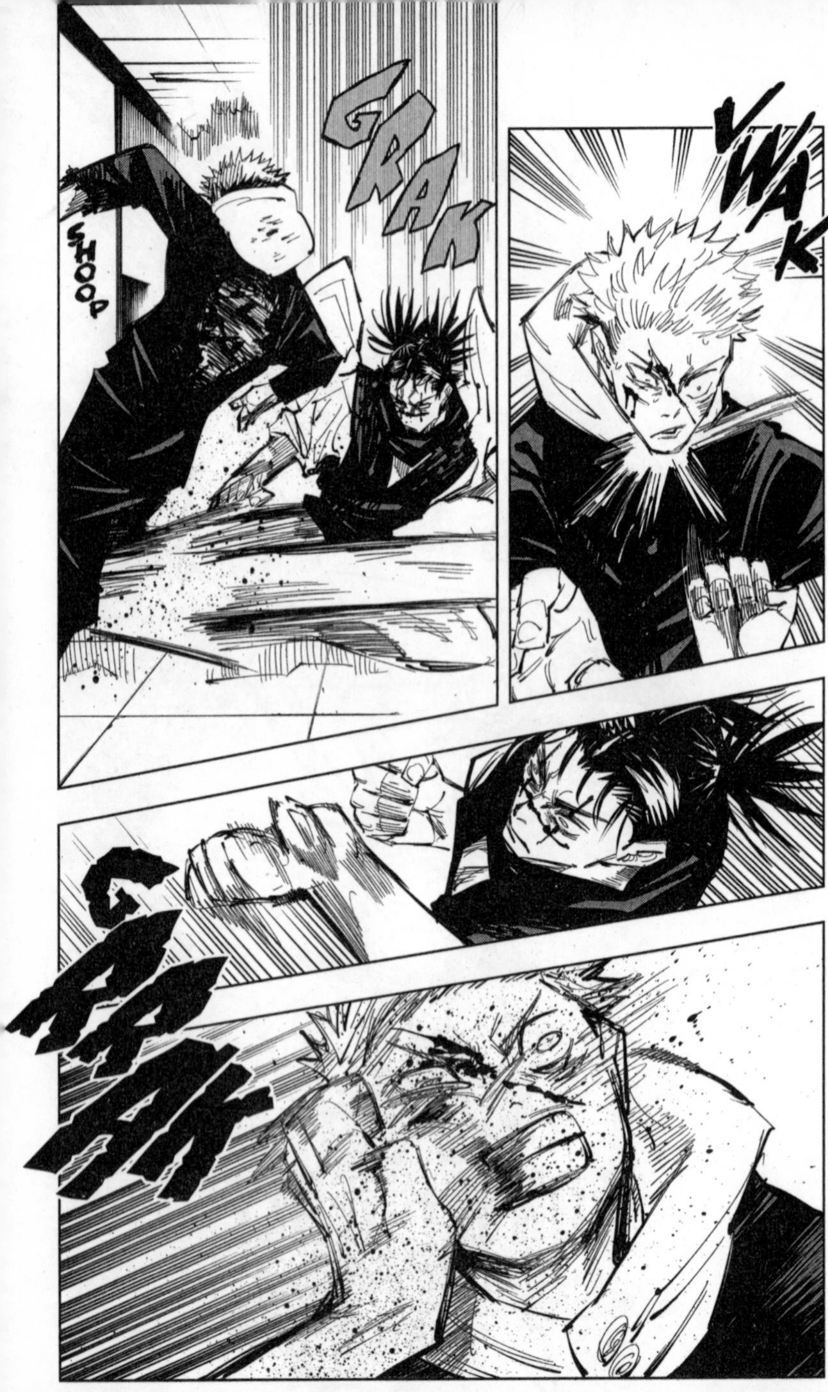
VWAK
GRAK
SHOOP
GRAK

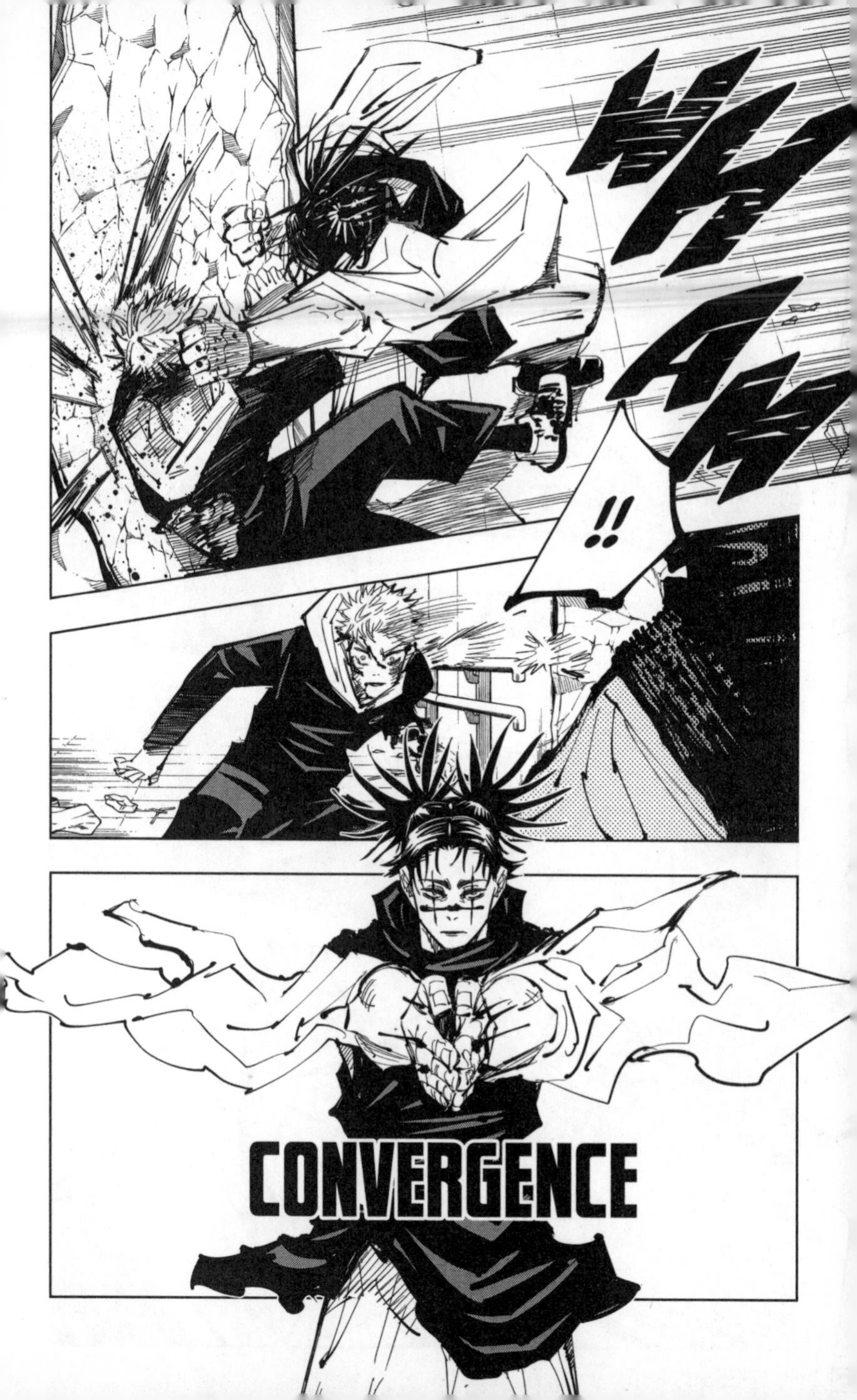
WHAM
!!
CONVERGENCE

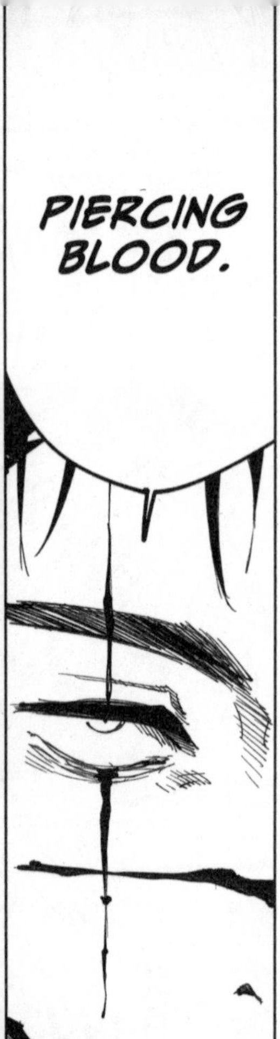
PIERCING BLOOD.
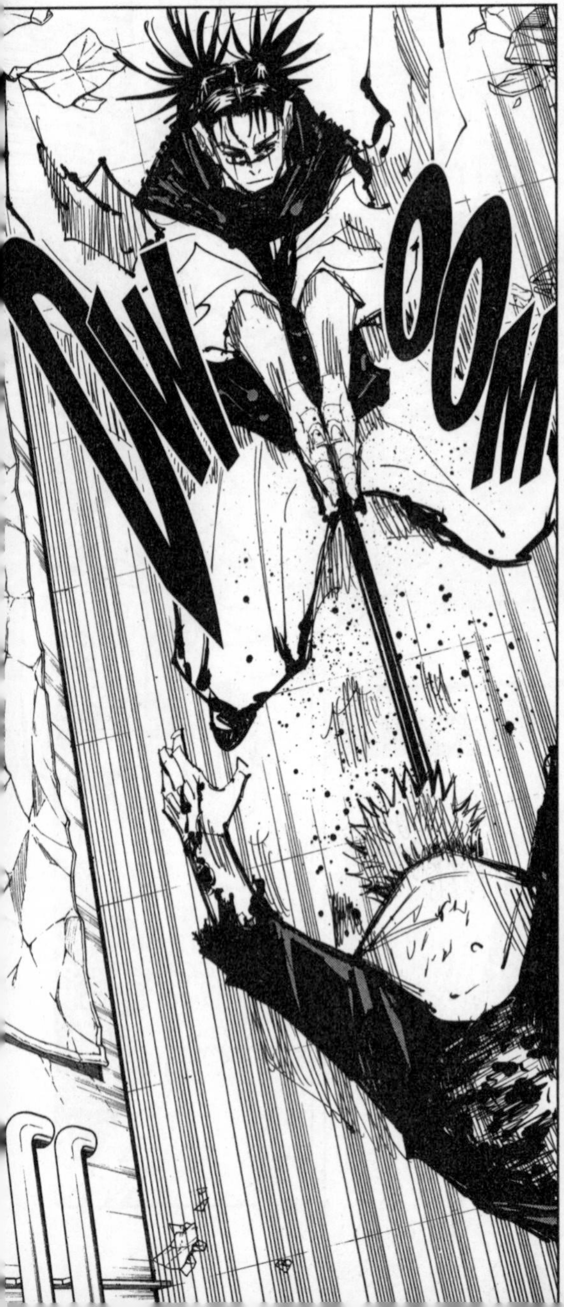
DWOOM

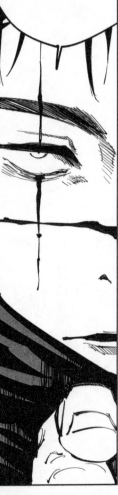

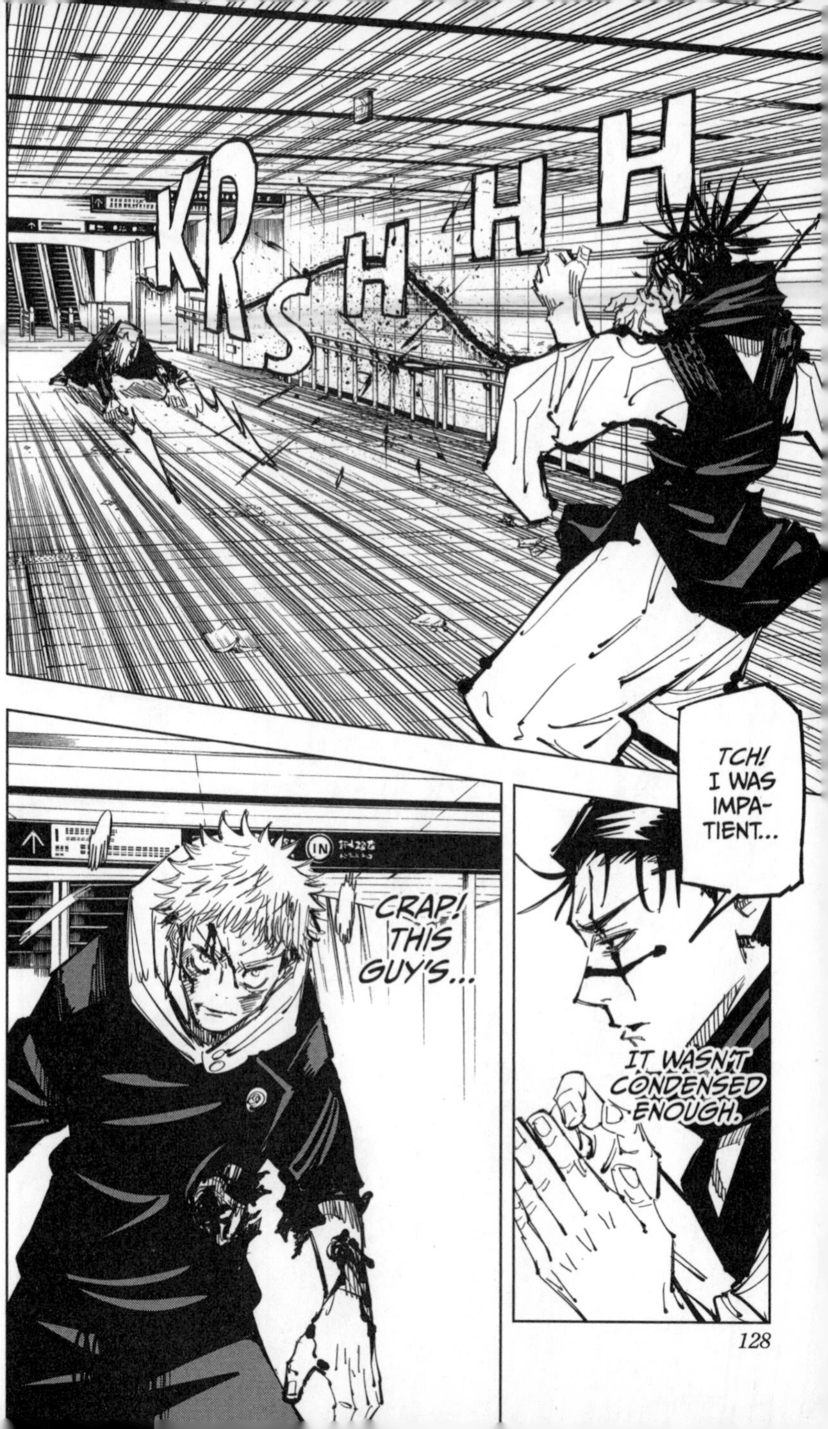
KRSHHH
TCH! I WAS IMPATIENT...
IT WASN'T CONDENSED ENOUGH.
CRAP! THIS GUY'S...
IN

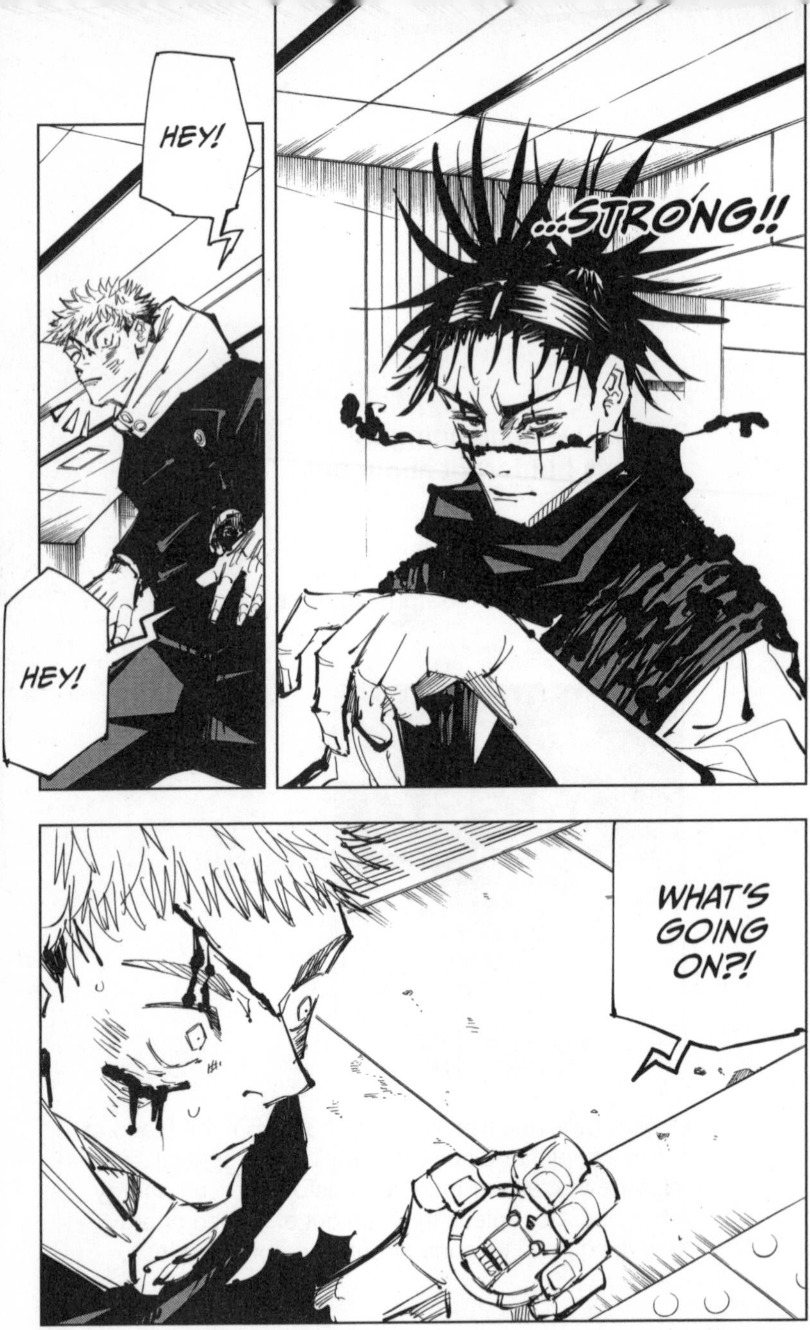
...STRONG!!
HEY!
HEY!
WHAT'S GOING ON?!

**Scenes I was planning to
address but forgot about until
now, part 5**

• Cursed Womb: Death Painting's blood

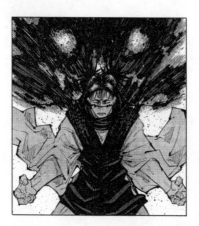

Choso, Eso, and Kechizu were born from the blood of
a cursed spirit and human. They have a special
attribute that allows them to transform cursed energy
into blood. So, unless they run out of cursed energy,
they don't have to worry about dying of blood loss.

Chapter 104: The Shibuya Incident, Part 22

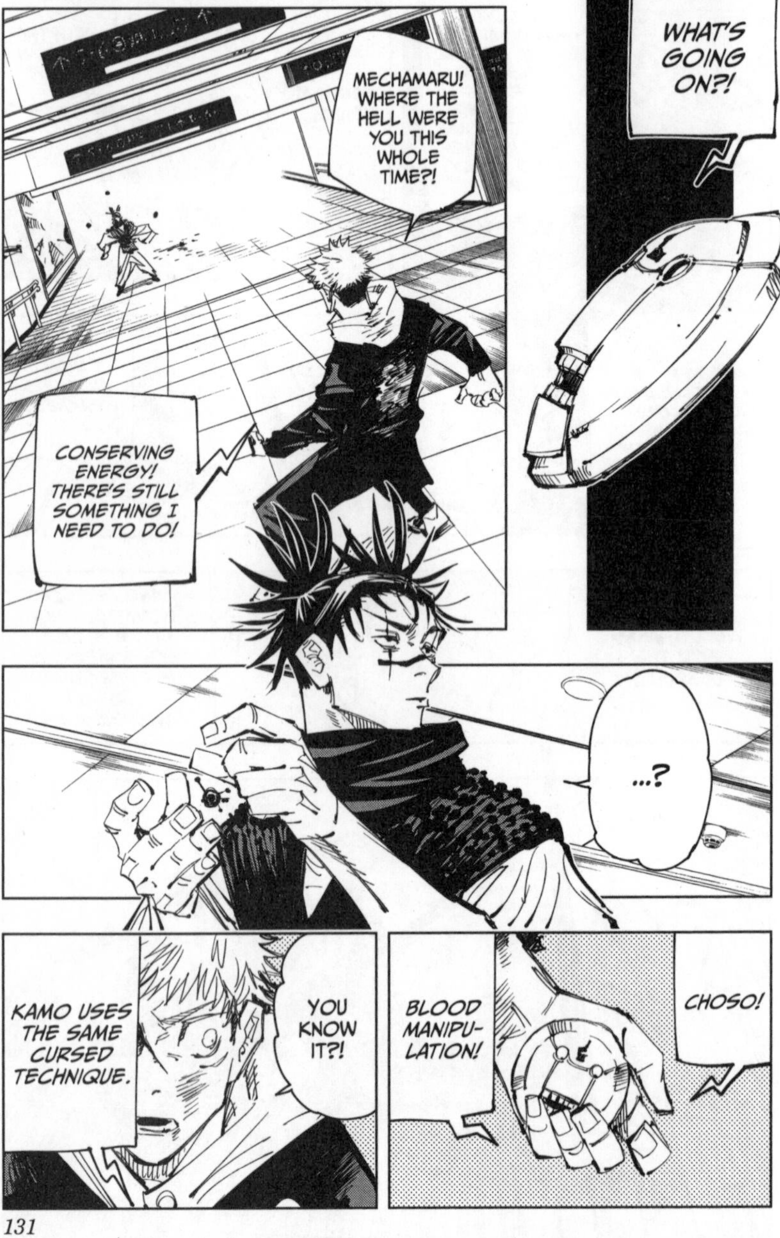
WHAT'S GOING ON?!
MECHAMARU! WHERE THE HELL WERE YOU THIS WHOLE TIME?!
CONSERVING ENERGY! THERE'S STILL SOMETHING I NEED TO DO!
...?
CHOSO!
BLOOD MANIPU-LATION!
YOU KNOW IT?!
KAMO USES THE SAME CURSED TECHNIQUE.

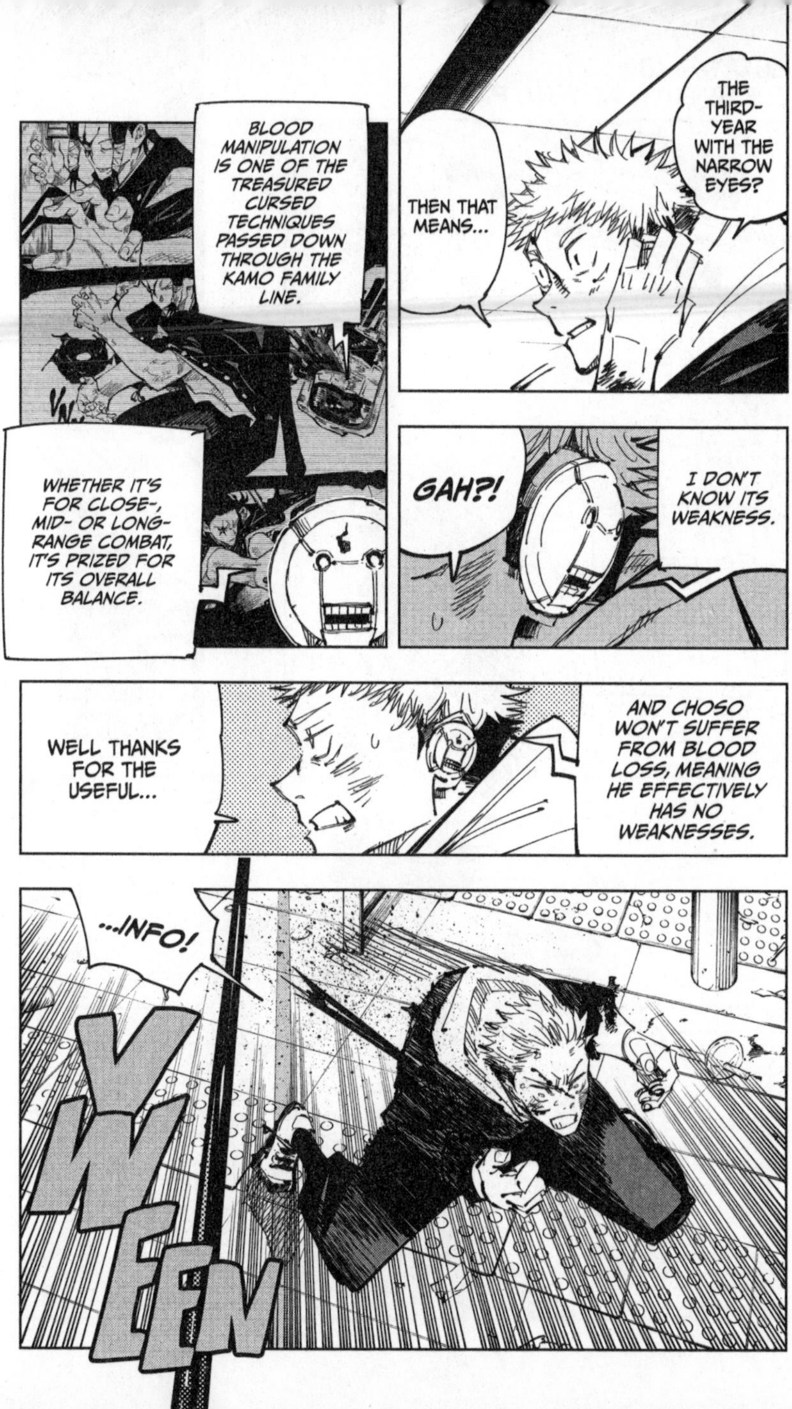
THE THIRD-YEAR WITH THE NARROW EYES?
THEN THAT MEANS...
I DON'T KNOW ITS WEAKNESS.
GAH?!
BLOOD MANIPULATION IS ONE OF THE TREASURED CURSED TECHNIQUES PASSED DOWN THROUGH THE KAMO FAMILY LINE.
WHETHER IT'S FOR CLOSE-, MID- OR LONG-RANGE COMBAT, IT'S PRIZED FOR ITS OVERALL BALANCE.
AND CHOSO WON'T SUFFER FROM BLOOD LOSS, MEANING HE EFFECTIVELY HAS NO WEAKNESSES.
WELL THANKS FOR THE USEFUL...
...INFO!

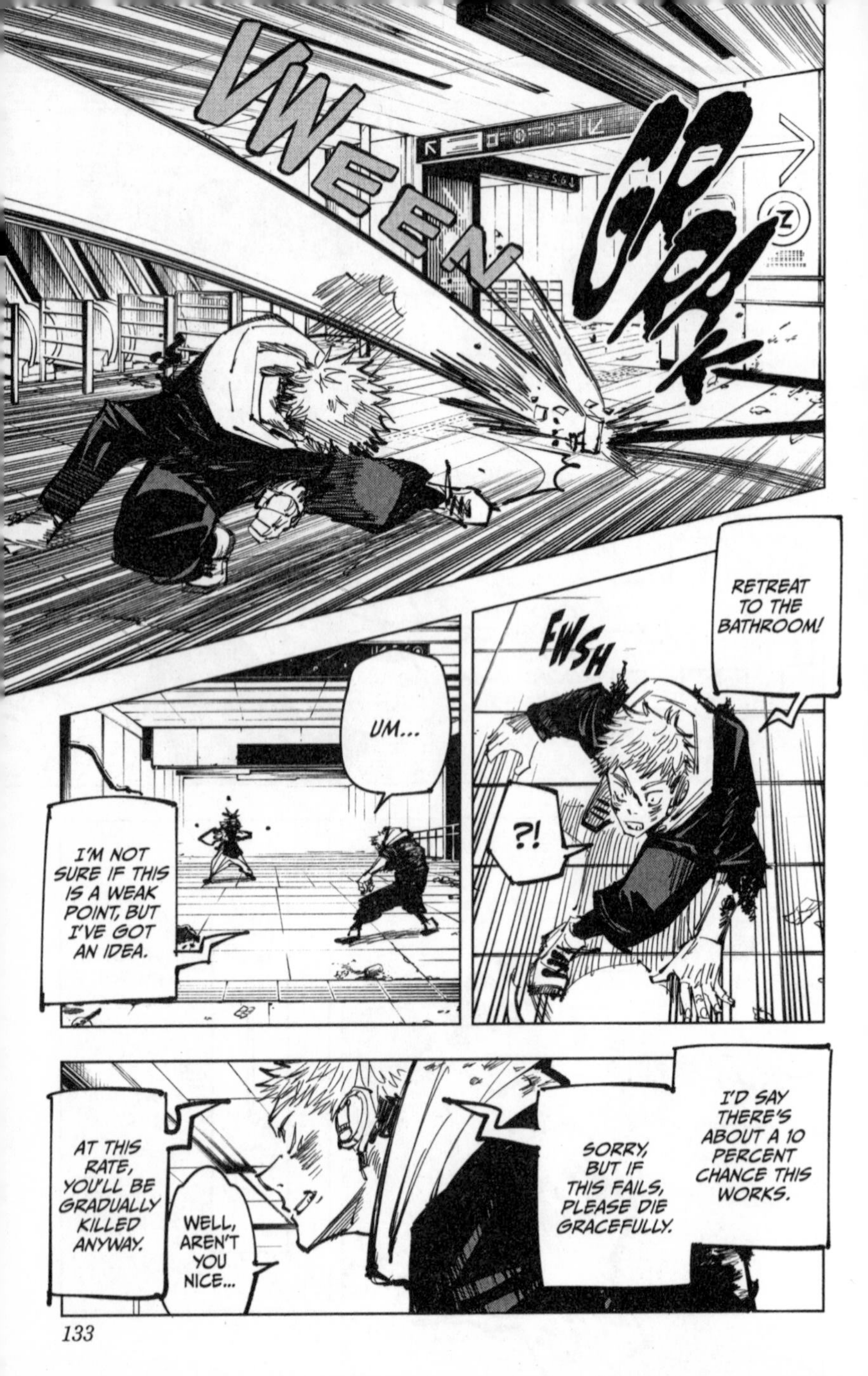
CRAK
VWEEN
RETREAT TO THE BATHROOM!
FWSH
?!
UM...
I'M NOT SURE IF THIS IS A WEAK POINT, BUT I'VE GOT AN IDEA.
I'D SAY THERE'S ABOUT A 10 PERCENT CHANCE THIS WORKS.
SORRY, BUT IF THIS FAILS, PLEASE DIE GRACEFULLY.
AT THIS RATE, YOU'LL BE GRADUALLY KILLED ANYWAY.
WELL, AREN'T YOU NICE...

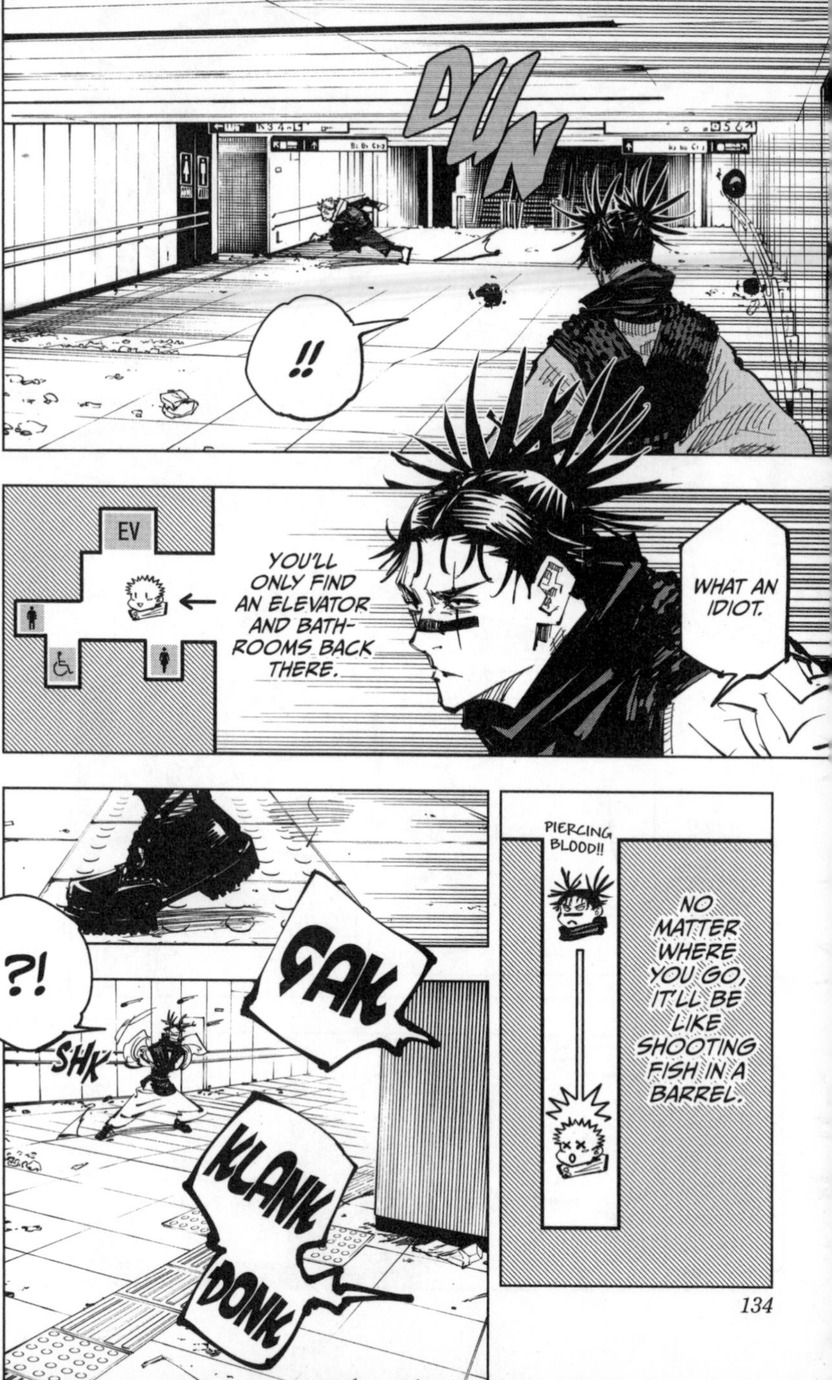
DUN
!!
WHAT AN IDIOT.
YOU'LL ONLY FIND AN ELEVATOR AND BATH-ROOMS BACK THERE.
EV
PIERCING BLOOD!!
NO MATTER WHERE YOU GO, IT'LL BE LIKE SHOOTING FISH IN A BARREL.
?!
GAK
SHK
KLANK
DONK

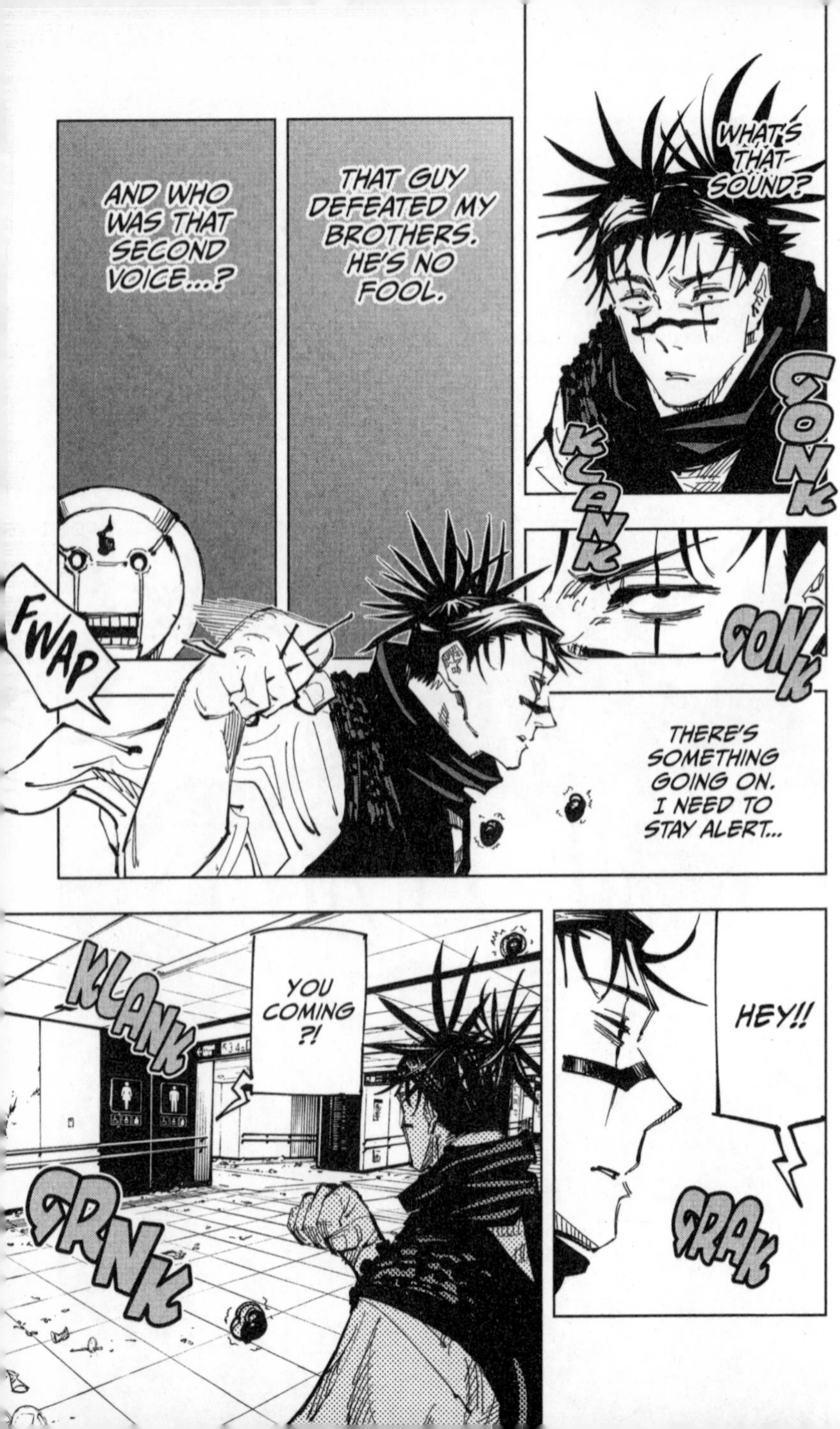
WHAT'S THAT SOUND?
GONK
KLANK
GONK
THERE'S SOMETHING GOING ON. I NEED TO STAY ALERT...
THAT GUY DEFEATED MY BROTHERS. HE'S NO FOOL.
AND WHO WAS THAT SECOND VOICE...?
FWAP
HEY!!
GRAK
YOU COMING?!
KLANK
GRNK

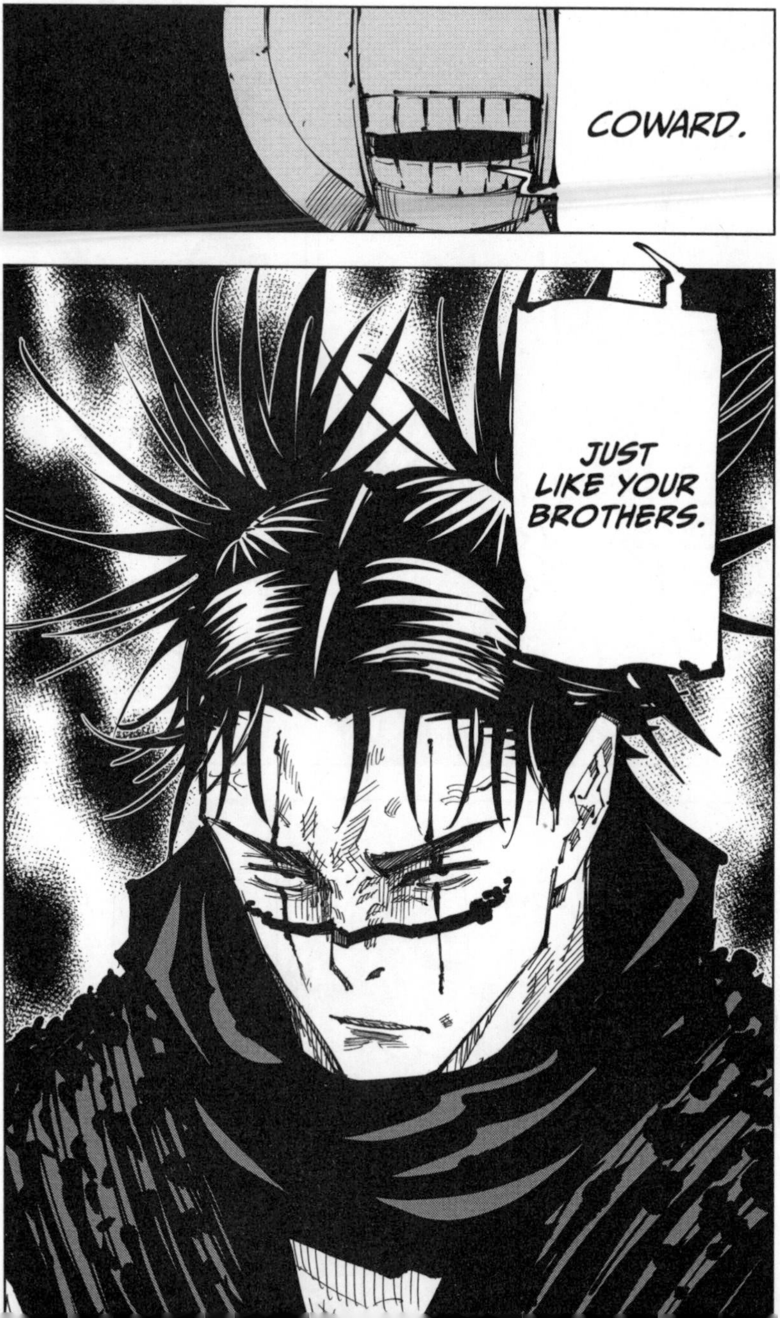
COWARD.
JUST LIKE YOUR BROTHERS.

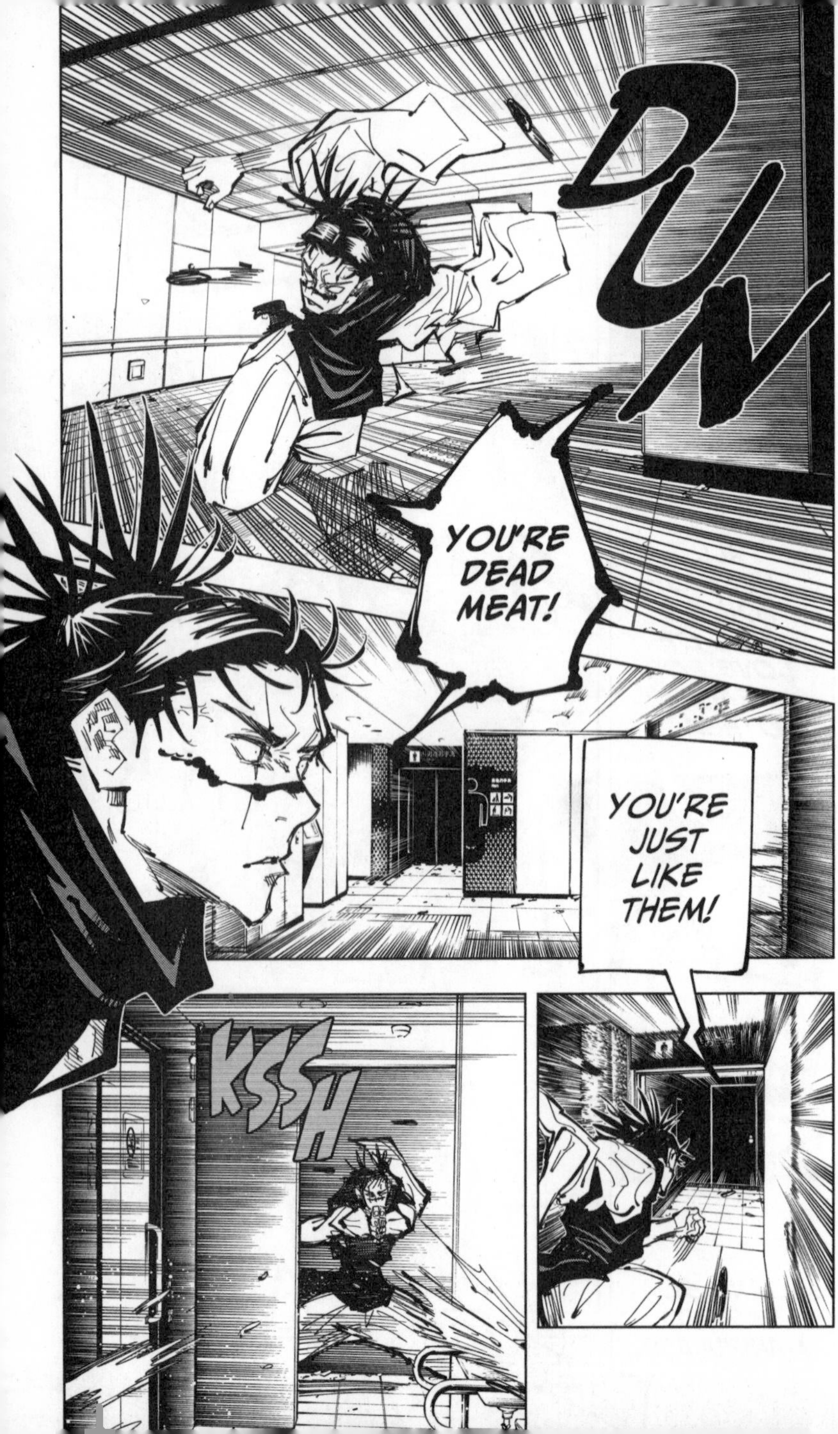
DUN
YOU'RE DEAD MEAT!
YOU'RE JUST LIKE THEM!
KSSH

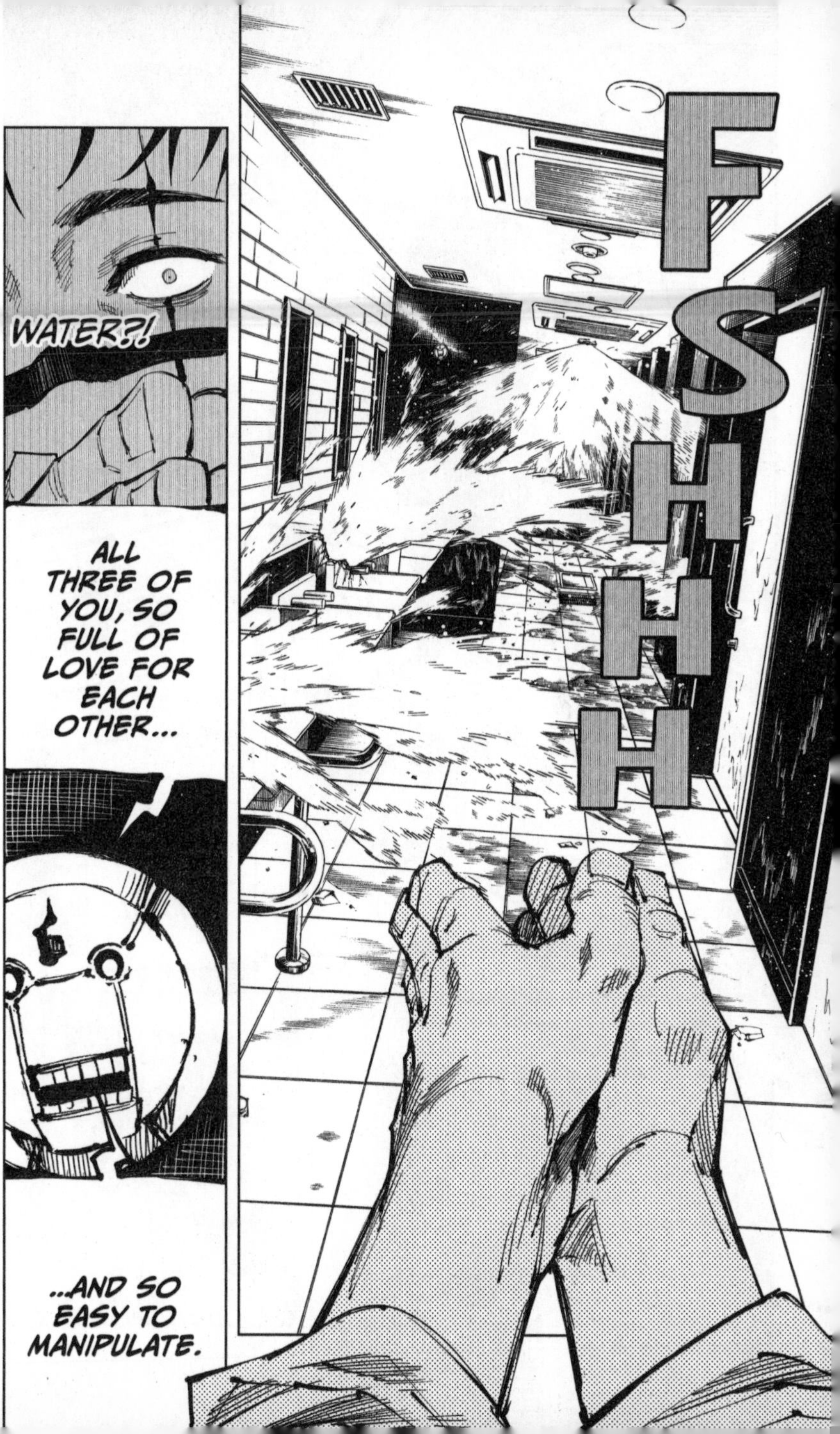
FSHHHH
WATER?!
ALL THREE OF YOU, SO FULL OF LOVE FOR EACH OTHER...
...AND SO EASY TO MANIPULATE.

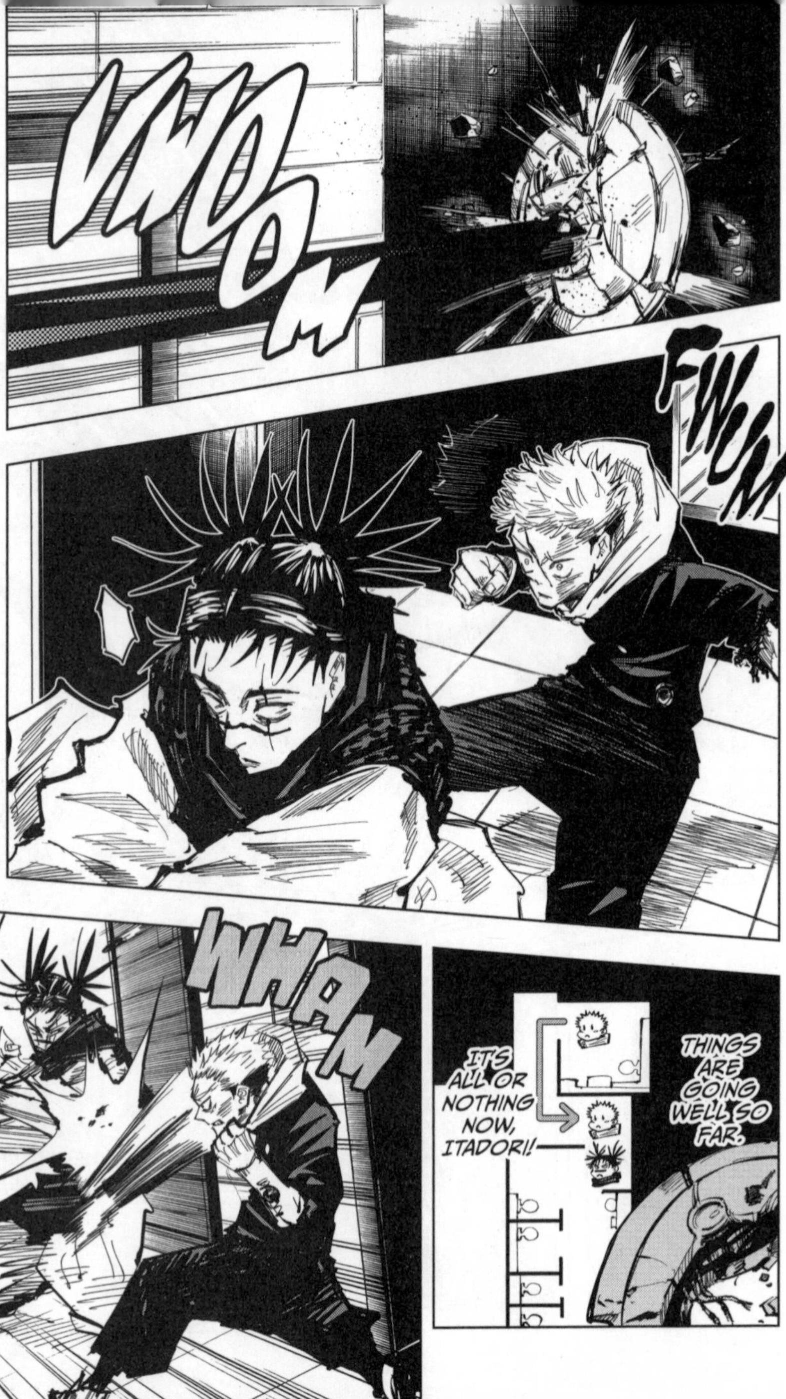
VWOOM
FWUM
THINGS ARE GOING WELL SO FAR.
IT'S ALL OR NOTHING NOW, ITADORI!
WHAM

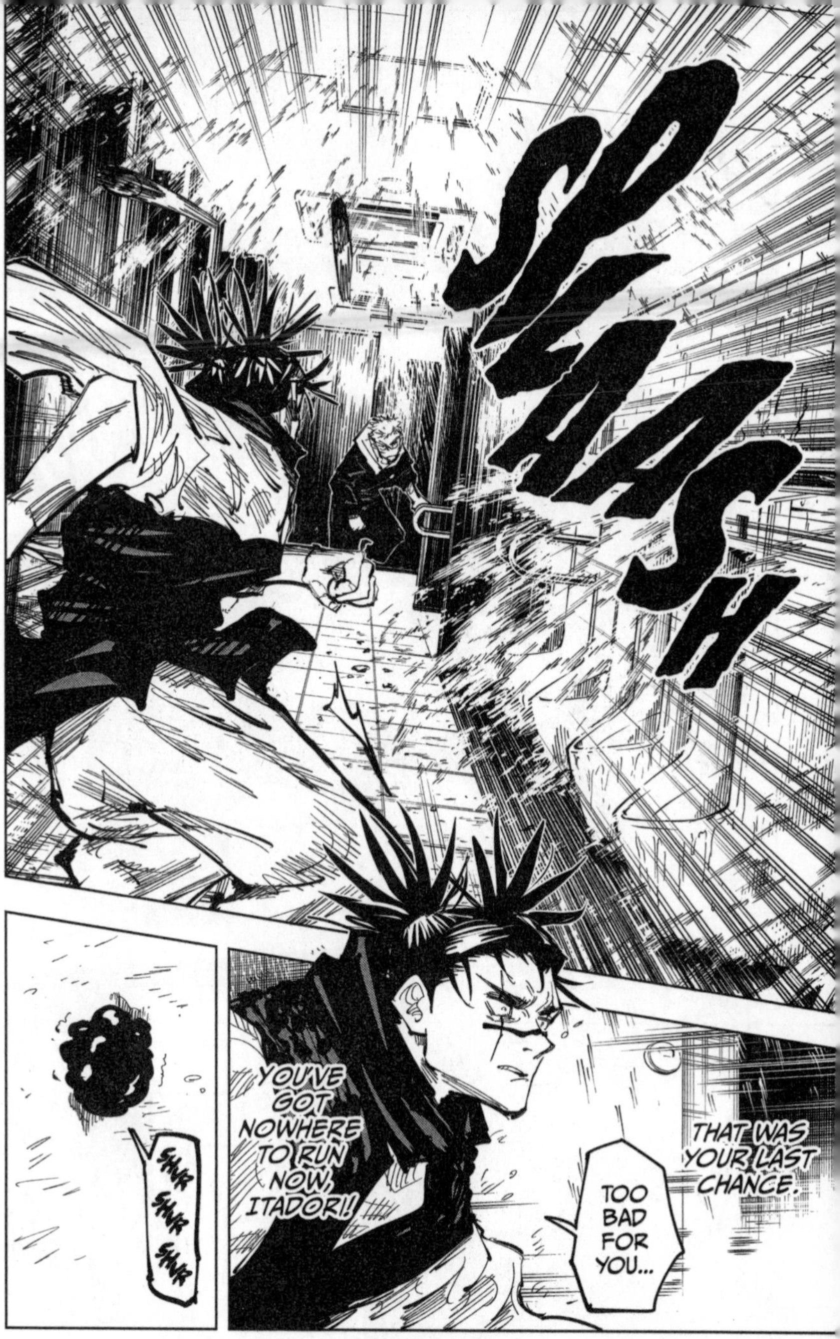
SMASH
THAT WAS YOUR LAST CHANCE.
TOO BAD FOR YOU...
YOU'VE GOT NOWHERE TO RUN NOW, ITADORI!
SHUR SHUR SHUR

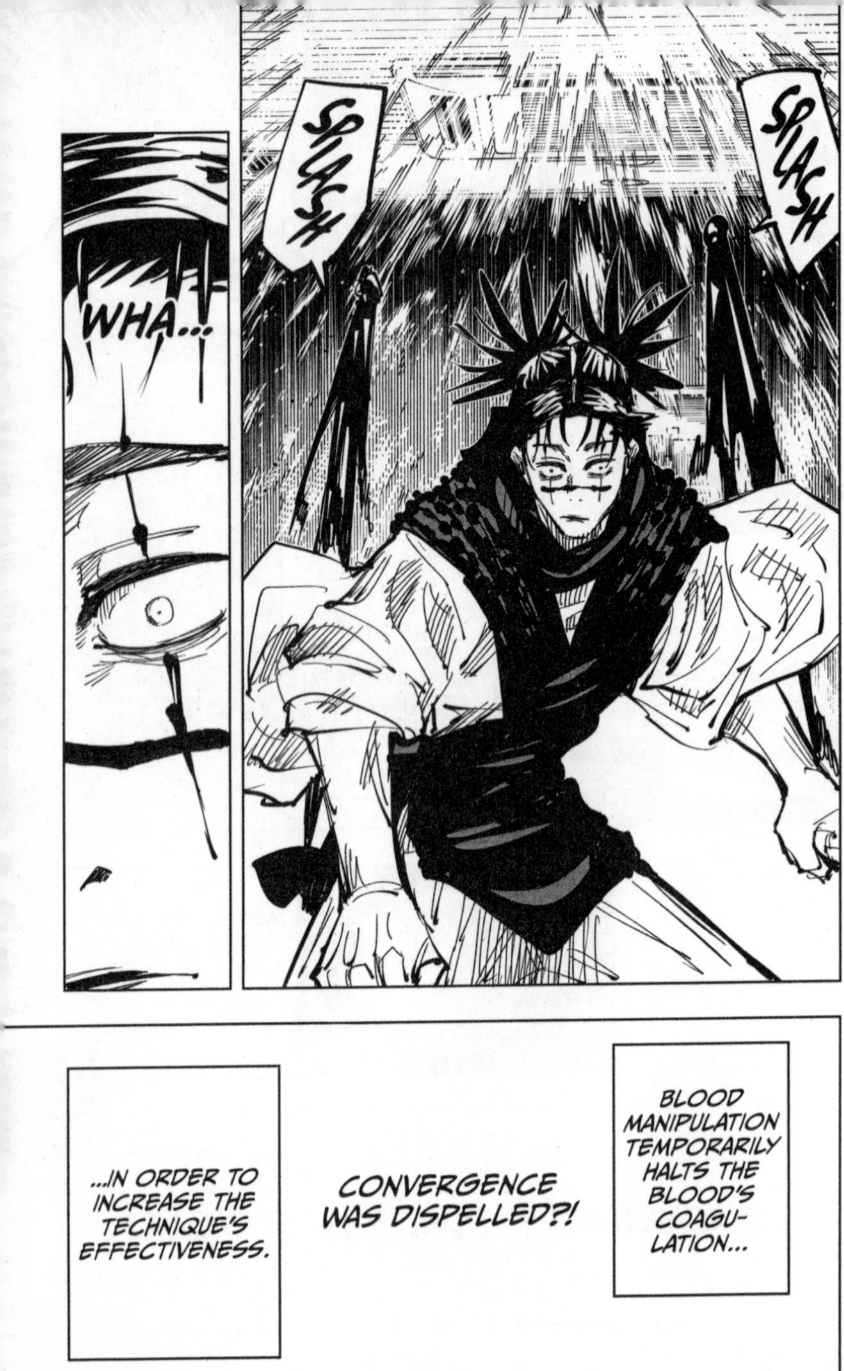
SPLASH
SPLASH
WHA...!
BLOOD MANIPULATION TEMPORARILY HALTS THE BLOOD'S COAGULATION...
CONVERGENCE WAS DISPELLED?!
...IN ORDER TO INCREASE THE TECHNIQUE'S EFFECTIVENESS.

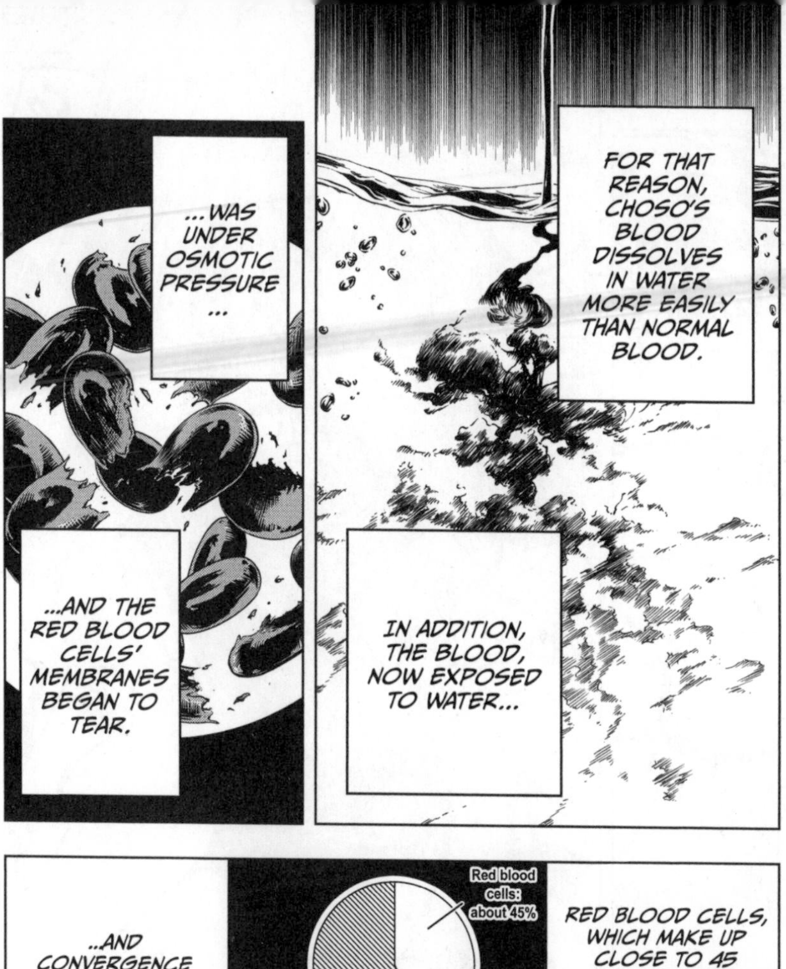
FOR THAT REASON, CHOSO'S BLOOD DISSOLVES IN WATER MORE EASILY THAN NORMAL BLOOD.
IN ADDITION, THE BLOOD, NOW EXPOSED TO WATER...
...WAS UNDER OSMOTIC PRESSURE...
...AND THE RED BLOOD CELLS' MEMBRANES BEGAN TO TEAR.
RED BLOOD CELLS, WHICH MAKE UP CLOSE TO 45 PERCENT OF BLOOD, BECAME UNCONTROLLABLE...
Red blood cells: about 45%
White blood cells and platelets
Blood plasma: about 55%
...AND CONVERGENCE WAS DISPELLED.
MECHAMARU'S HUNCH WAS RIGHT.

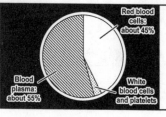

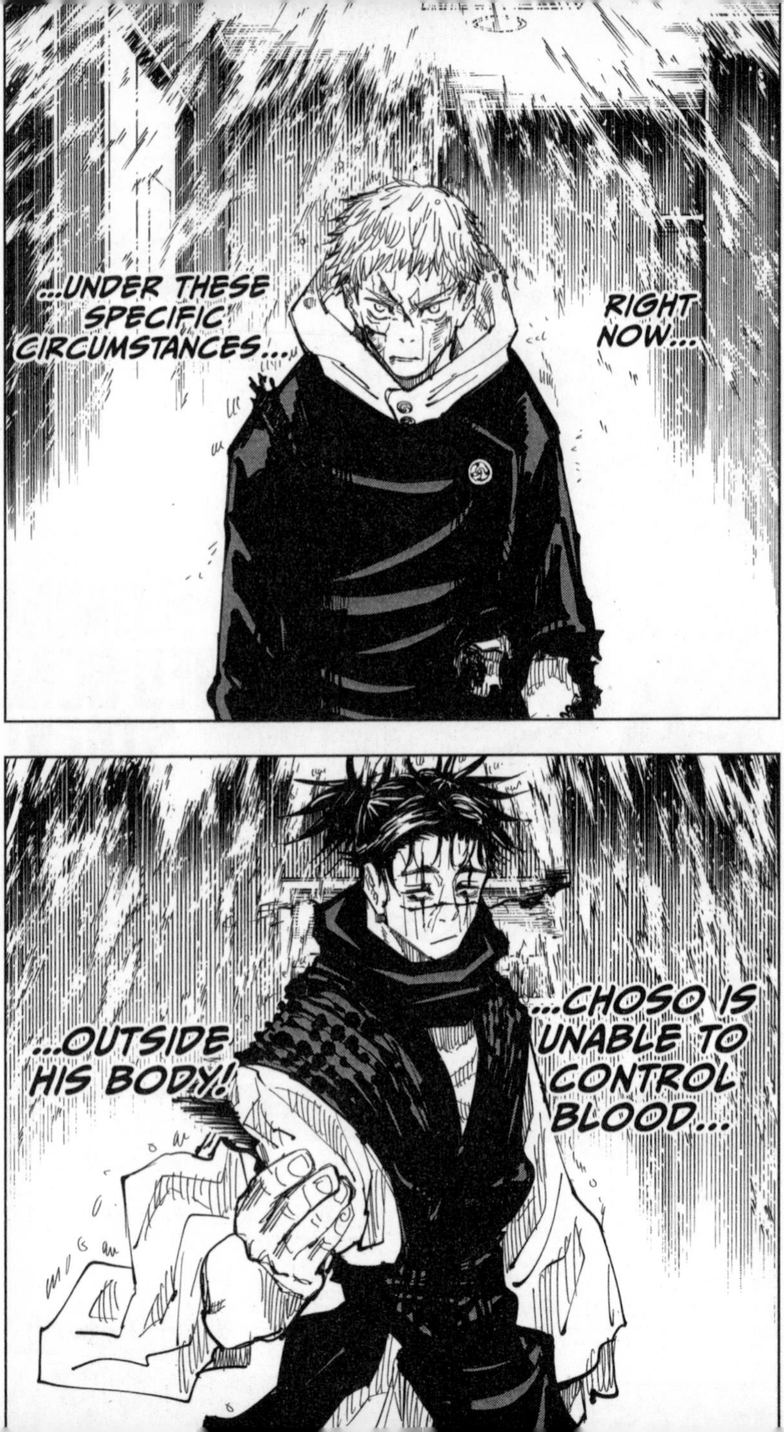
RIGHT NOW...
...UNDER THESE SPECIFIC CIRCUMSTANCES...
...CHOSO IS UNABLE TO CONTROL BLOOD...
...OUTSIDE HIS BODY!

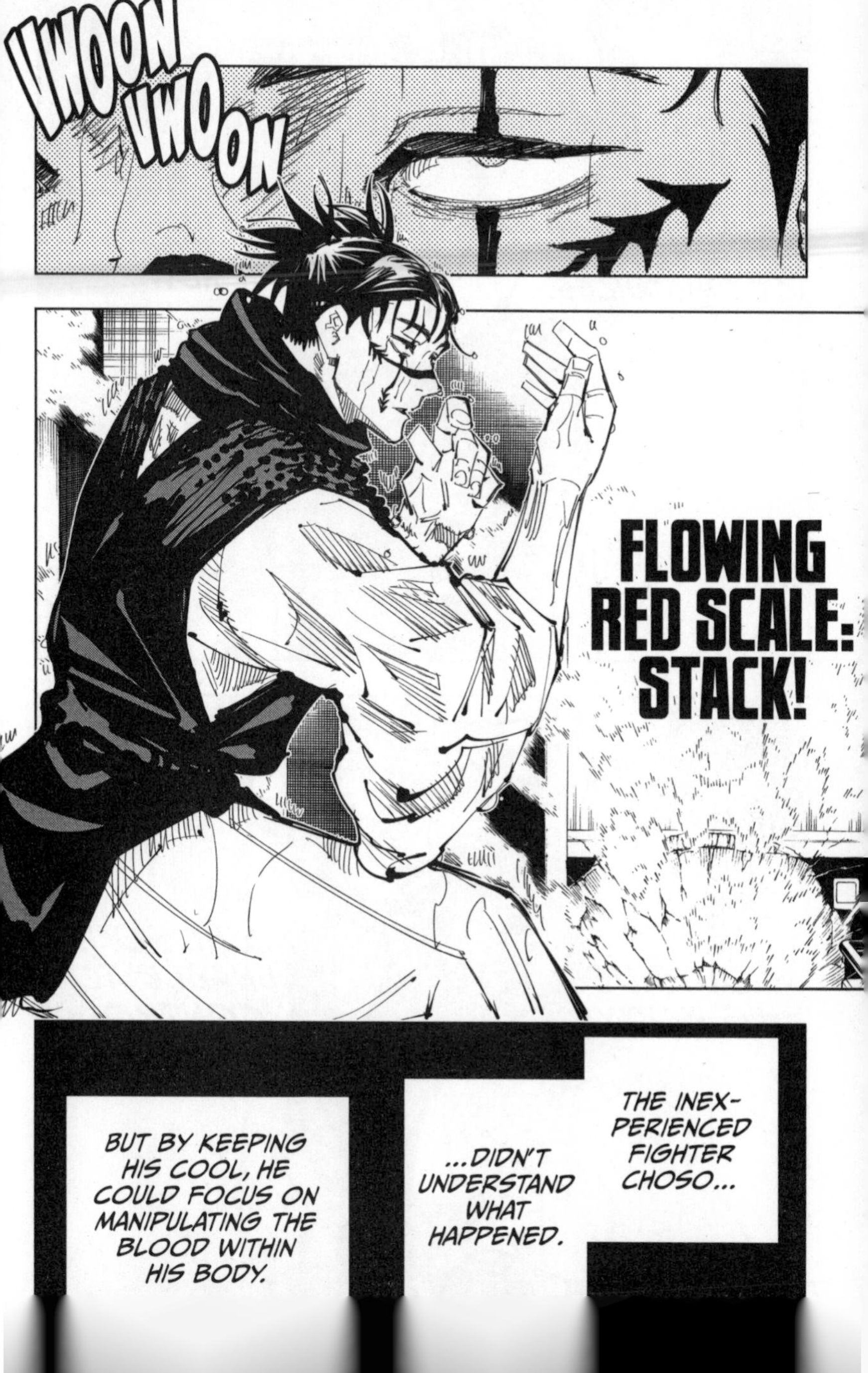
VWOON VWOON
FLOWING RED SCALE: STACK!
THE INEX-PERIENCED FIGHTER CHOSO...
...DIDN'T UNDERSTAND WHAT HAPPENED.
BUT BY KEEPING HIS COOL, HE COULD FOCUS ON MANIPULATING THE BLOOD WITHIN HIS BODY.

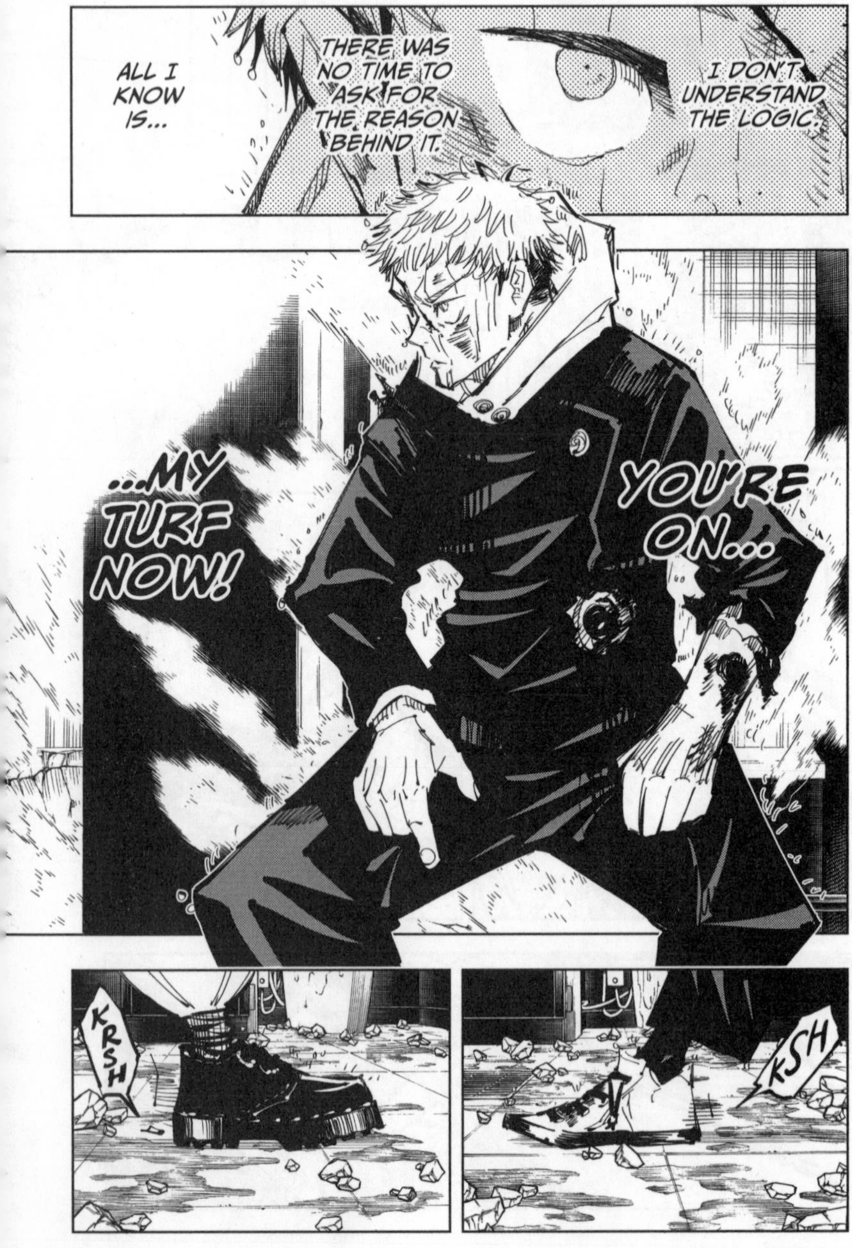
I DON'T UNDERSTAND THE LOGIC.
THERE WAS NO TIME TO ASK FOR THE REASON BEHIND IT.
ALL I KNOW IS...
YOU'RE ON...
...MY TURF NOW!
KSH
KRSH

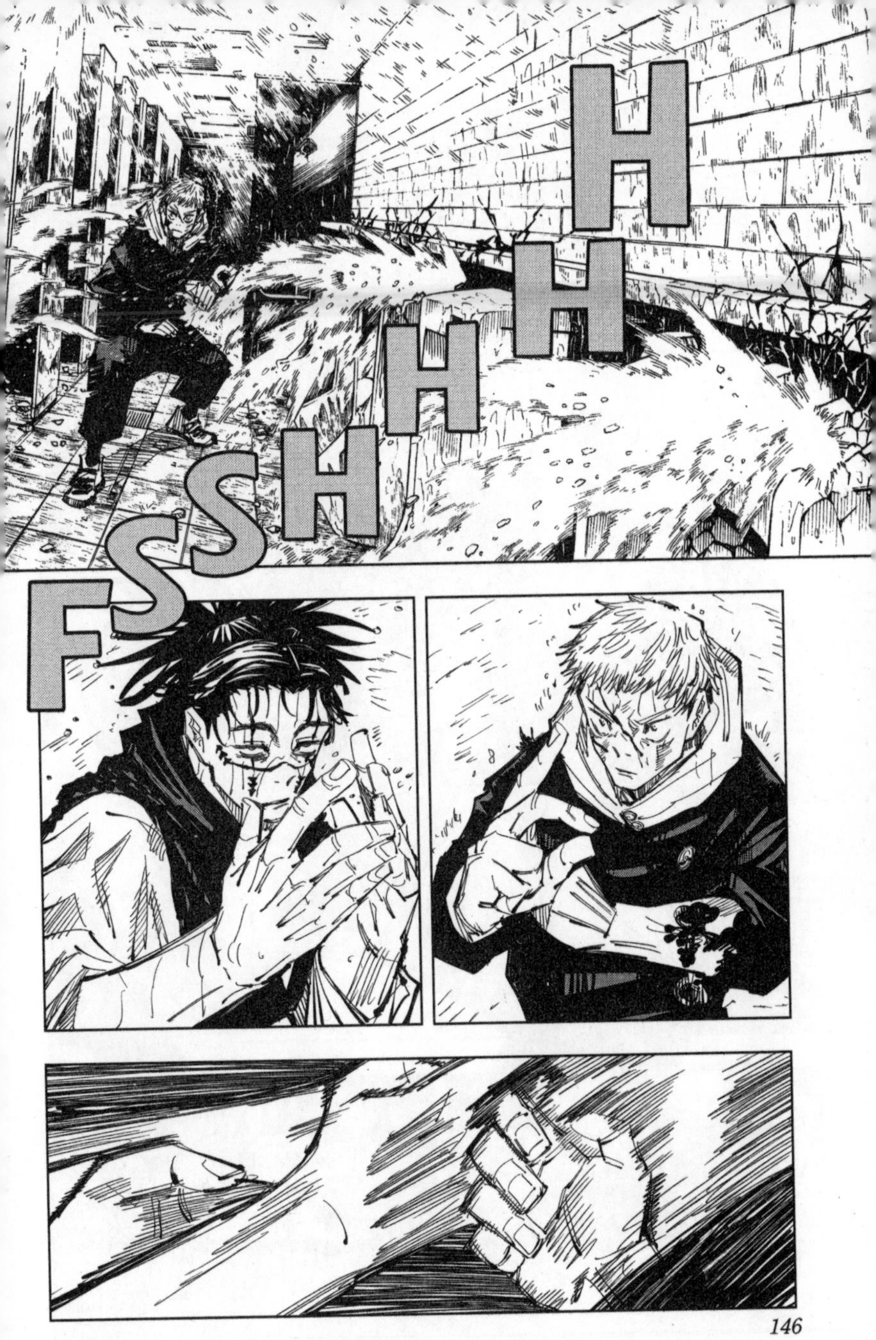
FSSHHHH

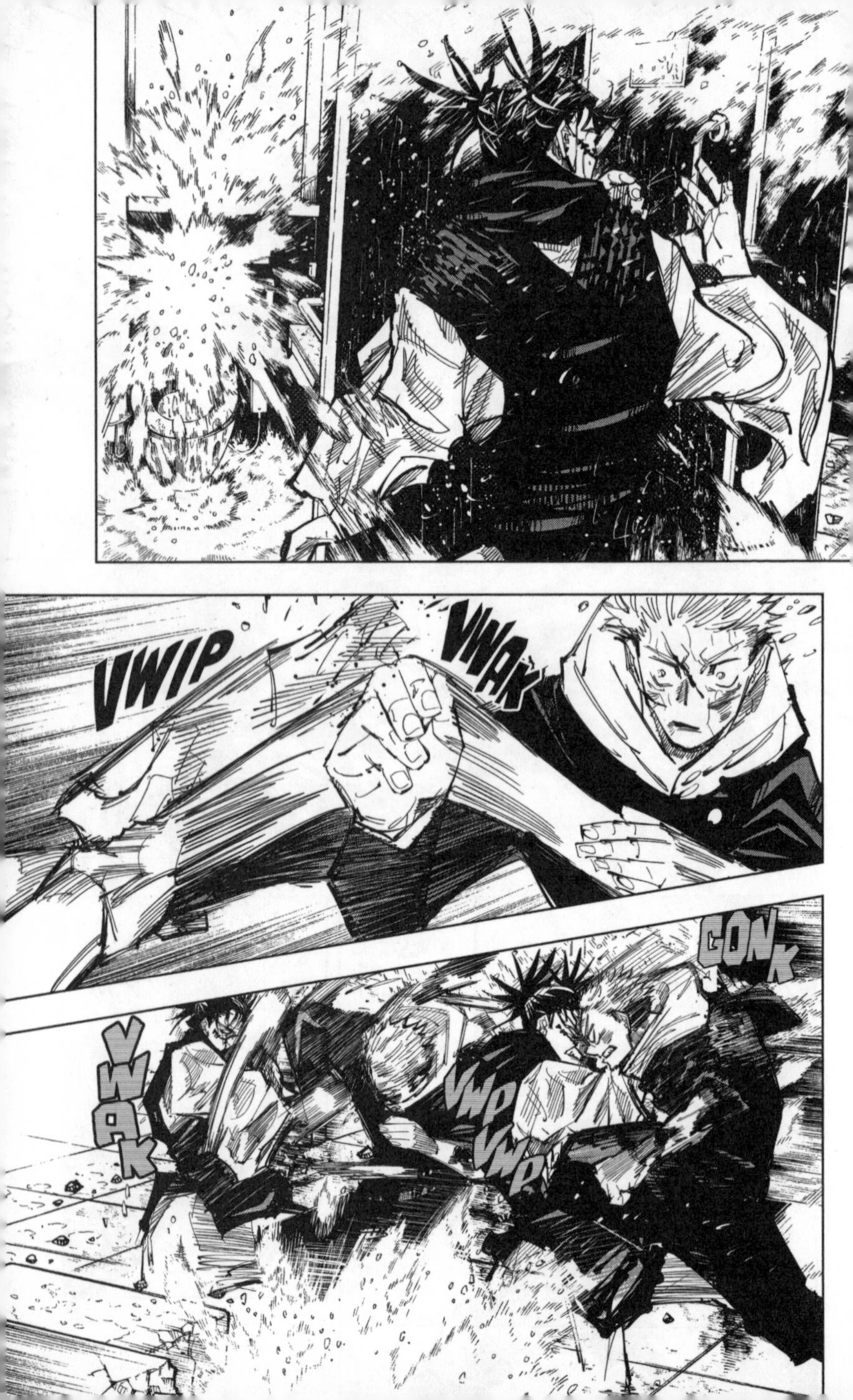

VWAK
VWIP
GONK
VWP VWP VWP
VWAK

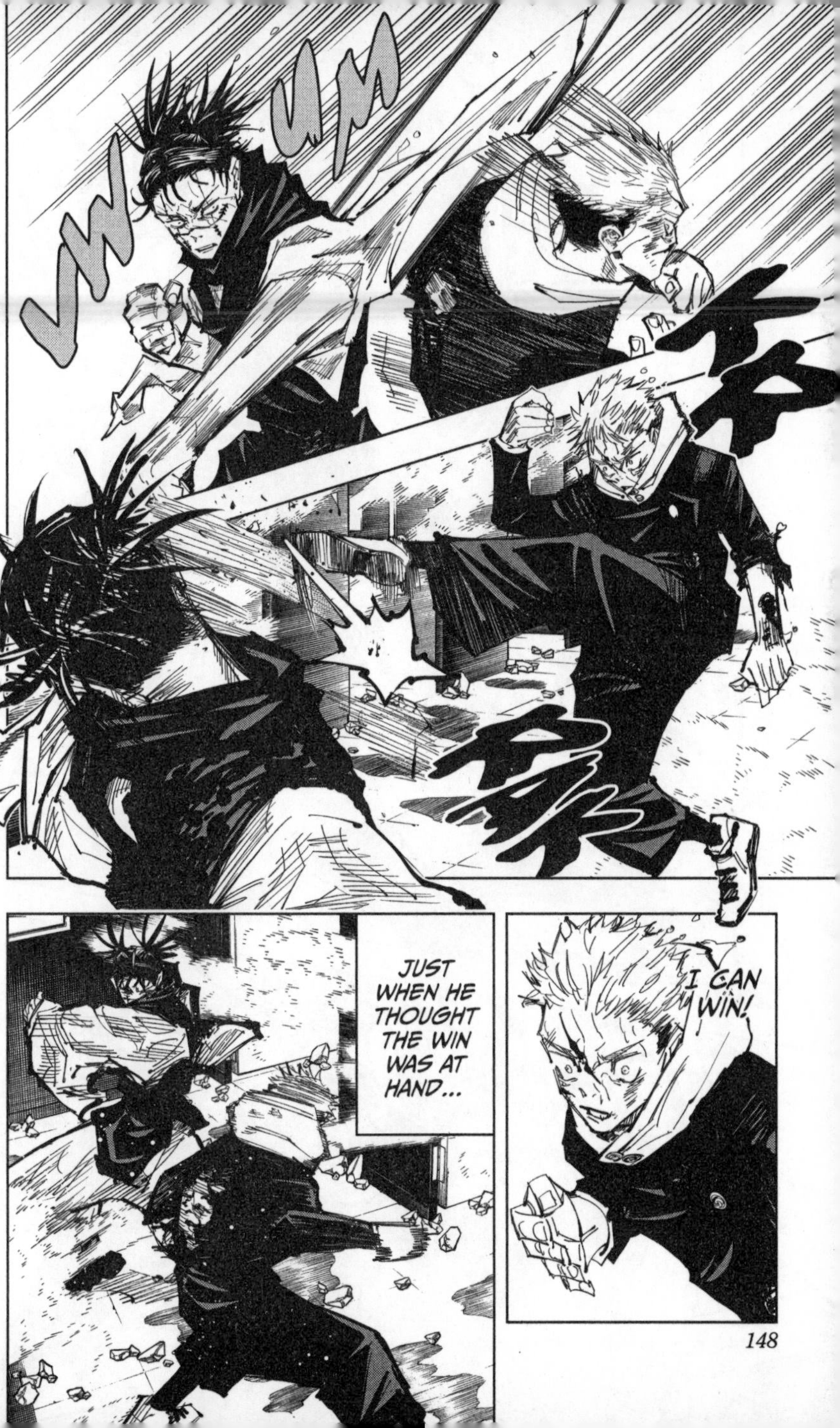
VWUM
I CAN WIN!
JUST WHEN HE THOUGHT THE WIN WAS AT HAND...

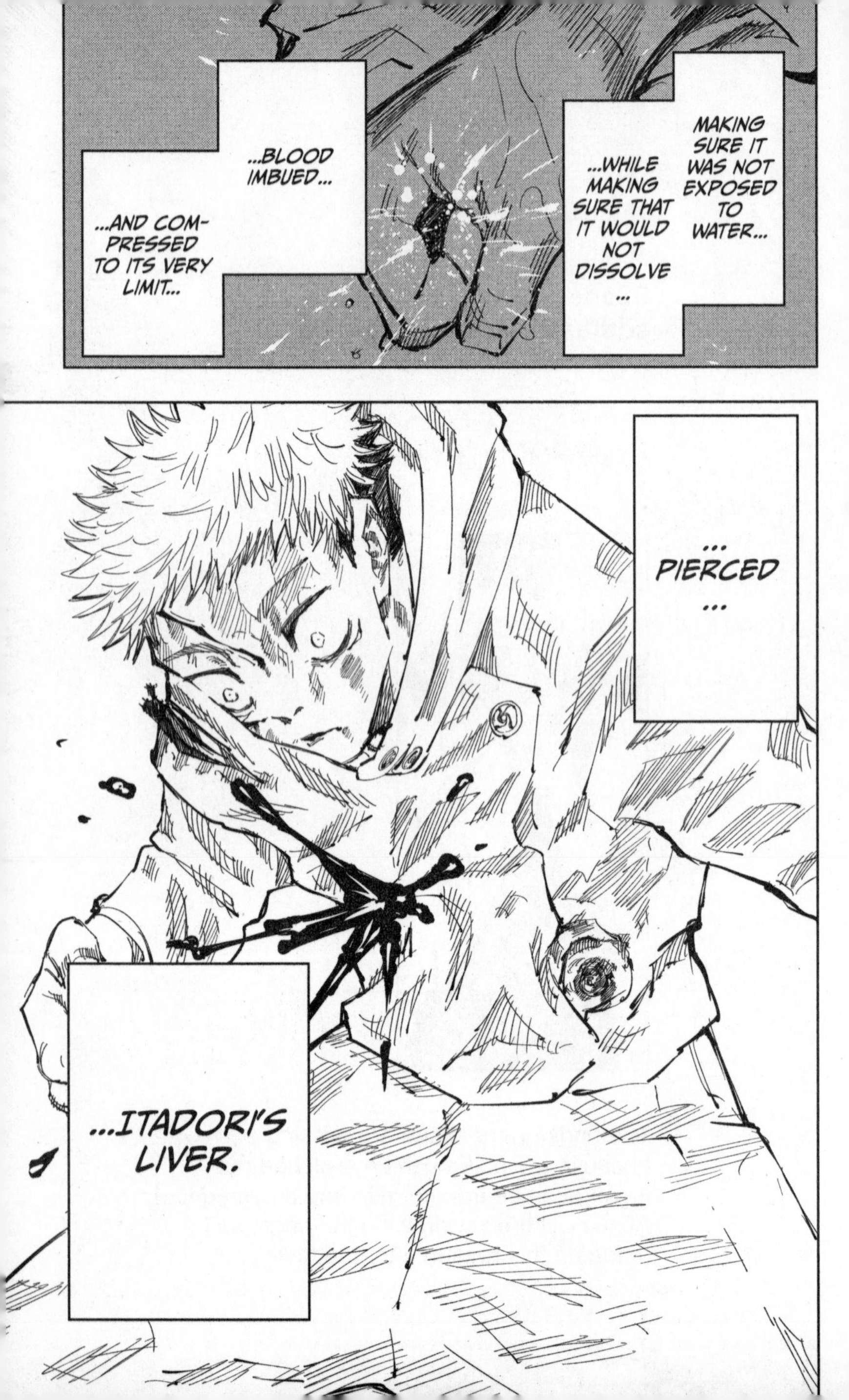
MAKING SURE IT WAS NOT EXPOSED TO WATER...
...WHILE MAKING SURE THAT IT WOULD NOT DISSOLVE...
...BLOOD IMBUED...
...AND COM-PRESSED TO ITS VERY LIMIT...
...PIERCED...
...ITADORI'S LIVER.

Scenes I was planning to address but forgot about until now, part 6

• Side Ponytail's sword

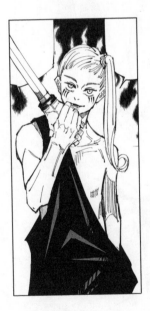

The rings on the blade are missing
because the blade can be switched out.
It can even be transformed into a cursed tool.
Also, I got tired of drawing the rings, so I
made up this reason after the fact.

Chapter 105: The Shibuya Incident, Part 23

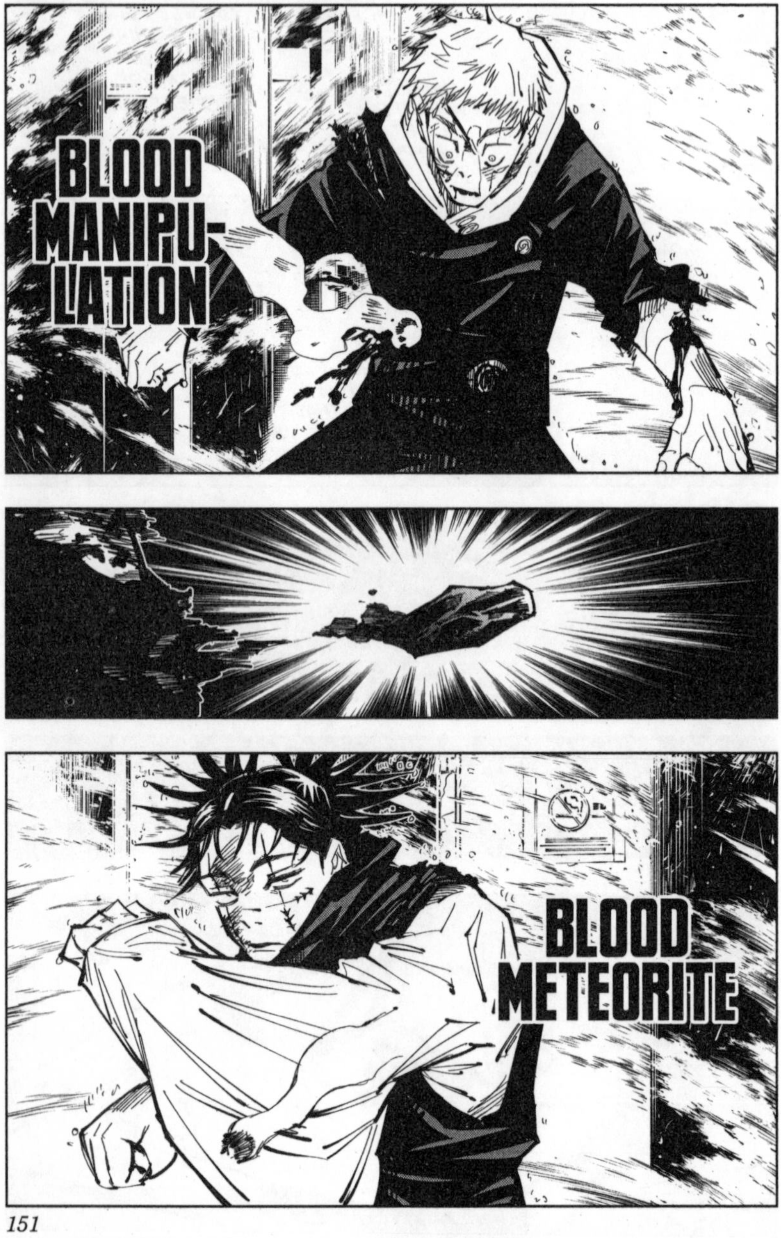
BLOOD MANIPU-LATION
BLOOD METEORITE

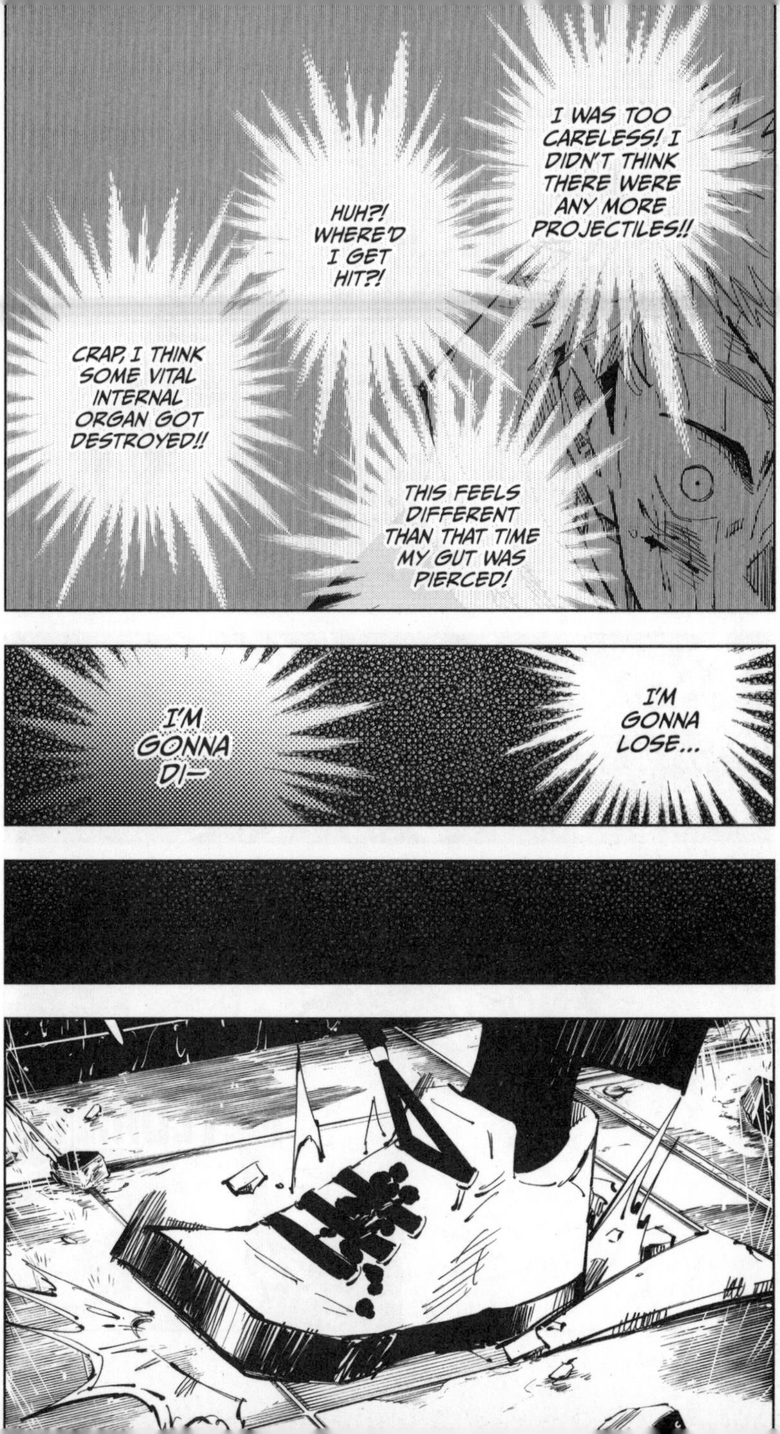
I WAS TOO CARELESS! I DIDN'T THINK THERE WERE ANY MORE PROJECTILES!!
HUH?! WHERE'D I GET HIT?!
THIS FEELS DIFFERENT THAN THAT TIME MY GUT WAS PIERCED!
CRAP, I THINK SOME VITAL INTERNAL ORGAN GOT DESTROYED!!
I'M GONNA LOSE...
I'M GONNA DI—

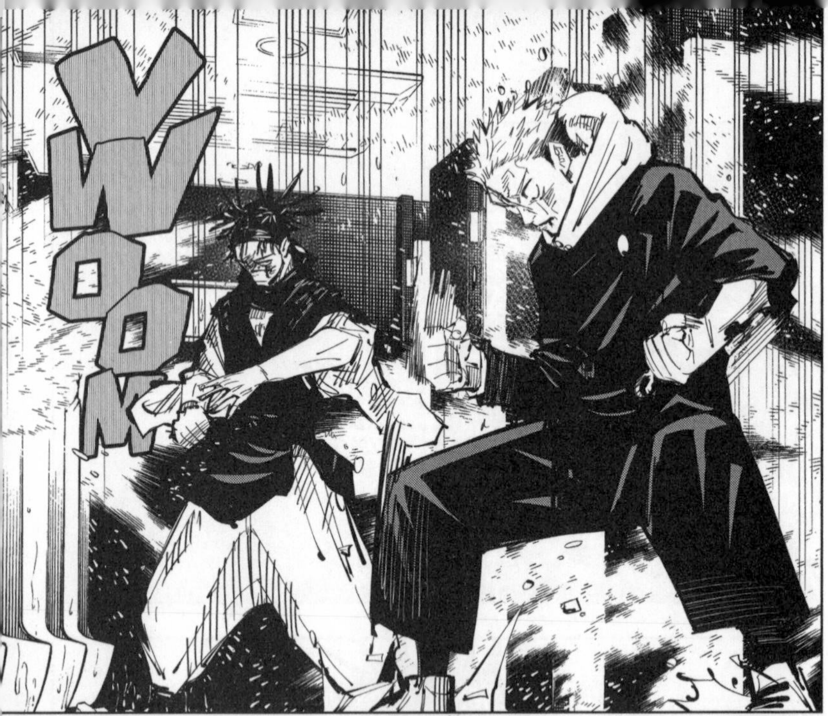
VWOOM

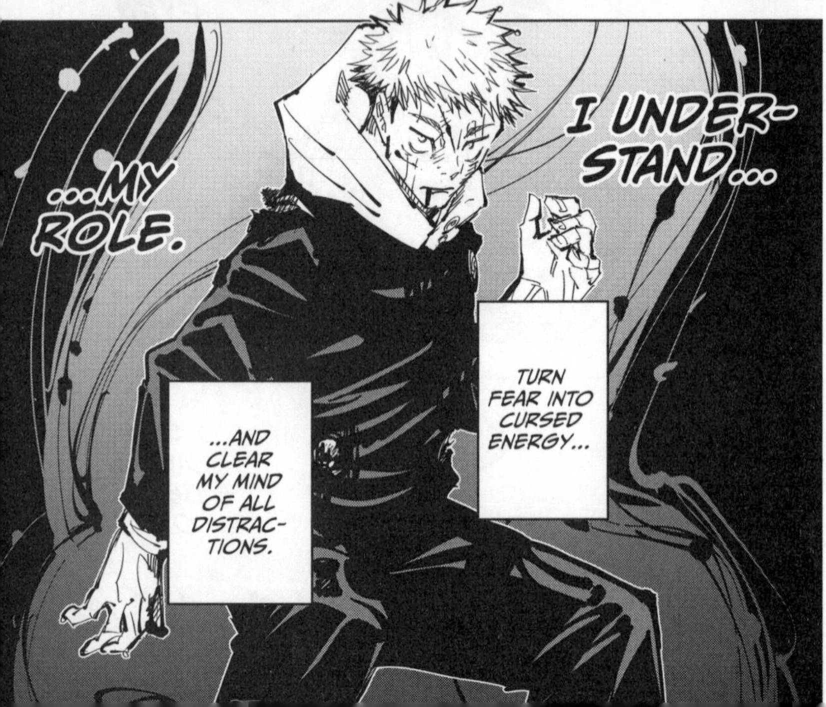
I UNDER-
STAND...
...MY
ROLE.
TURN FEAR INTO CURSED ENERGY...
...AND CLEAR MY MIND OF ALL DISTRACTIONS.

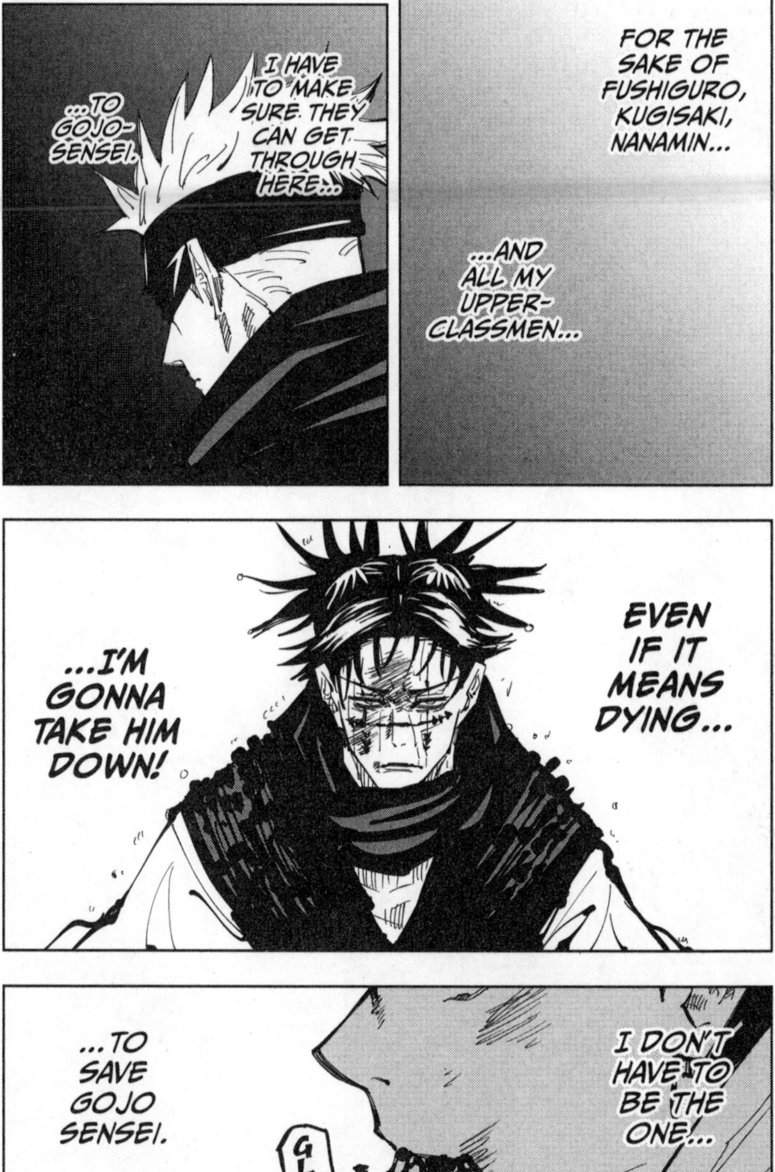
FOR THE SAKE OF FUSHIGURO, KUGISAKI, NANAMIN...
...AND ALL MY UPPER-CLASSMEN...
I HAVE TO MAKE SURE THEY CAN GET THROUGH HERE...
...TO GOJO-SENSEI.
EVEN IF IT MEANS DYING...
...I'M GONNA TAKE HIM DOWN!
I DON'T HAVE TO BE THE ONE...
GLUP
...TO SAVE GOJO SENSEI.

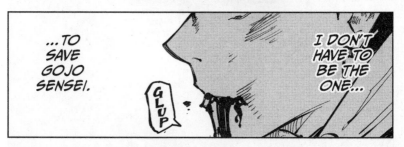

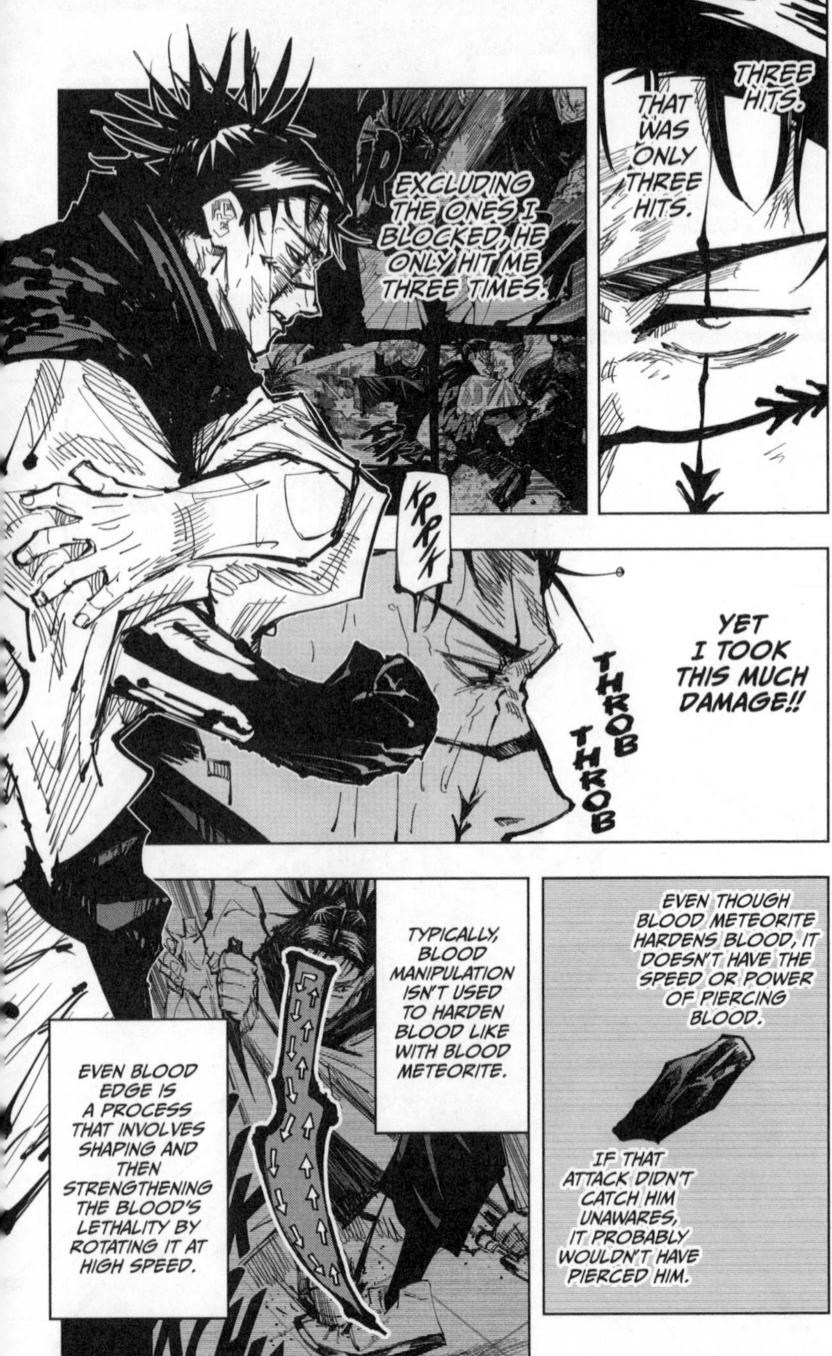
THREE HITS.
THAT WAS ONLY THREE HITS.
EXCLUDING THE ONES I BLOCKED, HE ONLY HIT ME THREE TIMES.
KRRIK
YET I TOOK THIS MUCH DAMAGE!!
THROB THROB
EVEN THOUGH BLOOD METEORITE HARDENS BLOOD, IT DOESN'T HAVE THE SPEED OR POWER OF PIERCING BLOOD.
IF THAT ATTACK DIDN'T CATCH HIM UNAWARES, IT PROBABLY WOULDN'T HAVE PIERCED HIM.
TYPICALLY, BLOOD MANIPULATION ISN'T USED TO HARDEN BLOOD LIKE WITH BLOOD METEORITE.
EVEN BLOOD EDGE IS A PROCESS THAT INVOLVES SHAPING AND THEN STRENGTHENING THE BLOOD'S LETHALITY BY ROTATING IT AT HIGH SPEED.

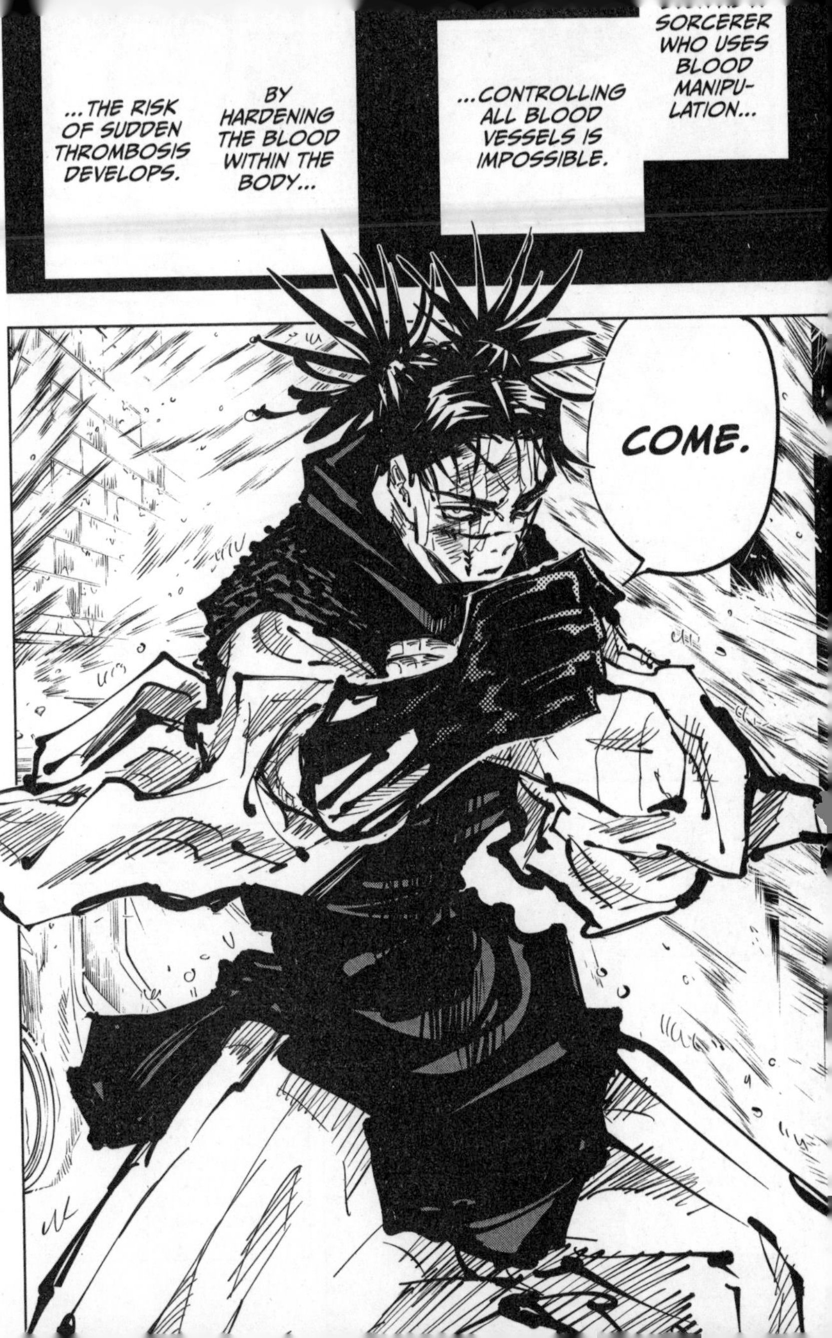
SORCERER WHO USES BLOOD MANIPU-LATION...
...CONTROLLING ALL BLOOD VESSELS IS IMPOSSIBLE.
BY HARDENING THE BLOOD WITHIN THE BODY...
...THE RISK OF SUDDEN THROMBOSIS DEVELOPS.
COME.

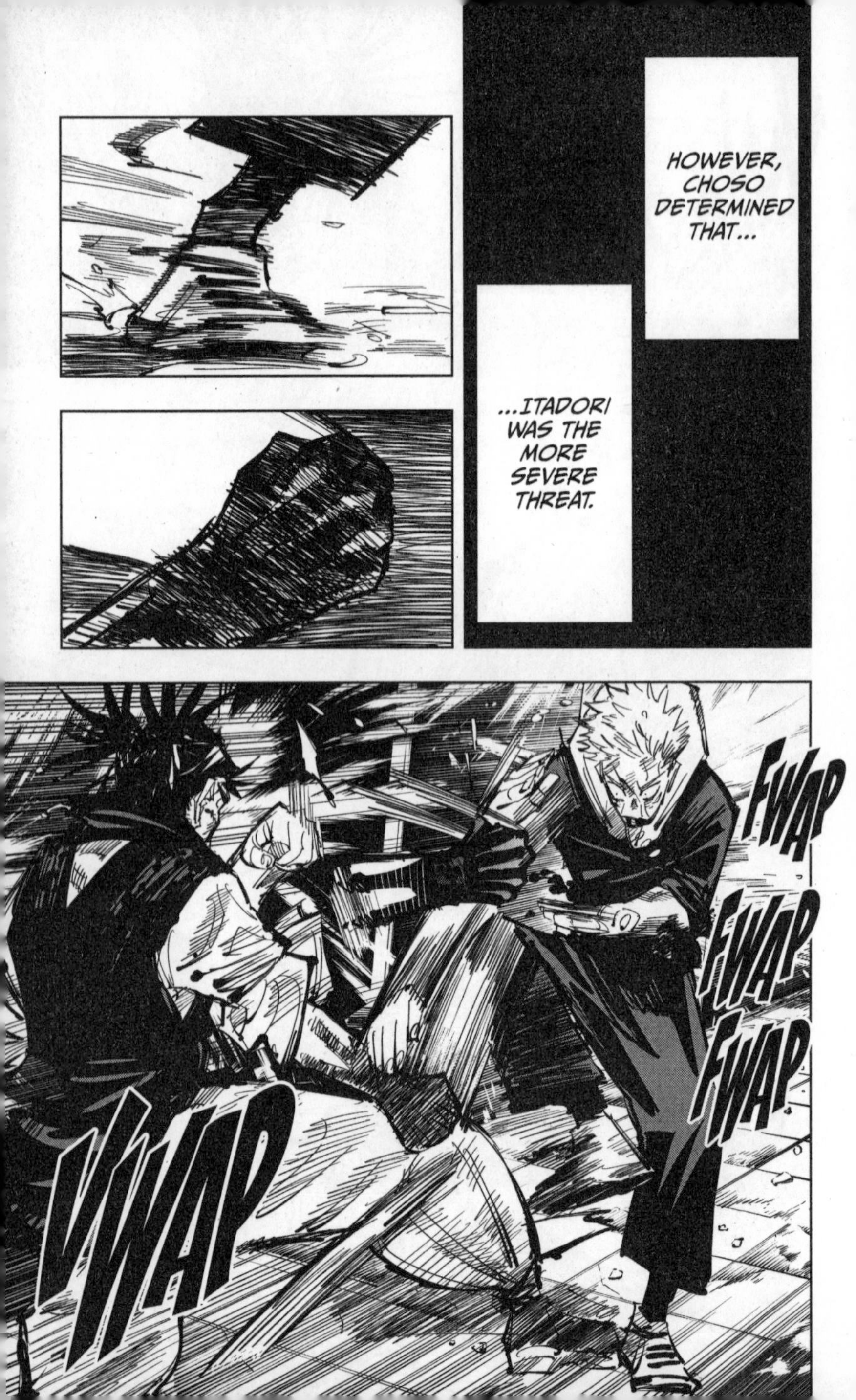
HOWEVER, CHOSO DETERMINED THAT...
...ITADORI WAS THE MORE SEVERE THREAT.
FWAP
FWAP
FWAP
VWAP

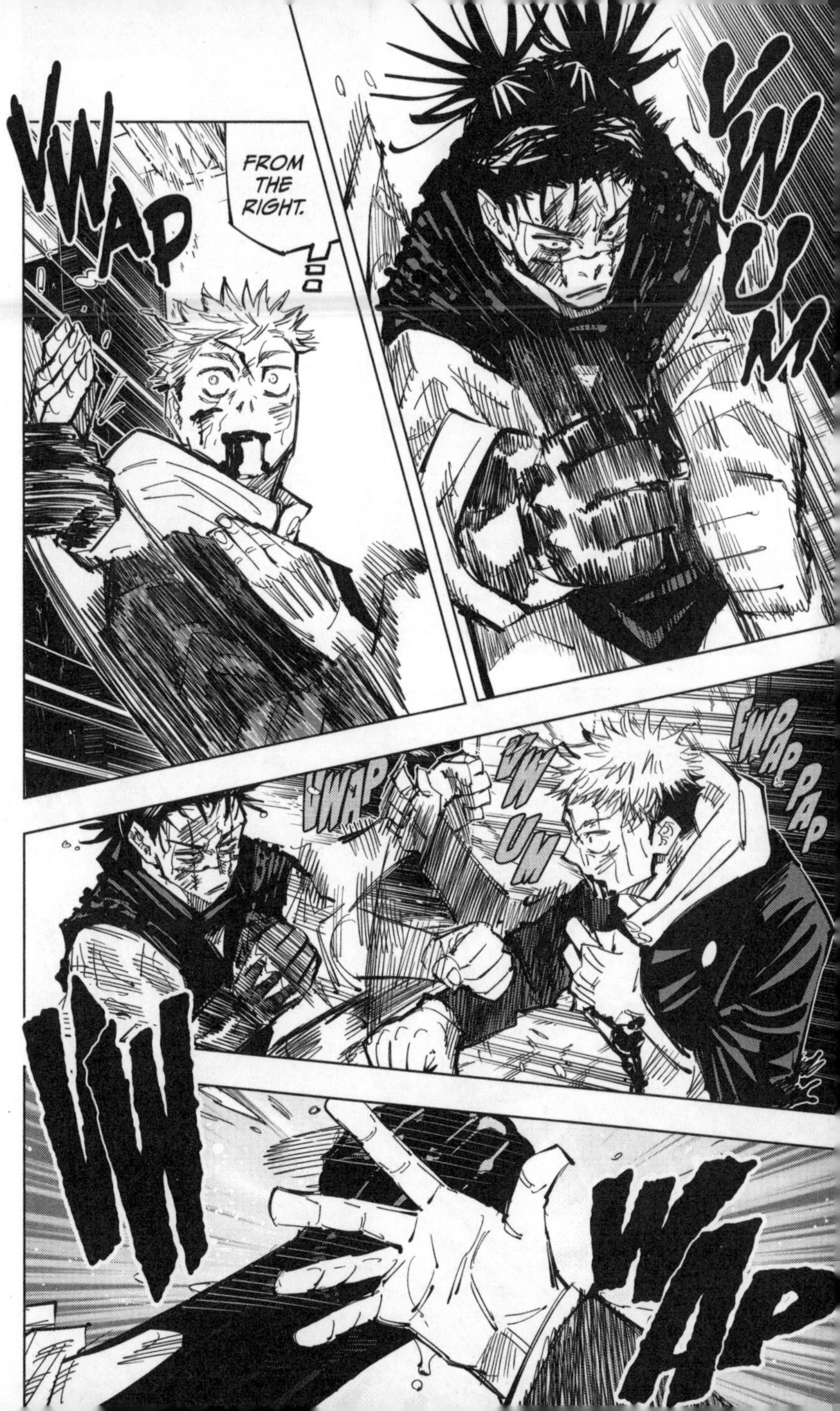
FROM THE RIGHT.
VWAP
FWAP PAP

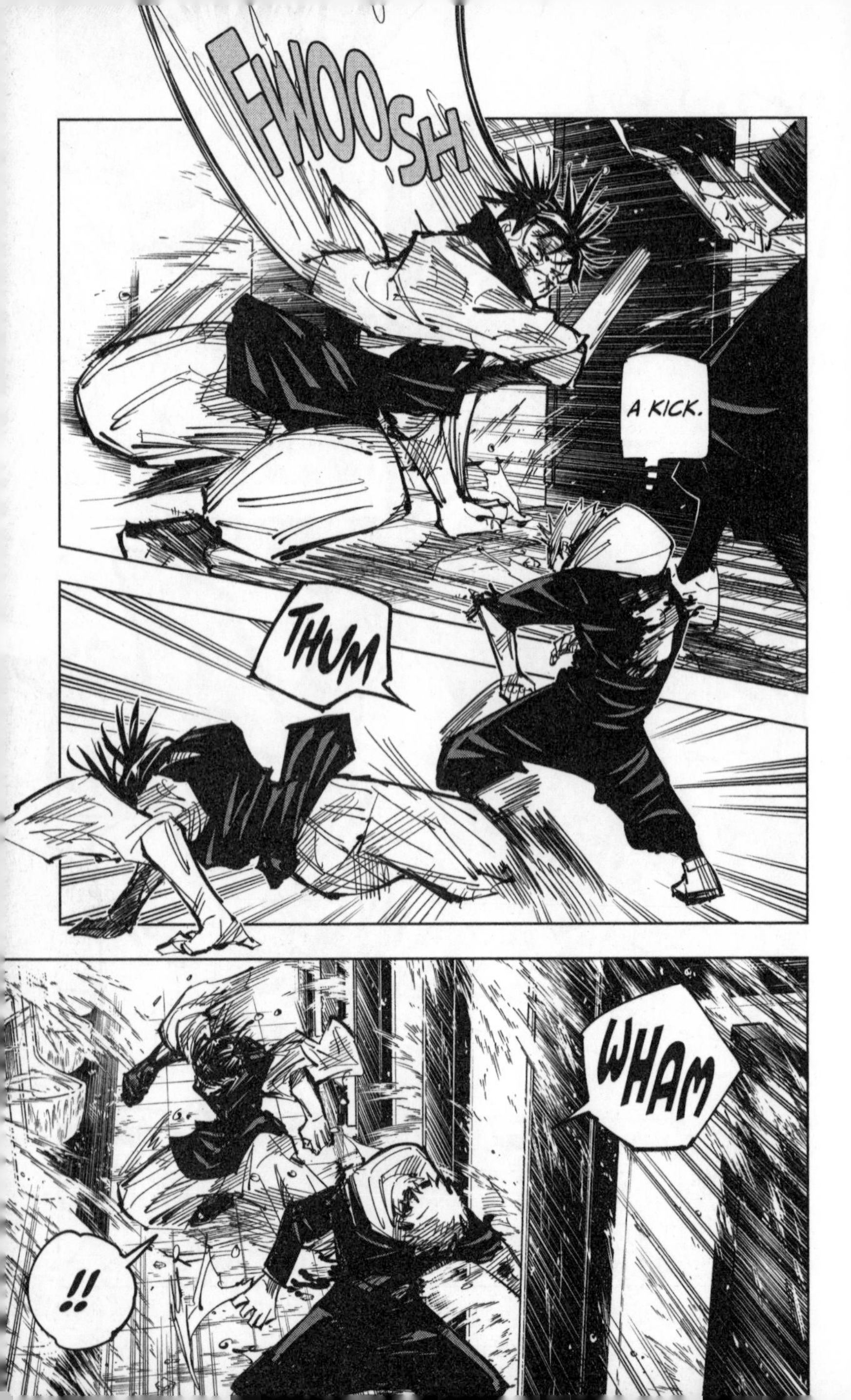
FWOOSH
A KICK.
THUM
WHAM
!!

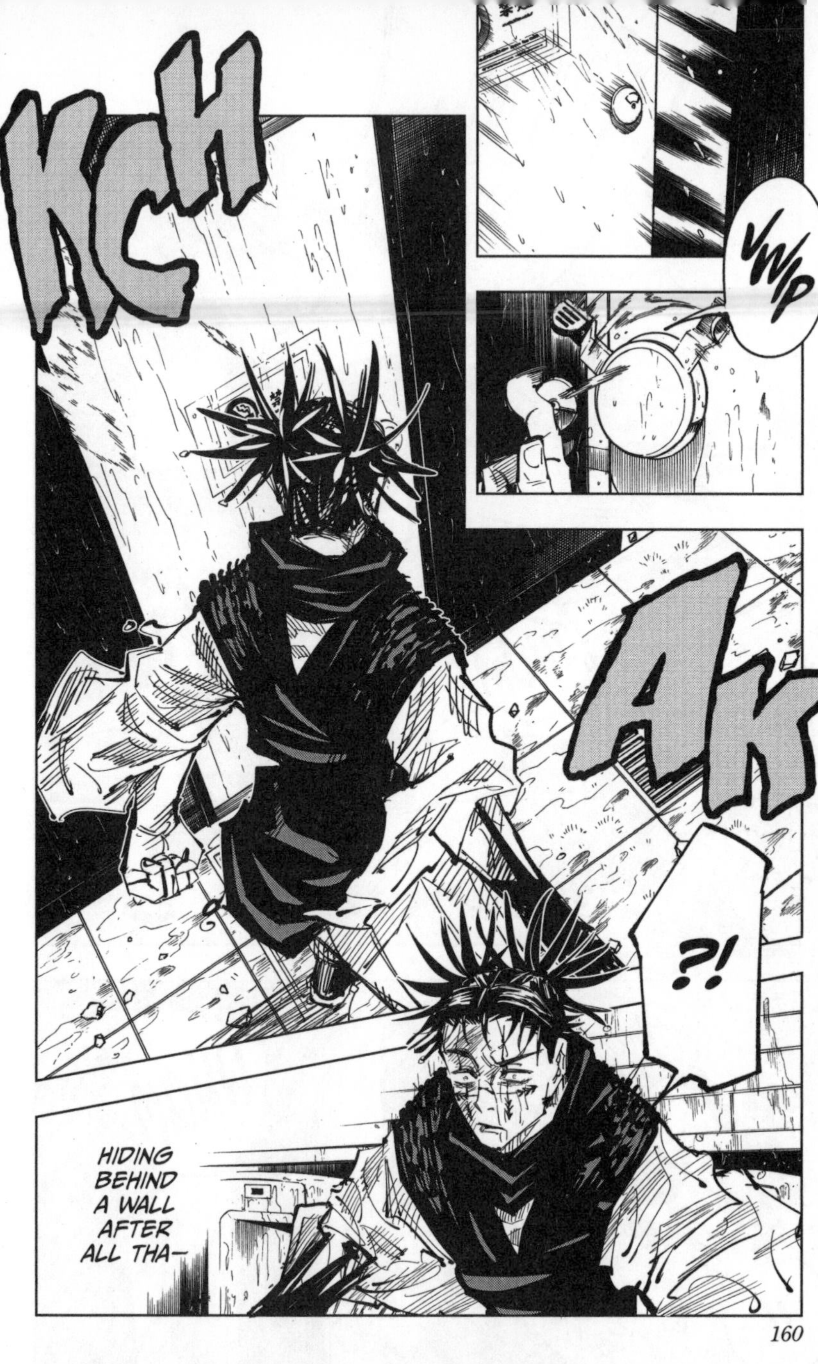
VWIP
KCH
AK
?!
HIDING BEHIND A WALL AFTER ALL THA—

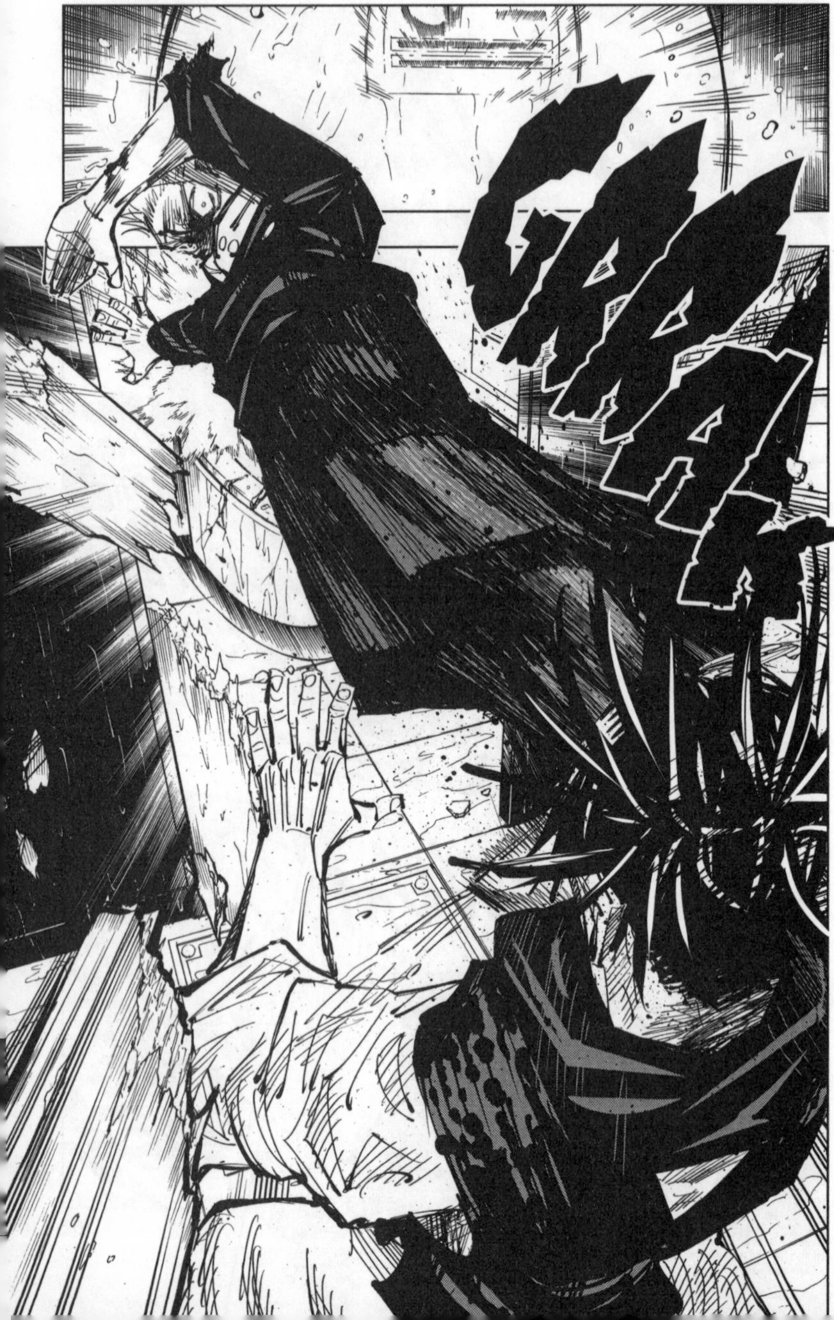

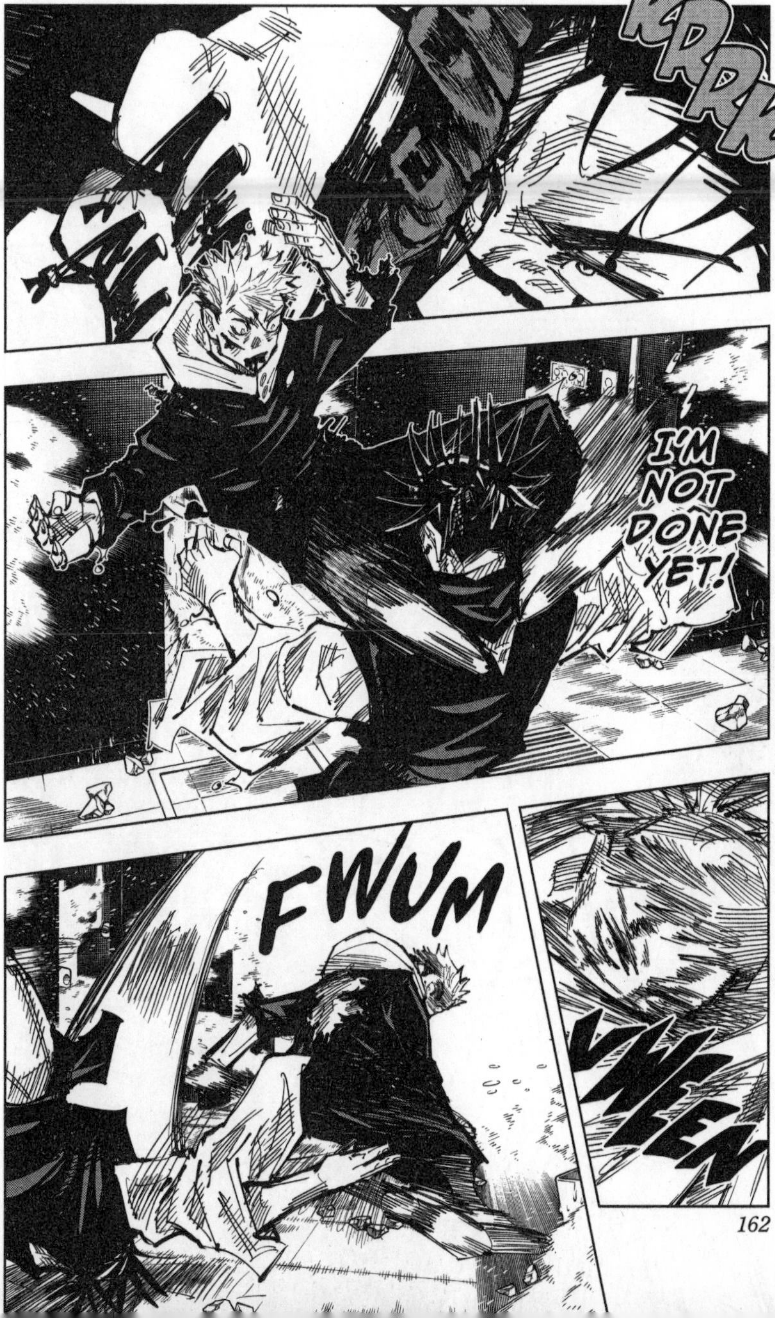
KRRK
I'M NOT DONE YET!
VWEN
FWUM

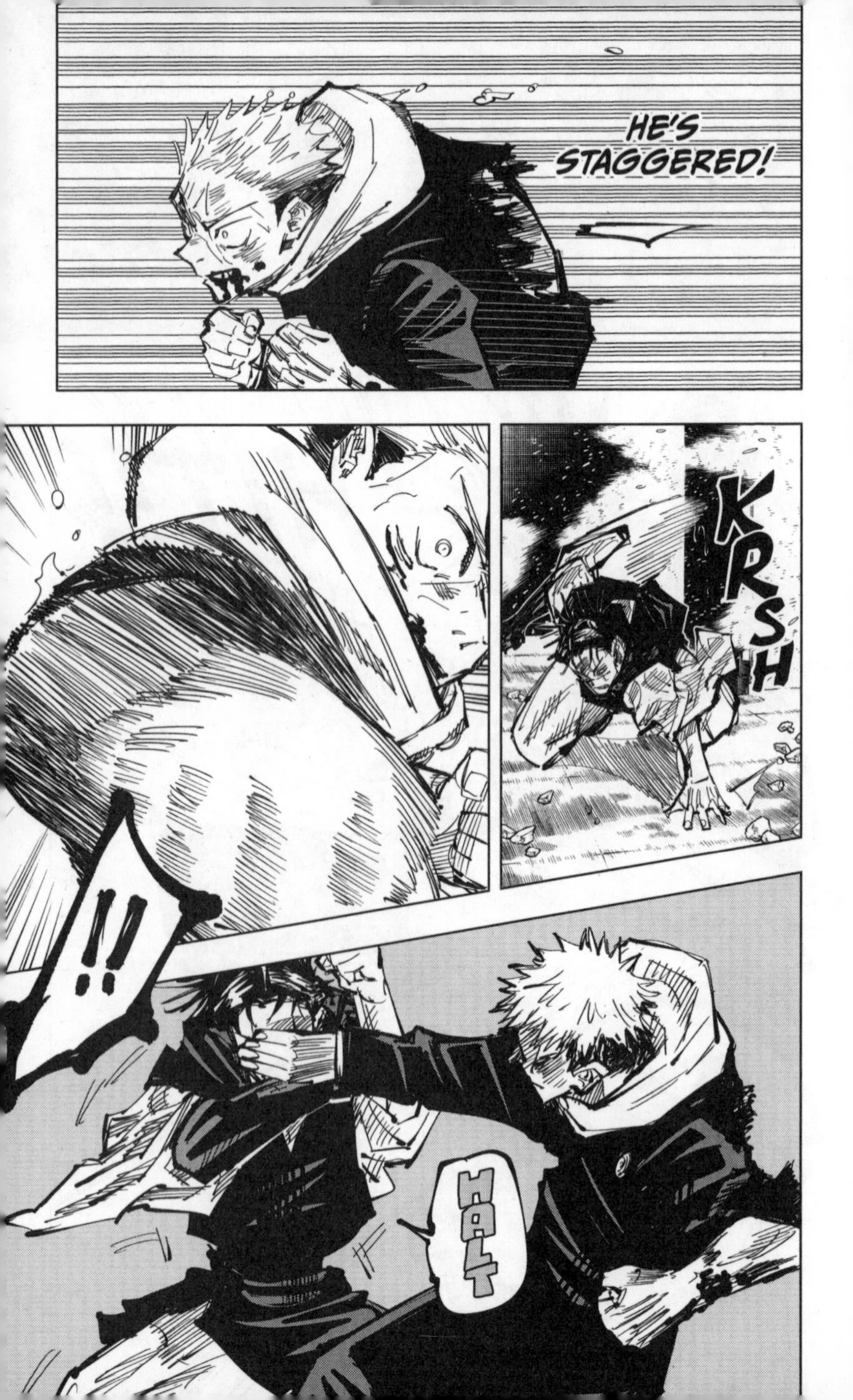
HE'S STAGGERED!
KRSH
!!
HALT

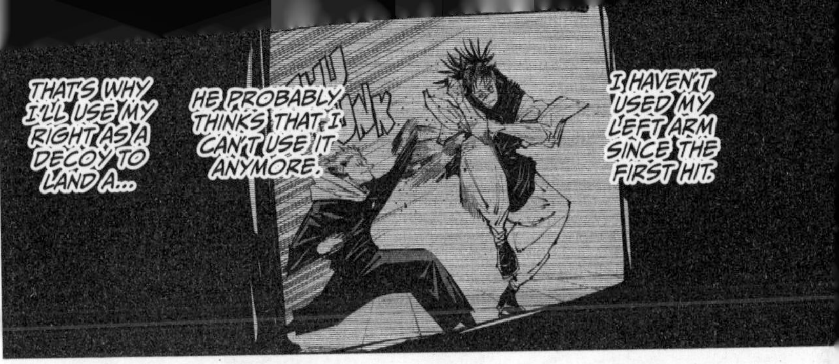
I HAVEN'T USED MY LEFT ARM SINCE THE FIRST HIT.
HE PROBABLY THINKS THAT I CAN'T USE IT ANYMORE.
THAT'S WHY I'LL USE MY RIGHT AS A DECOY TO LAND A...
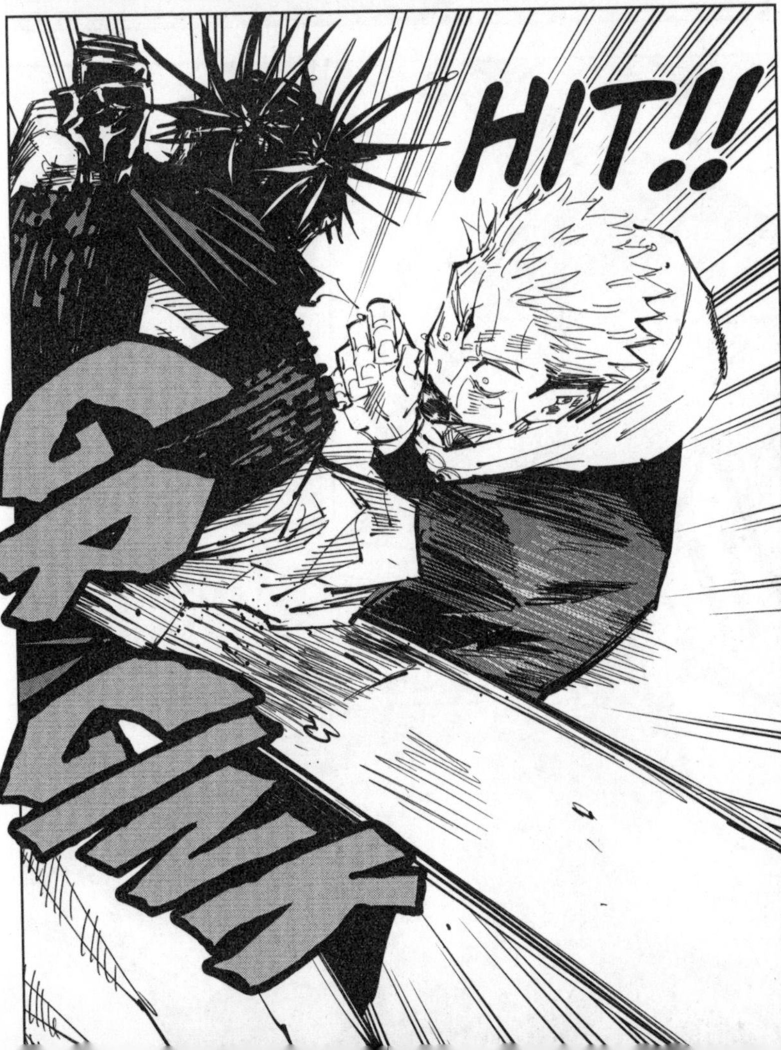
HIT!!

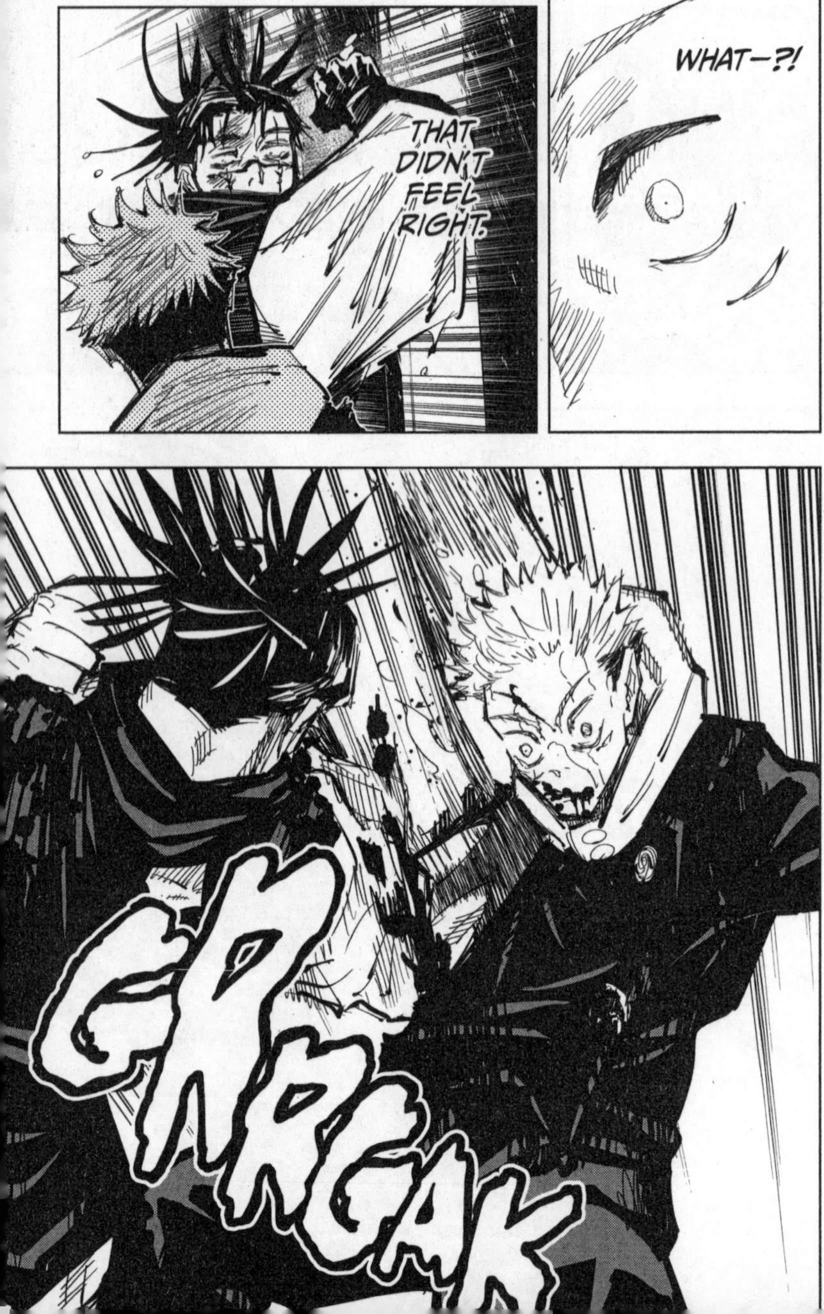
WHAT—?!
THAT DIDN'T FEEL RIGHT.

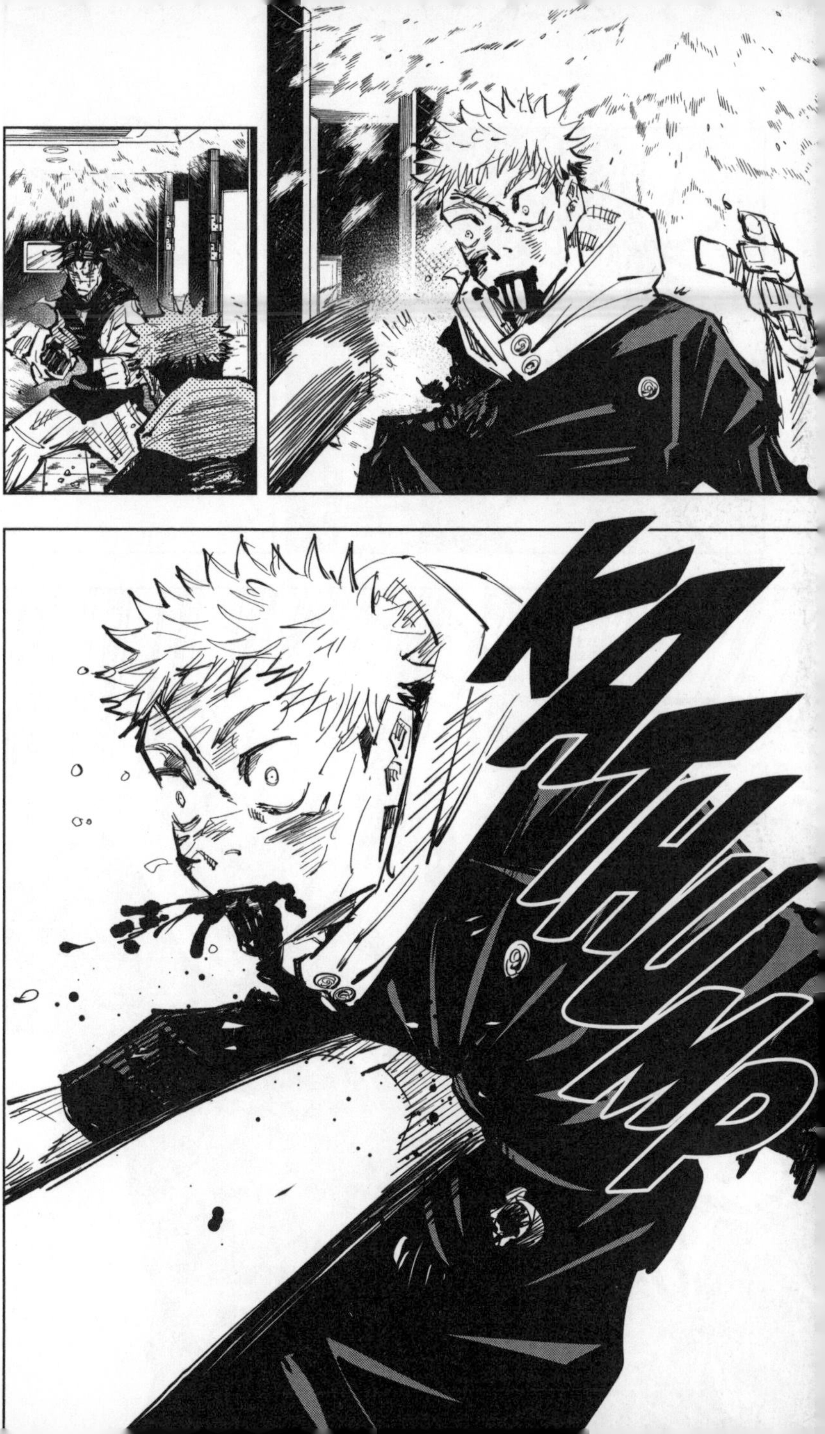
KATHUMP

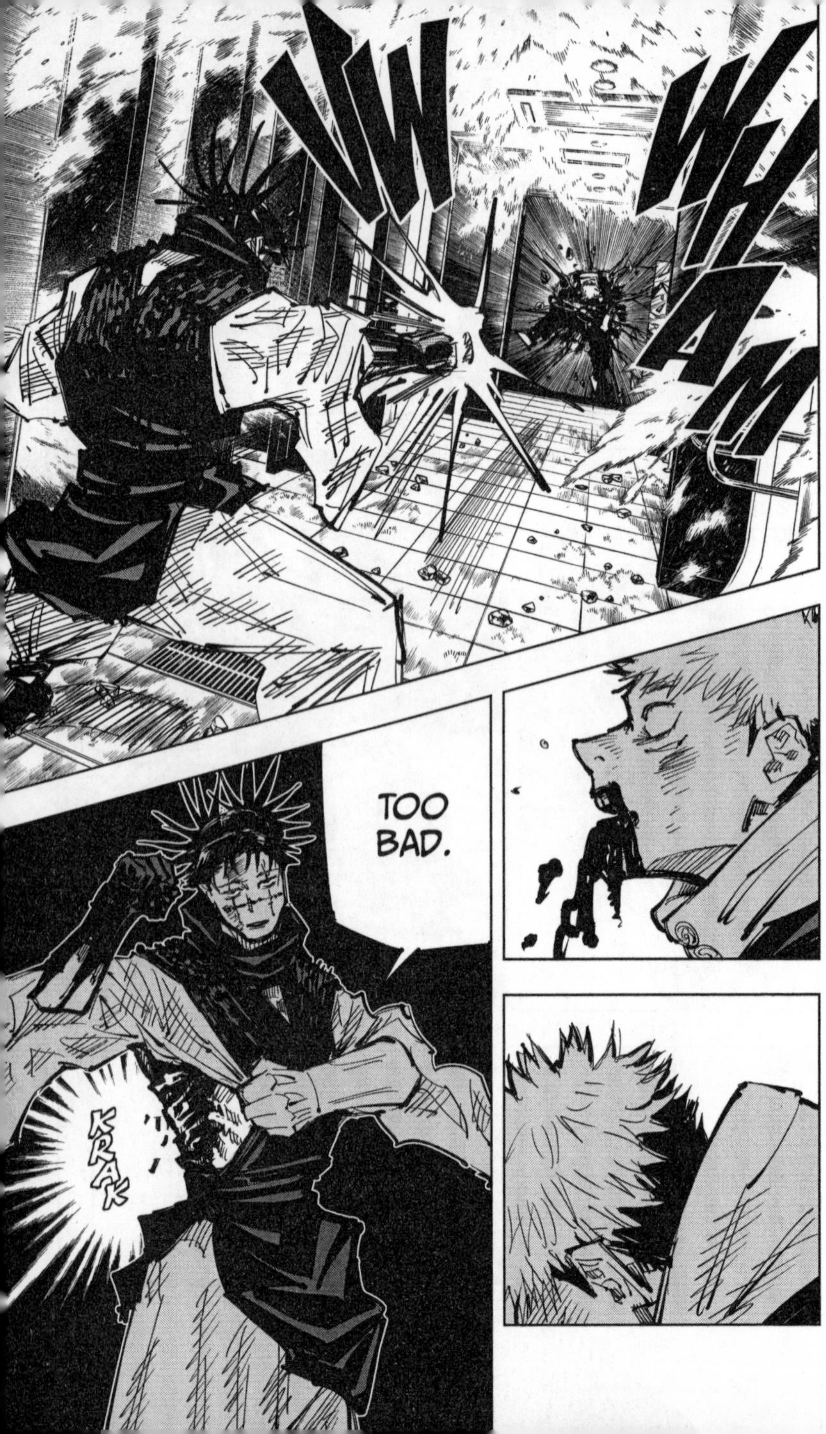
WHAM
TOO BAD.
KRAK

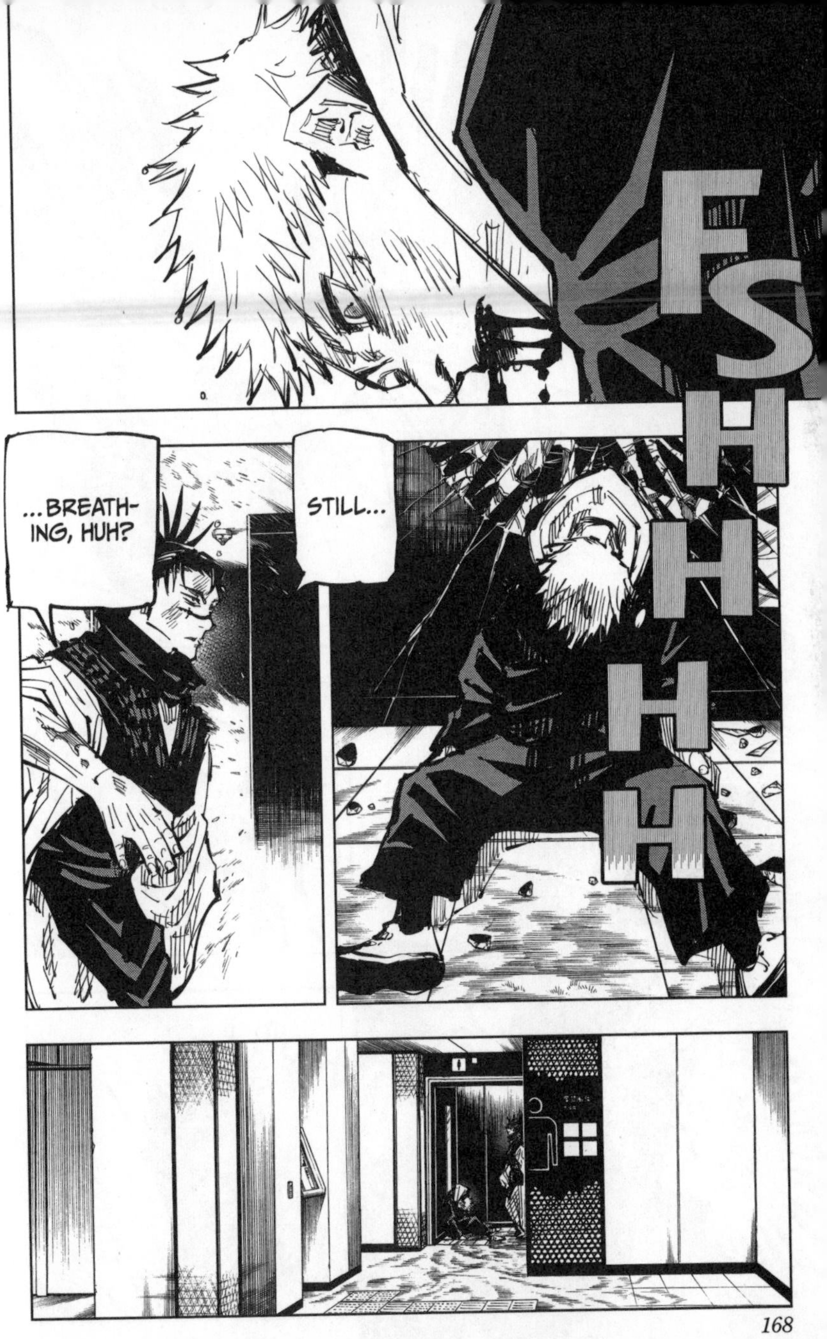
FSHHHHH
STILL...
...BREATH-ING, HUH?

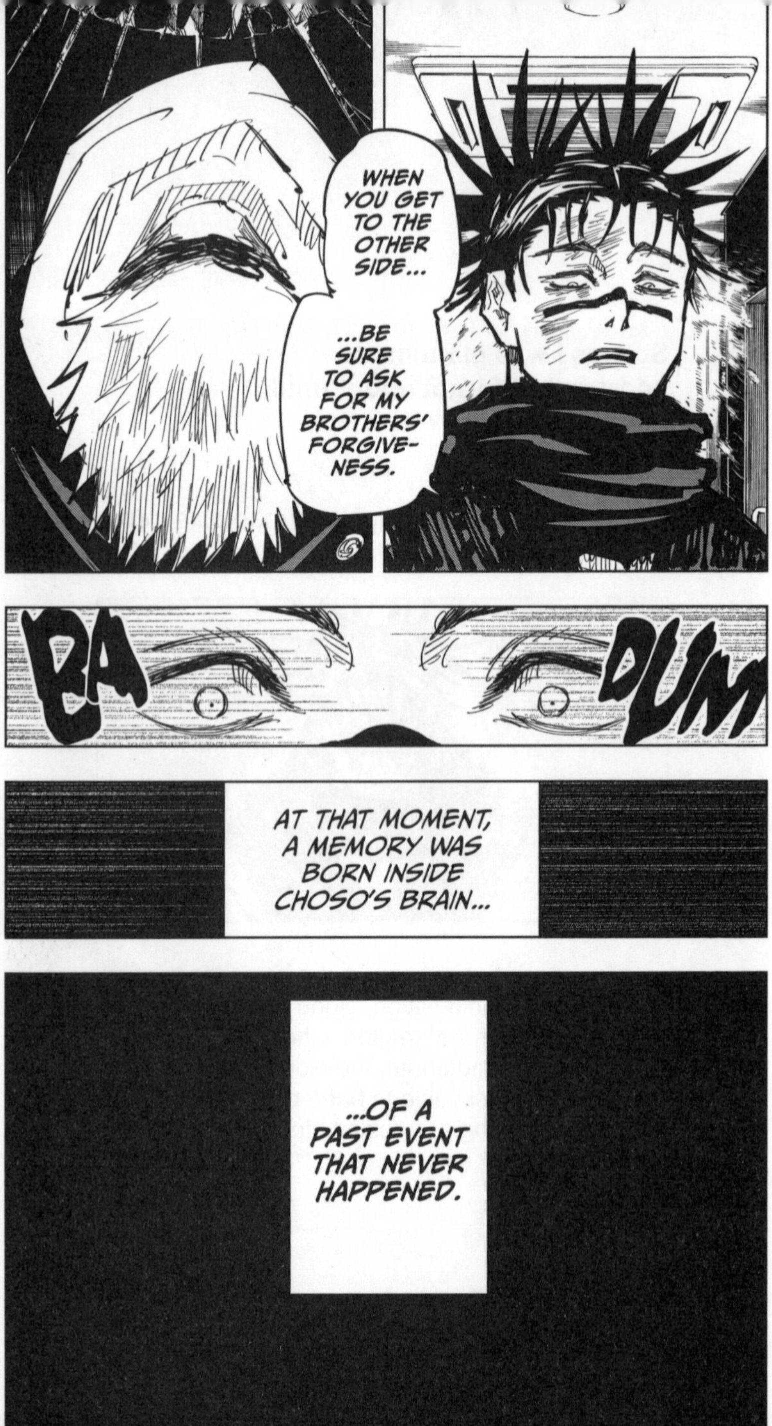
WHEN YOU GET TO THE OTHER SIDE...
...BE SURE TO ASK FOR MY BROTHERS' FORGIVE-NESS.
BA DUM
AT THAT MOMENT, A MEMORY WAS BORN INSIDE CHOSO'S BRAIN...
...OF A PAST EVENT THAT NEVER HAPPENED.

Scenes I was planning to address but forgot about until now, part 7

• Supplementary info on blood manipulation

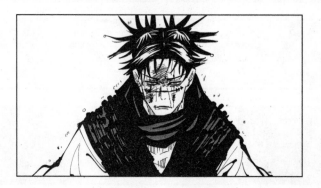

During blood manipulation, blood acts as if it's a single organ. For that reason, when using something like blood meteorite, the blood inside the body is also susceptible to hardening. Similarly, the idea of heating or freezing blood and using it is also extremely risky.

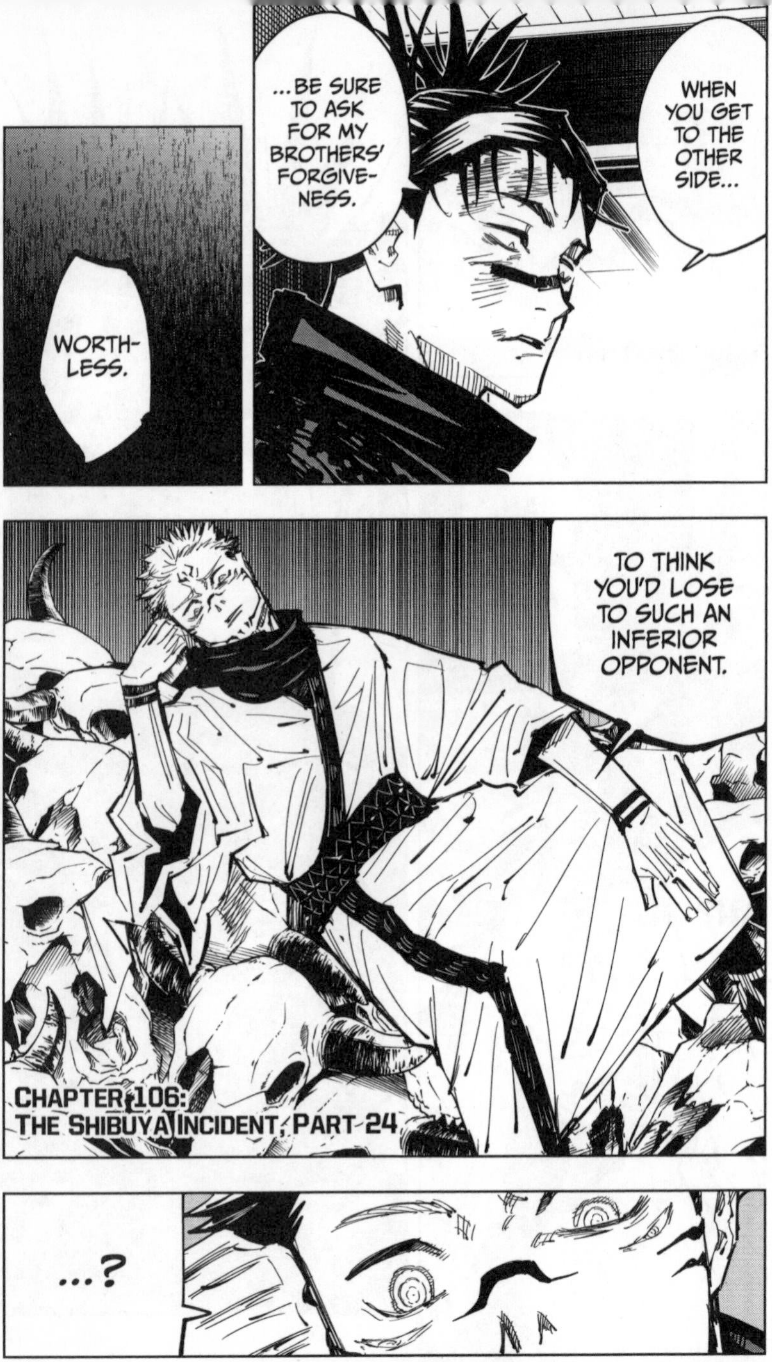
WHEN YOU GET TO THE OTHER SIDE...
...BE SURE TO ASK FOR MY BROTHERS' FORGIVE-NESS.
WORTH-LESS.
TO THINK YOU'D LOSE TO SUCH AN INFERIOR OPPONENT.
CHAPTER 106: THE SHIBUYA INCIDENT, PART 24
...?

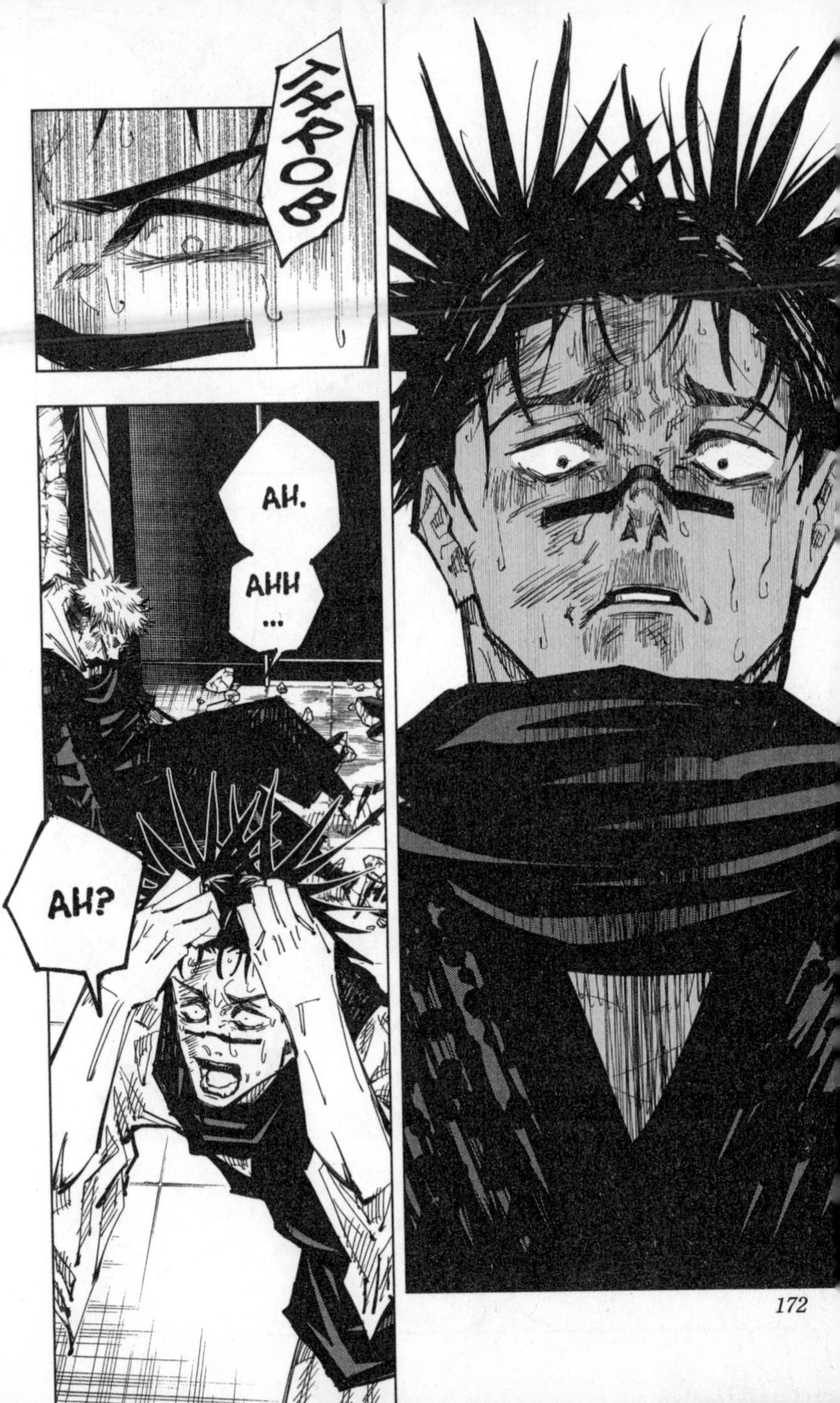
THROB
AH.
AHH ...
AH?

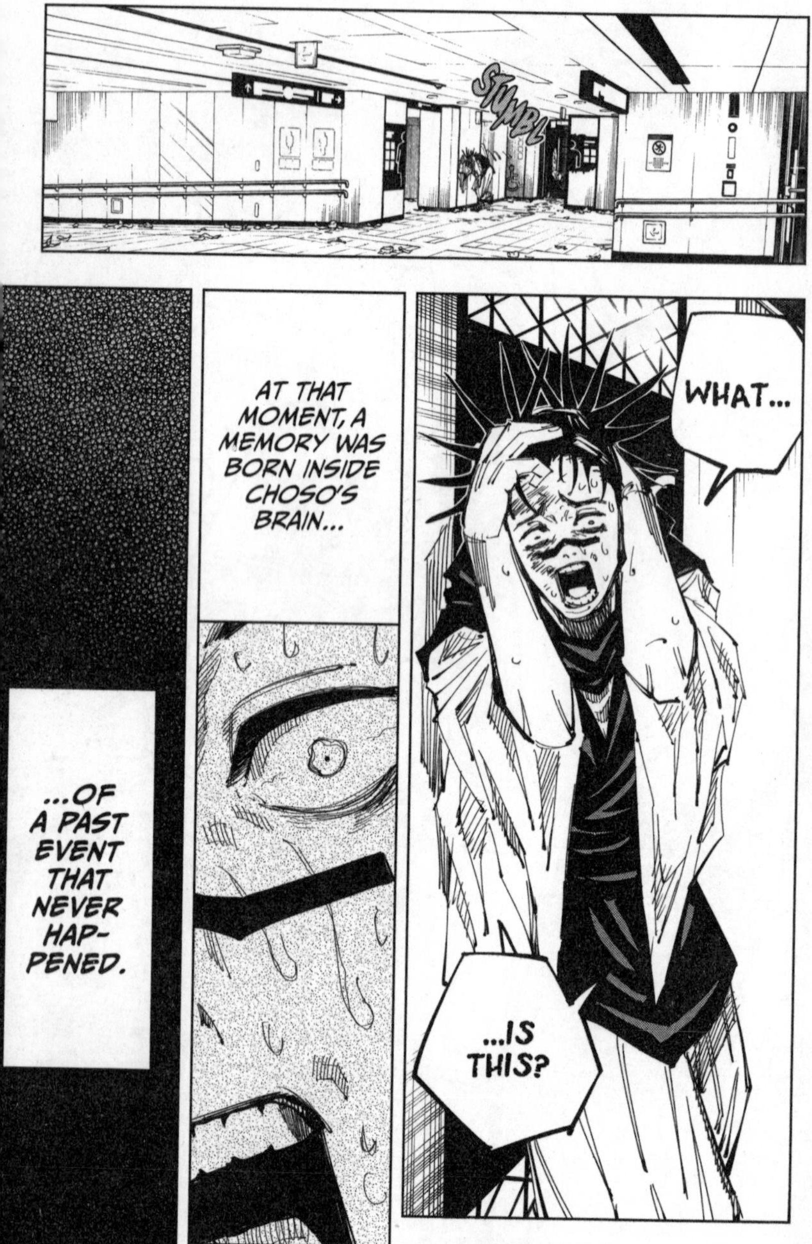
STUMBL
WHAT...
...IS THIS?
AT THAT MOMENT, A MEMORY WAS BORN INSIDE CHOSO'S BRAIN...
...OF A PAST EVENT THAT NEVER HAP-PENED.

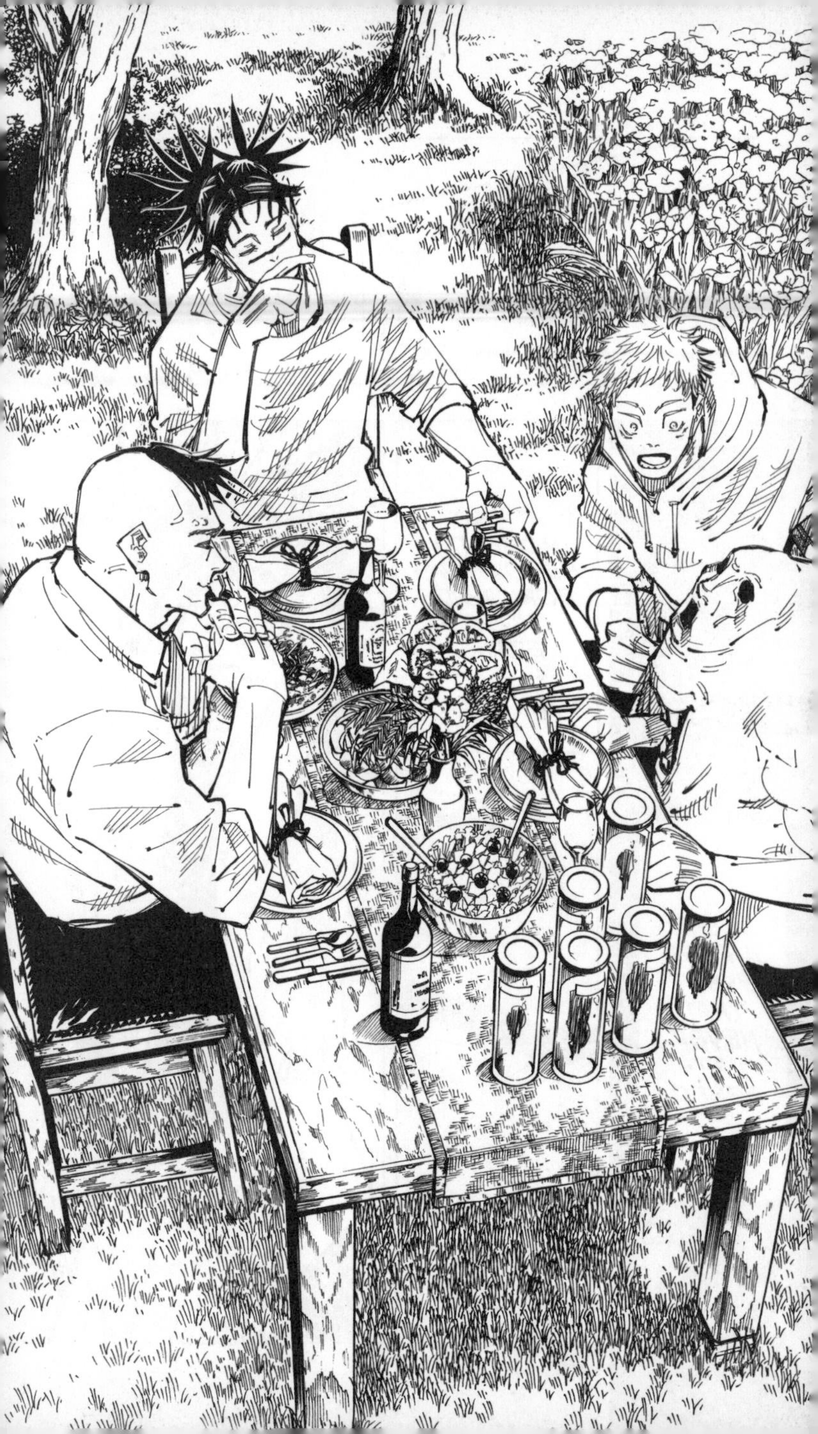

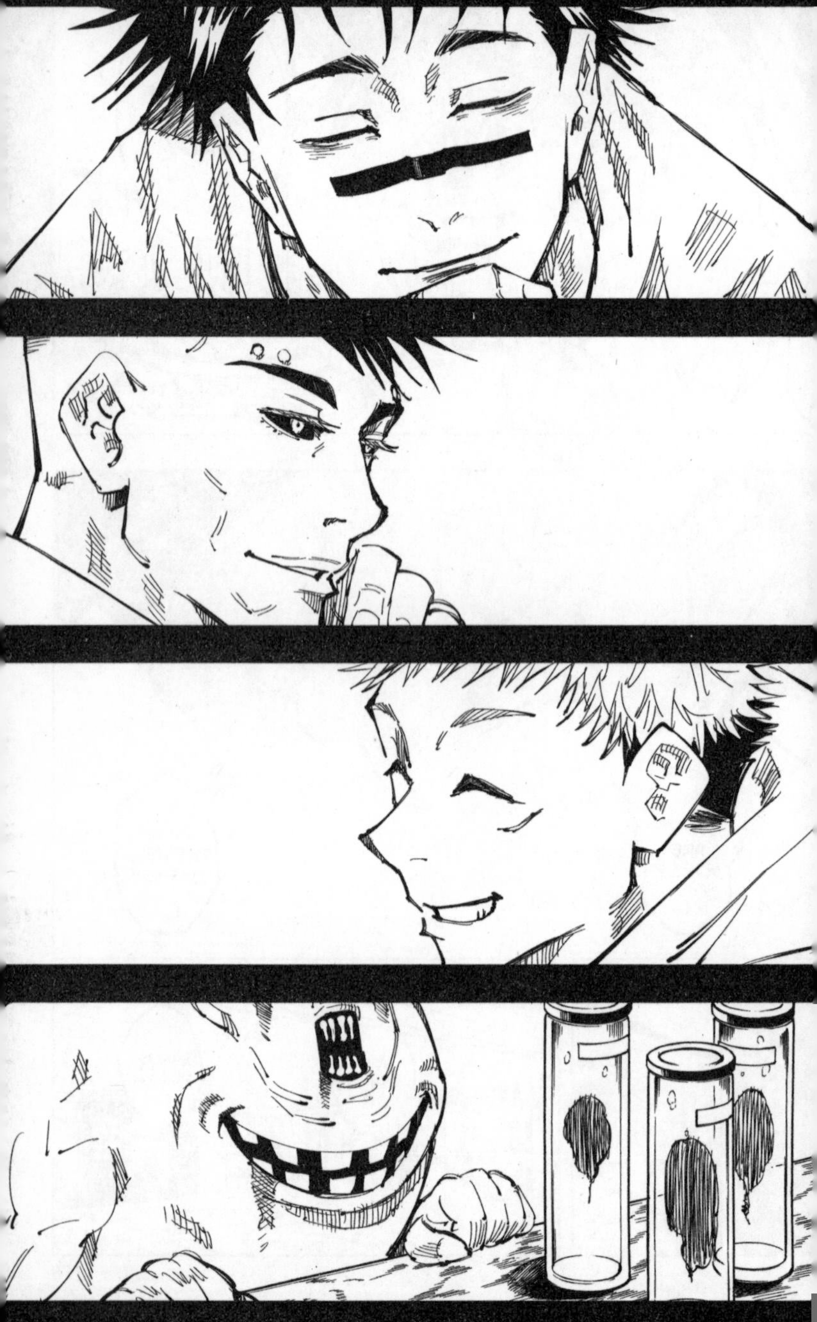

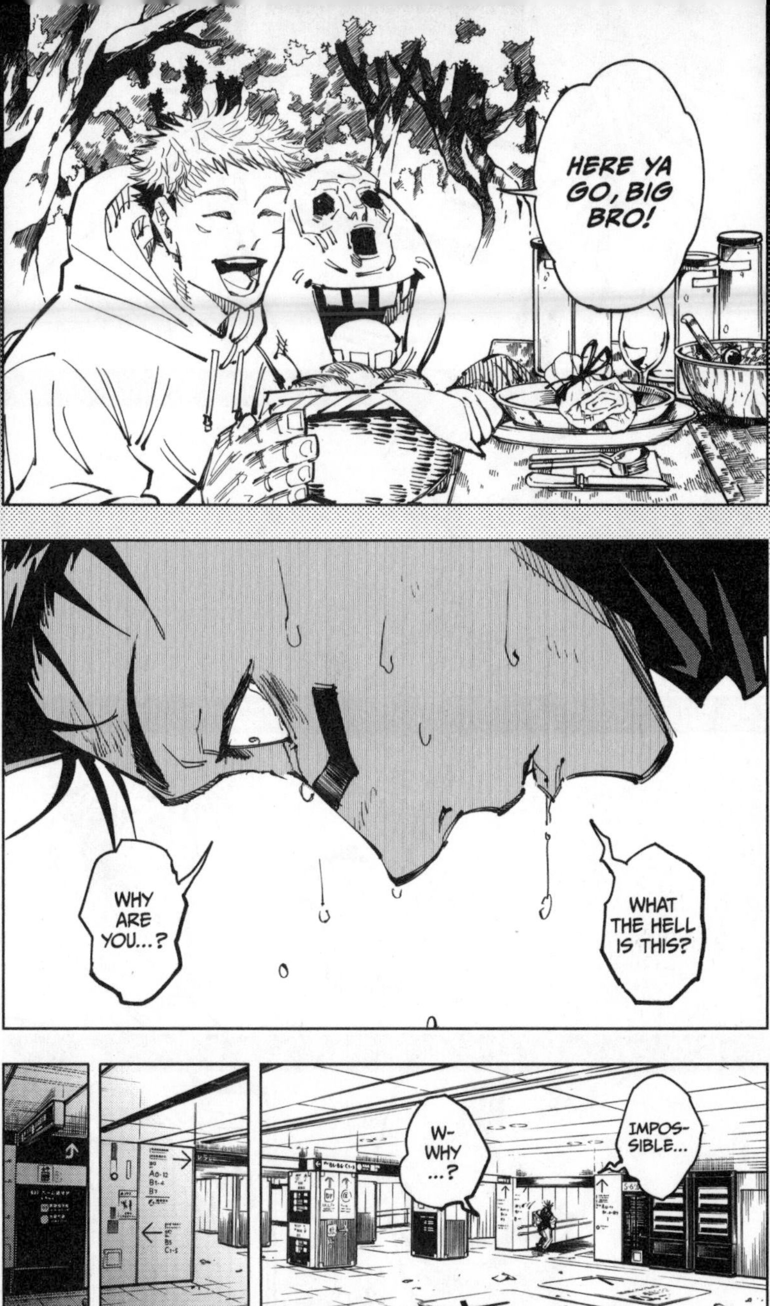
HERE YA GO, BIG BRO!
WHAT THE HELL IS THIS?
WHY ARE YOU...?
IMPOS-SIBLE...
W-WHY ...?

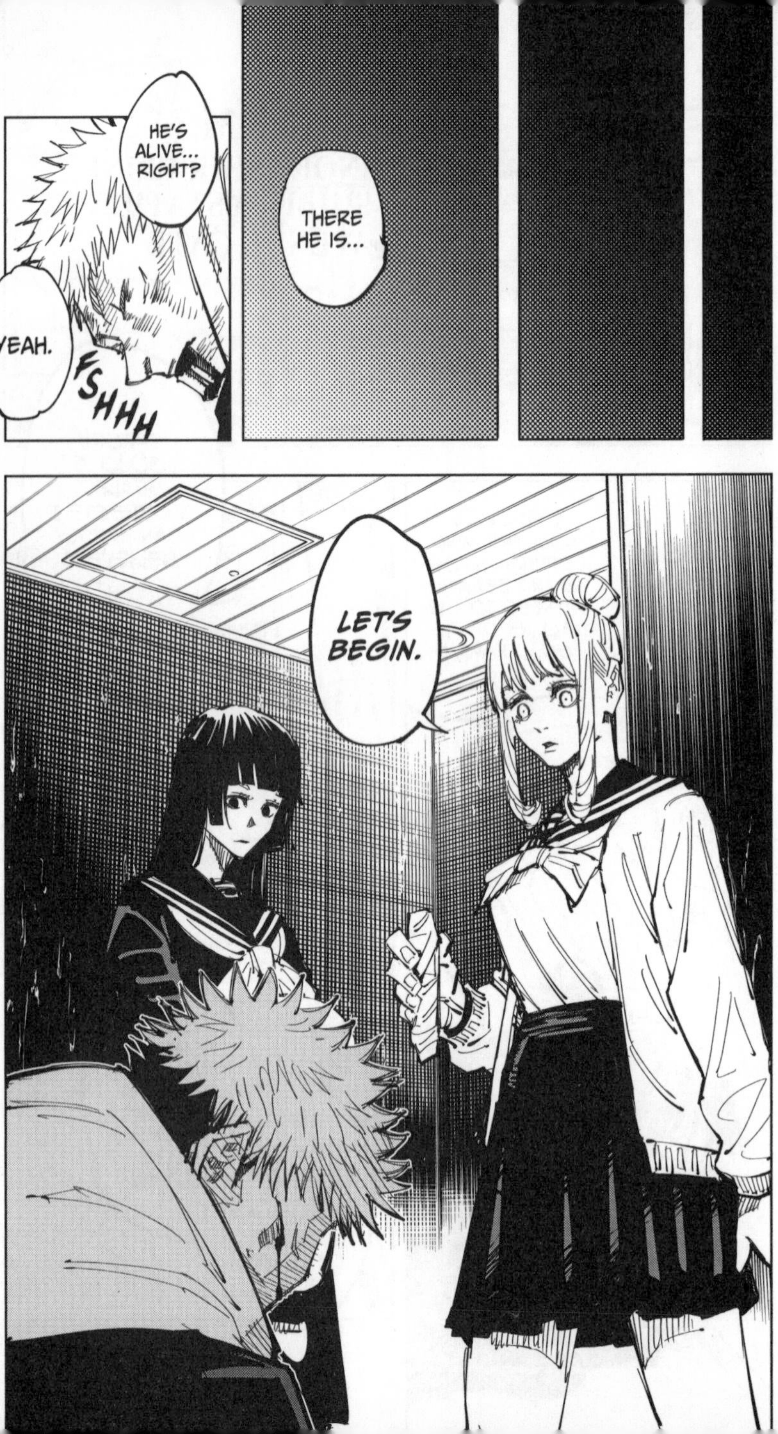
THERE HE IS...
HE'S ALIVE... RIGHT?
YEAH.
FSHHH
LET'S BEGIN.

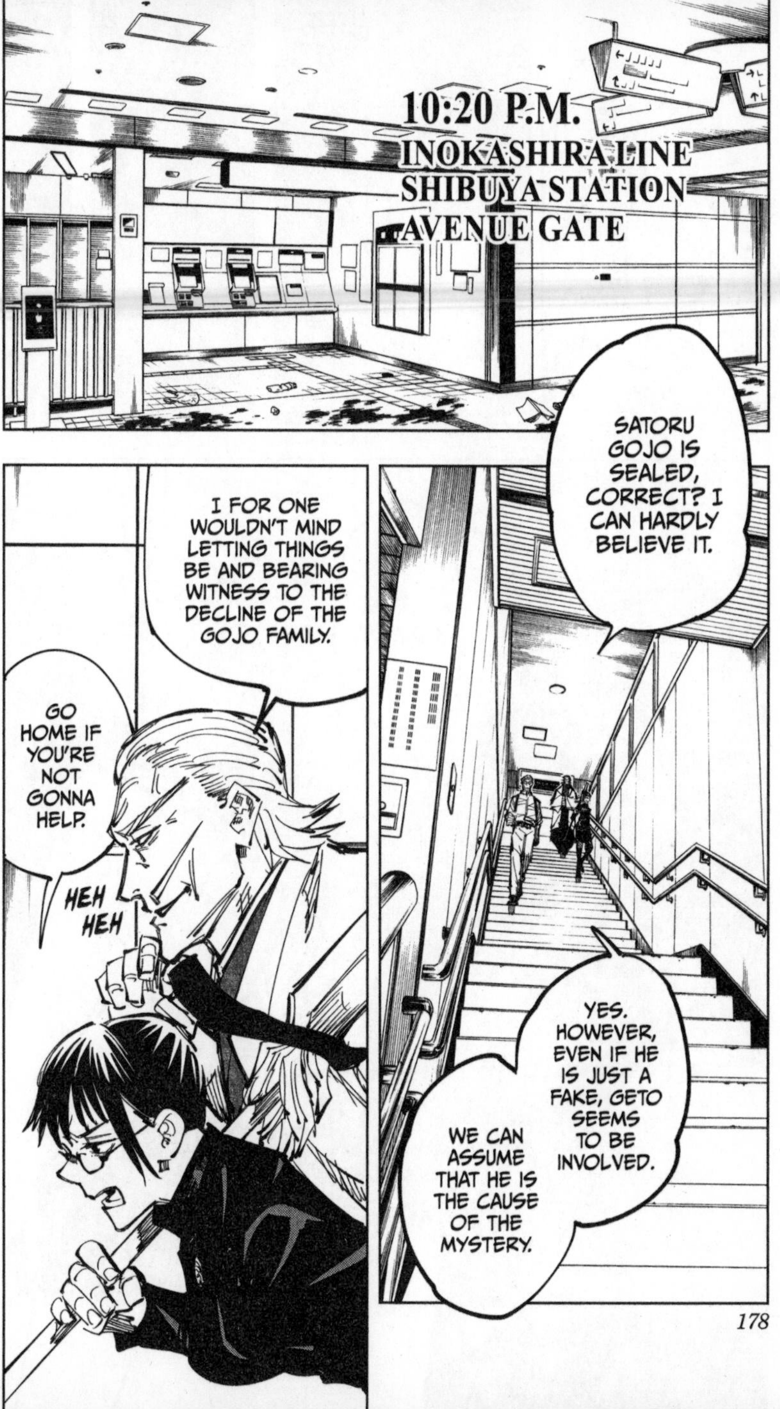
10:20 P.M.
INOKASHIRA LINE SHIBUYA STATION AVENUE GATE
SATORU GOJO IS SEALED, CORRECT? I CAN HARDLY BELIEVE IT.
YES. HOWEVER, EVEN IF HE IS JUST A FAKE, GETO SEEMS TO BE INVOLVED.
WE CAN ASSUME THAT HE IS THE CAUSE OF THE MYSTERY.
I FOR ONE WOULDN'T MIND LETTING THINGS BE AND BEARING WITNESS TO THE DECLINE OF THE GOJO FAMILY.
GO HOME IF YOU'RE NOT GONNA HELP.
HEH HEH

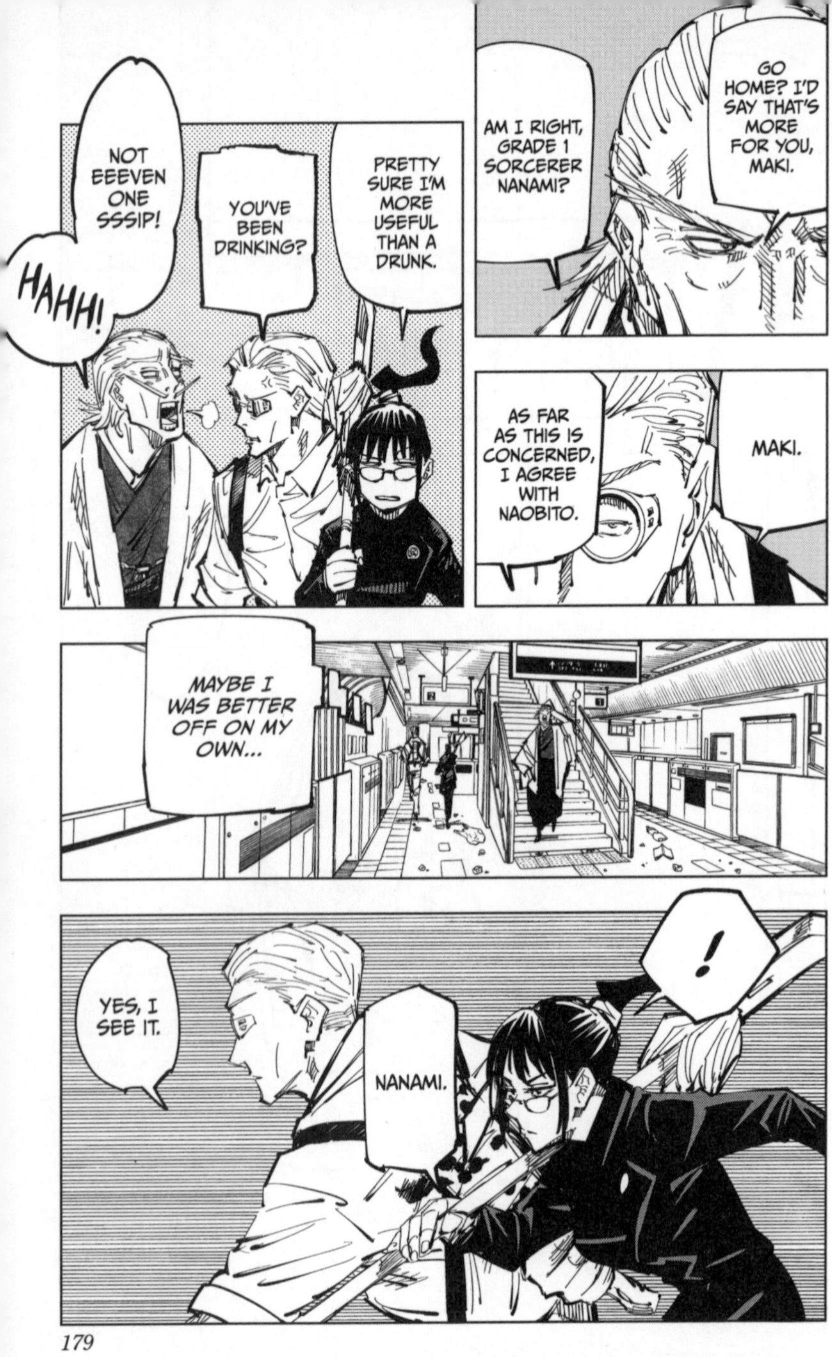
GO HOME? I'D SAY THAT'S MORE FOR YOU, MAKI.
AM I RIGHT, GRADE 1 SORCERER NANAMI?
MAKI.
AS FAR AS THIS IS CONCERNED, I AGREE WITH NAOBITO.
PRETTY SURE I'M MORE USEFUL THAN A DRUNK.
YOU'VE BEEN DRINKING?
NOT EEEVEN ONE SSSIP!
HAHH!
MAYBE I WAS BETTER OFF ON MY OWN...
!
NANAMI.
YES, I SEE IT.

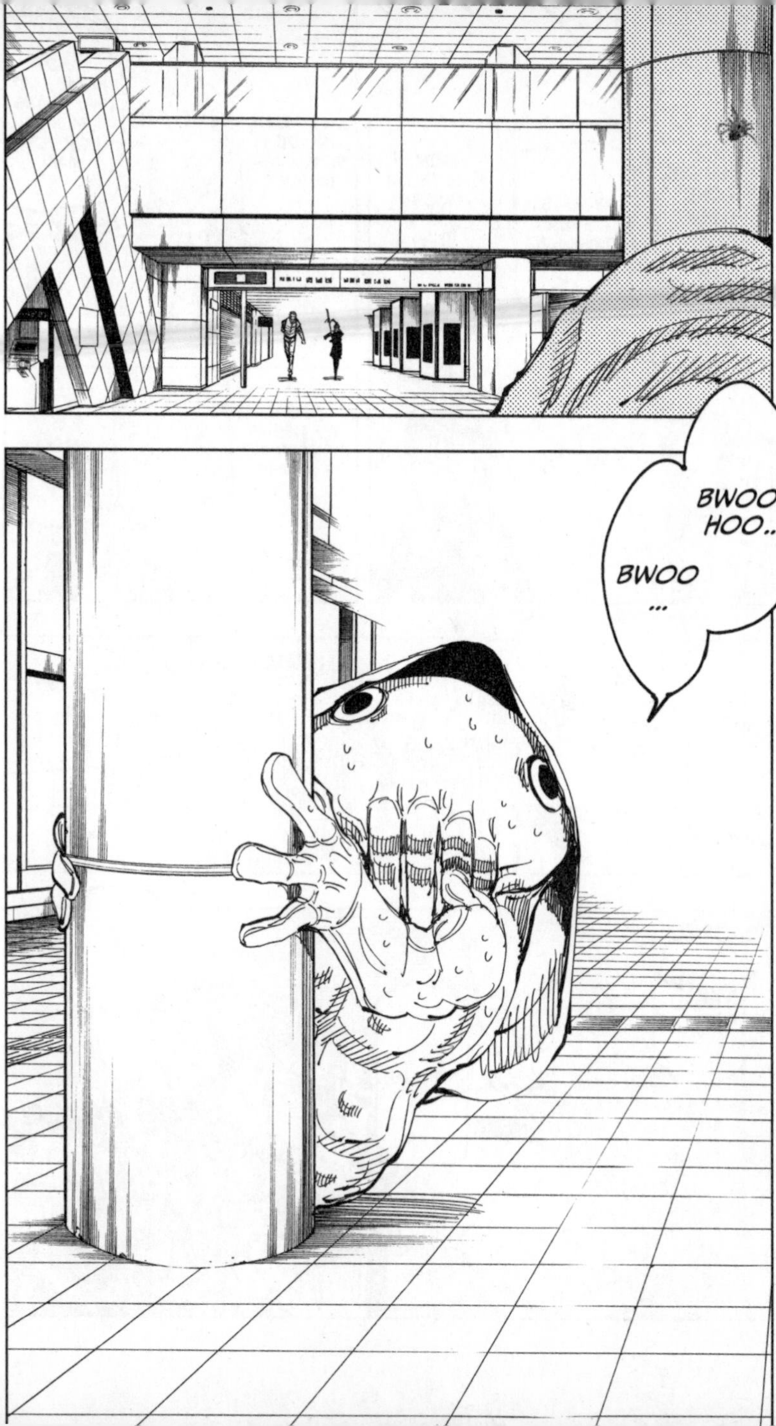
BWOO-HOO... BWOO ...

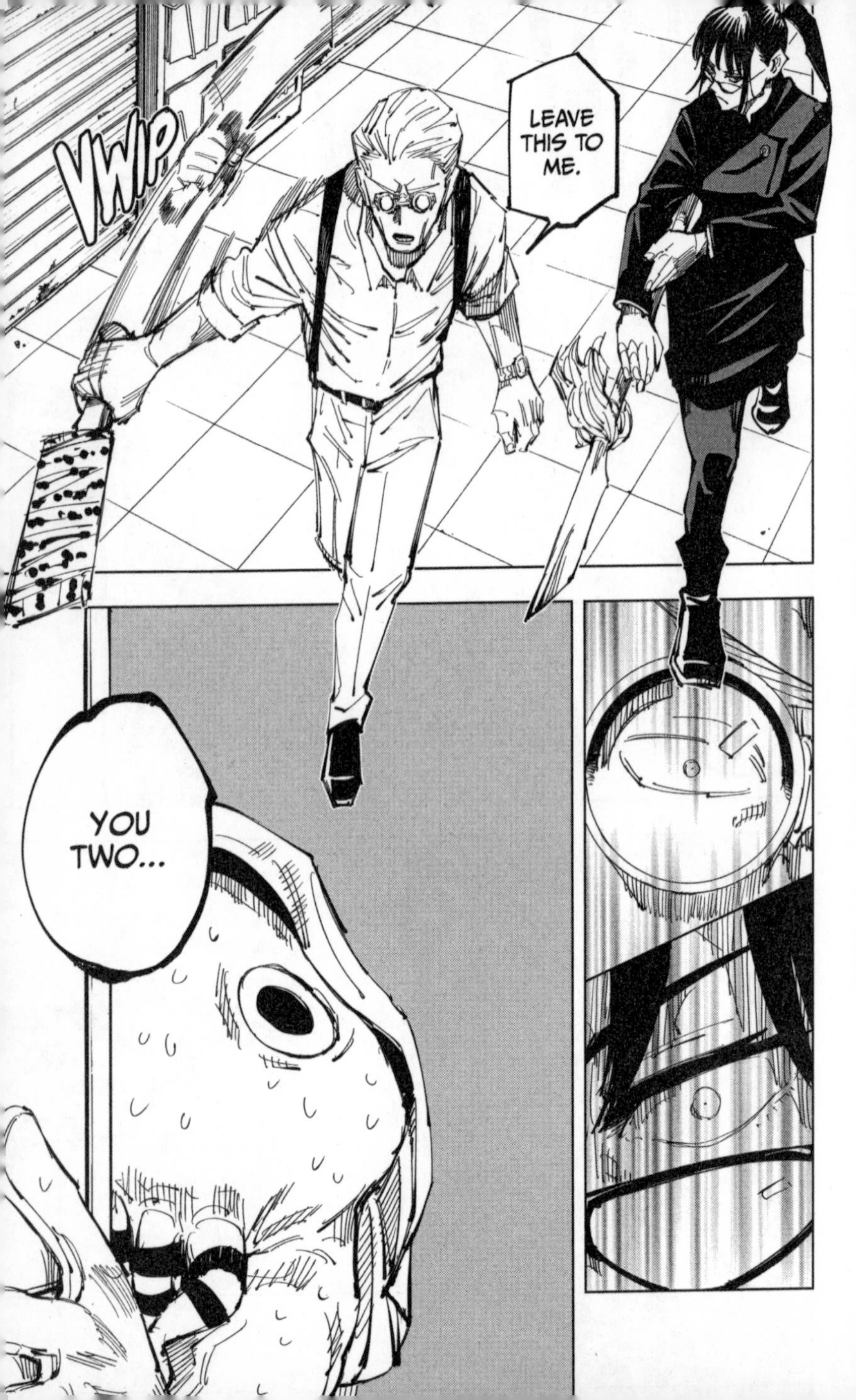
LEAVE THIS TO ME.
VWIP
YOU TWO...

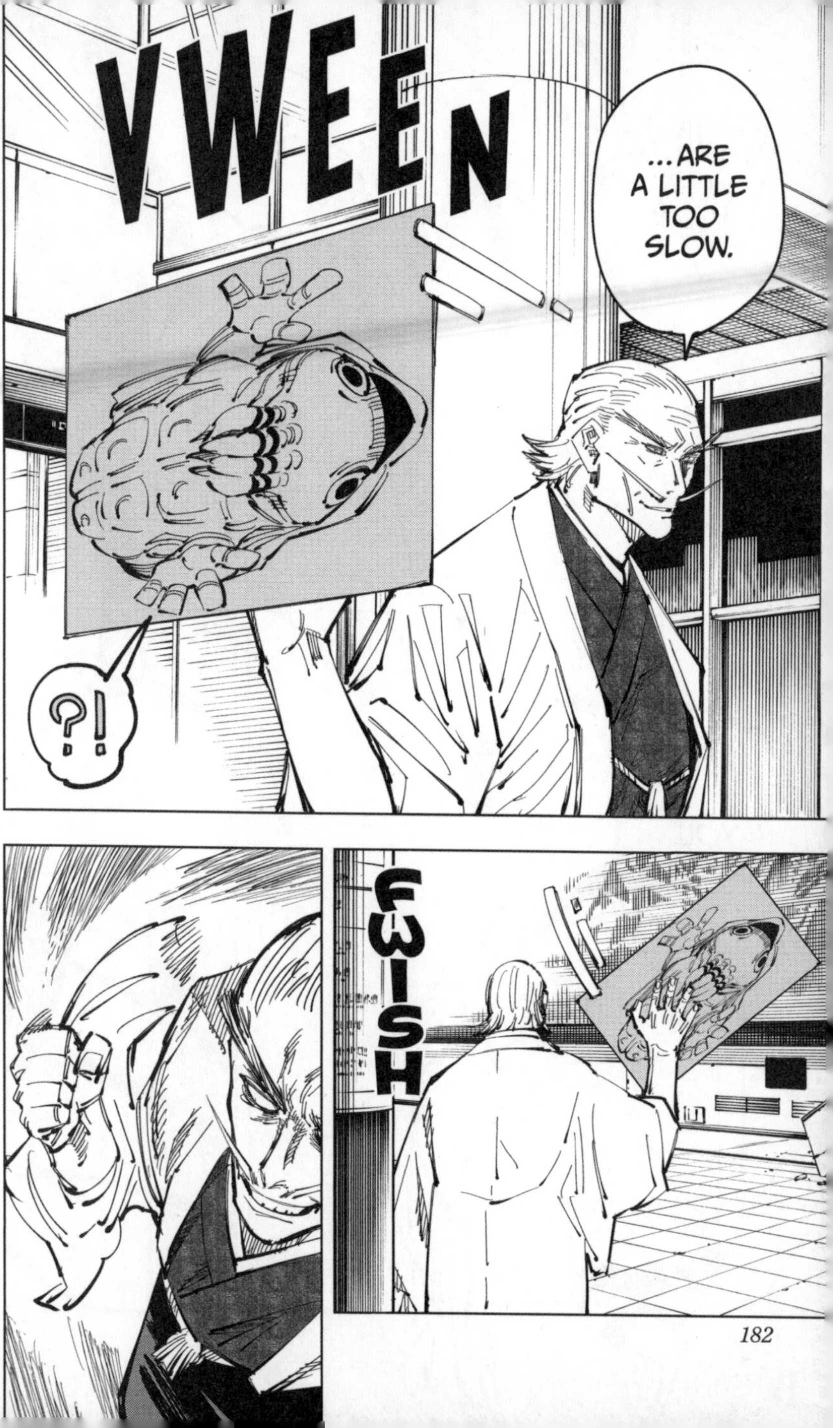
...ARE A LITTLE TOO SLOW.
VWEEN
?!
FWISH

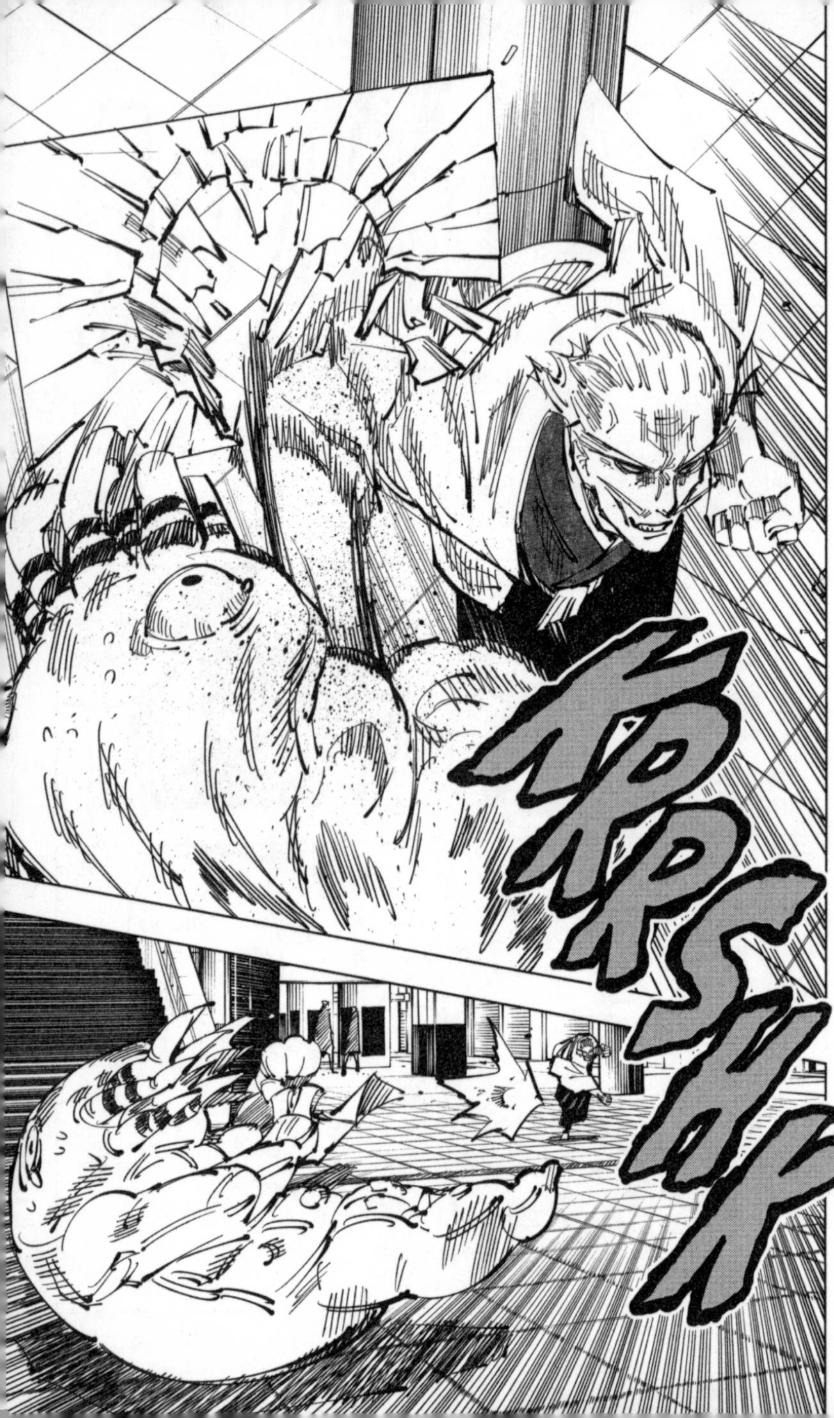
KRSHK

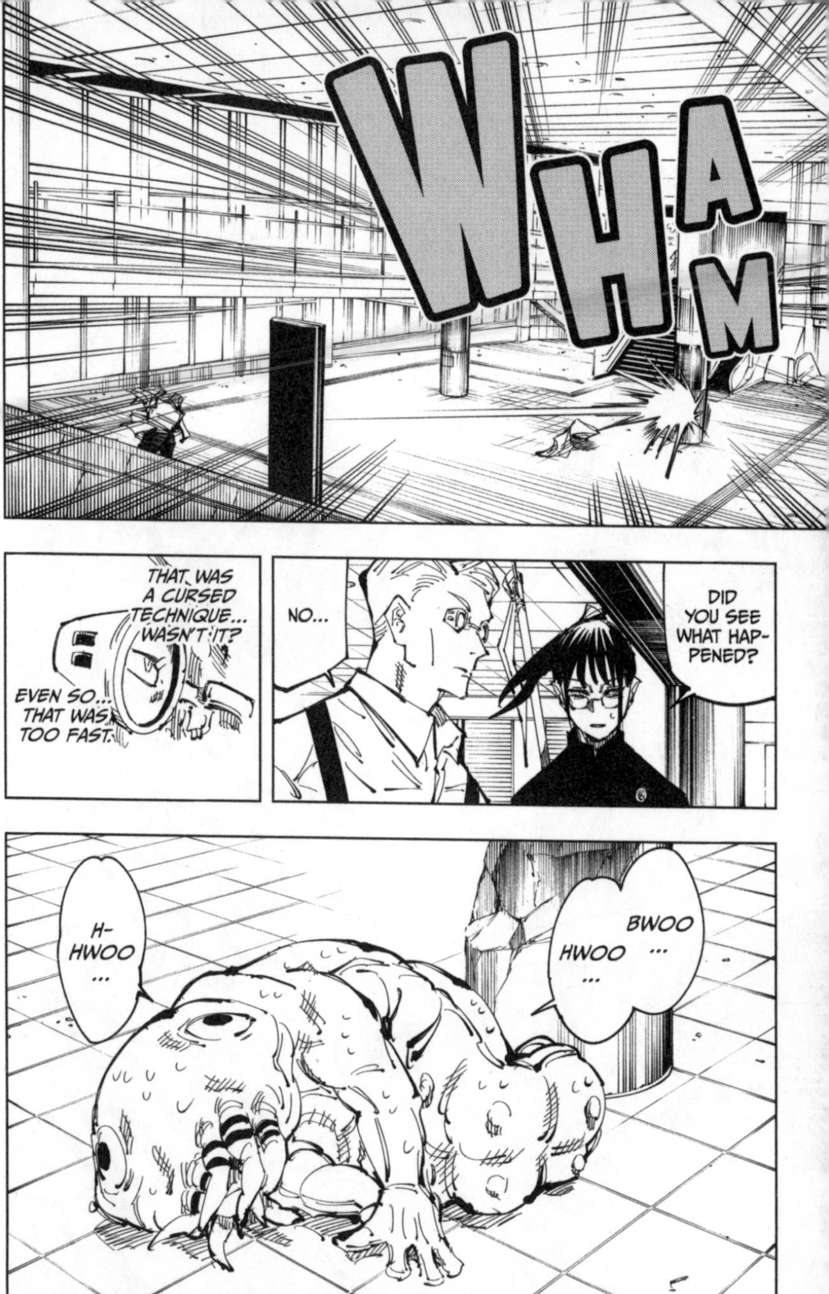
WHAM
DID YOU SEE WHAT HAPPENED?
NO...
THAT WAS A CURSED TECHNIQUE... WASN'T IT?
EVEN SO... THAT WAS TOO FAST.
BWOO...
HWOO...
H-HWOO...

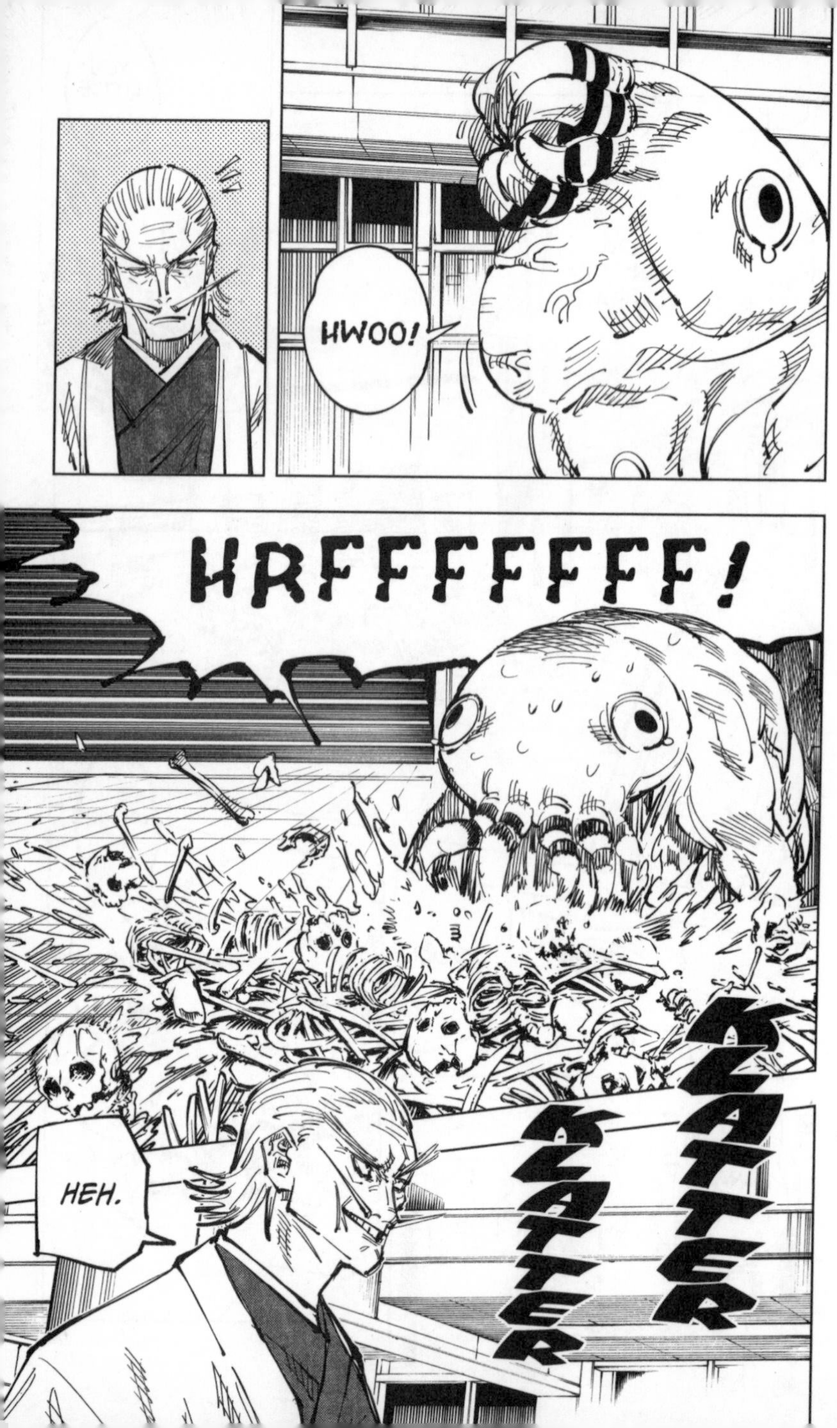

HWOO!
HRFFFFFFF!
KLATTER
KLATTER
HEH.

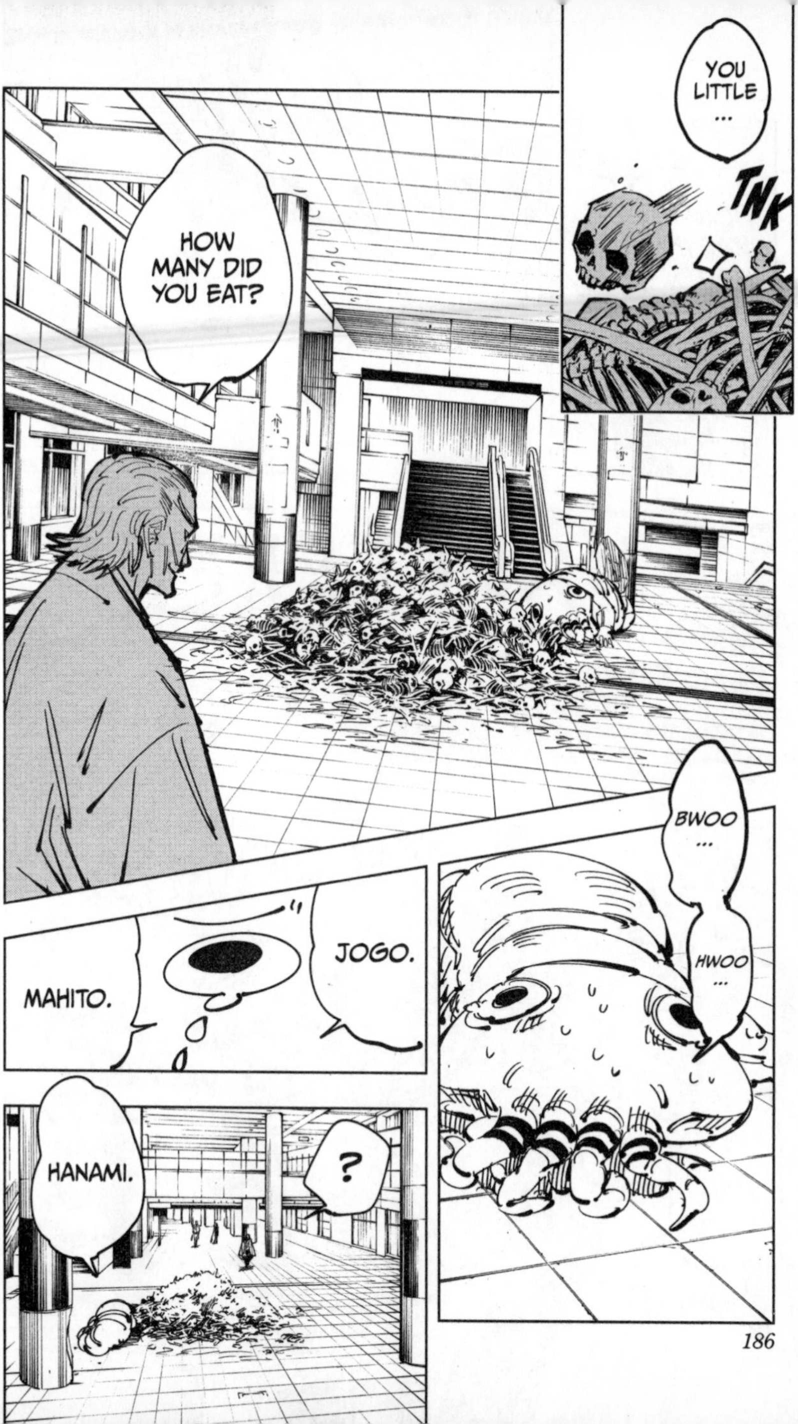
YOU LITTLE ...
TNK
HOW MANY DID YOU EAT?
BWOO ...
HWOO ...
JOGO.
MAHITO.
HANAMI.
?

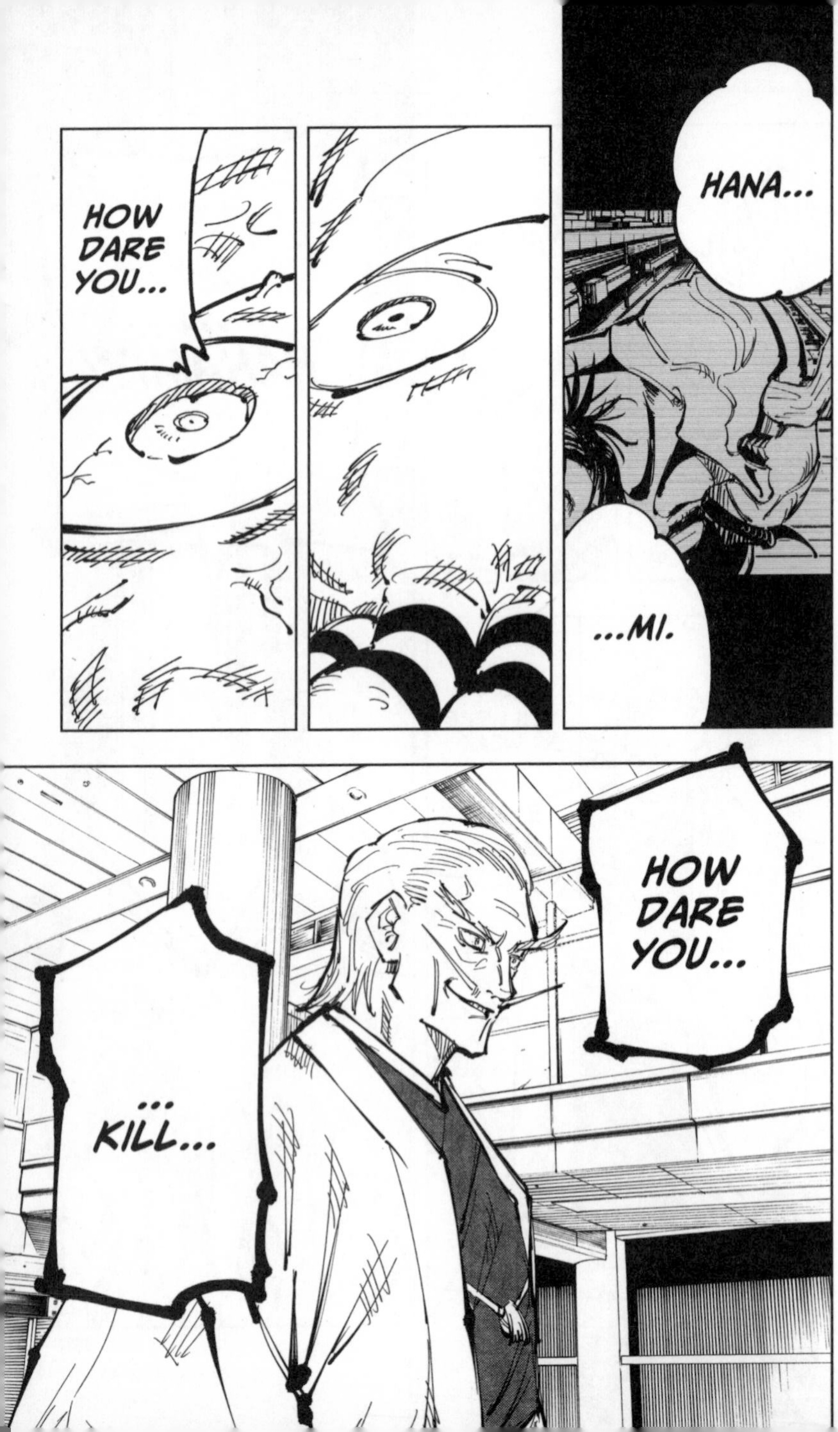
HANA...
...MI.
HOW DARE YOU...
HOW DARE YOU...
... KILL...

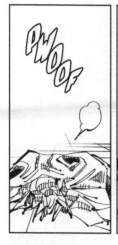

PWOOF

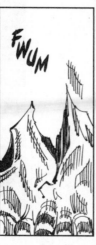

FWUM

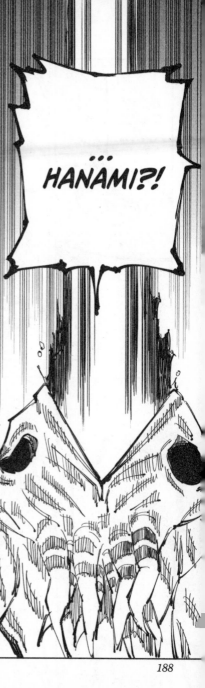

HANAMI!?!

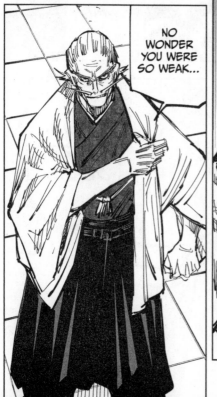

NO WONDER YOU WERE SO WEAK...

188

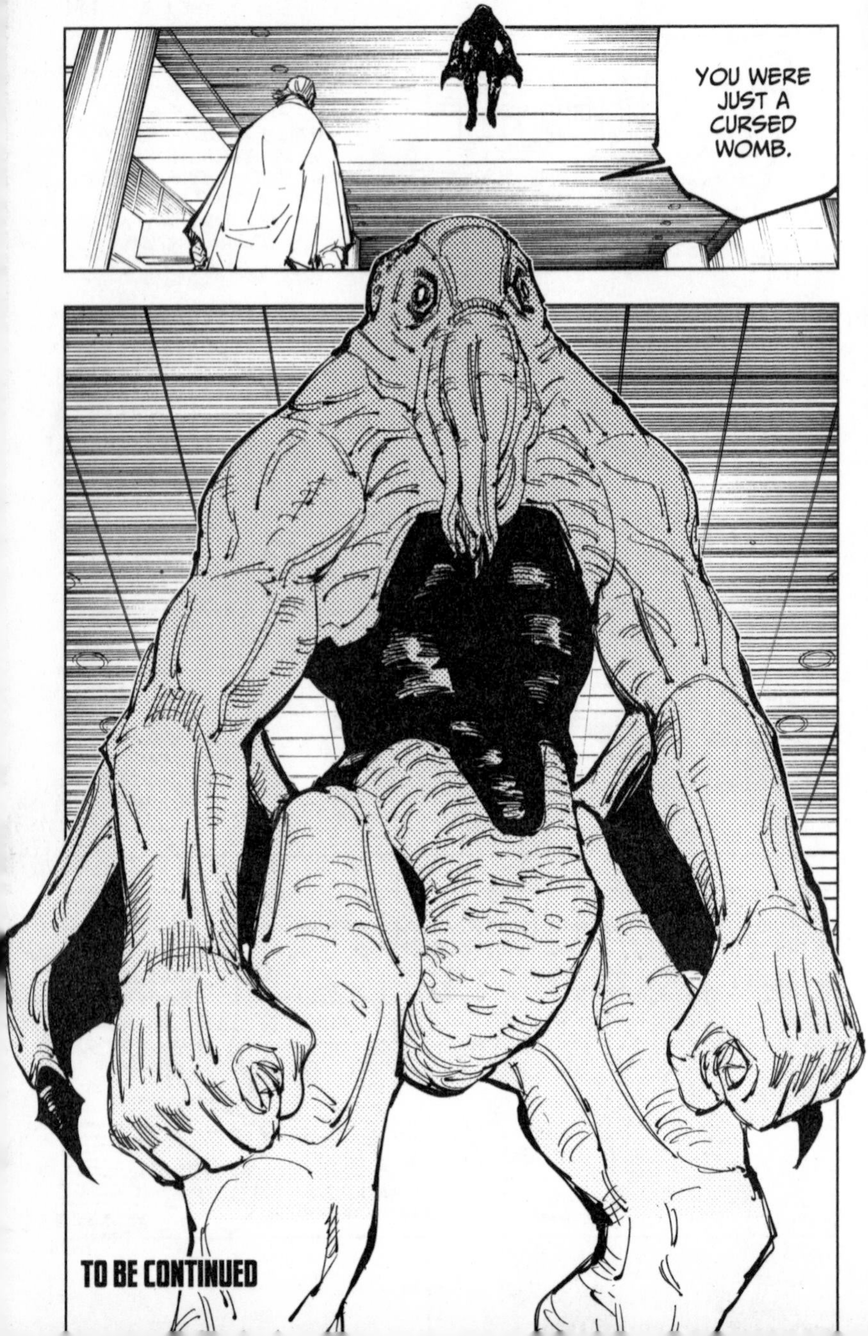
YOU WERE JUST A CURSED WOMB.
TO BE CONTINUED

AKUTAMI AT JUMP FESTA

A STORY ABOUT THE END OF 2019

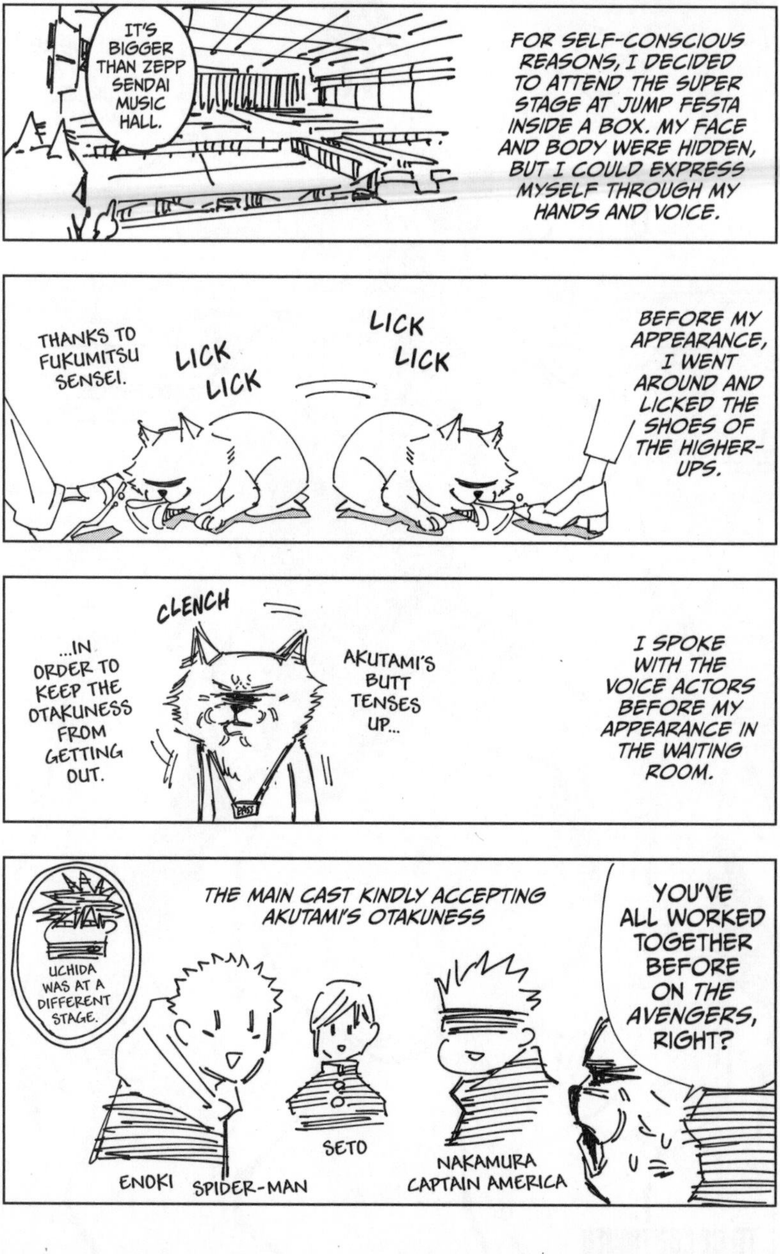
FOR SELF-CONSCIOUS REASONS, I DECIDED TO ATTEND THE SUPER STAGE AT JUMP FESTA INSIDE A BOX. MY FACE AND BODY WERE HIDDEN, BUT I COULD EXPRESS MYSELF THROUGH MY HANDS AND VOICE.
IT'S BIGGER THAN ZEPP SENDAI MUSIC HALL.
BEFORE MY APPEARANCE, I WENT AROUND AND LICKED THE SHOES OF THE HIGHER-UPS.
LICK
LICK
LICK
LICK
THANKS TO FUKUMITSU SENSEI.
I SPOKE WITH THE VOICE ACTORS BEFORE MY APPEARANCE IN THE WAITING ROOM.
CLENCH
AKUTAMI'S BUTT TENSES UP...
...IN ORDER TO KEEP THE OTAKUNESS FROM GETTING OUT.
YOU'VE ALL WORKED TOGETHER BEFORE ON THE AVENGERS, RIGHT?
THE MAIN CAST KINDLY ACCEPTING AKUTAMI'S OTAKUNESS
UCHIDA WAS AT A DIFFERENT STAGE.
NAKAMURA
CAPTAIN AMERICA
SETO
SPIDER-MAN
ENOKI

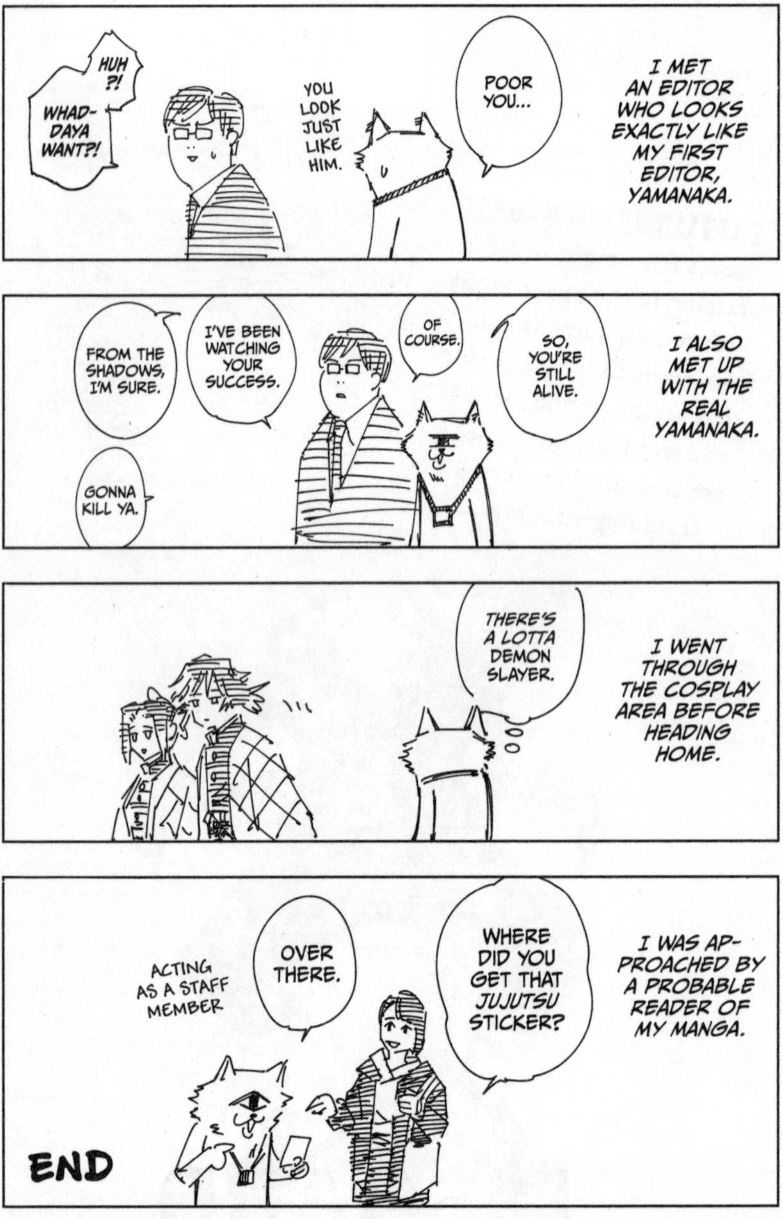
I MET AN EDITOR WHO LOOKS EXACTLY LIKE MY FIRST EDITOR, YAMANAKA.
POOR YOU...
YOU LOOK JUST LIKE HIM.
HUH ?!
WHAD-DAYA WANT?!
I ALSO MET UP WITH THE REAL YAMANAKA.
SO, YOU'RE STILL ALIVE.
OF COURSE.
I'VE BEEN WATCHING YOUR SUCCESS.
FROM THE SHADOWS, I'M SURE.
GONNA KILL YA.
I WENT THROUGH THE COSPLAY AREA BEFORE HEADING HOME.
THERE'S A LOTTA DEMON SLAYER.
I WAS AP-PROACHED BY A PROBABLE READER OF MY MANGA.
WHERE DID YOU GET THAT JUJUTSU STICKER?
OVER THERE.
ACTING AS A STAFF MEMBER
END

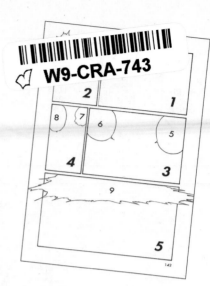

JUJUTSU KAISEN

reads from right to left, starting in the upper-right corner. Japanese is read from right to left, meaning that action, sound effects and word-balloon order are completely reversed from English order.

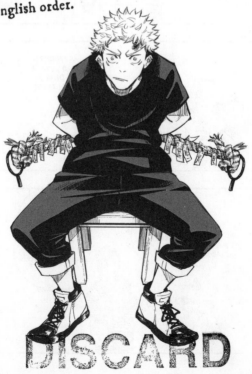